Advances in
Clinical Child
Psychology

Volume 19

ADVANCES IN CLINICAL CHILD PSYCHOLOGY

A Continuation Order Plan is available for this series. A continuation order will bring delivery of each new volume immediately upon publication. Volumes are billed only upon actual shipment. For further information please contact the publisher.

Advances in
Clinical Child
Psychology
Volume 19

Edited by

THOMAS H. OLLENDICK

Virginia Polytechnic Institute and State University
Blacksburg, Virginia

and

RONALD J. PRINZ

University of South Carolina
Columbia, South Carolina

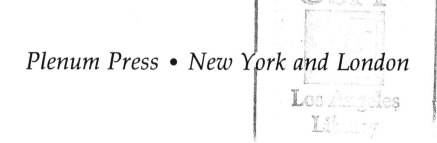

Plenum Press • *New York and London*

The Library of Congress cataloged the first volume of this title as follows:

Advances in clinical child psychology, v. 1–

New York, Plenum Press, ©1977–

v. ill. 24 cm.
Key title: Advances in clinical child psychology. ISSN 0149-4732

1. Clinical psychology—Collected works. 2. Child psychology—Collected works.
3. Child psychotherapy—Collected works.
RJ503.3.A37 618.9'28'9   77-643411

ISBN 0-306-45447-5

©1997 Plenum Press, New York
A Division of Plenum Publishing Corporation
233 Spring Street, New York, N.Y. 10013

10 9 8 7 6 5 4 3 2 1

Printed in the United States of America

Contributors

Judith V. Becker | *Department of Psychology, University of Arizona, Tucson, Arizona 85721*

Susan B. Campbell | *Department of Psychology, University of Pittsburgh, Pittsburgh, Pennsylvania 15260*

Joseph A. Durlak | *Department of Psychology, Loyola University, Chicago, Illinois 60626*

Aude Henin | *Department of Psychology, Temple University, Philadelphia, Pennsylvania 19122*

Stephen R. Hooper | *Center for Development and Learning, University of North Carolina, Chapel Hill, North Carolina 27599*

John A. Hunter, Jr. | *Department of Psychology, University of Arizona, Tucson, Arizona 85721*

Philip C. Kendall | *Department of Psychology, Temple University, Philadelphia, Pennsylvania 19122*

Sara G. Mattis | *Department of Psychology, Virginia Polytechnic Institute and State University, Blacksburg, Virginia 24061*

Thomas H. Ollendick | *Department of Psychology, Virginia Polytechnic Institute and State University, Blacksburg, Virginia 24061*

Charlotte J. Patterson | *Department of Psychology, University of Virginia, Charlottesville, Virginia 22903*

Michael G. Tramontana | *Division of Child and Adolescent Psychiatry, Vanderbilt University School of Medicine, Nashville, Tennessee 37212*

Holly B. Waldron   *Department of Psychology, University of
                          New Mexico, Albuquerque, New Mexico
                          87131*

Mark D. Weist   *Department of Psychiatry, University of Mary-
                          land, Baltimore, Maryland 21201*

Preface

This nineteenth volume of *Advances in Clinical Child Psychology* continues our tradition of examining a broad range of topics and issues that characterizes the continually evolving field of clinical child psychology. Over the years, the series has served to identify important, exciting, and timely new developments in the field and to provide scholarly and in-depth reviews of current thought and practices. The present volume is no exception.

In the opening chapter, Sue Campbell explores developmental pathways associated with serious behavior problems in preschool children. Specifically, she notes that about half of preschool children identified with aggression and problems of impulse control persist in their deviance across development. The other half do not. What accounts for these different developmental outcomes? Campbell invokes developmental and family influences as possible sources of these differential outcomes and, in doing so, describes aspects of her own programmatic research program that has greatly enriched our understanding of this complex topic.

In a similar vein, Sara Mattis and Tom Ollendick undertake a developmental analysis of panic in children and adolescents in Chapter 2. In recent years, separation anxiety and/or experiences in separation from attachment figures in childhood have been hypothesized as playing a critical role in the development of panic. This chapter presents relevant findings in the areas of childhood temperament and attachment, in addition to experiences of separation, that might predispose a child to development of panic. Furthermore, a conceptual model of the etiology of panic is proposed to account for diverse outcomes associated with varying developmental pathways.

A similar analysis of the development of obsessive–compulsive behavior is undertaken by Aude Henin and Phil Kendall in Chapter 3. In addition, these authors explore the implications of diverse developmental pathways for the clinical assessment and treatment of this difficult-to-treat disorder. In all three of these opening chapters, the focus is clearly centered on development and its role in the onset and expression of diverse behavior problems.

In Chapter 4, Stephen Hooper and Michael Tramontana provide us a rich glimpse of new advances in the neuropsychological bases of child and adolescent disorders. Following a sophisticated analysis of the neurological basis of emotion, they go on to explore the implications of this analysis for diverse child psychopathologies, including pervasive developmental disorder, attention-deficit/hyperactivity disorder, conduct disorder, depressive disorder, anxiety disorder, post-traumatic stress disorder, and

Tourette's disorder. They conclude their interesting and provocative chapter by proposing a set of ongoing issues and concerns for the field to address in the years ahead.

In the next three chapters, contemporary issues and problems related to adolescent sexual offenders (Judith Becker and John Hunter), adolescent substance abusers (Holly Waldron), and children of lesbian and gay parents (Charlotte Patterson) are examined in considerable detail. For example, Becker and Hunter conclude that important advances in the assessment and treatment of juvenile sexual offenders have been made; equally important, they lay out a clinical and research agenda for the future. Waldron reviews randomized trials that use a variety of family therapy procedures and, in general, concludes that these procedures are effective, at least in the short run. However, she too issues a call for systematic and programmatic research that uses long-term follow-up designs. Such a call seems more than justified given the increase in adolescent substance abuse in recent years. Patterson, in Chapter 7, asks the penetrating question: What kinds of home environments are best able to support children's psychological adjustment and growth? Following an insightful review of the literature, she concludes that a diversity of environments is associated with healthy outcome, including homes in which children are reared by lesbian and gay parents. Research in this area has the potential to contribute knowledge about nontraditional family forms and about their impact on children, encourage innovative approaches to the conceptualization of human development, and inform legal rulings and public policies relevant to children of gay and lesbian parents. Clearly, significant advances are being made in these exciting areas of inquiry.

In the final two chapters of this volume, Joe Durlak examines primary prevention programs in schools, and Mark Weist tackles the difficult topic of expanded mental health services in school settings. Durlak highlights a multitude of primary prevention programs that are effective but cautions us that much more specificity in the research is needed in order to answer basic questions such as "what, who, how, why, when, and where." He also suggests that more work is needed to achieve maximum and enduring preventative effects in these settings. Somewhat similarly, Weist reminds us of the limitations of current mental health service delivery systems for youth and strikes a chord for the advantages of school-based programs. Although not without its own set of limitations, the school setting presents many advantages for reaching youth by developing collaborative programs between schools and community agencies. These final two chapters present stimulating prospects for the future of clinical child psychology and illustrate to us, once again, that the field of clinical child psychology is extremely varied and defies narrow or rigid boundaries.

As with other volumes in this serires, the success of each volume is related in no small way to the calibre of the contributors. We have been fortunate to recruit some of the very best in the field today. We thank them for their timely, scholarly, and provocative contributions. We also wish to thank the editorial and production staffs of Plenum Press. They have been of invaluable assistance in bringing this volume to a timely completion. Nineteen in a row isn't all bad!

THOMAS H. OLLENDICK
RONALD J. PRINZ

Contents

Chapter 3. Obsessive–Compulsive Disorder in Childhood and Adolescence   75

Aude Henin and Philip C. Kendall

Chapter 4.   Advances in the Neuropsychological Bases of
Child and Adolescent Psychopathology: Proposed Models,
Findings, and Ongoing Issues   133

Stephen R. Hooper and Michael G. Tramontana

Chapter 5. Understanding and Treating Child and Adolescent Sexual Offenders 177

Judith V. Becker and John A. Hunter, Jr.

Chapter 6. Adolescent Substance Abuse and Family Therapy Outcome: A Review of Randomized Trials 199

Holly B. Waldron

Chapter 8. Primary Prevention Programs in Schools   283

Joseph A. Durlak

1

Behavior Problems in Preschool Children
Developmental and Family Issues

SUSAN B. CAMPBELL

1. Introduction

It has been shown that serious problems with aggression and impulse control that are apparent by the preschool years are relatively stable and often persist to school entry and beyond (for a review, see Campbell, 1995). However, not all children with early-appearing problems continue to have difficulties. Roughly half the children identified with problems by preschool age will continue on a path toward externalizing problems, but the other half will improve with development. These data are based on several prospective studies of problem preschoolers followed from ages 3–4 to early elementary school age (Campbell, 1994; Campbell, Ewing, Breaux, & Szumowski, 1986; Richman, Stevenson, & Graham, 1982). This indicates that identifying a young child as problematic at one point in time is not useful, in and of itself, in predicting outcome. Although problem behavior is somewhat stable, increasing the relative risk of a child developing a diagnosable disorder by school age, difficult behavior, such as tantrums, noncompliance, overactivity, or difficulty with peers may be an indicator of emerging behavior problems or an age-appropriate, short-lived manifestation of stress. Thus, there appear to be different developmental pathways: Some children with early-onset problems outgrow their difficulties; others have difficulties that either stabilize or worsen with development; still other children do not show problems in the preschool period but

SUSAN B. CAMPBELL • Department of Psychology, University of Pittsburgh, Pittsburgh, Pennsylvania 15260.

Advances in Clinical Child Psychology, Volume 19, edited by Thomas H. Ollendick and Ronald J. Prinz. Plenum Press, New York, 1997.

develop problems by school entry, middle childhood or even early adolescence. What accounts for these different developmental pathways?

2. Possible Sources of Individual Differences

Many researchers, of varying theoretical persuasions, agree that parental behavior and other aspect of the family environment may account for some of these differences in the timing of problem onset and its developmental course (e.g., Greenberg, Speltz, & DeKlyen, 1993; Patterson, DeBaryshe, & Ramsey, 1989; Reid, 1993). A developmental approach to psychopathology in young children is based on the premise that the origins of problems are frequently in evidence by toddlerhood and often emerge from, or are exacerbated by, qualities of the early parent–child relationship (e.g., Cicchetti, Toth, & Lynch, 1995; Greenberg et al., 1993; Sroufe, 1990). Characteristics of the child obviously play a role, for example, individual differences in arousal and irritability (e.g., Campos, Campos, & Barrett, 1989; Goldsmith & Campos, 1982). However, parenting is seen as central to the developmental process and may influence how successfully infants, toddlers, and preschoolers will meet developmental challenges (Kopp, 1989; Sroufe, 1979). Parental socialization strategies may be particularly relevant to understanding which preschoolers with early problems will demonstrate more serious and persistent disorders (Campbell, 1990, 1995), and which will outgrow early difficulties.

This argument seems especially compelling when one considers the dependence of the toddler and preschooler on parental guidance and support. Furthermore, many of the behaviors that are seen as symptoms as disorder when they occur in school-age children (e.g., noncompliance, temper tantrums, aggression toward peers) are quite common, even normative, in toddlers and preschoolers. These problem behaviors often reflect age-appropriate transitions and struggles over autonomy, rather than emerging signs of disorder. However, variations in parental warmth, support, and appropriate control may be major factors in determining whether a difficult toddler masters these developmental transitions or becomes a coercive and demanding preschooler with emerging behavior problems (Campbell, 1990; Greenberg et al., 1993; Shaw & Bell, 1993).

Thus, for example, some parents may skillfully help some hard-to-manage toddlers negotiate autonomy issues, whereas others may exacerbate conflict and fuel noncompliance. Similarly, difficulties cooperating and sharing toys with siblings or peers are hallmarks of normal development (e.g., Dunn, 1988; Shantz, 1987). Adults may manage this normal conflict with patience and appropriate limit setting or they may engender continued struggles that become aggressive. Longitudinal data and a process-oriented approach to understanding children, parents, and their interaction are needed before the different pathways toward and away from problem behavior are to be understood.

Whereas parenting has obvious and direct implications for the development of young children, other aspects of the family environment also are important to consider. These include maternal depression, marital distress, and stressful life events. These may have direct effects on the child, because they create a climate of tension and conflict in the home (Davies & Cummings, 1994). They also may have indirect effects on the child because of their disruptive effect on parenting, which in turn influences the child's behavior and sense of well-being (e.g., Hetherington, 1989; Miller, Cowan, Cowan, Hetherington, & Clingempeel, 1993; Patterson et al., 1989).

In this chapter, I will review some of the work suggesting that parental behavior during toddlerhood and the preschool years plays a significant role in determining which problem preschoolers will continue to have difficulties and which will outgrow their early problems. This review will include studies of nonclinical mother–child dyads, as well as studies of children at risk for psychopathology. The few studies that incorporate fathers will be discussed as well. In addition, studies that examine both compliance and other aspects of self-regulation and social competence, as well as more negative behaviors such as aggression and noncompliance, will be considered. Data from my own study of hard-to-manage preschool boys will be used to illustrate some of these issues.

3. Stability of Problem Behavior

Numerous studies have confirmed that problems in preschoolers are relatively stable (these studies are reviewed in Campbell, 1995). Stability is clearest at the extremes. Children who show only moderate and age-appropriate aggression or noncompliance, or only isolated symptoms, are much less likely to continue to have difficulties than children who show a range of more severe early problems that interfere with their social development and are reflected in deficits in self-control and cooperation with others. Children who are identified as meeting some criteria for problem behavior in the preschool period have about a 50:50 chance of continuing to have difficulties at school age. Findings have been consistent in several studies, despite variations in the way children were initially identified as showing problems, whether representative or high-risk samples were selected, and whether teacher and/or parent reports were used to designate problem status at follow-up (Campbell, Ewing, et al., 1986; Campbell, 1994; Egeland, Kalkoske, Gottesman, & Erickson, 1990; Fischer, Rolf, Hasazi, & Cummings, 1984; McGee, Silva, & Williams, 1984; Richman et al., 1982).

For example, in our own sample of hard-to-manage preschool boys followed from ages 4 through 6, the stability of externalizing behaviors as rated by mothers at both assessments was $r = .68, p < .0001$, when an initial rating of externalizing behavior (Behar Aggression + Hyperactivity; Behar, 1977) was correlated with the externalizing factor of the Child Behavior Checklist (Achenbach & Edelbrock, 1983) at age 6. We have also found, in two separate cohorts of problem children, that depending upon the stringency of criteria used to define problems, from 30% to 50% of preschoolers identified as hard-to-manage will meet criteria for externalizing problems at school entry (Campbell, Ewing, et al., 1986; Campbell, 1994). Furthermore, once problems are stable from preschool to school entry, they are even more likely to continue into adolescence (Ewing & Campbell, 1995).

However, the mere stability of symptomatic behaviors does not clarify the reasons why some children continue to have difficulties and others do not. Our work has focused on trying to identify family variables that are associated both with the early onset of problems by preschool age and their persistence over time. As already noted, two classes of variables may be especially important for understanding individual differences in outcome: parenting variables and indicators of family stress and dysfunction. These will be emphasized in the remainder of this chapter.

4. Parenting Practices and Socialization

Much research has focused on the quality of the early mother–child relationship, particularly maternal sensitivity and responsiveness in infancy, which in turn predicts a secure attachment relationship (Ainsworth, Blehar, Waters, & Wall, 1978; Bretherton, 1985). Attachment theory is based on the premise that infants have particular needs for warmth and nurturance from caregivers, as well as appropriate cognitive and social stimulation and timely responsiveness to their early attempts at social communication (Ainsworth et al., 1978; Bretherton, 1985; Sroufe, 1979; Tronick, 1989). Parents' responses to infant distress and to infant social initiations are seen as laying the groundwork for the development of an internal sense of self-efficacy and well-being, as well as positive relationships with others (Bretherton, 1985; Sroufe & Fleeson, 1986). According to this theoretical perspective, infants who are securely attached have learned that the world is a predictable place, that caregivers can be counted on to protect them from harm and to meet their emotional needs. In addition, attachment security in infancy and toddlerhood has been linked to compliance and prosocial behavior (Frankel & Bates, 1990; Londerville & Main, 1981; Matas, Arend, & Sroufe, 1978), and to social competence in the peer group in the preschool years (Sroufe, 1983; Waters, Wippman, & Sroufe, 1979).

Individual differences in infants also may play a role in the quality of the early parent–child relationship. Some children will be relatively positive in mood and easy to care for, whereas others may evidence irritable, negative, or difficult behavior (Bates, 1980; Goldsmith & Campos, 1982; Thomas, Chess, & Birch, 1968). In infancy or toddlerhood, irritability and fussiness may be a manifestation of characteristics of the child as well as a reflection of the caregiving environment (e.g., Crockenberg, 1981). Appropriate support and responsiveness may help the irritable infant to begin to regulate distress, whereas either limited responses on the part of caregivers or harsh control may serve to exacerbate difficulties with the control of negative affect (Calkins, 1994; Goldsmith & Campos, 1982; Thomas et al., 1968).

In addition to the warmth and involvement that seem especially important in infancy, by toddlerhood, parents must set limits and provide support as young children become more interested in exploring and mastering the physical world, expanding their cognitive, language, and social-cognitive abilities, practicing emerging motor skills, and learning about the world of peers. As their skills evolve and their worlds widen, toddlers require more leeway as well as more control, particularly as they begin to test their emerging autonomy and differentiate self from other. At the same time, the demands on parents for skilled, appropriately timed, and supportive interventions become more complex. In toddlerhood, children require firm limits and clear explanations and expectations. Parents of toddlers and preschoolers must balance appropriate limit setting with warmth and support.

Because this is a time of rapid developmental change during which young children are testing their limits, both internal and external, many behaviors that are considered problematic are also normative. Thus, the ability of parents to handle behaviors such as passive noncompliance, outright defiance, difficulty sharing, and aggression toward siblings or peers may set the stage for parent–child cooperation or ongoing conflict (Campbell, 1990, in press; Sroufe, 1979; Wenar, 1982). Toddlerhood and the early preschool years are important periods of developmental transition; parental management style and affective involvement may be especially salient for children's prosocial development, self-control, and internalization of behavioral standards. Studies of mother–child interaction during toddlerhood and the preschool period indicate quite clearly that the quality of parenting is important for overall socialization (e.g., Dunn, 1988; Kochanska, 1991; Kopp, 1989; Maccoby & Martin, 1983). Parents play the major role in inculcating values and standards, and children begin to internalize these standards and act accordingly during toddlerhood (Dunn, 1988; Kagan, 1981; Kopp, 1989). Developmental theorists place special importance on the toddler's growing awareness of the self as an active agent capable of making independent decisions (Kagan, 1981; Kopp, 1989). Although a sense of self is inextricably interwoven with the child's emerging self-regulation, this growing sense of autonomy also may be at odds with the socialization goals of parents. Crockenberg and Litman (1990) point out that one important facet of young children's growing social competence is their ability to balance their own striving for independence with adult expectations for cooperation and with the needs of others, especially family members.

By the second year, the toddler's tendency to say "no" or otherwise avoid adult requests may be seen as noncompliance or as an important developmental milestone: the establishment of autonomy (Erikson, 1963). Thus, some developmental researchers make distinctions between refusals that reflect self-assertion and are age-appropriate manifestations of autonomy, and outright defiance that reflects anger and noncompliance (e.g., Crockenberg & Litman, 1990; Wenar, 1982). Self-assertion is seen as a positive developmental achievement, whereas excessive defiance may herald the beginning of parent–child conflict. The way in which parents manage this challenging stage of development may have important implications for children's functioning. Parents may interpret an assertive "no" as a challenge to their authority and move in to enforce limits, or they may see it as an opportunity for their child to learn to cooperate in the family toward shared goals. In this context, Crockenberg and Litman (1990) discuss the balance between parental use of power to enforce limits and parents' ability to allow the child some sense of autonomy. The development of autonomy is seen as one indicator of early social competence (Crockenberg & Litman, 1990; Kopp, 1989), and parental management of autonomy strivings may set the stage for later cooperation or for escalating frustration and conflict.

A few studies have observed mother–toddler dyads in naturally occurring interactions in an attempt to study children's assertiveness, defiance, and compliance, and maternal management strategies. In general, these studies suggest that the use of less power-oriented and harsh methods are associated with children's assertiveness and their willingness to negotiate toward mutually agreeable outcomes. Moreover, when negotiation occurs, it is less likely to do so in the context of anger and other indicators of negative affect (Crockenberg & Litman, 1990; Kuczynski,

Radke-Yarrow, Kochanska, & Girnius-Brown, 1987; Lytton, 1980). On the other hand, when mothers issue strict commands, give few reasons or explanations, and leave no room for negotiation or discussion, toddlers are more likely to show anger and defiance (Kuczynski et al., 1987; Lytton, 1980).

For example, Crockenberg and Litman (1990) observed mother–toddler interactions during a laboratory cleanup task and at home during the dinner hour. Extensive coding of maternal and child behavior indicated that high levels of negative control (verbal and physical prohibitions, punishment, threats, criticism) were associated with outright defiance across settings. Guidance (redirects, suggestions, explanations, offers of assistance) was associated with self-assertion across settings, whereas moderate control (clear directives, rewards for compliance) was associated with compliance. When sequential analyses were undertaken, it was found that a mother's use of negative control was more often followed by defiance, whereas her use of moderate control plus guidance led to increased compliance; as in the correlational analyses, guidance was followed by children's assertive responses to requests.

Studies suggest that cooperation and social competence, as well as the establishment of shared goals, are facilitated when parents provide clear but positive limits. In addition, reasoning and explanations provide a context for the desired behavior (Crockenberg & Litman, 1990; Kuczynski et al., 1987; Lytton, 1980). Maternal support and warmth are also associated with greater cooperation and less frustration during problem-solving tasks in toddlerhood (Frankel & Bates, 1990; Matas et al., 1978) and with prosocial behavior and concern for others (Zahn-Waxler, Radke-Yarrow, & King, 1979). Finally, emotional understanding, empathy, and cooperation with peers also are facilitated by positive parental involvement paired with appropriate explanations and limit setting (e.g., Denham, Renwick, & Holt, 1991; Dunn, 1988; Hart, DeWolf, Wozniak, & Burts, 1992; Maccoby & Martin, 1983; Turner, 1991).

This style of parental behavior that combines high warmth, high involvement, clear limit-setting, and reasoning and explanations is akin to what Baumrind (1967) labeled "authoritative." Most studies of normal development suggest that this is the optimal style for inculcating moral values, internal controls, and prosocial behavior during the early stages of socialization (Dunn, 1988; Kochanska, 1991; Maccoby & Martin, 1983). A number of mechanisms have been hypothesized to account for these relationships. These include the probability that authoritative parents are more likely than more negative or uninvolved parents to model positive interactions, negotiating strategies and problem-solving styles in their encounters with their young children, as well as with other family members (Dunn, Brown, & Beardsall, 1991). In addition, much direct teaching goes on in the context on mother–child encounters that specifically involves concern for others, discussions of feelings, and suggestions about appropriate or expected ways of behaving in social situations (e.g., Denham, Renwick-Debardi, & Hewes, 1994; Dunn, 1988; Dunn et al., 1991; Zahn-Waxler et al., 1979). Thus, the young child is continuously given prescriptions for expected behavior in specific social situations. In the context of authoritative parenting, these expectations are conveyed to the child in a manner that respects autonomy, feelings, and goals. Moreover, much of this teaching and modeling occurs in a positive emotional context, with highly charged anger and negative affect reserved to convey only salient messages about serious transgressions (e.g., Zahn-Waxler et al., 1979).

In addition, it has been argued that the quality of the parent–child relationship is important in determining whether parental expectations for appropriate behavior will be met (e.g., Calkins, 1994; Crockenberg & Litman, 1990; Greenberg et al., 1993; Maccoby & Martin, 1983). When there is a warm, supportive relationship, toddlers and preschoolers have more to lose when they are irritable, noncompliant, or aggressive and more to gain when they are positive in mood and compliant. For example, Maccoby and Martin (1983) have suggested that supportive, sensitive parents balance demands and expectations for mature, competent, and cooperative behavior with their own compliance to their children's requests. In addition, in positive parent–child relationships, both partners get pleasure from ongoing harmonious interactions and are more likely to have shared goals. Mother–child reciprocity and shared positive affect are seen as important contributors to effective socialization.

Studies of children with behavior problems suggest that they rarely receive this type of positive, proactive parenting, either because parents are unable to provide it or because they themselves are more likely to elicit less optimal power-assertive parenting strategies (e.g., Gardner, 1987, 1989; Lee & Bates, 1985). Most research has focused on harsh, punitive discipline that has been widely associated with externalizing behavior in young children (Campbell, 1995; Greenberg et al., 1993; Patterson, 1980). Thus, it has been well documented that children who are seen as overactive, impulsive, aggressive, and noncompliant are more likely to engage in conflict-ridden and coercive interactions with their parents (Campbell, 1990; Patterson, 1980). Such children tend to be demanding, to ignore parental requests, and to engage in troublesome, defiant, and aggressive behavior (Campbell, 1990; Gardner, 1987, 1989; Lee & Bates, 1985; Patterson, 1980). Consistent with studies of nonclinical samples, negative parenting that is harsh, punitive, impatient, and uninvolved is associated with poorer self-regulation and lower peer competence in normal samples and in children with behavior problems. In addition, in the absence of either sufficient guidance and control from parents, or in the face of harsh control, problems may be more likely to persist. Moreover, some children may be more likely than others to suffer from the adverse impact of limited parental warmth and parental anger, and these may be the very children who are more likely to elicit harsh, negative parenting, because they are more excitable and prone to explosive and defiant behavior (e.g., Shaw & Bell, 1993).

In addition, the relationship history may also be important; high degrees of reciprocity and cooperation, as well as negative and coercive interactions, may be a result not only of the immediate dyadic situation, but also the expectations each member of the dyad has about the other's likely behavior (e.g., Dumas & LaFreniere, 1993). Thus, negative maternal control may also be one important factor in the maintenance of problems (Campbell & Ewing, 1990; Greenberg et al., 1993; Patterson et al., 1989). Harsh parenting has implications not only for concurrent parent–child relationships and socialization, but also for the quality of the ongoing relationship and the child's internalization of standards of behavior and self-regulation. For example, Feldman and Weinberger (1994) suggested that ineffective parenting observed earlier in development and characterized by rejection, power-assertive discipline, and inconsistency should have an impact on children's self-regulation, which in turn should predict behavior problems at a later date. Although they studied children making the transition from middle childhood to early adolescence, their data were consistent with this model. We also have examined ineffective parenting, operationalized as negative maternal control, as a predictor of continuing problems in hard-to-manage preschool children.

4.1. Negative Maternal Control and Child Behavior Problems: Illustrations from a Study of Hard-to-Manage Preschool Boys

4.1.1. Concurrent Relations

In our own work, we have reported that mother–child interaction in young children who are identified as hard to manage tends to be more conflict-ridden and negative. This was found in two cohorts of children observed in different situations with their mothers. Cohort 1 (44 parent-identified behavior-problem preschoolers and 22 comparison children) was observed in a structured play interaction meant to optimize maternal involvement with the child in a low-stress situation (Campbell, Breaux, Ewing, Szumowski, & Pierce, 1986). Mothers of problem 3-year-olds were more directive and more negative during this play interaction than comparison mothers, although their children did not exhibit more aggressive play or noncompliance. However, dyadic ratings of the quality of the interaction suggested that problem dyads engaged in less positive, harmonious interaction than comparison dyads, and that mothers of problem children were more intrusive, inappropriately overdirecting their children's play.

At a 1-year follow-up when children were 4, mothers of problem children continued to be more negative than mothers of control children, although they were less so than they had been initially. However, within the problem group, there was surprising stability in maternal behavior. For example, mothers who praised their children at the initial assessment also were more likely to do so at follow-up ($r = .41$, $p = .02$), and mothers who were more negative at intake were also more negative at follow-up ($r = .62$, $p < .001$). It is especially noteworthy that these maternal behaviors were observed in a relatively unstructured play interaction in which demands on the dyad were minimal.

In our second cohort of children, we observed mother–child interaction during a toy cleanup situation meant to elicit confrontation and noncompliance. Cohort 2 consisted of 112 preschool boys, 69 of whom had been identified at age 4 as hard to manage by mothers and/or teachers. After a 15-minute free-play period, boys were asked by their mothers to put all the toys away in a large basket (Campbell, 1994; Campbell, Pierce, March, Ewing, & Szumowski, 1994). Although the boys themselves did not differ consistently on measures of noncompliance, mothers of problem boys were more negative, impatient, and controlling than mothers of comparison boys. However, data obtained across contexts (home, school, lab) indicated that problem boys were more overactive, impulsive, and disruptive in all three settings than comparison boys and more noncompliant with their preshcool teachers (Campbell et al., 1994). Moreover, maternal negative control and child noncompliance were moderately correlated ($r = .45$, $p < .001$), underscoring the bidirectional and mutually regulated pattern of conflict that was apparent.

The onset of problems undoubtedly reflects a transaction between child characteristics and family factors (Campbell, 1990). We examined this empirically by computing multiple correlations to assess whether a combined set of measures of child problems and maternal behavior was associated with maternal and teacher ratings of boys' externalizing problems at age 4. The summed ratings of the aggression and hyperactivity scales of the Behar Preschool Behavior Questionnaire (Behar, 1977) were used as the index of externalizing problems obtained from both mothers and preschool teachers (teacher data were available on the 101 preschool attenders in the sample). A maternal-interview measure of difficult infant behavior at 3 months (alpha = .76) and 12 months (alpha = .64), derived from a structured interview, was utilized, and composite measures of child non-compliance (complaining, whining, not picking up toys) and negative maternal control (number of negative, irritable verbalizations and ratings of negative affect and intrusive control), derived from the cleanup observation (see Campbell, 1994; Campbell, Pierce, March, & Ewing, 1991, 1994; for details), were entered into a hierarchial regression analysis. We first controlled for social class and then entered the maternal interview composite of infant difficultness at 3 and 12 months. The observed noncompliance measure was entered next, followed by the negative maternal control composite score. The interaction between negative maternal control and child noncompliance was entered last. This interaction term was meant to capture the reciprocal and escalating nature of mother–child conflict. The multiple R of .50 (F [4, 106] = 8.85, $p <$ .0001) was significant. Together, early (reported) and concurrent (observed) child behavior problems accounted for 14% of the variance in material ratings of externalizing problems, and negative maternal control accounted for another 8% of the variance. The interaction term did not contribute additional variance. Thus, both child behavior and negative maternal control contributed *unique and independent* variance to maternal ratings of externalizing behavior problems at age 4.

A similar analysis was conducted at age 4 with teacher ratings as the dependent variable. Observed negative maternal control made the largest contribution to teacher ratings of externalizing behavior, accounting for 9% of the variance (F [3, 97] = 9.73, $p <$ .01). Concurrent child behavior in the laboratory during cleanup was not significant, and maternal reports of a difficult infancy were of borderline significance in the equation (R^2ch = .03, p = .075). These analyses, then, highlight concurrent relationships between negative maternal control and preschool children's externalizing behavior, as assessed by different informants in different settings.

4.1.2. *Negative Maternal Control and Children's Continuing Problems*

As noted earlier, negative maternal control may also predict persistent problems, possibly because it is an index of an impaired mother–child relationship and partly for other reasons, such as modeling inappropriate conflict-resolution styles. In our first cohort, we reported that maternal negative control observed during play was associated with continuing problems both at school entry (Campbell, Ewing, Breaux, 1986) at age 9 (Campbell & Ewing, 1990). However, in these data, this association was not independent of the severity and chronicity of children's problems.

The data from Cohort 2 also indicate that negative and conflicted early interaction predicts continuing problems. The correlation between negative maternal control observed in the laboratory at age 4 and ratings of externalizing problems at age 6 was significant across informants (mother reports: r (104) = .44, p < .001; father reports: r (86) = .31, p < .01; teacher reports: r (98) = .46, p < .001). These correlations highlight the predictive relations between children's problems and earlier more restrictive and negative maternal control. However, they do not indicate whether maternal control predicts later problems independent of initial problems or a third variable that might account for this association.

Therefore, hierarchical multiple regression analyses were conducted next to determine whether negative maternal control predicted adult ratings of behavior problems at age 6 *uniquely*, after controlling for relevant demographic measures and initial problem ratings. Mother, father, and teacher ratings of children's age 6 externalizing problems served as the three dependent variables. Mothers and teachers completed the appropriate versions of the Child Behavior Checklist (CBCL; Achenbach & Edelbrock, 1983; 1986) at age 6; the externalizing score was used in these analyses. Fathers completed a modified version (Campbell, 1994) of the Swanson, Nolan, and Pelham (SNAP) questionnaire (Pelham & Bender, 1982). An externalizing score was derived by summing the symptom ratings for oppositional disorder, attention deficit disorder, and peer problems. Preliminary analysis of demographic variables indicated that child age was not associated with age 6 ratings, social class [assessed with the Hollingshead (1975) four-factor index] was correlated with parent ratings of problems, and child IQ (assessed with the Stanford–Binet at intake) was associated with father and teacher ratings.

Initial problem levels were partialed out after social class in order to control for the stability of behavior problems per se. IQ was controlled when predicting teacher and father ratings. The negative maternal control composite score was entered next, followed by the interaction between negative maternal control and initial problem levels. The interaction term was included on the assumption that behavior problems and maternal negative control should have more than additive effects (reflected in the main effects); rather, the combination of high initial problems and high negative maternal control should be associated with particularly high rates of behavior problems at follow-up, a reflection of an escalating cycle of coercive interaction (Patterson, 1982). The results of these analyses are summarized in Table 1.

As can be seen in the table, there was a trend for maternal negative control to contribute independent variance to age 6 maternal ratings of externalizing problems on the CBCL, after first controlling for *socioeconomic status* (SES) and initial problem levels. Because 48% of the variance

TABLE 1

Demographic Variables, Initial Problem Ratings,
and Negative Maternal Control as Predictors
of Adult Reports of Externalizing Symptoms at Age 6

Predictor variable	Mother ($n = 105$) R^2ch	Father ($n = 84$) R^2ch	Teacher ($n = 95$) R^2ch
SES (Hollingshead)	.078***	.05*	a
Initial problems	.404****	.273****	.287****
IQ at intake	a	.071***	.031*
Maternal control	.014†	.001	.041**
Problems × maternal control	.006	.008	.027*

Note. The dependent variables include the externalizing scale of the Child Behavior Checklist and Teacher Report Form completed by mothers and teachers, respectively; fathers completed a modified version of the SNAP.
aDemographic variables were included only if they correlated at a significant level with the dependent variable. Therefore, SES was not included in the analysis of teacher ratings and IQ was not included in the analysis of mothers' ratings.
†$p = .09$; *$p < .05$; **$p < .02$; ***$p < .01$; ****$p < .001$.

was already accounted for by SES and the stability of maternal ratings from age 4 to 6, even a unique relationship of this magnitude is suggestive. The interaction between initial maternal ratings and maternal negative control did not approach significance, however. The overall R of .71 ($R^2 = .50$, $F [4, 100] = 25.38$, $p < .0001$) was highly significant. Fathers' ratings of problems were predicted only by the combination of SES, IQ, and initial maternal ratings ($R = .63$, $R^2 = .40$, $F [5, 78] = 10.52$, $p < .0001$).

The prediction of teacher ratings at age 6 was consistent with our underlying assumptions, however, and this is especially impressive, because these teachers were different from the preschool teachers who were involved initially in rating the children as problematic, and most children were in new schools. Even after controlling for appropriate demographics and initial problem ratings, both negative maternal control and the interaction between negative maternal control and initial problem ratings were significant in the equation. Overall, 38% of the variance in teacher ratings was accounted for by earlier measures ($R = .62$, $F [4, 90] = 14.09$, $p < .0001$).

The significant initial problem by maternal negative control interaction was followed up with a one-way ANOVA, based on a median split on both variables. Results indicated a significant main effect of group $F [3, 95] = 9.36$, $p < .0001$. A follow-up Newman–Keuls test indicated that the group with low scores on both negative maternal control and initial behavior problems received the lowest externalizing score from teachers at age 6

($M = 49.15$), differing significantly from all other groups. Boys high on only one factor received midrange scores (low maternal negative, high initial problems, $M = 56.00$; high maternal negative, low initial problems, $M = 55.10$). However, consistent with expectations, the boys with high scores on both initial maternal ratings of problems and negative maternal control at age 4 received the highest teacher ratings at follow-up ($M = 60.07$).

These data, then, provide support for the notion that negative maternal control may maintain problem behavior, and that bidirectional influences may be especially potent when the child is hard to manage and the mother is harsh and controlling. These data are consistent with findings reported on older children (e.g., Feldman & Weinberger, 1994; Olweus, 1980; Patterson, 1982). However, few studies have examined these issues in children making the transition from preschool to school. These findings are also noteworthy, because one set of follow-up measures was obtained from teachers, most of whom had not known the child at the initial assessment. Despite this independent assessment of problems at age 6, earlier child behavior and maternal negative control observed in the laboratory at age 4 were predictive of externalizing behavior rated by teachers, based on their observations of classroom behavior. This underscores the importance of the early mother–child interaction and suggests that a conflict-ridden relationship may set the stage for prolonged problems in self-control, as reflected in higher rates of aggression, noncompliance, and disruptive behavior, across contexts (home, school, laboratory; see Campbell, 1994; Campbell et al., 1994).

5. Family Stress and Children's Problems

A large body of data links family stress to children's problems. On the one hand, although young children may be buffered to some degree from the impact of distal family stress such as illness in extended family members, because they are more dependent on family members who are usually primary caregivers and because stress often has an impact on parenting, the role of family stress and dysfunction is important to examine. Research has focused on stressful life events and daily hassles, on maternal depression, and on marital conflict (e.g., Belsky, Crnic, & Gable, 1995; Egeland et al., 1990; Miller et al., 1993; Richman et al., 1982; Webster-Stratton, 1988). Not surprisingly in many studies, these have been correlated (see Kazdin & Kagan, 1995; Masten, Best, & Garmezy, 1991). However, these various indicators of family stress are more often looked at separately.

In general, higher rates of stressful events, higher levels of maternal depressive symptoms, and more marital conflict are associated with more behavior problems in young children (e.g., Richman et al., 1982; Miller et al., 1993; Snyder, 1991). Furthermore, the pathways from family stress to children's problems appear to be complex, including both direct effects of family disharmony and conflict on children's sense of well-being (see Davies & Cummings, 1994, for a theoretical discussion of this issue as it relates to marital conflict) and indirect effects that are mediated through their impact on the quality of parenting (e.g., Cummings & Davies, 1994; Miller et al., 1993; Zahn-Waxler, Iannotti, Cummings, & Denham, 1990).

Maternal depression has been examined in relation to maternal be-havior and has been associated with less responsive, involved parenting, more negative affect expression, and less effective enforcement of limits, which in turn predict behavior problems (see Cummings & Davies, 1994 for a review). In addition, maternal depression is associated with marital discord, suggesting that family conflict may account for some of these relationships (Downey & Coyne, 1990). For example, Miller et al. (1993) examined parental depression, marital conflict (observed and self-reported), and parent–child interaction (observed warmth and control) in relation to concurrent reports of externalizing problems in a sample of normal 3½-year-olds. Mothers who reported more depressive symptoms were also less positive in interaction with their husbands, and more conflict was observed in the marital relationship. Path analysis indicated a direct link between marital conflict and children's externalizing symptoms, while the effects of maternal depression were mediated by their relationship to negative affect expression and low warmth. The results for fathers indicate no direct relationship between marital conflict and children's problems; however, fathers who reported higher levels of depressive symptoms were less controlling with their children, who in turn showed more problems; moreover, as with mothers, there was a direct path from low parental warmth to children's problems.

Jouriles and colleagues (Jouriles et al., 1991) examined various facets of marital adjustment including general adjustment, specific disagree-ments over childrearing, and young children's exposure to marital conflict, and their relationships to children's behavior problems in 3-year-old boys. Childrearing disagreements had the clearest association with children's noncompliant and oppositional behavior as rated by mothers. In addition, childrearing disagreements accounted for variance in behavior problem ratings after controlling for general marital adjustment and for the fre-quency with which children witnessed marital conflict.

In a recent study, Belsky et al. (1995) obtained measures of parental personality, childrearing attitudes, and family stress, as reflected in daily hassles, and observed family interaction in the home in the early evening.

Mothers, fathers, and their 15-month-olds were observed and the quality of coparenting was coded from narrative accounts of ongoing interactions. Surprisingly, attitudes toward discipline were not associated with the quality of coparenting; however, unsupportive–emotional coparenting episodes, characterized by negative affect and statements that undermined or contradicted the partner, were predicted by differences in personality style and exacerbated by daily hassles; that is, when there were large differences in affect expression and extraversion between parents, along with high levels of daily stresses, cooperative parenting was most likely to be undermined, and parents were least likely to work together to socialize their toddler. This is the type of interparental disagreement that would be expected to predict more noncompliance and testing of limits in toddlers, and possibly to be associated with the onset of behavior problems in early childhood.

Whereas the Jouriles et al. (1991) study examines maternal reports of parenting disagreements and children's behavior problems, the Belsky et al. (1995) study targets observations of parental interaction around childrearing. Both studies underscore the importance of examining the family as a system and understanding more about how stresses in the marital relationship impact upon the quality of parent–child relationships and parental cooperation around shared childrearing goals. Although very few studies have examined coparenting of young children, it seems likely that arguments and conflicts around child management, parental expectations, and maturity demands, especially when they occur in the context of an unsupportive marital relationship and in concert with other stresses, will be associated with children's behavior problems.

Taken together, then, a growing body of evidence links various indicators of family stress and conflict to less effective, warm, involved, and appropriate parenting, and to children's behavior problems. Furthermore, studies document both direct effects of family stress and conflict on children and indirect effects reflecting the negative impact of stress and dysphoria on parenting competence (Belsky et al., 1995; Miller et al., 1993; Snyder, 1991).

5.1. Illustrations from a Study of Hard-to-Manage Preschool Boys

In my own work, I also have included maternal reports of depressive symptoms, marital distress, and stressful life events, and examined their associations with children's problems. Stressful life events were operationalized as the sum of negative ratings on the Life Experiences Survey (Sarason, Johnson, & Siegel, 1978). Depressive symptoms were assessed with the Center for Epidemiologic Studies Depression Scale (CES-D; Radloff, 1977) at intake and follow-up. The marital dysfunction measure at intake was made up of a composite score derived from an interview measure of spousal support and the Dyadic Adjustment Scale (Spanier, 1976); the spouse support scale from the Parenting Stress Index was obtained at age 6 (Abidin, 1986). (Details may be found in Campbell et al., 1991, and Campbell, 1994.)

Not surprisingly, mothers of boys who were seen as problem preschoolers reported more stressful life events; there was also a trend for mothers of problem boys to report less marital satisfaction and support, and more separation/divorce than was reported by comparison mothers (Campbell et al., 1991). Moreover, concurrent family stress was associated with maternal reports of externalizing problems at initial assessment, independent of observed child behavior and negative maternal control; the addition of life stress in the hierarchical regression examining concurrent associations between family variables and children's problems increased the multiple correlation from $R = .50$ to $R = .53$ (Fch [5,106] = 4.49, $p < .05$), although maternal depression was not associated with problem ratings independent of other measures.

At intake, these three measures of family stress were moderately correlated with one another. Thus, women who reported more negative life events also reported higher levels of depressive symptoms ($r = .38$, $p < .001$) and less positive relationships with their spouses ($r = -.39$, $p < .001$). Higher levels of depressive symptoms were also associated with less positive marriages ($r = -.27$, $p < .01$). At the age 6 follow-up, stress measures showed a rather marked degree of stability in all three domains: negative life events, $r = .56$, $p < .001$; depressive symptoms, $r = .50$, $p < .001$; marital stress, $r = .37$, $p < .01$. They were likewise related to each other (r's from $-.35$ to $.37$, all $p < .001$). Thus, family difficulties that continue may be especially important to understanding the persistence of children's problems.

So far, we have demonstrated that family stress is associated with the identification of children as showing externalizing behavior problems at age 4, and that various indicators of family stress and dysfunction are moderately correlated and stable over time. We also examined whether initial family stress measures predicted *later* problem ratings. After first controlling for initial problem levels and demographics, we again examined main effects of each of the measures of family stress first, followed by their interaction with initial child problems. We hypothesized that the synergistic effects of high levels of family stress or dysfunction paired with high rates of initial child problems might exacerbate problem levels at follow-up. These data are summarized in Table 2. As before, appropriate demographic measures and initial child problems were entered first in

TABLE 2
Demographic Variables, Initial Problem Ratings,
and Family Stress Measures as Predictors
of Adult Reports of Externalizing Symptoms at Age 6

Predictor variable	Mother ($n = 105$) R^2ch	Father ($n = 84$) R^2ch	Teacher ($n = 95$) R^2ch
SES (Hollingshead)	.078***	.05*	b
Initial problems	.404****	.273****	.287****
IQ at intake	b	.071***	.031*
Maternal depression	.058****	.056***	.009
Problems × depression	.000	.011	.003
Stressful events	.018†	.016	.036*
Problems × events	.001	.003	.010
Marital distress[a]	.042***	.007	.004
Problems × marital	.000	.009	.003

Note. The dependent variables include the externalizing scale of the Child Behavior Checklist and Teacher Report Form completed by mothers and teachers, respectively; fathers completed a modified version of the SNAP.
[a]The n's differ for the analyses of marital distress because only women with partners were included (mother report, $n = 91$; father report, $n = 82$; teacher report, $n = 82$). In addition, because of the somewhat smaller sample, the changes in r^2 for the demographic and initial behavior problem measures also vary slightly from those reported in the table for the other analyses.
[b]Demographic variables were included only if they correlated at a significant level with the dependent variable. Therefore, SES was not included in the analyses of teacher ratings, and IQ was not included in the analyses of mothers' ratings.
†$p = .09$; *$p < .05$; **$p < .02$; ***$p < .01$; ****$p < .001$.

each equation. Although significant main effects were obtained, none of the interaction terms even approached significance, providing support for additive but not multiplicative effects of preschool boys' initial problems and family stress as predictors of continuing problems

Maternal reports of depressive symptoms at intake predicted continuing problems as reported both by mothers and by fathers (for mothers: $R = .74$, $F [4, 100] = 29.44$, $p < .0001$; for fathers: $R = .68$, $F [5, 78] = 13.33$, $p < .0001$) Indeed, in both equations, mothers' depressive symptoms accounted for between 5% and 6% of the variance in later problem ratings, after controlling for demographics and initial problems. Maternal reports of marital distress at intake also predicted later behavior problem ratings by mothers, accounting for 4% of the variance ($R = .68$, $F [4, 86] = 18.98$, $p < .0001$). Finally, stressful life events predicted both maternal and teacher ratings of problems 2 years later (for mothers: $R = .71$, $F [4, 100] = 25.14$, $p < $

.0001; for teachers: $R = .60$, $F [4, 90] = 12.88$, $p < .0001$). These data are consistent with numerous studies suggesting that children with problems are more likely to continue to have difficulties in the context of more stressful, less supportive, and less stable family environments (Egeland et al., 1990; McGee et al., 1984; Patterson et al., 1989; Richman et al., 1982).

One follow-up analysis was conducted to determine whether both maternal depression at intake and marital distress contributed to maternal ratings of problems at follow-up or whether maternal depression mediated the relation between stressful events and problem ratings. The analysis was conducted only on the two-parent families ($n = 91$), first controlling for initial problem levels and then examining the contributions made by each variable with the other controlled. When depression was entered into the equation after behavior problems, it accounted for 10% ($Fch [2, 88] = 16.82$, $p < .0001$), and marital distress accounted for another 3% of the variance ($F [3, 87] = 5.90$, $p < .02$) in problem ratings. When the order was reversed, marital distress accounted for 6% ($Fch [2, 88] = 10.07$, $p < .01$), and depression still accounted for 7% of the variance ($Fch [3, 87] = 12.29$, $p < .001$) in maternal ratings of externalizing problems. Thus, although depression appeared to account for some of the impact of marital distress, both were predictive of ratings of children's problems at follow-up. Again, consistent with an additive rather than an interactive model, only main effects were significant. The interaction term of marital distress and maternal depression scores was not significant in the equation.

Finally, we asked whether concurrent measures of stress contributed unique variance to measures of age 6 problems. Marital distress and maternal depressive symptoms were associated with age 6 ratings of problems even after controlling for initial measures of children's problems and initial family stress. Each of these variables at age 6 accounted for another 5% of the variance in maternal ratings ($p < .01$). This supports the view that both early ongoing family difficulties predict continuing problems at school entry.

Additional follow-up analyses were conducted to examine subgroups of children with consistently high levels of stress, as compared to moderate and low levels. For each subject, a stress index was computed for the initial and 2-year follow-up assessment. At each time, stressful life events were weighted as 0, 1, or 2, based on the sum of the negative ratings (highest 25% = 2; middle 50% = 1; lowest 25% = 0). Maternal depression was likewise weighted as 0, 1, or 2 at each assessment, following a similar distribution (CES-D greater than 14 = 2; CES-D between 14 and 4 = 1; CES-D less than 4 = 0). Solo parenting or marital satisfaction below the median was weighted a 1. A stress score was then computed for the initial and follow-up period (range = 0–5). Families with scores above the median of

2 at both times were considered to evidence chronic stress; those with only one score above the median were considered to be experiencing intermittent stress; those with scores below 2 at both assessments were considered to be in a relatively low-stress environment. Within the problem group, the breakdown was as follows: chronic stress, n = 23; intermittent stress, n = 20; low stress, n = 21. Within the control group, 9, 11, and 20 families were classified as chronic, intermittent, and low, respectively. Surprisingly, the distributions did not vary systematically by group.

We then examined the stress index in children with and without elevated scores on the CBCL (defined as a T-score at or above 63 on the externalizing scale as completed by mothers). As can be seen in Figure 1, high levels of chronic stress are associated with both the persistence of problems and their onset. Over half the problem boys with persistently high levels of symptoms at follow-up were living in chronically stressful homes. Of the 6 boys in the control group with newly emerging problems, all experienced high levels of family stress at intake, and 5 out of 6 (83%) continued to experience high family stress at follow-up. On the other hand, relatively low levels of chronic stress were associated with the absence of problems at follow-up in both groups: the problem children who improved and the control group without problems. The fact that these relationships are found in both problem and control groups suggests that

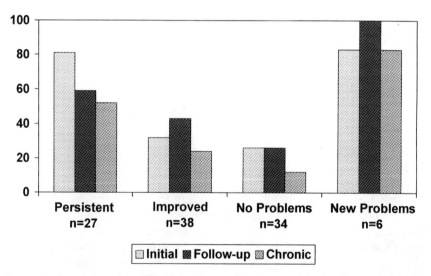

FIGURE 1. Proportion of families above the median stress index as a function of CBCL (T > 63) scores at age 6.

chronic stress has an impact not only on boys with early-appearing problems, but also on boys who were not identified as problems at preschool age but are beginning to show emerging problems by school entry. In earlier analyses of this same data set, we reported that boys with new problems, as defined by adult ratings above a critical cutoff, came from families in which mothers reported more depressive symptoms and less marital satisfaction at follow-up.

These data linking family adversity to the onset of problems, as well as to their persistence, are also supported by other studies. Both Richman et al. (1982) and Egeland et al. (1990) reported that maternal depressive feelings and other indicators of family adversity, including stressful life events and marital difficulties, were associated with newly emerging problems. In all three studies, these findings are based on small samples, and may be seen as hypothesis generating and suggestive.

6.   Combined Effects of Negative Maternal Control and a Stressful Family Environment

It has already been suggested that family stress may have direct effects on children's functioning or be mediated by the relationship between family stress and parenting. In the current data set, we were able to examine these possibilities with the teacher data at follow-up, since both negative maternal control and stressful life events in the family predicted later teacher ratings when examined singly. In prior analyses, we reported that family stress predicted higher levels of negative maternal behavior (Campbell et al., 1991), a finding that has been reported by others as well (Snyder, 1991). Indeed, once maternal negative control was entered into a regression analysis prior to stressful life events, events were no longer significant in the equation, indicating that maternal negative control accounted for this association. Women experiencing more stress were more negative with their preschool boys during the observation of toy cleanup, and these youngsters were in turn more noncompliant and overactive. These boys were then rated as more problematic by teachers at follow-up. Results were similar when the family stress index was substituted for the life events score in the regression equation. Thus, from the perspective of the teachers, boys who had experienced more negative maternal control were more likely to be seen as problematic at age 6. This suggests that women feeling stressed are more likely to be harsh and negative with their preschool boy, who becomes more difficult to manage in other contexts as well.

On the other hand, it is interesting that in the regression equations predicting maternal ratings, negative maternal control accounted for less than 2% of the variance, and this minimal effect was totally eliminated when various indicators of stress were entered first. Indeed, when the family stress index at ages 4 and 6 were included, together they accounted for 13% of the variance in maternal ratings of externalizing problems. Thus, from the perspective of mothers of young boys, family stress, especially chronic family stress, was a critical factor in perceptions of children's problems.

7. Different Developmental Pathways

The research reviewed from both our own study and others suggests that children do follow different developmental pathways. Our data indicate that one group of boys was seen as hard to manage at age 4 by both mothers and teachers. When initial symptoms were more severe, mothers were more negative and controlling, and family stress was more severe and chronic, problems were more likely to persist. A second group of hard-to-manage preschool boys was living in less stressful family circumstances, and their mothers were initially more patient and less negative. These boys emerged with fewer problems at age 6, possibly because their less-stressed mothers were able to provide them with more support and guidance as they made the transition to school, and early problems were not exacerbated. A third small group of boys, not seen as problems by their preschool teachers, developed problems by age 6. This group of boys was living in particularly dysfunctional family circumstances with more depression, negative life events, and marital distress, although their mothers were not more negative and controlling when observed at age 4. Finally, boys with low levels of initial problems living in normal family environments continued on a normal developmental trajectory. These findings highlight the importance of childrearing practices and family context in understanding the course of problem behavior in young children. Research that teases apart these complex aspects of socialization and childrearing, and that takes into account family circumstances, especially marital harmony and coparenting, will be necessary to clarify their role in children's early development, both normal and abnormal.

8. References

Abidin, R. R. (1986). *Parenting Stress Index manual* (2nd ed.) Charlottesville, VA: Pediatric Psychology Press.

Achenbach, T. M., & Edelbrock, C. (1983). *Manual for the Child Behavior Checklist and the Child Behavior Profile*. Burlington, VT: University of Vermont, Department of Psychiatry.

Achenbach, T. M., & Edelbrock, C. (1986). *Manual for the Teacher's Report Form and Teacher Version of the Child Behavior Profile*. Burlington, VT: University of Vermont, Department of Psychiatry.

Ainsworth, M. D. S., Blehar, M., Waters, E., & Wall, S. (1978). *Patterns of attachment*. Hillsdale, NJ: Erlbaum.

Bates, J. E. (1980). The concept of difficult temperament. *Merrill–Palmer Quarterly, 26*, 299–319.

Baumrind, D. (1967). Child care practices anteceding three patterns of preschool behavior. *Genetic Psychology Monographs, 75*, 43–88.

Behar, L. (1977). The Preschool Behavior Questionnaire. *Journal of Abnormal Child Psychology, 5*, 265–276.

Belsky, J., Crnic, K., & Gable, S. (1995). The determinants of co-parenting in families with toddler boys: Spousal differences and daily hassles. *Child Development, 66*, 629–642.

Bretherton, I. (1985). Attachment theory: Retrospect and prospect. In I. Bretherton & E. Waters (Eds.), Growing points of attachment theory and research. *Monographs of the Society for Research in Child Development, 50*, (Serial No. 209), 3–35.

Calkins, S. (1994). Origins and outcomes of individual differences in emotion regulation. In N. A. Fox (Ed.), *The development of emotion regulation* (pp. 53–72). *Monographs of the Society for Research in Child Development, 59* (2–3).

Campbell, S. B. (1990). *Behavior problems in preschool children: Clinical and developmental issues*. New York: Guilford Press.

Campbell, S. B. (1994). Hard-to-manage preschool boys: Externalizing behavior, social competence, and family context at two-year follow-up. *Journal of Abnormal Child Psychology, 22*, 147–166.

Campbell, S. B. (1995). Behavior problems in preschool children: A review of recent research. *Journal of Child Psychology and Psychiatry, 36*, 113–149.

Campbell, S. B. (in press). Developmental perspectives on child psychopathology. In T. H. Ollendick & M. Hersen (Eds.), *Handbook of clinical child psychology* (3rd ed.). New York: Plenum Press.

Campbell, S. B., Breaux, A. M., Ewing, L. J., Szumowski, E. K., & Pierce, E. W. (1986). Parent identified problem preschoolers: Mother–child interaction during play at intake and one-year follow-up. *Journal of Abnormal Child Psychology, 14*, 425–440.

Campbell, S. B., & Ewing, L. J. (1990). Hard-to manage preschoolers: Adjustment at age nine and predictors of continuing symptoms. *Journal of Child Psychology and Psychiatry, 31*, 871–889.

Campbell, S. B., Ewing, L. J., Breaux, A. M., & Szumowski, E. K. (1986). Parent-referred problem three-year-olds: Follow-up at school entry. *Journal of Child Psychology and Psychiatry, 27*, 473–488.

Campbell, S. B., Pierce, E., March, C., & Ewing, L. J. (1991). Noncompliant behavior, overactivity, and family stress as predictors of negative maternal control in preschool children. *Development and Psychopathology, 3*, 175–190.

Campbell, S. B., Pierce, E., March, C., Ewing, L. J., & Szumowski, E. K. (1994). Hard-to-manage preschool boys: Symptomatic behavior across contexts and time. *Child Development, 65*, 836–851.

Campos, J. J., Campos, R. G., & Barrett, K. C. (1989). Emergent themes in the study of emotional development and emotion regulation. *Developmental Psychology, 25*, 394–402.

Cicchetti, D., Toth, S. L., & Lynch, M. (1995). Bowlby's dream comes full circle: The application of attachment theory to risk and psychopathology. In T. H. Ollendick & R. J. Prinz (Eds.), *Advances in clinical child psychology*, volume 17 (pp. 1–76) New York: Plenum Press.

Crockenberg, S. B. (1981). Infant irritability, mother responsiveness, and social support influences on the security of mother–infant attachment. *Child Development, 52,* 857–865.

Crockenberg, S., & Litman, C. (1990). Autonomy as competence in 2-year-olds: Maternal correlates of child defiance, compliance and self-assertion. *Developmental Psychology, 26,* 961–971.

Cummings, E. M., & Davies, P. T. (1994). Maternal depression and child development. *Journal of Child Psychology and Psychiatry, 35,* 73–112.

Davies, P., & Cummings, E. M. (1994). Marital conflict and child adjustment: An emotional security hypothesis. *Psychological Bulletin, 116,* 387–441.

Denham, S. A., Renwick, S. M., & Holt, R. W. (1991). Working and playing together: Prediction of preschool social–emotional competence from mother–child interaction. *Child Development, 62,* 242–249.

Denham, S. A., Renwick-DeBardi, S. M., & Hewes, S. (1994). Emotional communication between mothers and preschoolers: Relations with emotional competence. *Merrill–Palmer Quarterly, 40,* 488–508.

Downey, G., & Coyne, J. (1990). Children of depressed parents: An integrative review. *Psychological Bulletin, 108,* 50–76.

Dumas, J. E., & LaFreniere, P. J. (1993). Mother-child relationships as sources of support or stress: A comparison of competent, average, aggressive, and anxious dyads. *Child Development, 64,* 1732–1754.

Dunn, J. (1988). *The growth of social understanding.* Cambridge, MA: Harvard University Press.

Dunn, J., Brown, J., & Beardsall, L. (1991). Family talk about emotions, and children's later understanding of others' emotions. *Developmental Psychology, 27,* 448–455.

Egeland, B., Kalkoske, M., Gottesman, N., & Erickson, M. F. (1990). Preschool behavior problems: Stability and factors accounting for change. *Journal of Child Psychology and Psychiatry, 31,* 891–909.

Erikson, E. (1963). *Childhood and society.* New York: Norton.

Ewing, L. J., & Campbell, S. B. (1995, April). *Hard to manage preschoolers: Social competence, externalizing behavior, and psychopathology at early adolescence.* Poster presented at the Society for Research in Child Development, Indianapolis, IN.

Feldman, S. S., & Weinberger, D. A. (1994). Self-restraint as a mediator of family influences on boys' delinquent behavior: A longitudinal study. *Child Development, 65,* 195–211.

Fischer, M., Rolf, J. E., Hasazi, H. E., & Cummings, L. (1984). Follow-up of a preschool epidemiological sample: Cross-age continuities and predictions of later adjustment with internalizing and externalizing dimension of behavior. *Child Development, 55,* 137–150.

Frankel, K. A., & Bates, J. E. (1990). Mother–toddler problem solving: Antecedents in attachment, home behavior, and temperament. *Child Development, 60,* 810–819.

Gardner, F. E. (1987). Positive interaction between mothers and conduct-problem children: Is there training for harmony as well as fighting? *Journal of Abnormal Child Psychology, 15,* 283–293.

Gardner, F. E. (1989). Inconsistent parenting: Is there evidence for a link with children's conduct problems? *Journal of Abnormal Child Psychology, 17,* 223–233.

Goldsmith, H. H., & Campos, J. J. (1982). Toward a theory of infant temperament. In R. N. Emde & R. J. Harmon (Eds.), *The development of attachment and affiliative systems* (pp. 161–193). New York: Plenum Press.

Greenberg, M. T., Speltz, M. L., & DeKlyen, M. (1993). The role of attachment in the early development of disruptive behavior problems. *Development and Psychopathology, 5,* 191–213.

Hart, C. H., DeWolf, D. M., Wozniak, P., & Burts, D. C. (1992). Maternal and paternal disciplinary styles: Relations with preschoolers' playground behavioral orientation and peer status. *Child Development, 63,* 879–892.

Hetherington, E. M. (1989). Coping with family transitions: Winners, losers, and survivors. *Child Development, 60,* 1–14.

Hollingshead, A. B. (1975). *Four-factor index of social status.* New Haven, CT: Yale University, Department of Sociology.

Jouriles, E. N., Murphy, C. M., Farris, A. M., Smith, D. A., Richters , J. E., & Waters, E. (1991). Marital adjustment, parental disagreements about child rearing, and behavior problems in boys: Increasing the specificity of the marital assessment. *Child Development, 62,* 1424–1433.

Kagan, J. (1981). *The second year: The emergence of self-awareness.* Cambridge, MA: Harvard University Press.

Kazdin, A. E., & Kagan, J. (1995). Models of dysfunction in developmental psychopathology. *Clinical Psychology: Science and Practice, 1,* 35–52.

Kochanska, G. (1991). Socialization and temperament in the development of guilt and conscience. *Child Development, 62,* 1379–1392.

Kopp, C. B. (1989). Regulation of distress and negative emotions: A developmental view. *Developmental Psychology, 25,* 343–354.

Kuczynski, L., Radke-Yarrow, M., Kochanska, G., & Girnius-Brown, O. (1987). A developmental interpretation of young children's noncompliance. *Developmental Psychology, 23,* 799–806.

Lee, C. L., & Bates, J. E. (1985). Mother–child interaction at age two years and perceived difficult temperament. *Child Development, 56,* 1314–1325.

Londerville, S., & Main, M. (1981). Security of attachment, compliance, and maternal training methods in the second year of life. *Developmental Psychology, 17,* 289–299.

Lytton, H. (1980). *Parent–child interaction: The socialization process observed in twin and singleton families.* New York: Plenum Press.

Maccoby, E. E., & Martin, J. A. (1983). Socialization in the context of the family: Parent–child interaction. In P. Mussen (Series Ed.), & E. M. Hetherington (Vol. Ed.), *Handbook of child psychology*: Vol. 4. *Socialization, personality, and social development* (4th ed., pp. 1–102). New York: Wiley.

Masten, A., Best, K., & Garmezy, N. (1990). Resilience and development: Contributions from the study of children who overcome adversity. *Development and Psychopathology, 2,* 425–444.

Matas, L., Arend, R. A., & Sroufe, L. A. (1978). Continuity of adaptation in the second year: The relationship between quality of attachment and later competence. *Child Development, 49,* 547–556.

McGee, R., Silva, P. A., & Williams, S. (1984). Perinatal, neurological, environmental, and developmental characteristics of children with stable behavior problems. *Journal of Child Psychology and Psychiatry, 25,* 573–586.

Miller, N. B., Cowan, P. A., Cowan, C. P., Hetherington, E. M. & Clingempeel, W. G. (1993). Externalizing behavior in preschoolers and early adolescents: A cross-study replication of a family model. *Developmental Psychology, 29,* 3–18.

Olweus, D. (1980). Familial and temperamental determinants of aggressive behavior: A causal analysis. *Developmental Psychology, 16,* 644–660.

Patterson, G. R. (1980). Mothers: The unacknowledged victims. *Monographs of the Society for Research in Child Development, 45* (whole no. 186).

Patterson, G. R. (1982). *A social learning approach: 3. Coercive family process.* Eugene, OR: Castalia.

Patterson, G. R., DeBaryshe, B. D., & Ramsey, E. (1989). A developmental perspective on antisocial behavior. *American Psychologist, 44,* 329–335.

Pelham, W., & Bender, M. E. (1982). Peer relations in hyperactive children: Description and treatment. In K. Gadow & I. Bialer (Eds.), *Advances in learning and behavioral disabilities* (Vol. 1, pp. 365–436). Greenwich, CT: JAI Press.

Radloff, L. (1977). The CES-D Scale: A self-report depression scale for research in the general population. *Journal of Applied Psychological Measurement, 1,* 385– 401.

Reid, J. (1993). Prevention of conduct disorder before and after school entry: Relating interventions to developmental findings. *Development and Psychopathology, 5,* 243–262.

Richman, N., Stevenson, J., & Graham, P. (1982). *Preschool to school: A behavioural study.* London: Academic Press.

Sarason, I. G., Johnson, J. A., and Siegel, J. M. (1978). Assessing the impact of life changes: Development of the Life Experiences Survey. *Journal of Consulting and Clinical Psychology, 46,* 932–946.

Shantz, C. (1987). Conflicts between children. *Child Development, 58,* 283–305.

Shaw, D. S., & Bell, R. Q. (1993). Developmental theories of parental contributors to antisocial behavior. *Journal of Abnormal Child Psychology, 21,* 493–518.

Snyder, J. (1991). Discipline as a mediator of the impact of maternal stress and mood on child conduct problems. *Development and Psychopathology, 3,* 263–276.

Spanier, G. B. (1976). Measuring dyadic adjustment: New scales for assessing the quality of marriage and similar dyads. *Journal of Marriage and the Family, 38,* 15–28.

Sroufe, L. A. (1979). The coherence of individual development. *American Psychologist, 34,* 834–841.

Sroufe, L. A. (1983). Infant–caregiver attachment and patterns of adaptation in preschool: The roots of maladaptation and competence. In M. Perlmutter (Ed.), *Minnesota Symposium on Child Psychology* (Vol. 16, pp. 41–79). Hillsdale, NJ: Erlbaum.

Sroufe, L. A. (1990). Considering normal and abnormal together: The essence of developmental psychopathology. *Development and Psychopathology, 2,* 335–347.

Sroufe, L. A., & Fleeson, J. (1986). Attachment and the construction of relationships. In W. Hartup & Z. Rubin (Eds.), *The nature and development of relationships.* (pp. 51–76) Hillsdale, NJ: Erlbaum.

Thomas, A., Chess, S., & Birch, H. G. (1968). *Temperament and behavior disorders in children.* New York: New York University Press.

Tronick, E. Z. (1989). Emotions and emotional communication in infants. *American Psychologist, 44,* 112–119.

Turner, P. J. (1991). Relations between attachment, gender, and behavior with peers in preschool. *Child Development, 62,* 1475–1488.

Waters, E., Wippman, J., & Sroufe, L. A. (1979). Attachment, positive affect, and competence in the peer group: Two studies in construct validation. *Child Development, 50,* 821–829.

Webster-Stratton, C. (1988). Mothers' and fathers' perceptions of child deviance: Roles of parent and child behaviors in parent adjustment. *Journal of Consulting and Clinical Psychology, 56,* 909–915.

Wenar, C. (1982). Developmental psychopathology: Its nature and models. *Journal of Clinical Child Psychology, 11,* 192–201.

Zahn-Waxler, C., Iannotti, R. J., Cummings, C. M., & Denham, S. (1990). Antecedents of problem behaviors in children of depressed mothers. *Development and Psychopathology, 2,* 271–291.

Zahn-Waxler, C., Radke-Yarrow, M., & King, R. A. (1979). Childrearing and children's responses to victims of distress. *Child Development, 50,* 319–330.

2

Panic in Children and Adolescents
A Developmental Analysis

Sara G. Mattis and Thomas H. Ollendick

1. Introduction and Purpose

Recent literature investigating the prevalence and nature of panic in children and adolescents has suggested that separation anxiety and/or experiences of separation from significant attachment figures in childhood may play an important role in the development of panic (Alessi & Magen, 1988, Biederman, 1987; Bradley & Hood, 1993, Faravelli, Webb, Ambonetti, Fonnesu, & Sessarego, 1985; Hayward, Killen, & Taylor, 1989; Moreau, Weissman, & Warner, 1989; Warren & Zgourides, 1988). The purpose of this chapter is to explore a pathway through which separation in early childhood, conceptualized as a possible source of stress within Barlow's (1988) model of panic disorder, may lead to the development of panic in later childhood and adolescence. Specifically, variables related to temperament, attachment, and the relationship of these two constructs to the onset of panic disorder will be explored. It will be suggested that such variables may mediate the effects of separation, affecting the likelihood that components of panic etiology, as defined in Barlow's (1988) model, will develop.

1.1. The Relationship between Separation and Panic

The body of literature exploring the etiology, prevalence, and nature of panic attacks and/or panic disorder has included several recent reports suggesting a link between separation-related phenomena and the devel-

Sara G. Mattis and Thomas H. Ollendick • Department of Psychology, Virginia Polytechnic Institute and State University, Blacksburg, Virginia 24061.

Advances in Clinical Child Psychology, Volume 19, edited by Thomas H. Ollendick and Ronald J. Prinz. Plenum Press, New York, 1997.

opment of panic in childhood and adolescence. In one of the first studies, Faravelli and colleagues (1985) interviewed 31 adult patients with a diagnosis of agoraphobia with panic attacks regarding the occurrence of separation-related phenomena in childhood (i.e., death of or separation from one or both parents, divorce or separation of parents, death of a cohabitating relative, and childhood illness that interfered with normal social development). Sixty-five percent of the agoraphobic subjects reported experiencing at least one of these events prior to the age of 15, relative to 26% of a matched control group. Separation from one parent for any reason was reported significantly more often by the agoraphobic group, who also reported a higher parental divorce rate and a higher rate of maternal separation relative to controls.

An initial, normative study of panic attacks in children and adolescents was conducted by Warren and Zgourides (1988) through the administration of a Panic Attack Survey to 388 high school students aged 12 to 19 years. Of 203 students reporting at least one panic attack, 72% reported interpersonal conflict while 53% reported loss-related events (i.e., loss of someone cared about, parental separation or divorce, move to a different house or town) as antecedents to their first experience of panic. Rates of interpersonal conflict and loss-related events for nonpanickers were not given in this study.

Hayward et al. (1989) interviewed a sample of 95 ninth graders, of which 11.6% reported experiencing at least one four-symptom panic attack. The incidence of divorced or separated parents was significantly higher among panickers than nonpanickers (61% vs. 29%). The authors suggested that early loss, or sensitivity to separation, may be a risk factor for the subsequent development of panic attacks.

In a clinical study, Alessi and Magen (1988) assessed 136 consecutive referrals to a child psychiatric unit. Four boys and 3 girls, ranging in age from 7 to 12 years, were diagnosed with panic disorder. While 4 of the 7 children also had depressive disorders, 6 of the 7 were diagnosed with comorbid separation anxiety disorder. The authors interpreted this result as strongly suggesting that a subpopulation of children with separation anxiety disorder also evidence panic disorder during childhood.

Bradley and Hood (1993) also reported an association between separation anxiety and panic in a sample of 28 adolescents, aged 11 to 18 years, who met criteria for clinically significant panic attacks. Of these subjects, 48.1% reported a history of significant separation anxiety. In addition, psychosocial stressors, including family conflict, peer problems, death of a relative, and school pressures, were reported by 26 of the 28 adolescents.

Moreau et al. (1989) investigated panic disorder in 220 children, adolescents, and young adults, aged 6 to 23 years, who were identified as being at high or low risk for depression based on parents' diagnosis. Four girls and 3 boys, ranging in age from 11 to 23 years, evinced panic symptoms, and 6 of these 7 children were diagnosed with panic disorder. Major depression and separation anxiety disorder were identified as the most common comorbid diagnoses, each occurring in 5 of the 7 cases. The authors reported that the onset of panic disorder occurred either concurrently with separation anxiety disorder or major depression, or was preceded by at least several months by the onset of separation anxiety disorder.

Finally, a set of three case reports by Biederman (1987) identified two 11-year-old children (1 male and 1 female) and one 8-year-old male with a diagnosis of panic disorder. Symptoms included school refusal, separation difficulties, fear of falling asleep and insistence that parents be present throughout the night, fear of catastrophic events befalling self or family, recurrent shaking, palpitations, sweating, and muscle tension. In the case of one 11-year-old boy, Biederman reported that increasing separation difficulties since the age of 4 were compatible with a diagnosis of separation anxiety disorder, although clinical presentation was also consistent with the diagnostic criteria of "adult-type panic-like symptoms with agoraphobia" (Biederman, 1987, p. 39).

2. Barlow's Model of the Etiology of Panic

Although the extant literature provides evidence suggesting a possible link between separation anxiety and/or experiences of separation and the development of panic, exploration of a pathway through which such development may occur rests upon the conceptualization, delineation, and description of the role played by separation-related phenomena and mediating variables within the etiology of panic. Barlow's (1988) model of the etiology of panic disorder, presented in Figure 1, will next be described, with the goal of conceptualizing temperament, attachment, and separation in early childhood as phenomena that may have important implications for the development of panic in children and adolescents.

2.1. Biological Vulnerability and Stress

Barlow's (1988) model of the etiology of panic disorder posits the tendency to be neurobiologically overreactive to the stress of negative life events as an initial vulnerability. Such a biological response sets the stage for "an initial hard-wired alarm reaction" (p. 366). Barlow suggested that this alarm reaction to stress is false, since there is no real danger, as there

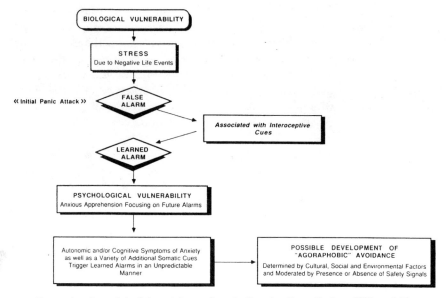

FIGURE 1.   A model of the etiology of panic disorder (from Barlow, 1988, p. 367).

would be in the event of a true alarm, and thus the "fight or flight" action tendencies triggered by the alarm serve no function. This biological vulnerability, or tendency to react to negative life events with inappropriate false alarms associated with exaggerated neurobiological activity, is regarded as genetically based within this model.

2.2.   Learned Alarms to Somatic Cues

According to Barlow's (1988) model, the tendency to be neurobiologically overreactive to stress would diminish in the absence of the subsequent association between false alarms and interoceptive cues, which results in learned alarms to somatic cues. Specifically, in his discussion of the origins of panic, Barlow analyzed the alarm system of fear, distinguishing between true alarms, false alarms, and learned alarms. True alarms involve the emotion of fear in response to relevant threats and mobilize the individual both physically and cognitively to either counter the source of threat or escape quickly (i.e., "fight or flight"). False alarms, on the other hand, refer to marked fear or panic (i.e., feelings of great apprehension and impending doom in association with a broad range of distressing physical symptoms) occurring in the absence of any "real" threat or dangerous stimulus. Barlow cited biological dysregulation, a history of separation anxiety, and stress as possible causes of false alarms. Finally, learned alarms result from the process of fear conditioning, whereby a neutral stimulus (CS) acquires the capacity to elicit the fear response (CR) after pairing with a fear-arousing stimulus, false alarm, or original source of fear (UCS). Barlow stressed that this association does not occur randomly. Rather, conditioning is more likely to occur when certain evolutionarily prepared stimuli are involved and in situations (e.g., crowded malls, airplanes, bridges) that block "the overwhelmingly powerful and ethologically ancient action tendency of escape" (p. 228). Such situations are hypothesized to potentiate learning by intensifying and prolonging the false alarm.

Whereas Barlow (1988) argued that alarms, both true and false, seem to play an important role in the development of anxiety disorders in general, he proposed that the conditioning of false alarms to interoceptive or somatic cues is especially critical in the development of panic disorder. In considering the role of false alarms in panic disorder, both with and without agoraphobia, Barlow stated that the majority of individuals with this disorder are unable to identify a specific cue for their alarms, although agoraphobics typically report fear of various diffuse situations that often involves the perception of being "trapped" away from a safe place. He suggested that individuals with panic disorder may have learned an association between internal or interoceptive cues (i.e., physiological sensations) and false alarms. These internal cues then serve the same function that external cues do for simple phobics (i.e., signaling the possibility of another false alarm). Furthermore, according to Barlow, an individual who has learned to associate interoceptive cues with false alarms will become extremely sensitive to somatic sensations that may signal the beginning of another alarm.

2.3. Psychological Vulnerability

Barlow's (1988) model of panic disorder proposes that the learned association between false alarms and interoceptive cues must be followed by the development of anxious apprehension over the possibility of future alarms. The tendency to develop such anxiety over negative events or additional alarms is regarded as a critical psychological vulnerability arising from developmental experiences with predictability and control. Barlow proposed that the focus of anxious apprehension is partly determined by the nature of the negative event experienced, including the associated alarm, although a more important determinant may be a preexisting tendency to focus anxiety on internal somatic events.

Psychological vulnerability, or the tendency to focus anxious apprehension on negative events, future alarms, and/or internal somatic events that may signal the possible occurrence of an alarm, is similar to the construct of anxiety sensitivity. Reiss, Peterson, Gursky, and McNally (1986) defined *anxiety sensitivity* as "an individual difference variable consisting of beliefs that the experience of anxiety/fear causes illness, embarrassment, or additional anxiety ... which should increase alertness to stimuli signaling the possibility of becoming anxious, increase worry about the possibility of becoming anxious, and increase motivation to avoid anxiety-provoking stimuli" (p. 2). Reiss and colleagues suggested that the construct of anxiety sensitivity is causally related to the development of anxiety disorders, as it may increase the aversiveness of an anxiety experience. Using the Anxiety Sensitivity Index (ASI; Reiss et al., 1986), they demonstrated that agoraphobics scored higher relative to patients with other anxiety disorders, who received higher scores than normals. These findings are consistent with Barlow's (1988) model of panic disorder in which the notion of sensitivity to false alarms plays an important role.

2.4. Possible Development of Agoraphobia

The degree and extent to which avoidance behavior develops is considered within Barlow's (1988) model to be a function of the particular coping skills an individual employs to deal with unexpected panic. Experiential and cultural factors are thought to at least partially determine the development of avoidance behavior, and fluctuations in such behavior are regarded as functions of perceptions of safety. Specifically, Barlow's model of panic disorder proposes that the possible development of "agoraphobic" avoidance is moderated by the presence or absence of safety signals (i.e., the perception that a place or person exists where or with whom it is relatively safe to have a panic attack).

2.5. Summary

Barlow's (1988) model of the etiology of panic disorder thus proposes a biological vulnerability, or a tendency to display neurobiological lability in response to negative life events. There is a predisposition to focus anxiety on internal somatic events, and a psychological vulnerability characterized by anxious apprehension over the possibility of future alarms. Finally, avoidance behavior may develop as a coping response moderated by perceptions of safety. Later in this chapter, we will focus on describing a pathway through which separation-related phenomena in childhood may serve as a source of stress within this model, thus playing a role in the etiology of panic. First, however, let us consider individual differences in temperament as a source of biological vulnerability that might predispose the individual to develop panic disorder.

3. Individual Differences in Temperament as a Biological Vulnerability

The concept of temperament provides a framework for exploring the origins of cognitive and affective structures, and the relationship of these structures to underlying physiological systems associated with reaction and regulation (Rothbart & Derryberry, 1981). By considering individual differences in temperament, we can begin exploring developmental patterns of experience that may shed light on the origins and development of biological vulnerability (i.e., the tendency to be neurobiologically over-reactive to stress).

3.1. Definition and Components

Temperament has been defined as "individual differences in reactivity and self-regulation assumed to have a constitutional basis" (Rothbart & Derryberry, 1981, p. 40). Within this definition, "constitutional" refers to the biological makeup of the organism, which is relatively enduring and influenced over time by factors of heredity, maturation, and experience. "Reactivity" encompasses the characteristics of excitability, responsivity, and arousability through which the organism reacts to environmental changes. These responses are located in the behavioral and physiological systems, including the somatic, endocrine, and autonomic nervous systems of the organism. Finally, "self-regulation" involves the neural and behavioral processes that serve to modulate reactivity, including attentional and behavioral sequences of approach–avoidance. The development of temperament may be viewed in light of the relationship between reactivity and self-regulation, and changes in the balance between these two dimensions over time. Rothbart and Derryberry described five response characteristics that capture the dynamics of reactivity, as well as self-regulatory mechanisms that modulate reactivity. Their description of such temperamental variables provides a framework for understanding individual differences in neurobiological reactivity that may make the individual vulnerable to stress.

3.2. Response Characteristics

In describing the dynamics of individual responsivity, Rothbart and Derryberry (1981) considered both *intensive* and *temporal* characteristics of the response. The intensive characteristics of a response include its threshold and intensity; the temporal characteristics of a response consist of its latency, rise time, and recovery time.

3.2.1. Intensive Characteristics

The characteristic of threshold captures the degree of sensitivity displayed by the infant in response to stimulation of low intensity. Individual differences in sensory sensitivity are evident as early as the newborn period. Although some researchers have argued for a general threshold that is stable across different modalities (e.g., auditory, tactile, visual, etc.), Escalona (1968) has suggested that some children evidence greater sensitivity in particular modalities. For instance, some may be highly responsive to tactile stimulation, whereas others may show heightened sensitivity to visual or auditory stimulation. Still other infants may evidence heightened reactivity to internal physiological cues, such as those that characterize bodily need states (e.g., hunger, fatigue, stress).

The response characteristic of intensity captures the "peak of responsivity" (Rothbart & Derryberry, 1981, p. 43) or the "energy level of response" (Thomas & Chess, 1977, p. 21) evident within various behaviors, ranging from smiling and laughter to distress. Research has examined intensity in several modalities, including motor, vocal, and autonomic reactivity. Rothbart and Derryberry suggested that, like the characteristic of threshold, response magnitude shows variability across response systems.

3.2.2. Temporal Characteristics

Latency of response describes individual differences in time required to orient to a stimulus. For instance, some 3-month-old infants will orient toward the sound of a bell almost instantly, whereas others require several seconds, and still others show little or no orienting response. Such response latencies reflect the broader behavioral dimension of "alertness" (Rothbart & Derryberry, 1981).

Individual variability is also evident in the rise time of a response, or the time required for a response to reach maximum intensity. In the presence of a stimulus, some babies show rapid increases in excitation, whereas others will reach the same level of excitation more gradually. Rothbart and Derryberry (1981) suggested that a more gradual rising phase allows greater possibility for the alleviation of distress both through the opportunity to process more information and to allow for caregiver intervention to impact on reactivity before it has reached its peak.

Finally, time required for recovery from peak reactivity varies across individuals, impacting their interactions with the environment. Sooth-ability and self-comforting ability have been suggested as individual dif-ferences in infancy that relate to the seeking of comfort from others in childhood (Rothbart & Derryberry, 1981). Recovery time is also important in the degree to which unpleasant levels of reactivity are experienced. Specifically, infants characterized by somatic and autonomic resiliency may experience fewer prolonged episodes of distress-evoking excitation relative to infants with less resiliency and greater recovery time.

3.3. Self-Regulation

Self-regulation refers to "the functioning of multilevel processes serv-ing to increase, decrease, maintain, and restructure the patterning of re-activity in either an anticipatory or correctional manner" (Rothbart & Derryberry, 1981, p. 51). Behavioral processes reflecting individual differ-ences in the capacity for self-regulation include approach and avoidance behavior, attention, and "self-stimulatory" or "self-soothing" behaviors.

3.3.1. Approach and Avoidance Behavior

Approach and avoidance behaviors are a primary source of self-regulation, impacting the amount and quality of stimulation with which the child is confronted. Infants show wide variability in both avoidance and approach responses. In the presence of an unpleasant stimulus, some babies display inhibited approach, others lean away cautiously, and still others turn away immediately. Similarly, some babies will engage in pro-longed and extensive attempts to obtain an attractive toy, whereas others approach with moderate intensity or simply look at the toy. Variability in the thresholds at which either approach or avoidance is initiated is also evident, with some individuals requiring low levels of a stimulus for response elicitation, whereas others begin to self-regulate reactivity only at greater intensities or durations of stimulation. Finally, individual differ-ences in latency of approach (i.e., some children reach immediately for a new toy, whereas others examine it cautiously before initiating approach) have been viewed as reflecting an underlying dimension of "wariness" when confronted with novelty. Alternatively, such behavior may result from a less intense approach tendency or one that rises more slowly (Rothbart & Derryberry, 1981).

3.3.2. Attention

Attentional mechanisms are a second important means of self-regula-tion. The temperamental categories of distractibility, attention span, and persistence capture individual differences in attentional processes (Thomas, Chess, Birch, Hertzig, & Korn, 1963). First, more distractible children may be more readily soothed, as they are better able to regulate arousal through attentional shifts and may be more responsive to a caregiver's interventions (e.g., redirecting their attention to a toy). Second, the dimension of attention span reflects individual differences in duration of orienting. Such differences may indicate variability in the degree to which infants are able to disengage themselves from a stimulus. Finally, persistence is a third attentional variable that captures individual differences in the pursuit of an obstructed goal.

3.3.3. Self-Stimulation and Self-Soothing

Additional self-regulating variables include different body behaviors (e.g., thumb sucking, rocking) that affect the impact of environmental stimuli on the child, often reducing distress so that continued processing of incoming information is possible. Infants differ in their use of these behaviors, both in terms of the stimuli required to elicit them and their effectiveness as a means of self-regulation.

3.4. The Relationship between Reactivity and Self-Regulation

Reactivity and self-regulation may be viewed as interacting complementary processes, with regulatory systems structuring and shaping the nature of reactivity by influencing the intensive and temporal characteristics of the individual's response. In turn, regulatory processes are a function of underlying reactivity from which they derive their own intensive and temporal qualities (Rothbart & Derryberry, 1981). This critical interaction between the temperamental factors of reactivity and self-regulation is hypothesized to form the basis of biological vulnerability, or the tendency to be neurobiologically overreactive to stress (Barlow, 1988).

3.5. Temperament and Anxiety

Recent literature has addressed the relationship between temperamental variables and anxiety, including panic. Clark, Watson, and Mineka (1994) described a tripartite model of anxiety and depression in which a general distress factor of negative affectivity is conceptualized as "a stable, heritable, and highly general trait dimension with a multiplicity of aspects ranging from mood to behavior" (p. 104), with a temperamental sensitivity to negative stimuli as the underlying factor. Clark et al. described the work of Fowles (1993) as offering a theory linking negative affectivity with biological systems of motivation drawn from animal literature and the work of Gray (1982, 1987). This theory focuses on the behavioral inhibition system (BIS) as "an aversive motivational system" that serves to increase nonspecific arousal, promoting attention to and appraisal of stimuli that are conditioned to be threat-relevant. Such a system thus inhibits behavior to avoid punishment associated with threat-relevant stimuli and prepares the organism for action if necessary. Although originally viewed as a neuropsychological theory of anxiety by Gray, Fowles regarded the BIS as a "negative motivational–affective system" that plays an important role in both anxiety and depression (Clark et al., 1994, p. 104).

Heightened physiological or autonomic arousal is presented as the anxiety-specific factor in the tripartite model. This factor is viewed as having critical importance in panic disorder (Barlow, 1988), including such symptoms as shortness of breath, racing heart, and dizziness. The theory of Fowles links Gray's flight–fight reaction described earlier with the alarm system of fear described by Barlow, suggesting that both are associated with enhanced sensitivity to internal physiological stimuli. Clark and colleagues (1994) suggested that such a sensitivity, particularly characteristic of panic disorder, possesses a temperamental quality. Specifically, while Barlow proposed that panic disorder results from the development of anxious apprehension surrounding future panic attacks after the experience of an initial alarm reaction, Fowles argued that proneness to the development of anxious apprehension is found in those with heightened negative affectivity. Clark et al. suggested that the combination of negative affectivity and anxious arousal may be the critical factor in the development of panic disorder.

3.6. Behavioral Inhibition

Previous literature (Biederman et al., 1990; Rosenbaum et al., 1988) has also suggested an association between behavioral inhibition, as described by Fowles (1993), and panic disorder. Rosenbaum and colleagues suggested that separation anxiety disorder reflects an underlying temperamental quality predisposing children to school avoidance and adults to panic disorder and agoraphobia. Specifically, they investigated the notion that behavioral inhibition in response to unfamiliar stimuli is a predisposing factor in children at risk for the development of panic disorder (PD) and agoraphobia (PDAG), as defined by parental manifestation of this disorder. Their results supported this hypothesis, indicating that children of parents with PDAG were more likely to show behavioral inhibition, measured as high latency to speak to an unfamiliar examiner and reduced frequency of spontaneous comments, relative to a comparison group.

Rosenbaum et al. (1988) suggested that a lower threshold of arousal in the limbic system in response to unfamiliar events explains the link between behavioral inhibition in children and adult PD. They proposed that such excessive arousal, with accompanying vigilance, withdrawal, and reduced exploratory behavior, comprises a diathesis, with separation as one potential source of challenge or stress. Indeed, they reported that, although repeated threats of separation can elicit "anxiety" in monkeys, Suomi and colleagues (Suomi, Kraemer, Baysinger, & DeLizio, 1981) have proposed genetic loading for the trait of high reactivity as the most important predictor of developing behavior characterized by persistent anxiety-like features. Similarly, Biederman et al. (1990) reported higher rates of multiple anxiety disorders in inhibited versus noninhibited children, suggesting that behavioral inhibition, or the underlying tendency to display excessive arousal when confronted with novelty, may be a predisposing factor for childhood anxiety disorders.

3.7. Temperament, Development, and Individual Differences

The nature and development of individual differences in temperament has been an important area of inquiry and has shed light on the interaction of environmental and temperamental factors throughout the course of development. In a study of individual reactivity, Worobey and Lewis (1989) found that infants who were highly reactive at birth in response to phenylketonuria (PKU) screening showed high reactivity at 2 months of age, whereas low to moderately reactive infants showed little consistency. The authors suggested that differences in parental soothing may have had a greater influence on babies with lower initial levels of reactivity, whereas highly reactive infants may remain high regardless of parental responses.

Fox (1989) reported individual differences in emotional reactivity and sociability over the first year of life associated with varying degrees of vagal tone (heart-rate variability). Specifically, 5-month-old infants with high vagal tone displayed more emotional reactivity in response to both positive (peekaboo) and negative (arm restraint) stimuli, while exhibiting more sociable and approach behaviors in response to novel stimuli at 14 months. These babies spent less time close to their mothers, although displaying more reactivity to maternal separation (i.e., shorter latency to cry). In contrast, infants with low vagal tone showed less emotional reactivity at 5 months and greater wariness and less sociability in response to novel situations at 14 months. The author suggested that, whereas the reactive babies seemed to develop an increase in approach responses to novel stimuli combined with increased ability to regulate arousal, babies with low responsivity seemed to have learned to respond passively to novel or stressful stimuli. Furthermore, this passive avoidance was accompanied by physiological arousal (i.e., high heart rate and low heart-rate variability). Thus, individual variability both in reactivity and self-regulatory capacities influenced the extent to which exploratory or inhibited responses were evidenced in the face of novel or stressful stimuli.

The studies described here emphasize the interaction of environmental and temperamental factors and their joint impact on the course of development. Indeed, the manner in which factors of temperament, or biological vulnerability, influence the child's response to stress (e.g., separation) should be strongly affected by the child's history of interactions within his or her social system. As attachment provides an important framework for exploring social development, let us examine this construct at this time.

4. Attachment

Although the consideration of temperament provides an understanding of biological vulnerability, Barlow's (1988) model proposes that the tendency to be neurobiologically overreactive to stress would diminish without the subsequent association between false alarms and interoceptive cues that results in learned alarms to somatic cues. Furthermore, this model of the etiology of panic proposes that such learning must be followed by the development of anxious apprehension over the possibility of future alarms. Such anxious apprehension is regarded as a critical psychological vulnerability arising from developmental experiences with predictability and control. Attachment has been defined as "an affectional tie that one person forms to another specific person, binding them together in space and enduring over time" (Ainsworth, 1973, p. 1). Let us explore the manner in which this tie might impact on and interact with developmental experiences of predictability and control, and then examine the implications of these experiences for psychological vulnerability and the etiology of panic.

4.1. Attachment Theory

The partnership of Bowlby and Ainsworth, reflected in theory and research spanning from the early 1950s to Bowlby's death in 1990, led to the development of a theory of attachment that has guided recent clinical research in the area of developmental psychopathology (Ainsworth & Bowlby, 1991). Within attachment theory, the existence of attachment is inferred from consistent behaviors that promote proximity to or contact with a particular figure. These attachment behaviors include signaling behavior (e.g., crying), orienting behavior (e.g., looking), locomotions in relation to another (e.g., following or approaching), and physical contact behaviors (e.g., clinging). Such behaviors serve to initiate and maintain interaction while avoiding separation from the attachment figure. Furthermore, they facilitate protection and reassurance from the attachment figure in the presence of a frightening stimulus (Ainsworth, 1973).

Bowlby (1969, 1973) first noted the importance of equilibrium between attachment behavior and other behavioral systems (e.g., exploration and play). Although environmental stimuli characterized by novelty or complexity tend to elicit approach and promote learning, a certain degree of proximity to the attachment figure will be maintained by the activation of attachment behavior, and is affected by the infant's experience (e.g., alarm or distress promote proximity). Thus, Bowlby (1969) argued that a primary function served by an attachment object is to provide a secure base from which the infant can explore the environment, returning to the attachment object for comfort when confronted with a frightening stimulus.

4.2. The Development of Attachment

Attachment develops over the course of early childhood. Four major phases in this development have been identified by Ainsworth (1973): (1) undiscriminating social responsiveness; (2) discriminating social responsiveness; (3) active initiative in seeking proximity; and (4) goal-corrected partnership. Although the criteria used to define attachment vary, Ainsworth regards the third stage, occurring at a median age of 7 months, as the point at which the child is finally "attached." In describing the nature of this phenomenon, she states that "once formed, this attachment is amazingly persistent, and is capable of enduring an extraordinary amount of absence, neglect, or abuse—although these adverse conditions are likely to affect both the quality of a child's attachment relationship and his subsequent personality development" (p. 13).

In contrast, Cairns (1977, 1979) has emphasized plasticity, flexibility, and adaptation in the development of attachment. He has argued that social preferences will evolve to the extent that events within the environment support and become synchronized with the behavior of the young. For instance, Cairns (1979) described an unpublished study in which a wastebasket was wired to make a soft sound in response to the movement of isolated lambs. Within 24 hours, the lambs demonstrated attachment behaviors toward the basket, remaining close to it and displaying species-typical separation distress upon removal of the basket. Based on such evidence, Cairns concluded that no single behavior (e.g., suckling, contact) is, in and of itself, critical to the development of social preferences in young animals. Instead, the most important factor seems to be predictable behavioral interdependency between the reactive tendencies of the young organism and an environmental "object," whether that be the caregiver or an inanimate stimulus.

Furthermore, Main, Kaplan, and Cassidy (1985) advanced our understanding of attachment by focusing on the development of an internal working model of attachment. These researchers conceptualized individual differences in attachment as stemming from variability in mental representations of the self relative to attachment. Such a conceptualization has contributed to the study of attachment in older children and adults by extending the focus to the level of representation and language. Indeed, Main et al. have reported a strong relation between security of infant attachment to the mother and the nature of both verbal and nonverbal representations at 6 years of age. For instance, children who were securely attached as infants responded to the question of what they would do during a 2-week separation from their parents with answers indicating effective behavior directed toward others (e.g., express disappointment to the parents, persuade them not to leave), thus showing a working model of accessibility pertaining to the attachment figures. Main et al. suggested that such an internal sense would help the child deal with real separations. Insecurely attached infants, however, indicated at 6 years of age that they did not know what they would do during a 2-week separation from their parents, although some gave responses characterized by inflicting harm on themselves or their parents. Such responses would actually decrease accessibility of the attachment figures and are consistent with an internal working model of inaccessibility with regard to attachment figures. Let us now consider attachment classification, its implications for understanding developmental psychopathology, and its relevance to the development of panic disorder.

4.3. Attachment Classification

Three distinct attachment categories have been described by Ainsworth (1973) based primarily on behavioral observations of young children in the Strange Situation, a laboratory procedure designed to activate the attachment system of the infant via minor stressors (e.g., an unfamiliar environment, introduction to a stranger, brief experiences of separation from the caregiver). A summary of the attachment categories and their characteristic features as summarized by Cicchetti, Toth, and Lynch (1995) is presented in Table 1.

TABLE 1
Attachment Classification[a]

Attachment category	Characteristic features
Type A: Insecure–avoidant	Readily separate to explore a new environment Little affective sharing with caregiver Affiliative behavior toward stranger Avoid proximity and positive affect with caregiver upon reunion after separation Active avoidant behavior (e.g., turning, looking, moving away, ignoring the caregiver) No avoidance of stranger
Type B: Secure	Use of the caregiver as a secure base from which to explore the environment Separate easily to investigate toys, and engage caregiver in affective sharing during play Affiliative to stranger in caregiver's presence Seek proximity and interaction with caregiver upon reunion If upset, seek to gain and maintain contact that is effective in terminating distress prior to resumption of exploratory/play behavior
Type C: Insecure–ambivalent/resistant	Difficulty separating from caregiver to explore the environment Seek contact prior to separation Display wariness in response to novel environmental stimuli, including people Notable separation distress Proximity seeking mixed with resistant behavior (e.g., hitting, kicking) upon reunion Difficulty being comforted by contact with caregiver Persistent fussy or angry behavior that interferes with a return to play
Type D: Disorganized–disoriented	Failure to display an "organized coping mechanism" in the Strange Situation Display behavior characteristic of two or more of the other categories (e.g., strong avoidance following strong proximity seeking upon reunion) Contradictory behavior patterns Dazed, disoriented behavior (e.g., stereotypes, asymmetrical movements, unusual postures, apprehension directed toward caregiver) upon reunion

[a]Adapted from Cicchetti, Toth, and Lynch (1995).

According to Ainsworth (1973), insecure–avoidant babies (Type A) comprise approximately 20% of normative samples. These children readily separate from their caregivers to explore a new environment and engage in little affective sharing with them. Although evidencing affiliative behavior toward the stranger in the Strange Situation, these babies tend to avoid proximity and positive affect with their caregivers upon reunion after separation. This active avoidant behavior includes turning, looking, or moving away, as well as ignoring the caregiver, although such behaviors are not directed necessarily toward the stranger.

Approximately 70% of normative samples are coded as securely attached (Type B) babies, thus composing the largest group described by Ainsworth. These babies are characterized by their use of the caregiver as a secure base from which to explore the environment. They separate easily to investigate toys and engage the caregiver in affective sharing during play. Type-B babies demonstrate affiliative behavior toward strangers, but only when caregivers are present. Following brief separations, these babies respond in an unambivalent fashion toward their caregivers, actively seeking proximity or interaction by greeting or approaching them. If upset, these babies seek to gain and maintain contact, which is readily effective in terminating distress prior to the resumption of exploratory and/or play behavior.

Insecure–ambivalent/resistant babies (Type C) comprise the remaining 10% of infants classified within Ainsworth's original system. These children have difficulty separating from their caregivers to explore the environment, seeking contact prior to separation and displaying wariness in response to novel environmental stimuli, including the stranger. Separation distress is notable and, although these babies show proximity seeking upon reunion with their caregivers, it may be mixed with resistant behavior (e.g., hitting, kicking). The inability to be comforted by contact with their caregivers is accompanied by persistent fussy or angry behavior that interferes with a return to play.

A fourth attachment category, disorganized–disoriented (Type D), was proposed by Main and her colleagues (Main & Hesse, 1990; Main & Solomon, 1986) in order to classify children who could not be coded using Ainsworth's criteria, as they failed to display an "organized coping mechanism" in the Strange Situation. Rather, their reunion behavior was characterized by a blend of behaviors characteristic of two or more of the other categories (e.g., strong avoidance following strong seeking of proximity), or they displayed dazed, disoriented behavior (e.g., stereotypes, asymmetrical movements, unusual postures, apprehension directed toward the caregiver) upon reunion.

4.4. Attachment and Developmental Psychopathology

Cicchetti and colleagues (1995) noted that the emergence of developmental psychopathology as a field of study over the last decade has promoted investigation of attachment, risk, and psychopathology while facilitating the clinical application of attachment theory. These authors reviewed studies examining "the continuum of caretaking casualty" (Sameroff & Chandler, 1975) as it relates to the development of attachment, as well as the relationship between attachment and emergent psychopathology. Specifically, they stated that caregiver problems, including psychiatric dysfunction or child maltreatment, have been shown to produce distributions of attachment classification that are more deviant relative to child problems of a biological nature (e.g., Down's syndrome). Comparing the attachment classifications of 12-month-old maltreated infants with a sample of nonmaltreated babies, Carlson, Cicchetti, Barnett, and Braunwald (1989) reported that, of the maltreated sample, 14% were securely attached, 82% were Type D, and 4% were classified as Type A. In contrast, of the nonmaltreated infants, 52% were securely attached, 19% were Type D, and the remaining 29% were either Type A or Type C.

Cicchetti and colleagues (1995) also explored the relationship between attachment and both depression and externalizing disorders. Specifically, they reported that a study by Egeland and Sroufe (1981) found that 100% of a sample of 18-month-old children with depressed and psychologically unavailable mothers were insecurely attached. Another study of 7-year-olds who had been exposed to maternal depression as infants found a 45% rate of insecure attachment (19% A, 12% C, 14% D). Of this sample, securely attached children evidenced fewer internalizing and externalizing symptoms based on both mother and teacher ratings, with 83% of the insecure group scoring in the clinical range relative to 45% of securely attached children. Finally, a study of 25 children diagnosed with oppositional defiant disorder (ODD) and 25 matched controls, aged 3 to 6 years, revealed that 84% of children with ODD were insecurely attached, compared with 28% of the controls. Specifically, children with ODD evidenced a significantly greater likelihood of protesting in response to maternal separation and were more likely to search for their mothers after they had departed.

4.5. Attachment, Temperament, and the Development of Psychological Vulnerability

The construct of attachment, with its implications for psychopathology, may play an important role in the development of psychological vulnerability as described in Barlow's (1988) model of the etiology of panic. Barlow defined *psychological vulnerability* as the tendency to develop anxious apprehension over negative events or the possibility of future alarms. He further viewed this phenomenon as arising from developmental experiences with predictability and control. To the extent that the quality of attachment is formed by such experiences in the context of the child–caregiver relationship, and that the nature of attachment itself impacts the child's expectations within that context, it should affect the development of psychological vulnerability. For instance, in discussing the implications of child maltreatment and Type-D attachment relationships, Cicchetti et al. (1995) stressed that the erratic tendencies inherent in parental maltreatment of children lead to difficulty in a child's ability to predict parental behavior, resulting in chronic anxiety and uncertainty. Similarly, insecure–ambivalent (Type C) children evidence difficulty relying on their caregiver as a source of comfort in times of stress (e.g., separation), thus decreasing their ability to escape from the fear aroused by a stressful experience (as securely attached children are able to do via caregiver contact). The alarm reaction is therefore intensified and prolonged for Type-C children, increasing the likelihood that they will learn to associate the experience of stress with increasing negativity, accompanied by lack of predictability and control, thus potentiating the development of anxious apprehension over the possibility of future alarms and or experiences of stress/anxiety.

Cicchetti and colleagues (1995) stressed the importance of analyzing mechanisms affecting the outcome of risk factors throughout development, noting that linear models do not capture the links between insecure attachment and childhood psychopathology. With the knowledge that not all insecurely attached children will evidence pathology or psychological vulnerability, and an emphasis on individual differences in temperament and attachment relationships, let us next examine the relationship between these two phenomena and how it may direct the child's pathway toward or away from maladaptive outcomes in response to the stress of separation.

5.   The Relationship between Temperament and Attachment

The development of an attachment relationship in which the caregiver serves as a source of comfort or security depends on both caregiver sensitivity to the infant's needs and signals, and individual differences in the infant's temperament, affecting the degree to which the infant requires such security (Rothbart & Derryberry, 1981). For instance, infants characterized by reactivity that is low or quick in recovering may need less adult intervention due to reduction in the experience of "felt insecurity" (p. 67). Other infants who are relatively reactive may require less intervention due to effective self-regulatory capacities. Another group of infants whose reactivity is high or poorly modulated may have difficulty reducing distress, even with caregiver intervention. Indeed, Rothbart and Derryberry proposed that the conceptualization of the caregiver as a source of comfort is most likely to develop in relatively reactive infants who seek security or regulation through attachment behaviors, perhaps as a result of less efficient self-regulatory processes. The quality of attachment is thus impacted by individual differences in reactive and regulatory processes in response to stress or insecurity, as well as differences in infants' construction of their caregiver as a source of comfort.

The temperament of the caregiver and his or her role in the developing attachment relationship must also be considered. Variability exists between caregivers in sensitivity to the signals of their infants, as well as the capacity to tailor their actions to meet their baby's needs. Rothbart and Derryberry (1981) noted that these characteristics influence the extent to which an infant will perceive the caregiver as a source of comfort. Similarly, caregivers will differ in the degree to which their infants become a source of comfort and stimulation to them, depending on the caregiver's own temperamental qualities of reactivity and self-regulation.

The developing attachment relationship may thus be understood as "a function of two intricate and flexible interactional systems, which can achieve a 'balance' in a number of different ways" (Rothbart & Derryberry, 1981, p. 68). Specifically, individual differences in infant temperament, including the capacity to modulate one's own reactivity, combine with the caregiver's sensitivity, flexibility, and temperamental qualities. These systems interact in a bidirectional manner, determining the extent to which each is constructed as a source of comfort or stimulation, distress or pleasure, in the perception of the other.

In a recent discussion of temperament and personality development, Rothbart and Ahadi (1994) reviewed several studies suggesting a relationship between differences in distress-proneness in infancy and later assessment of attachment security. Distress-prone northern European infants, for instance, were more likely to be later classified as insecure–avoidant (Type A) relative to their less distress-prone counterparts (Grossman, Grossman, Spangler, Suess, & Unzner, 1985). In contrast, distress-prone Japanese infants and, to a lesser extent, those from the United States were more likely to develop insecure–ambivalent (Type C) attachments (Goldsmith & Alansky, 1987; Miyake, Chen, & Campos, 1985). Rothbart and Ahadi (1994) noted that these cross-cultural results supported the notion of temperamental effects on behavior in the Strange Situation, as well as the importance of cultural experiences in shaping the expression of attachment behavior. Rothbart and Ahadi (1994) also reviewed two longitudinal studies conducted by van den Boom (1989) that further investigated these factors through examination of low socioeconomic status (SES) mother–infant dyads from the Netherlands.

Van den Boom's (1989) initial study found that distress-proneness at 15 days of age predicted attachment classification at one year, particularly Type A (i.e., insecure–avoidant). Although maternal behavior was not predictive of attachment classification, van den Boom observed that mothers tended to increasingly ignore and play less with distress-prone infants over time. Her second study thus contained an experimental group in which mothers of distress-prone infants participated in a training program, learning how to soothe and play with their babies. More positive and less negative affect was displayed in the home by experimental infants relative to controls, as was greater involvement with their mothers and higher levels of exploratory play. Furthermore, 68% of the experimental group were classified as securely attached at 12 months, compared with only 28% of the control infants.

Rothbart and Ahadi (1994) interpreted van den Boom's (1989) initial study as supporting temperament as a strong predictor of later attachment classification, whereas the second study showed the importance of parental skills in influencing the developing, "interacting" attachment relationship. Considered together, both studies described "the way in which an interaction between infant predisposition and mother behavior may develop into a trajectory of experience for the child, with important outcomes" (Rothbart & Ahadi, 1994, p. 59).

Several other researchers have studied the relationship between temperament and attachment security. Belsky and Rovine (1987) examined the relationship between infant temperament, assessed during the newborn period and again at 3 months, and infant–parent attachment, assessed in the Strange Situation at 12–13 months. In their analyses, these researchers compared the traditional A-B-C classification scheme with an attachment scheme designed to capture temperamental differences in emotional expression (see Table 2 for a summary of this classification system). Specifically, four secure classification subgroups were identified, with infants classified as B1 displaying distal modes and babies in subgroup B2 showing somewhat more proximal modes of contact. These babies were classified with Type-A (A1 and A2) babies in terms of similarity in emotional expression. Subgroups B3 and B4 evidenced increasingly proximal modes of interactive behavior in the Strange Situation, characterized by a high degree of contact seeking/maintaining, and were thus grouped with Type-C (C1 and C2) babies.

TABLE 2

Attachment Security and Temperament: An Alternative Classification Scheme[a]

Attachment category	Reunion behavior	Temperament
A1—Insecure–avoidant	Notable avoidance	Low distress
A2—Insecure–avoidant	Combined approach–avoidance	Low distress
B1—Secure	Positive–distal	Low distress
B2—Secure	Positive/tendency to approach	Low distress
B3—Secure	Actively seeks/maintains contact	High distress
B4—Secure	Maintains strong contact	High distress
C1—Insecure–ambivalent	Simultaneously seeks–resists contact	High distress
C2—Insecure–ambivalent	Notable passivity and resistance	High distress

[a]Adapted from Fish and Belsky (1991).

Belsky and Rovine (1987) reported the A1-B2 versus B3-C2 classification scheme to be more sensitive to temperamental differences than the traditional A-B-C scheme of Ainsworth, with infants classified as A1-B2 at 12–13 months displaying greater autonomic stability during the newborn period (measured via tremulousness, amount of startle, and motor maturity) than those classified as B3-C2. The only difference evident with the traditional classification was that in one of two samples studied, insecure–resistant infants showed less autonomic stability during the newborn period relative to all other infants. Similar results were obtained from analyses of maternal report at 3 months. Specifically, infants later classified in the A1-B2 group were rated as "easier" than those in group B3-C2, whereas no reliable differences were found using traditional A-B-C classification. Belsky and Rovine concluded that newborns characterized by less central nervous system organization were more likely to express insecurity in a resistant rather than an avoidant manner, whereas an opposite pattern was evidenced in infants with more organized behavioral systems. Furthermore, infants with more difficult temperaments expressed security by crying, approaching, and clinging to attachment figures in the Strange Situation (i.e., B3, B4), whereas more distal means of expressing security were evident in babies who were less temperamentally vulnerable to stress (i.e., B1, B2).

In a similar study, Vaughn, Lefever, Seifer, and Barglow (1989) examined temperamental correlates of behaviors in the Strange Situation, focusing particularly on *emotionality* (defined as distress during separation and reunion). Maternal perceptions of infant temperament were assessed at 5–8 months of age, and babies were observed with their mothers in the Strange Situation at 12–14 months. Although no significant relationship between temperament and attachment was found, frequency of crying during separation was significantly correlated with maternal ratings of temperamental difficulty.

In a more recent study, Vaughn et al. (1992) explored the relationship between temperament and attachment security across six samples, drawn from the United States, Canada, and England, of children assessed during infancy and early childhood. Significant negative correlations were found between security of attachment and temperamental negative reactivity/ affective activation (i.e., negative emotionality or arousal intensity) in five of the six samples. The researchers further reported a strong association between the child's age and correlational magnitude, with older children evidencing a stronger relationship between negative reactivity/affective activation and attachment security relative to their younger counterparts. Vaughn and colleagues (1992) interpreted this finding of a consistent association between attachment security and negative emotionality/affective activation, increasing with development, as indicative of overlap between the behavioral domains of temperament and attachment. They argued that such a conceptualization of a shared boundary between attachment and temperament facilitates an understanding of both domains as contributing to affective expression and control, and the development of personality.

Finally, Calkins and Fox (1992) examined the relationship between temperament, attachment security, and behavioral inhibition during the first 2 years of life in 52 full-term infants. First, distress reactivity during the neonatal period was significantly correlated with secure versus insecure attachment at 14 months, with insecure infants more likely to cry as newborns in response to pacifier withdrawal than secure babies. Second, infants who evidenced a high frequency of reunion crying in the Strange Situation at 14 months were more likely to show behavioral inhibition at 24 months, assessed via proximity to mother during play, and latency to vocalize, approach, and cry in response to different stimuli. Calkins and Fox also reported a significant difference in behavioral inhibition among the three attachment groups at 24 months, with Type-C infants more inhibited that Type A. Finally, a significant interaction between attachment and frustrated reactivity was reported. Specifically, Type-C infants who did not cry in response to arm restraint at 5 months were likely to show greater inhibition relative to their Type-C counterparts who did cry, as well as to all Type-A infants.

These provocative findings suggest a complex process of development relating temperament, attachment security, and behavioral inhibition. Specifically, two possibilities were presented by Calkins and Fox (1992) as examples of pathways that may develop from early distress reactivity. First, infants who evidence high reactivity in response to frustration or limitations may show greater activity and arousal, eliciting a caregiver response that provides few limits and greater independence of autonomous movement. These children may show avoidance in the Strange Situation, and, if the environment remains unstructured, with few limitations, may evidence undisciplined, active behavior in response to later social requirements. A second possible pathway centers around the infant who has a low threshold to respond to novelty, including environmental changes, and is easily aroused although less active. Some caregivers cope ineffectively with such infants' fussiness, attentional demands, and irritability in response to relatively low levels of stimulation. The result may be resistant infant behavior in the Strange Situation and progressive withdrawal from situations characterized by novelty, including unfamiliar people, or change.

The role of self-regulatory mechanisms was also considered by Calkins and Fox (1992), who suggested that some highly reactive children may regulate arousal in response to frustration or controls by engaging in heightened exploratory behavior, spending less time close to parents, and thus being viewed as uninhibited. However, children who have difficulty regulating arousal in response to novelty may withdraw, showing avoidance and fear responses when confronted with unfamiliar people or objects. Such difficulty regulating arousal may make such children difficult to soothe in a novel situation, while the reactive tendency may be exacerbated by an insecure attachment relationship that fails to reduce the stress of the fear-eliciting environment. Such an interaction would likely amplify the tendency to withdraw from novelty. Thus, Calkins and Fox concluded that children who evidence difficulty with self-regulation of reactivity, and who lack confidence in their attachment figure as a source of security (or stimulation reduction) when confronted with stress, are more likely to experience fear relative to children who are either able to self-regulate arousal or consistently rely on the attachment figure for security.

6. Effects of Separation in Childhood

The previous discussion supports the notion of individual differences in distress reactivity and is consistent with Barlow's (1988) conceptualization of biological vulnerability, or the tendency to be neurobiologically overreactive to stress, as "an initial hard-wired alarm reaction" (p. 366). Furthermore, there is empirical evidence that distress reactivity interacts with characteristics of the attachment relationship, affecting the likelihood that fearful, inhibited behavior will be evidenced in the presence of novel or fear-inducing stimuli. Conceptualization of separation from attachment figures as a possible source of stress within Barlow's model of the etiology of panic facilitates understanding of the alarm system of fear in childhood and its interaction with systems of temperament and attachment.

6.1. Social Separation in Mammals

Some comparative research provides a base from which to understand the effects of separation experiences on young mammals, including human children. In their review of social separation in monkeys, Mineka and Suomi (1978) described a "biphasic protest–despair reaction" that they compared to Bowlby's (1973) description of the behavior of young human children in response to prolonged physical separation from their mothers. Specifically, Bowlby described a phase of high agitation and distress, which he labeled *protest*, occurring immediately after separation. This phase was then followed by a period of dejection and withdrawal, or *despair*. Mineka and Suomi reviewed primate studies that confirmed a similar behavior pattern in monkeys in response to separation from their caregivers. In these studies, protest was characterized by hyperactivity and excessive vocalizations, whereas despair consisted of sharp decreases in play and socialization, accompanied by increases in passive, self-directed behavior. Finally, a review of studies investigating physiological and psychophysiological concomitants of monkeys' response to separation suggested an association between behavioral protest and physiological stress. Based on their review, Mineka and Suomi concluded that "an individual who has experienced the unpleasant experience of separation from an attachment object is not likely to forget it and may well develop a fear that at some time in the future separation will again occur" (p. 1390).

Cairns (1979) examined the effects of both brief and longer term separation on young mammals, and argued for the importance of plasticity in social development, focusing on the creation of "new social competencies" as a young organism adapts to and is altered by changes in its caretaking environment (pp. 59–60). Specifically, he considered the immediate effects of brief mother–infant separations, observing that forced separation from their mothers is an experience characterized by trauma and behavioral disorganization for most young mammals. However, Cairns noted a general pattern of adaptation characterized by a return to preseparation levels of behavior after extended periods of separation. Such a pattern of adaptation differs across both species and individuals, with some orphaned primate infants evidencing a prolonged "mourning" state, occurring after agitation and preceding recovery. Cairns argued that such variability in the course of adaptation, including time course and manifestation of deviant responses (e.g., withdrawal or motor depression), is influenced by interactional characteristics and the social environment in which the young animal is placed. This argument is supported by research examining different responses to maternal separation in two species of macaque monkeys (Cairns, 1979). According to this research, pigtail macaques typically respond to maternal separation with high agitation followed by depression (e.g., greatly diminished activity, withdrawal, nonresponsiveness), and finally evidence gradual recovery to preseparation behaviors. In contrast, bonnet monkeys typically evidence no depressive behavior, returning to preseparation levels of activity after a period of agitation. Such variability is related to differences in the infants' interactions with nonmaternal adult animals after separation from their mothers. Specifically, although adult pigtail macaques respond little to the infants, adult bonnet macaques interact with the young freely, thus creating a different postseparation experience. Cairns also noted the potential effects of differences in mother–infant interaction prior to separation on postseparation behavior (e.g., pigtail mothers show higher levels of restraint and guarding behavior relative to bonnets). Variability in patterns of adaptation to separation may thus be influenced by the nature of the interactional system before separation as well as the social environment that is present after separation.

6.2. The Role of Temperament and Attachment in Children's Response to Separation

Recent empirical literature has examined the role played by temperament and attachment in determining the impact of separation on children. In a study designed to investigate the relationship between infant regulatory behavior in the Strange Situation and both reactivity and attachment classification in eighteen 12-month-old infants, Braungart and Stifter (1991) found significant differences in reactivity between attachment groups during separation and reunion, but not preseparation. Specifically, B1-B2 (secure–low distress) infants were less distressed than both Type-A (insecure–avoidant) infants and B3-B4 (secure–high distress) infants during separation and reunion. Type-A infants showed less distress than B3-B4 infants during separation but not reunion, and Type-C (insecure–ambivalent) infants showed more distress relative to the B3-B4 group during reunion, but not separation.

Braungart and Stifter (1991) also explored differences between attachment groups on each of four regulatory behaviors (i.e., people orientation, object orientation, self-comforting, toy exploration) during separation and reunion. Type-A (insecure–avoidant) infants displayed more self-comforting during separation relative to B1-B2 (secure–low distress) babies, who evidenced less people orientation during separation, less object orientation during reunion, and more toy exploration during reunion compared to B3-B4 (secure–high distress) infants. Babies in the B3-B4 group showed a tendency toward more object orientation relative to Type-C (insecure–ambivalent) infants. Finally, Type-A infants showed less people orientation, more self-comforting during separation, less object orientation, and more toy exploration during reunion than B3-B4 babies.

Braungart and Stifter (1991) concluded that individual differences in patterns of self-regulation during a stressful situation, characterized by maternal separation and reunion, depended on the level of negative reactivity experienced as well as the nature of the attachment relationship. Thus, B1-B2 (secure–low distress) infants showed low levels of both negative reactivity and self-regulation throughout the Strange Situation, including the stressful episodes of separation and reunion. Braungart and Stifter interpreted this finding as consistent with Rothbart and Derryberry's (1981) statement that infants with low or quickly recovering levels of reactivity may not experience the arousal necessary to trigger self-regulatory behaviors. In contrast, B3-B4 (secure–high distress) infants evidenced high levels of negative reactivity during separation, but were quickly calmed by both their mother's return and self-regulatory behavior. Braungart and Stifter referred to the belief of attachment theorists that the ability to receive comfort from the caregiver contributes to a secure attachment. Thus the perception of the caregiver as a secure base allowed the distress of B3-B4 infants to be effectively reduced upon reunion, whereas the high levels of proximity and contact-seeking behaviors evidenced by these children may be conceptualized as a form of regulation.

Infants classified as Type A (insecure–avoidant) in this study displayed moderate levels of distress in response to separation and reunion. Furthermore, these babies evidenced more self-comforting behaviors during separation relative to both B groups, and showed nearly twice as much toy play during reunion than similarly distressed B3-B4 babies. Braungart and Stifter (1991) interpreted these findings as indicating that Type-A infants depend more on self-regulation as opposed to seeking comfort from others. They suggested that such behavior may have been learned from earlier interactions with their caregiver, and noted that caregivers of Type-A infants have been observed by researchers to be rejecting and unresponsive, while evidencing higher levels of temperamental reactivity. These babies may thus learn to avoid contact and reliance on others for comfort (p. 362).

Finally, similarities were observed between Type-C (insecure–ambivalent) and B3-B4 (secure–high distress) infants in intense negative reactivity during separation, as well as high people orientation during separation and low toy play during reunion. However, striking differences were evident during reunion, in that Type-C babies failed to show similar recovery and displayed less regulatory behavior (e.g., object orientation) compared to B3-B4 infants. Braungart and Stifter (1991) suggested two interpretations of the intense distress, coupled with a failure to regulate reactivity, either through their own means or the comfort of a caregiver, that characterized the Type-C babies. First, a temperamental proneness to high-distress reactivity may make such babies very difficult to soothe; second, unresponsive caregivers may lead to poor development of self-regulatory capacity. Braungart and Stifter concluded that regulation may be an important component of reactivity and attachment, with greater distress intensity requiring the intervention of more regulatory behaviors, whereas the amount and type of regulation depends on the nature of the attachment relationship.

In a study of 98 mother–child pairs, Fish and Belsky (1991) analyzed the contribution of temperament and attachment security to separation intolerance at age 3. The "temperament-based" attachment classification scheme (i.e., A1-B2 vs. B3-C2), with attachment assessed at 12 months, most reliably discriminated between children, with the B3-C2 group most likely to be intolerant of separation at 3 years. Furthermore, it was the secure (B3-B4) children in this group who were almost three times as likely as all other groups to show separation intolerance at age 3. Within the B3-B4 group, children who evidenced separation intolerance had cried with greater frequency during a mother–infant observation at 3 months, compared with B3-B4 children who were tolerant of separation.

In light of these findings, Fish and Belsky (1991) investigated the possibility that separation intolerance may, in fact, be an effective coping strategy for children who are secure and prone to distress. Data on emotional expression during separation and postseparation tasks were analyzed to test two hypotheses: (1) that insecure children were not less likely to experience distress upon separation, but, rather, less likely to overtly express their feelings in order to end the separation episode; and (2) that protest serving to terminate separation represented adaptive coping for children who were both securely attached and temperamentally vulnerable.

In support of their hypothesis, Fish and Belsky (1991) found that insecure children who showed separation tolerance were more likely to appear uncomfortable (i.e., anxious, withdrawn, depressed) compared to secure children who tolerated the episode. Indeed, 65% of insecurely attached children received low scores on positive affect, compared to only 39% of secure children, although they were not more likely to engage in overt expressions of negative affect.

The second hypothesis was partially supported through comparison of the B3-B4 children who were both separation intolerant at 3 years and evidenced a high frequency of crying at 3 months, with insecure, separation-tolerant children matched on the basis of gender and crying during the 3-month mother–infant observation. The results showed that during a postseparation teaching task including the mother (although not during a cleanup episode), secure children who were temperamentally vulnerable and showed separation intolerance displayed more positive affect, whereas insecure children with similar temperament who tolerated separation evidenced more negative affect. Fish and Belsky (1991) interpreted these results as consistent with an affective cost–gain hypothesis, in which less positive functioning results from tolerance of separation in distress-prone children, while subsequent positive behavior follows intolerance of separation for children with such a temperamental vulnerability.

Fish and Belsky (1991) regarded the findings of this study as inconsistent with the common view that separation intolerance among preschoolers represents insecurity or immature dependence. They argued that separation intolerance in their study by distress-prone children with secure attachment histories reflected a tendency toward open expression of negative affect, promoting effective regulation and coping. Specifically, they suggested that caregivers who are sensitive and responsive to their infant's distress may encourage the overt expression of negative affect in temperamentally vulnerable infants and contribute to the child's belief that his or her needs will be met. Conversely, caregivers of insecure, distress-prone infants may fail to provide such consistent responsiveness, thus limiting the child's perception that expressing distress will facilitate his or her needs being met. Indeed, Fish and Belsky suggested that the suppression of distress may delay the development of self-regulatory capacities, arguing that "it is principally via the open expression of negative affect and the acknowledgment and acceptance of it during early childhood that the temperamentally vulnerable child eventually develops the capacity to manage his or her affect" (p. 426).

Gunnar and colleagues (Gunnar, Larson, Hertsgaard, Harris, & Broderson, 1992) examined the impact of temperament and social context on the stressfulness of separation for 9-month-old infants, noting that social context and the interaction between infant and environmental characteristics have received little empirical attention as potential determinants of separation-related stress. These researchers compared the effects of two types of caregiving, designated as "Caregiver" and "Playmate." The Caregiver protocol, designed to simulate the behavior of the stranger in the Strange Situation, was characterized by sensitive responsiveness to infant fussiness with no interaction under nondistressed conditions. In contrast, the Playmate protocol involved continuous nonintrusive play in addition to sensitive responsiveness to distress.

Thirty-eight infants participated in two sessions, one in which the mother was present (No Separation) and one in which she was absent (Separation). Babies were randomly assigned to condition, and the mother behaved consistently with the assigned protocol during the No Separation session. Saliva samples were obtained for the purpose of cortisol analysis, and mothers completed the Rothbart Infant Behavior Questionnaire (IBQ; Rothbart, 1981).

Analysis of positive and negative affect revealed a significant effect of Separation in addition to a Condition X Separation interaction. The Separation effect was significant for both positive and negative affect, whereas the interaction was only significant for negative affect. Specifically, less positive affect was evident during Separation than No Separation sessions, and Separation produced increased negative affect in the Caregiver but not the Playmate condition.

A significant effect of Separation as well as a significant Separation X Condition interaction were also found for cortisol levels. Specifically, Caregiver Separation posttest levels were significantly higher than all other mean values of this variable. Finally, examination of the Fear of Novelty and Distress to Limits scales of the IBQ produced only one significant multivariate effect, namely the interaction of Condition and Distress to Limits. This interaction was significant for the three measures of Separation positive affect, Separation negative affect, and Separation cortisol.

These findings suggest that the degree to which an infant responds with stress to separation is influenced by the substitute caregiver's behavior. Specifically, substitute caregiving characterized by sensitive responsiveness to distress with no additional interaction produced infant increases in both cortisol and negative affect. However, when the caregiver interacted continuously with the baby, neither adrenocortical nor negative affective responses to separation differed from responses in the mother's presence. Gunnar et al. (1992) concluded that these findings were consistent with the conceptualization that separation stress results from both loss of the attachment object, or disruption of affiliation, and from anxiety or fear surrounding the postseparation environment. They suggested that babies in the Playmate condition experienced less of a disruption of affiliation. From a neurophysiological perspective, Gunnar et al. proposed that such positive social interaction may reduce stress through the activation of opioid pathways, noting that injections of opioids have been found to reduce separation distress in infant monkeys. Alternatively, these researchers suggested that the effects may have been due to the degree of control provided to the infant over the separation environment in the

Playmate condition. They noted that control and lack of control have been shown to greatly impact the adrenocortical stress response. Furthermore, although temperamental fear of novelty has been found to predict negative affect in response to separation, distress to limits predicts postseparation cortisol levels (Gunnar, 1990). Since distress to limits may be interpreted as negative reactivity in response to loss of control over desired events and/or behavioral freedom, the Playmate condition may have reduced stress by increasing the social control of the infant during separation, thus buffering the loss of access to the attachment figure. Gunnar et al. (1992) stressed that the results of the temperamental analysis supported this hypothesis, as differences between the two conditions were attributable to stress reduction in the Playmate condition for infants whose mothers reported that they responded with a high level of distress when confronted with limits. No differences were evident in either cortisol or behavior for infants with low distress to limits scores on the IBQ.

Gunnar and colleagues (1992) concluded that the stress of brief maternal separations is more closely related to substitute-care characteristics as opposed to the mother's absence, and that infants with one temperamental profile may respond with stress to a separation situation that may not be stressful for infants with different temperamental characteristics. For instance, infants who react with high distress to limits fuss more and show a heightened physiological stress response to separation, while tending to benefit most from an interactive and sensitive substitute caregiver. Gunnar and colleagues also proposed that other individual difference factors (e.g., quality of the primary attachment relationship; amount, quality, and variety of previous separation experiences) may mediate the stress reactions of infants to different separation contexts, with the interaction of such variables with temperamental aspects perhaps the most important predictor of the infant's ability to adapt. In conclusion, Gunnar et al. stated that individual differences in infant temperament can predict the stressfulness of separation, while "depending on the behavior of the caregiver, separation into an unfamiliar setting with an unfamiliar caregiver need not be highly stressful for infants who are, nonetheless, of the age and temperament to be stressed by separation" (p. 302).

7. Implications for the Etiology of Panic

Barlow's (1988) model of the etiology of panic disorder suggests several requisite conditions (e.g., biological vulnerability, learned alarms to somatic cues, psychological vulnerability) for the development of panic. The literature reviewed up to this point presents intriguing findings that offer insight into this developmental process, beginning in the newborn period and extending into childhood. The purpose of this section is to integrate findings in the area of childhood temperament, attachment, and separation within the context of Barlow's model (see Figures 1 and 2). In so doing, we will first explore the process of biological vulnerability that sets the stage in early infancy from which alternative outcomes unfold, thus guiding a child away from or along Barlow's etiological pathway.

7.1. Temperament as Biological Vulnerability

Biological vulnerability is described as an initial vulnerability within Barlow's (1988) model, and refers to the tendency to react to the stress of negative life events with inappropriate false alarms associated with exaggerated neurobiological activity. Consideration of individual differences in temperament sheds light on the critical components of this initial vulnerability.

A newborn who displays high distress reactivity, or high reactivity in response to negative events, may be conceptualized as evidencing biological vulnerability. Indeed, an experience of separation from a caregiver usually produces immediate distress and behavioral disorganization in young organisms (Cairns, 1979), and may thus be considered a possible source of stress within Barlow's (1988) model. Klein (1980) regarded this tendency to display distress in response to separation as an "innate affective control" mechanism with the evolutionary function of causing the vulnerable offspring to produce signals likely to promote retrieval by its mother. However, the expression of this mechanism in infants who evidence temperamental vulnerability (i.e., high negative reactivity) is characterized by intense and sometimes prolonged distress, with accompanying physiological arousal, in separation-relevant situations (Braungart & Stifter, 1991) that typically lack a true threat or danger (e.g., being left by parent with a competent substitute caregiver). Such heightened distress may be considered a false alarm within Barlow's model.

Although thorough consideration of the origins of high distress reactivity is beyond the scope of this chapter, this temperamental characteristic may be regarded as genetically based, as Barlow (1988) conceptualizes biological vulnerability, or it may result from developmental patterns of experience both before and after birth (Hofer, 1981). Of course, the nature of the reactivity displayed is a function of individual differences in both response characteristics and response systems. For instance, threshold and intensity of response may vary across different modalities (e.g., some children show high reactivity to tactile and others to interoceptive stimulation), with high reactivity to interoceptive stimulation being specifically

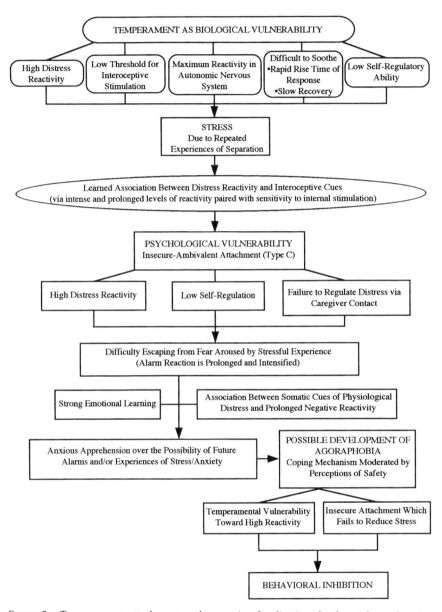

FIGURE 2.   Temperament, attachment, and separation: Implications for the etiology of panic.

central to the development of panic. Similarly, individual variability in temporal characteristics of response (e.g., rise and recovery time) shape the nature of the alarm reaction and affect soothability. Finally, individual differences in response systems impact the patterning of reactivity (e.g., some individuals evidence maximum reactivity in the cardiovascular, whereas others are more reactive in the electrodermal system). Individual differences in the nature and manifestation of reactivity thus affect the characteristics of the alarm reaction described within Barlow's (1988) model.

Barlow (1988) further suggested that this initial tendency to be neuro-biologically overreactive to stress would diminish without the subsequent association between false alarms and interoceptive cues that results in learned alarms to somatic cues. Escalona (1968) suggested individual differences in thresholds for interoceptive stimulation, with some infants evidencing heightened reactivity to internal physiological cues, such as those that characterize bodily need states (e.g., hunger, fatigue). Other infants evidence maximum reactivity, which may take the form of hyper-arousal, in the autonomic nervous system. Such infants, upon repeated exposure to stress (e.g., experiences of separation) may learn to associate distress reactivity, or alarms, with interoceptive cues. This learning would occur through repeated pairing of previously neutral interoceptive stimuli (e.g., heartbeat, rate of breathing) with the alarm reaction of heightened distress over the course of several experiences of separation. Barlow (1988) referred to this process as fear conditioning and suggested that the previously neutral interoceptive stimuli should, after pairing with the fear-arousing stimulus or false alarm, acquire the capacity to elicit the fear response. He further emphasized that such conditioning is more likely to occur in situations that block "the overwhelmingly powerful and etho-logically ancient action tendency of escape" (p. 228), thus potentiating learning by intensifying and prolonging the false alarm. One of the most critical variables in determining the intensity and duration of heightened reactivity, and the ability of the infant to easily "escape" from a heightened distress reaction, is individual differences in soothability and self-regulation. Thus, infants who evidence high distress differ in ability to reduce reac-tivity. For instance, infants with high reactivity characterized by rapid rise time would have less opportunity to benefit from caregiver intervention prior to reaching peak reactivity. This factor, coupled with low self-regulatory ability (via approach–avoidance, attentional mechanisms, and self-stimulation/self-soothing), would promote the experience of intense and prolonged levels of reactivity. Within Barlow's model, such a pattern-ing of temperamental variables should prevent the diminution of biolog-ical vulnerability, while beginning the conditioning process of associating false alarms with interoceptive cues.

Consistent with Barlow's (1988) emphasis on the combination of an initial biological vulnerability followed by the learned association between alarms and interoceptive cues is Clark et al.'s (1994) description of the tripartite model. This model proposes a general dimension of negative affectivity, with an underlying factor of temperamental sensitivity to negative stimuli, which combines, in the development of anxiety, with a specific factor of autonomic hyperarousal, a factor with critical importance in panic disorder. Thus, children with distress reactivity characterized by high intensity, combined with a patterning of responsiveness that evidences maximum reactivity (i.e., hyperarousal) within the autonomic nervous system and a low threshold for (or sensitivity to) interoceptive stimulation, may be at risk for the development of panic.

Similarly, behavioral inhibition has been suggested as a predisposing factor for childhood anxiety disorders (Biederman et al., 1990) and has been found to be highly prevalent among offspring of parents with panic disorder and agoraphobia (PDAG; Rosenbaum et al., 1988). It has been suggested that this characteristic, reflective of an underlying tendency to display excessive arousal when confronted with novelty, may predispose children to separation anxiety disorder and adults to PDAG. Fox (1989) reported that passive avoidance was accompanied by physiological arousal, and Suomi and colleagues' (1981) observation of primates suggested genetic loading for the trait of high reactivity, underlying behavioral inhibition, as the most important predictor of developing persistent anxiety-like features.

Studies of temperament, development, and individual differences (Fox, 1989; Worobey & Lewis, 1989) have suggested the importance of considering the interaction of environmental and temperamental factors in determining likely outcomes. As Rothbart and Derryberry (1981) stated, "The infant's developing reactivity and self-regulation must be viewed within the larger caregiver–infant social system" (p. 65). Individual differences in interactional history, conceptualized in the framework of attachment, will interact with biological vulnerability, impacting the child's response to stress (e.g., separation) and determining whether he or she will continue along Barlow's (1988) etiological pathway, with the subsequent development of additional fear conditioning, psychological vulnerability, and the possible development of agoraphobia.

7.2. Attachment, Temperament, and the Development of Psychological Vulnerability

Barlow's (1988) model proposes the development of anxious apprehension over the possibility of future alarms as a critical component in the etiology of panic that follows the initial learning of an association between false alarms and interoceptive cues. It further suggests that this tendency, or psychological vulnerability, arises from developmental experiences with predictability and control. The child's primary attachment relationship with his or her caregiver provides the setting within which such early developmental experiences unfold and may thus be considered, in conjunction with temperament, as having important implications for the development of psychological vulnerability and the etiology of panic.

Cairns (1979) described the most important factor in the development of attachment as the predictable behavioral interdependency between the reactive tendencies of the young organism and an environmental "object," which is most often the caregiver. This notion of predictable interdependency captures the bidirectional nature of the relationship between temperament and attachment, with the reactive tendencies, or temperament, of both caregiver and child influencing the nature of the attachment relationship that, in turn, provides the stimulus context within which temperamental variables are expressed. Main et al. (1985) have suggested that attachment-related experiences, including those relevant to predictability and control, are captured within internal working models representing the rules of the relationship and guiding behavior within its context.

The four attachment categories summarized in Table 1 provide a means of classifying the nature of predictable behavioral interdependency within a caregiver–child relationship, while capturing developmental experiences of predictability and control that may promote the development of psychological vulnerability. For instance, Type-A babies evidence an interactional style with their caregivers characterized by avoidance, actively turning away from them upon reunion, and not requiring or seeking proximity from them in order to manage distress/reactivity. Such children may have a developmental experience or internal working model of their caregiver characterized by predictable patterns of rejection or overstimulation, in which they felt little sense of control over the interaction, thus learning to avoid as a means of self-regulation. In contrast, Type-B babies display behavioral interdependency within the attachment relationship characterized by security, using the caregiver as a base from which to explore the environment and seeking contact/proximity that is effective in terminating distress. The history of such a relationship is most likely characterized by sensitive, consistent caregiving through which the infant learns that his or her needs/signals will be appropriately responded to, thus promoting a sense of control and predictability. The behavior of Type-C babies has been viewed as reflecting ambivalence and resistance. Specifically, these children show difficulty separating from the caregiver to explore the environment and display resistant behavior upon reunion, with little ability to reduce distress via contact/proximity with the caregiver.

The behavioral interdependency and internal working model that characterize this type of attachment relationship often reflect parental insensitivity and inconsistency (Isabella, 1993), contributing little predictability and control to the baby's developmental experience. Similarly, the Type-D category, characterized by disorganized/disoriented behavior, is typically evidenced in samples of maltreated children, again reflecting erratic tendencies in parental behavior, or lack of predictability and control from the perspective of the child.

Cicchetti et al. (1995) suggested that erratic parental tendencies which lack predictability and control, and often characterize the Type-D attachment relationship, result in chronic childhood anxiety and uncertainty. Type-C relationships also have important implications for the development of anxiety and may particularly promote psychological vulnerability. Specifically, alarm reactions are typically intensified and prolonged for these children, as they have difficulty relying on their caregiver as a source of comfort in times of stress (e.g., separation), thus decreasing their ability to escape from the fear aroused by a stressful experience (as securely attached children are able to do via caregiver contact). It is therefore likely that Type-C children may learn to associate the experience of stress with prolonged and heightened negative reactivity from which there is little means of escape, contributing to the conceptualization of separation and associated alarms as frightening experiences and the development of anxious apprehension over the possibility that they will recur. The process of fear conditioning described earlier, whereby interoceptive cues become associated with alarms, may continue throughout the acquisition of psychological vulnerability, with strong emotional learning prompted by difficulty escaping from the alarm reaction via regulation, and the resulting experience of prolonged and intense reactivity. Indeed, interoceptive cues may become a focus of anxious apprehension, as described later within the construct of anxiety sensitivity. It is also significant that Type-C babies tend to display wariness in response to novel stimuli, reflecting high reactivity in response to novelty. In order to further explore the potential contribution of temperament and attachment to the etiology of panic, let us examine the manner in which temperamental variables may interact with attachment, affecting the nature of the developing relationship as well as the likelihood that psychological vulnerability and other components of panic will be manifested.

Rothbart and Derryberry (1981) suggested that individual differences in temperament, particularly reactivity in response to stress and capacity for self-regulation, play an important role in the development of attachment. Thus, beyond setting the stage for the progression along Barlow's (1988) pathway via biological vulnerability and their initial role in fear conditioning (i.e., the association of distress reactivity/false alarms with interoceptive cues), temperamental variables interact with attachment to impact the likelihood that psychological vulnerability, and possibly agoraphobia, will develop.

One of the central roles played by temperament in the developing attachment relationship is its impact, via individual differences in reactivity and self-regulation, on the degree to which the baby requires proximity or contact with its caregiver in order to regulate distress. This role has important implications for both fear conditioning and the development of psychological vulnerability, as individual differences in the child's temperament interact with the nature of the attachment relationship to determine whether reactivity is effectively regulated, thus allowing the child to learn that distress is something that can be reasonably controlled, or not, resulting in prolonged experiences of heightened distress reactivity (i.e., false alarms). Thus, infants who have low or quickly recovering reactivity experience less distress and require less caregiver intervention, as do babies who have effective self-regulatory capacities. It is babies whose reactivity is high *and* capacity for self-regulation is low who are most dependent on the attachment relationship as a source of distress reduction that will prevent the experience of prolonged, intense reactivity. From this perspective, one can begin to conceptualize the process whereby individual differences in infant temperament combine with the caregiver's sensitivity, flexibility, and temperamental qualities to impact fear conditioning and affect the likelihood that psychological vulnerability, and possibly agoraphobia, will develop.

Recent research exploring the link between temperament and attachment sheds light on the interactive and behavioral characteristics of children in the context of attachment-relevant situations (e.g., the Strange Situation) and brings to mind possibilities for the early identification of children who may be developing along Barlow's (1988) etiological pathway of biological and psychological vulnerability. For instance, van den Boom (1989) reported that mothers of distress-prone infants tended to ignore and play less with them over time, thus illustrating the impact that an infant's newborn temperament can have on maternal behavior, which, in turn, affects the infant's perception of security within the attachment relationship. Belsky and Rovine (1987), investigating temperamental differences characteristic of attachment classifications, reported less autonomic stability during the newborn period in infants later classified as B3-C2 relative to those classified as A1-B2. Furthermore, Type-C infants showed less autonomic stability relative to all other infants, and mothers classified A1-B2 infants as easier than those in group B3-C2. Indeed, infants with less central nervous system organization (defined in this study as more tremors, startles, and less motor maturity) tend to be most vulnerable to behavioral disorganization, including distress reactivity when confronted with stress. In B3-B4 babies, this temperamental vulnerability is expressed by actively seeking and maintaining contact with the caregiver in order to effectively regulate distress. Thus, these babies experience predictable reduction of reactivity via the attachment relationship. In contrast, Type-C children evidence less autonomic stability yet fail to achieve reduction of distress through proximity or contact with their caregiver. It is these highly reactive children who seem to be most at risk for the experience of prolonged episodes of heightened reactivity from which there is difficulty escaping, thus promoting fear conditioning and psychological vulnerability.

Support for the association between negative reactivity and the development of an insecure attachment relationship is also evident in the studies of Vaughn and colleagues (1989, 1992) and Calkins and Fox (1992). Specifically, Vaughn and colleagues reported temperamental difficulty to be associated with negative emotionality during separation episodes of the Strange Situation, and found significant negative correlations, increasing in magnitude with age, between security of attachment and negative reactivity/affective activation (i.e., negative emotionality or arousal intensity). They interpreted these results as indicating that both attachment and temperament contribute to affective expression/control and the development of personality. Similarly, Calkins and Fox (1992) found a significant correlation between newborn distress reactivity and insecure attachment at 14 months. In addition, they reported an association between reunion crying in the Strange Situation and behavioral inhibition at 24 months, with Type-C children evidencing the most inhibited behavior, and Type-A children the most uninhibited. These authors suggested that patterns of reactivity might be modified or amplified by caregiving characteristics, and that infant differences in distress reactivity interact with type of attachment relationship, resulting in a specific inhibited or uninhibited behavioral style (e.g., an infant with a low threshold to respond to novelty will show distress in response to low levels of stimulation that, combined with frequently ineffective caregiver intervention, may result in resistant behavior and progressive withdrawal from novelty as a means of regulating distress).

It appears that the biological vulnerability of negative reactivity is a risk factor for the development of an insecure attachment relationship. Although neither temperamental vulnerability nor insecurity of attachment will, in and of themselves, lead to the development of panic, the regulatory components of the attachment relationship may, in conjunction with individual differences in reactivity and capacity for self-regulation, either promote or prevent the development of psychological vulnerability. Let us examine these processes in the context of separation as a common childhood experience that may be conceptualized as a source of stress within Barlow's (1988) model.

7.3. Separation as a Source of Stress

Barlow (1988) has defined *psychological vulnerability* as a critical component of the etiology of panic, characterized by the tendency to develop anxious apprehension over negative events or future alarms and arising from developmental experiences with predictability and control. He has further proposed that the focus of anxious apprehension is determined by the nature of the negative event experienced. The experience of separation from one's caregiver has been found to evoke high agitation and distress reactivity in primates as well as humans, although the intensity and duration of this type of alarm reaction is determined by several factors, including individual differences in temperament, attachment, and the post-separation context. Let us explore the implications of these variables for the identification of children who appear to be at risk via their developmental experiences for the development of psychological vulnerability focused on separation.

In their review of social separation in monkeys, Mineka and Suomi (1978) concluded that an individual who has had the negative experience of separation from an attachment figure will be unlikely to forget it and will probably develop a fear that separation will occur again in the future. However, recent literature exploring individual differences in response to separation has provided evidence that such anxious apprehension, which is an important component of separation anxiety in childhood, is likely to develop only given a particular constellation of variables. Cairns (1979) emphasized that adaptation is the typical response displayed by young organisms after the immediate stress of separation, although variability in paterns of adaptation may be influenced by the nature of the interactional system prior to separation as well as the social environment after separation. It is evident that temperamental differences may also contribute to this variability. For instance, Braungart and Stifter (1991) reported that individual differences in patterns of self-regulation during a stressful situation, characterized by maternal separation and reunion, depended on the level of negative reactivity experienced as well as the nature of the attachment relationship. Specifically, B1-B2 babies displayed low levels of both negative reactivity and self-regulation, whereas B3-B4 infants showed high levels of negative reactivity that were effectively reduced upon reunion via proximity and contact-seeking behavior directed toward the caregiver. Type-A babies displayed moderate levels of distress combined with heightened levels of self-regulation (e.g., self-comforting and toy play). It was suggested that these babies may have learned to depend more on self-regulation as opposed to seeking comfort from others due to a developmental history of rejecting, unresponsive interactions with their caregiver. Finally, Type-C babies evidenced intense disress coupled with a failure to regulate reactivity either through their own means or the comfort of a caregiver. The authors concluded that a temperamental proneness to high distress reactivity may make such babies very difficult to soothe, or unresponsive caregiving may lead to poor self-regulatory development. It is this combination of attachment characteristics and temperamental variables that may interct with the stress of separation experiences to promote the development of psychological vulnerability.

Fish and Belsky (1991) argued that separation intolerance via protest represents an adaptive coping response for children who are both securely attached and temperamentally vulnerable (i.e., distress prone). Specifically, secure children who evidenced proneness to distress were more likely to show separation intolerance followed by more positive affect, whereas insecure children with similar temperament who tolerated separation evinced more negative affect. It was suggested that sensitive, responsive caretaking may encourage the overt expression of negative affect in temperamentally vulnerable infants and contribute to the child's belief that his or her needs will be met. Such a developmental experience of predictability and control, in which the child learns that high reactivity will be effectively regulated via caregiver contact if he or she cries or engages in other proximity-promoting behavior, is unlikely to lead to psychological vulnerability (i.e., the conceptualization that a stressful situation leads to heightened reactivity that cannot be managed, thus producing anxious apprehension focused on the recurrence of this experience). In contrast, Fish and Belsky suggested that insecure, distress-prone infants whose caregivers do not provide such consistent responsiveness fail to learn that expressing distress will facilitate their needs being met, resulting in suppression of distress, which may delay the development of self-regulatory capacities. It is this very developmental experience of the inability to effectively reduce or control reactivity in a predictable manner that is hypothesized to promote anxious apprehension surrounding the experience of heightened reactivity in response to stress (e.g., separation).

Finally, Gunnar and colleagues (1992) have shed light on the process by which environmental characteristics may interact with individual difference variables to affect a child's response to the stressfulness of separation. Specifically, while substitute caregiving characterized by sensitive responsiveness to distress with no additional interaction produced infant increases in both cortisol and negative affect, the presence of a substitute caregiver who continuously interacted with the baby produced responses to separation that were no different from those evidenced in the mother's presence. The authors interpreted these differences as possibly due to the degree of control provided to the infant over the separation environment in this Playmate condition. Significantly, differences between the two conditions were attributable to stress reduction in the Playmate condition for infants whose mothers reported that they responded with a high level of distress when confronted with limits.

Delineation of the constellation of variables necessary for the development of anxious apprehension must take into consideration developmental experiences with predictability and control, from which Barlow (1988) views this psychological vulnerability as arising. It is suggested that the temperamental factor of distress-proneness or high negative reactivity interacts with capacity for self-regulation and the nature of the primary attachment relationship (including the degree of predictability and control it provides) to determine the extent to which heightened and prolonged levels of reactivity will be experienced in response to stress. Barlow has suggested that situations that intensify and prolong an alarm reaction potentiate learning. Indeed, separation may be conceptualized as such a stressor for Type-C infants, as it typically provokes notable distress reactivity in the absence of self-regulatory ability, coupled with failure to rely on the caregiver as a source of comfort. Type-C babies thus experience heightened and prolonged distress reactions in response to separation-relevant stress. It is suggested that repeated exposure to this stressor will potentiate the learning of an association between separation and heightened negative reactivity, thus increasing the likelihood that anxious apprehension focused on separation-related experiences (i.e., separation anxiety) will develop. One caveat, of course, is the nature of the separation environment, with substitute caregiving that allows for interaction and provides the child a degree of control within its context likely to reduce negative reactivity, thus serving as a protective factor against the development of psychological vulnerability.

7.4. Psychological Vulnerability, Anxiety Sensitivity, and Fear Conditioning

Psychological vulnerability, defined as the tendency to focus apprehension on negative events, future alarms, and/or internal somatic events that may signal the possible occurrence of an alarm, has been conceptualized as similar to the construct of anxiety sensitivity (Barlow, 1988). As an individual-difference variable comprising the belief that the experience of anxiety or fear causes illness, embarrassment, or additional anxiety, anxiety sensitivity should increase alertness to stimuli that signal the possibility of becoming anxious, including internal somatic events. Indeed, Barlow has suggested a preexisting tendency to focus anxiety on internal somatic events as an important determinant in the development of anxious apprehension and panic disorder.

The pairing of behavioral protest and physiological stress in monkeys experiencing social separation (Mineka & Suomi, 1978) suggests that children may learn, via repeated pairing, to associate internal cues of physiological arousal with distress reactivity and anxious apprehension. However, it is also apparent that some children evidence a low threshold and/or high reactivity in response to interoceptive stimulation, thus appearing particularly sensitive to these cues. Furthermore, individual differences exist in the patterning of reactivity across response modalities, with some children evidencing maximum reactivity (e.g., hyperarousal) within the autonomic nervous system. As in fear conditioning, characterized by a learned association between alarms and interoceptive cues, children who experience prolonged and intense distress reactivity in a repeated stressful situation, and who evidence sensitivity to interoceptive stimulation or hyperarousal within the autonomic nervous system, may develop a learned association between somatic cues and the experience of anxiety. Such a conditioning experience is likely to increase alertness to internal somatic events that signal the possibility of becoming anxious, thus reflecting anxiety sensitivity and promoting the development of panic.

7.5. The Possible Development of Agoraphobia

The development of avoidance behavior is conceptualized, within Barlow's (1988) model, as a function of the coping skills an individual employs to deal with unexpected panic. Specifically, the development of agoraphobic avoidance is moderated by perceptions of safety and the presence or absence of safety signals. The development of such a coping mechanism may be reflected in the behavioral inhibition displayed by children who cannot regulate arousal in response to novelty. As Calkins and Fox (1992) suggested, this inability to cope with high reactivity may lead to withdrawal from novelty and avoidance/fear of unfamiliar people and objects. Additionally, such temperamental vulnerability toward high reactivity may be exacerbated by an insecure attachment relationship that fails to reduce the stress of a fear-provoking situation, increasing the likelihood of behavioral inhibition in novel or stressful situations. Thus, "children who have difficulty regulating their arousal, and who are not confident that their primary attachment figure will provide security (and a reduction of stimulation) in a time of stress, will likely experience more fear than children who are either able to regulate their own arousal or can comfortably depend on their attachment figure for security" (p. 1470).

8. Conclusion

Separation anxiety and/or experiences of separation from attachment figures in childhood has been hypothesized, in recent literature, as playing a role in the development of panic. This chapter has presented relevant findings in the areas of childhood temperament, attachment, and the relationship of these two constructs, which suggest a pathway through which separation-relevant experiences may contribute to the etiology of this disorder. The conceptualization of this pathway is based on Barlow's (1988) model of the etiology of panic, viewing separation as one possible source of stress within this framework. Specifically, Barlow proposed an initial biological vulnerability, or a tendency to evidence exaggerated neurobiological activity in response to stress, followed by fear conditioning (i.e., learned alarms to somatic cues). Psychological vulnerability characterized by anxious apprehension over the possibility of future alarms is another central component of this model, with the possible development of avoidance behavior as a coping response moderated by perceptions of safety. Figure 2 presents the proposed integration of temperament, attachment, and separation within the context of Barlow's model of the etiology of panic. Specifically, it has been suggested that the temperamental individual-difference variables of high distress reactivity, low threshold for interoceptive stimulation or maximum reactivity in the autonomic nervous system, difficult soothability, and low self-regulatory ability form an initial biological vulnerability and set the stage for the learned association between distress reactivity and interoceptive cues given repeated experiences of stress (e.g., separation). Barlow has argued that fear conditioning or learning is potentiated in situations from which escape is difficult, thus intensifying and prolonging alarm reactions. Children who evidence high distress reactivity combined with low self-regulatory ability *and* failure to regulate distress through caregiver contact (i.e., Type-C insecure–ambivalent children) are seen as most at risk for the experience of heightened distress reactivity from which escape is blocked, or at least difficult. It is proposed that these children, upon exposure to repeated experiences of separation within which they evidence prolonged and heightened reactivity, will conceptualize separation and associated alarms as frightening experiences, thus developing anxious apprehension (i.e., psychological vulnerability) over the possibility that they will recur. Furthermore, the process of fear conditioning, or the association of interoceptive cues with alarms, is likely to continue, leading to the development of anxiety sensitivity (e.g., anxious apprehension focused on internal somatic events). Finally, behavioral inhibition may develop as a coping mechanism characterized by withdrawal from fear-evoking stimuli in order to regulate high reactivity in the absence of other self-regulatory mechanisms combined with an insecure attachment relationship that fails to reduce distress.

Consideration of the developmental processes underlying panic disorder is a relatively new undertaking in the field of anxiety disorders. As Barlow (1988) stated, "We have only just begun to collect information on the nature of panic ... but the accumulating evidence points to a complex biopsychosocial process" (p. 209). Understanding such a process requires integration of the biological, psychological, and social systems, as well as their interrelationships and impact on the course of development. The pathway suggested in this chapter presents one possible route whereby such systems, expressed through individual differences in temperament, attachment, and response to the stress of separation, contribute to the complex process involved in the etiology of panic.

9.   References

Ainsworth, M. D. S. (1973). The development of infant–mother attachment. In B. M. Caldwell & H. N. Ricciuti (Eds.), *Review of child development research: Volume 3. Child development and social policy* (pp. 1–94). Chicago: University of Chicago Press.

Ainsworth, M. D. S., & Bowlby, J. (1991). An ethological approach to personality development. *American Psychologist, 46,* 333–341.

Alessi, N. E., & Magen, J. (1988). Panic disorder is psychiatrically hospitalized children. *American Journal of Psychiatry, 145,* 1450–1452.

Barlow, D. H. (1988). *Anxiety and its disorders: The nature and treatemnt of anxiety and panic.* New York: Guilford Press.

Belsky, J., & Rovine, M. (1987). Temperament and attachment security in the strange situation: An empirical rapprochement. *Child Development, 58,* 787–795.

Biederman, J. (1987). Clonazepam in the treatment of prepubertal children with panic-like symptoms. *Journal of Clinical Psychiatry, 48* (Suppl. 10), 38–41.

Beiderman, J., Rosenbaum, J. F., Hirshfeld, D. R., Faraone, S. V., Bolduc, E. A., Gersten, M., Meminger, S. R., Kagan, J., Snidman, N., & Reznick, S. (1990). Psychiatric correlates of behavioral inhibition in young children of parents with and without psychiatric disorders. *Archives of General Psychiatry, 47,* 21–26.

Bowlby, J. (1969). *Attachment and loss: Volume 1. Attachment.* New York: Basic Books.

Bowlby, J. (1973). *Attachment and loss: Volume 2. Separation: Anxiety and anger.* New York: Basic Books.

Bradley, S. J., & Hood, J. (1993). Psychiatrically referred adolescents with panic attacks: Presenting symptoms, stressors, and comorbidity. *Journal of the American Academy of Child and Adolescent Psychiatry, 32,* 826–829.

Braungart, J. M., & Stifter, C. A. (1991). Regulation of negative reactivity during the strange situation: Temperament and attachment in 12-month-old infants. *Infant Behavior and Development, 14*, 349–364.

Cairns, R. B. (1977). Beyond social attachment: The dynamics of interactional development. In T. Alloway, P. Pliner, & L. Krames (eds.), *Attachment behavior* (pp. 1–24). New York: Plenum Press.

Cairns, R. B. (1979). *Social development: The origins and plasticity of interchanges.* San Francisco: W. H. Freeman.

Calkins, S. D. & Fox, N. A. (1992). The relations among infant temperament, security of attachment, and behavioral inhibition at twenty-four months. *Child Development, 63*, 1456–1472.

Carlson, V., Cicchetti, D., Barnett, D., & Braunwald, K. (1989). Disorganized/disoriented attachment relationships in maltreated infants. *Developmental Psychology, 25*, 525–531.

Cicchetti, D., Toth, S. L., & Lynch, M. (1995). Bowlby's dream comes full circle: The application of attachment theory to risk and psychopathology. In T. H. Ollendick & R. Prinz (eds.), *Advances in clinical child psychology* (Vol. 17, pp. 1–75). New York: Plenum Press.

Clark, L. A., Watson, D. & Mineka, S. (1994). Temperament, personality, and the mood and anxiety disorders. *Journal of Abnormal Psychology, 103*, 103–116.

Egeland, B., & Sroufe, L. A. (1981). Developmental sequelae of maltreatment in infancy. *New Directions for Child Development, 11*, 77–92.

Escalona, S. K. (1968). *The roots of individuality: Normal patterns of development in infancy.* Chicago: Aldine.

Faravelli, C., Webb, T., Ambonetti, A., Fonnesu, F., & Sessarego, A. (1985). Prevalence of traumatic early life events in 31 agoraphobic patients with panic attacks. *American Journal of Psychiatry, 142*, 1493–1494.

Fish, M., & Belsky, J. (1991). Temperament and attachment revisited: Origin and meaning of separation intolerance at age three. *American Journal of Orthopsychiatry, 61*, 418–427.

Fowles, D. C. (1993). A motivational theory of psychopathology. In W. Spaulding (Ed.), *Nebraska Symposium on Motivation: Integrated views of motivation, cognition and emotion* (Vol. 41, pp. 181–238). Lincoln: University of Nebraska Press.

Fox, N. A. (1989). Psychophysiological correlates of emotional reactivity during the first year of life. *Developmental Psychology, 25*, 364–372.

Goldsmith, H. H., & Alansky, J. A. (1987). Maternal and infant predictors of attachment: A meta-analytic review. *Journal of Consulting and Clinical Psychology, 55*, 805–816.

Gray, J. A. (1982). *The neuropsychology of anxiety: An enquiry into the functions of the septa-hippocampal system.* Oxford, UK: Clarendon Press.

Gray, J. A. (1987). *The psychology of fear and stress* (2nd ed.). Cambridge, UK: Cambridge University Press.

Grossman, K., Grossman, K. E. Spangler, G., Suess, G., & Unzner, L. (1985). Maternal sensitivity and newborn orientation responses as related to quality of attachment in northern Germany. *Monographs of the Society for Research in Child Development, 50* (1-2, Serial No. 209), 233–256.

Gunnar, M. (1990, January). *Activity of the pituitary-adrenocortical system in normal infants and children: A review with an eye to individual differences, vulnerability and temperament.* Paper given at meetings of the W. T. Grant Foundation Research Consortium on the Developmental Psychobiology of Stress, UCLA.

Gunnar, M. R., Larson, M. C., Hertsgaard, L., Harris, M. L., & Brodersen, L. (1992). The stressfulness of separation among nine-month-old infants: Effects of social context variables and infant temperament. *Child Development, 63*, 290–303.

Hayward, C., Killen, J. D., & Taylor, C. B. (1989). Panic attacks in young adolescents. *American Journal of Psychiatry, 146*, 1061–1062.

Hofer, M. A. (1981). *The roots of human behavior: An introduction to the psychobiology of early development.* New York: W. H. Freeman.

Isabella, R. A. (1993). Origins of attachment: Maternal interactive behavior across the first year. *Child Development, 64*, 605–621.

Klein, D. F. (1980). Anxiety reconceptualized. *Comprehensive Psychiatry, 21*, 411–427.

Main, M., & Hesse, P. (1990). Parents' unresolved traumatic experiences are related to infant disorganized attachment status: Is frightened and/or frightening parent behavior the linking mechanism? In M. Greenberg, D. Cicchetti, & E. M. Cummings (Eds.), *Attachment in the preschool years* (pp. 161–182). Chicago: University of Chicago Press.

Main, M., Kaplan, N., & Cassidy, J. (1985). Security in infancy, childhood, and adulthood: A move to the level of representation. *Monographs of the Society for Research in Child Development, 50*, 66–104.

Main, M., & Solomon, J. (1986). Discovery of a disorganized/disoriented attachment pattern. In T. B. Brazelton & M. W. Yogman (Eds.), *Affective development in infancy* (pp. 95–124). Norwood, NJ: Ablex.

Mineka, S., & Suomi, S. J. (1978). Social separation in monkeys. *Psychological Bulletin, 85*, 1376–1400.

Miyake, K., Chen, S., & Campos, J. J. (1985). Infant temperament, mother's mode of interaction, and attachment in Japan: An interim report. *Monographs of the Society for Research in Child Development, 50* (1-2, Serial No. 209), 276–297.

Moreau, D. L., Weissman, M., & Warner, V. (1989). Panic disorder in children at high risk for depression. *American Journal of Psychiatry, 146*, 1059–1060.

Reiss, S., Peterson, R. A., Gursky, D. M., & McNally, R. J. (1986). Anxiety sensitivity, anxiety frequency and the prediction of fearfulness. *Behaviour Research and Therapy, 24*, 1–8.

Rosenbaum, J. F., Biederman, J., Gersten, M., Hirshfeld, D. R., Meminger, S. R., Herman, J. B., Kagan, J., Reznick, S., & Snidman, N. (1988). Behavioral inhibition in children or parents with panic disorder and agoraphobia. *Archives of General Psychiatry, 45*, 463–470.

Rothbart, M. K. (1981). Measurement of temperament. *Child Development, 52*, 569–578.

Rothbart, M. K., & Ahadi, S. A. (1994). Temperament and the development of personality. *Journal of Abnormal Psychology, 103*, 55–66.

Rothbart, M. K., & Derryberry, D. (1981). Development of individual differences in temperament. In M. E. Lamb & A. L. Brown (Eds.), *Advances in developmental psychology* (Vol. 1, pp. 37–86). Hillsdale, NJ: Erlbaum.

Sameroff, A. J., & Chandler, M. J. (1975). Reproductive risk and the continuum of caretaking casualty. In F. D. Horowitz (Ed.), *Review of child development research* (Vol. 4, pp. 187–244). Chicago: University of Chicago Press.

Suomi, S. J., Kraemer, G. W., Baysinger, C. M., & DeLizio, R. D. (1981). Inherited and experiential factors associated with individual differences in anxious behavior displayed by Rhesus monkeys. In D. F. Klein & J. Rabkin (Eds.), *Anxiety: New research and changing concepts* (pp. 179–200). New York: Raven Press.

Thomas, A., & Chess, S. (1977). *Temperament and development.* New York: Brunner/Mazel.

Thomas, A., Chess, S., Birch, H. G., Hertzig, M. E., & Korn, S. (1963). *Behavioral individuality in early childhood.* New York: New York University Press.

van den Boom, D. C. (1989). Neonatal irritability and the development of attachment. In G. A. Kohnstamm, J. E. Bates, & M. K. Rothbart (Eds.), *Temperament in childhood* (pp. 299–318). Chichester, UK: Wiley.

Vaughn, B. E., Lefever, G. B., Seifer, R., & Barglow, P. (1989). Attachment behavior, attachment security, and temperament during infancy. *Child Development, 60*, 728–737.

Vaughn, B. E., Stevenson-Hinde, J., Waters, E., Kotsaftis, A., Lefever, G. B., Shouldice, A., Trudel, M., & Belsky, J. (1992). Attachment security and temperament in infancy and early childhood: Some conceptual clarifications. *Developmental Psychology, 28,* 463–473.

Warren, R., & Zgourides, G. (1988). Panic attacks in high school students: Implications for prevention and intervention. *Phobia Practice and Research Journal, 1,* 97–113.

Worobey, J., & Lewis, M. (1989). Individual differences in the reactivity of young infants. *Developmental Psychology, 25,* 663–667.

3

Obsessive–Compulsive Disorder in Childhood and Adolescence

Aude Henin and Philip C. Kendall

1. Introduction

Although Janet (1903) identified obsessive–compulsive neurosis in children as young as 5 years of age, the disorder has since remained largely unexamined: a mere handful of single case studies or small clinical samples of children diagnosed with obsessive–compulsive disorder (OCD) and little research regarding the clinical presentation or treatment exists. It is only in the past 10 years that OCD has been recognized as a serious psychopathology of childhood and that significant attention has been mounted toward its study. This recent interest has been inspired, in great part, by the finding that a large percentage of adult sufferers of OCD (33–50%) report onset of the disorder prior to age 15 (Beech, 1974), and has been fueled by subsequent studies demonstrating that the prevalence rate of the disorder is significantly higher in children than previously believed.

The purpose of this chapter is to examine the literature on childhood OCD while maintaining a focus on the characteristics of childhood OCD that may differentiate it from its adult counterpart. We begin with a general description of the disorder, its epidemiology and course, as well as patterns of comorbidity with other childhood disorders. Next, we address the assessment of the disorder, emphasizing structured clinical interviews and self-report inventories that have been developed for use with children. We then examine two dominant conceptualizations of childhood OCD—neurobiological and cognitive-behavioral explanations—and review the

Aude Henin and Philip C. Kendall • Department of Psychology, Temple University, Philadelphia, Pennsylvania 19122.

Advances in Clinical Child Psychology, Volume 19, edited by Thomas H. Ollendick and Ronald J. Prinz. Plenum Press, New York, 1997.

evidence for each, as well as related treatment approaches. Finally, we offer a summary of the relevant issues in the study of childhood OCD and provide suggestions for future research.

2. Definition and Clinical Presentation

OCD involves the presence of recurrent obsessions or compulsions that are significantly time-consuming, cause distress, or lead to an impairment in the individual's occupational/scholastic or social functioning (American Psychiatric Association, 1994). *Obsessions* consist of intrusive thoughts, images, or impulses that may be perceived as senseless or inappropriate and cause marked anxiety or distress, whereas *compulsions* are defined as repetitive behaviors whose primary aims are to reduce or eliminate anxiety or distress, rather than provide pleasure or gratification.

Despite controversy regarding the classification of OCD as an anxiety disorder (Insel, Zahn, & Murphy, 1985), the general definition of the disorder has changed little during the last three revisions of the *Diagnostic and Statistical Manual of Mental Disorders* (DSM), and has been employed consistently by researchers in the field. This consistency, in turn, has served to maintain the relevance of earlier OCD research.

The DSM definition of OCD has asserted continuity between the clinical presentation of adults and children. The only prominent developmental distinction in DSM criteria for OCD concerns a reportedly high level of insight by adult patients into the senselessness or excessiveness of their symptoms. However, the recent recognition that a large percentage of adult patients may have very little insight into their obsessive–compulsive symptoms, and the addition in DSM-IV of a "poor insight" specification has lessened the relevance of this distinction. Explicit etiological differences among those with little insight (either children or adults) have not been explored in the literature, and the relevance of insight as a diagnostic feature remains unclear.

2.1. Content of Obsessions and Compulsions

Certain patterns in the contents of obsessions and compulsions have been established across several epidemiological studies of childhood OCD. Common themes in obsessions include fears of contamination and dirt, death, violence and aggression, potential harm and danger, or moral and religious violations. Examples of obsessions include intrusive thoughts of family members dying in a car crash; recurrent intrusive thoughts of having been contaminated by dirt and germs from strangers; or recurrent impulses to blurt out obscenities in public, accompanied with the thought that the individual might actually have done this (De Silva & Rachman, 1992). Similarly, frequently reported compulsions involve ritualistic cleaning, repetition, ordering and arranging, hoarding, and counting rituals. Less frequently, instances of primary obsessional slowness have been reported, in which the primary features of the disorder are an exaggerated slowness, rigidity, and meticulousness when carrying out simple tasks of daily living (Bolton, Collins, & Steinberg, 1983; De Silva & Rachman, 1992; Toro, Cervera, Osejo, & Salamero, 1991).

In one of the largest prospective studies of pediatric OCD, Swedo, Rapoport, Leonard, Lenane, and Cheslow (1989) examined the clinical phenomenology of 70 consecutive cases of children and adolescents with primary OCD, utilizing a battery of standardized behavior ratings as well as standardized parent–child clinical interviews. The authors reported that rituals were more frequently reported by children than obsessions, with instances of "pure" obsessional disorder being a relatively rare phenomenon. These findings are consistent with those of preceding child studies, in which a predominance of compulsive behaviors was also reported, and, in this regard, are different from the adult presentation of the disorder, in which there are reportedly fairly even rates of obsessions and compulsions (Rasmussen & Tsuang, 1986).

Washing rituals were most frequently reported in the Swedo et al. (1989b) sample, with 85% displaying some form of excessive or ritualized hand washing, showering, or grooming. Repeating rituals (e.g., repeatedly crossing doorways) and checking rituals (e.g., checking doors, appliances, or homework) were also common, with 51% and 46% of the sample displaying these behaviors. Ordering, hoarding, or counting rituals were far less frequently displayed. Similarly, the most frequently reported obsessions involved a concern with dirt, germs, or environmental toxins (40% of the sample), or a fear of something terrible happening either to oneself or a loved one (24% of the sample). There appeared to be two broad themes in the content of obsessions and compulsions: a preoccupation with cleanliness, grooming, and averting danger; and a secondary theme of pervasive doubting, or being unable to know that one is "right" (Swedo et al., 1989b).

The findings of Swedo et al. (1989b) have been corroborated in subsequent reports. A study of 21 patients (ages 7.8 to 16.9 years) diagnosed with OCD at the Yale Child Study Center found that the most commonly reported obsessions surrounded thoughts of contamination (52% of patients), and aggressive/violent images and somatic obsessions, which were found in 38% of patients. Repeating rituals (76% of patients), washing rituals (67%), ordering and arranging (62%), and checking (57%) were the most commonly reported compulsions (Riddle et al., 1990). As Hanna

(1995) reported, however, more "unusual" obsessions/compulsions are also frequently encountered in obsessive–compulsive youth. Twenty-six percent of his sample of 31 OCD children and adolescents (ages 7.7–18.0) acknowledged sexual obsessions, whereas 26% and 23% reported magical (e.g., special numbers, colors, words) or religious obsessions. Similarly, a large percentage evidenced touching rituals (58%), counting rituals (42%), or mental rituals (39%).

In addition to contamination fears of dirt or "germs," case reports of obsessive fears of Acquired Immune Deficiency Syndrome (AIDS) contamination in childhood have recently appeared in the literature (Fisman & Walsh, 1994; Wagner & Sullivan, 1991). These fears appear to be similar to other contamination fears, although the central concern is contracting the HIV virus through such things as public toilets, social contacts, or hospital waste. Increased awareness and concern about AIDS in the general public, and misinformation concerning AIDS, may have promoted the appearance of these specific fears. These cases are of particular interest from a theoretical standpoint because they seem to point to an interaction between the content of obsessions/compulsions and social/environmental influences.

2.2. Prevalence

What would now be considered outdated reports provided very low prevalence rates for OCD in children (e.g., 2%). Berman (1942), based on over 3,000 pediatric cases over a 5-year period, identified only six cases of OCD. Similarly, Hollingsworth, Tanguay, Grossman, and Pabst (1980) examined 8,367 child and adolescent records over a 16-year period with only 17 cases (.2%) meeting the authors' stringent criteria (i.e., a well-defined constellation of obsessive–compulsive symptoms of sufficient severity to interfere with the child's general functioning in the absence of any other major psychiatric disorders). These estimates are substantially lower than the 6-month and lifetime prevalence rates of 1.6% and 2.5% that have been cited for adults (American Psychiatric Association, 1994; Karno, Golding, Sorenson, & Burnam, 1988).

Recent epidemiological results suggest that the rates of the disorder are higher in children and adolescents than previously believed. The first of these studies, conducted by Flament et al. (1988), was part of a broader, two-stage epidemiological study to assess eating, depressive, and anxiety symptoms in high school students in which over 5,500 students were surveyed. The first stage consisted of a survey questionnaire that included a 20-question inventory of obsessive–compulsive symptomatology (Leyton Obsessional Inventory–Child Version [LOI-CV]; Flament et al., 1988).

In the second stage, students selected on the basis of their scores on the questionnaires were interviewed by clinicians using a semistructured interview (Diagnostic Interview for Children and Adolescents [DICA]; Herjanic & Reich, 1982). A total of 18 cases of OCD were found among the 356 adolescents who participated in Stage 2, representing 0.35% of the population surveyed in Stage 1. An additional 2 subjects reported past histories of OCD. Thus, the authors propose a minimum point prevalence of .35 % and a lifetime prevalence of 0.40% of OCD in adolescents. When the sample was weighted to reflect the stratified sampling design, prevalences for current and lifetime OCD rose to 1 ($\pm$ 0.5)% and 1.9 ($\pm$ 0.7)% respectively (Flament et al., 1988).

In addition, Flament et al. (1988) reported a sizable "subclinical OCD" group (14 cases) in which subjects acknowledged one or two obsessive–compulsive symptoms that had a sudden onset and were viewed as undesirable but did not meet full diagnostic criteria for OCD. Despite the emergence of studies supporting the existence of a sizable subclinical population (Valleni-Basile et al., 1994), the importance of this subgroup, either as part of an obsessive–compulsive spectrum, as a precursor to the more severe disorder, or as a childhood variant of obsessive–compulsive personality disorder (Flament et al., 1988) has not been researched, nor have questions about etiological factors differentiating this milder variant from clinical OCD been addressed.

Epidemiological studies conducted outside the United States have supported the higher prevalence of childhood OCD, although the rates obtained by these international researchers have tended to be higher than that found by Flament et al. (1988) and closer to the adult prevalences of the disorder. For example, Zohar et al. (1992) screened over 560 Israeli 16- to 17-year-old inductees into the Israeli army with a DSM-III-R structured diagnostic interview, obtaining a prevalence rate for OCD of 3.56 $\pm$ 0.72%. Although Zohar and colleagues argue that this figure represents an accurate estimate because of the high motivation by the youths to present as physically and mentally healthy, they admit that approximately 50% of the youths diagnosed with OCD reported the presence of obsessions only. This finding distinguishes Zohar et al.'s sample from clinical samples in which the majority of children report the presence of both obsessions and compulsions. When individuals with obsessions only were excluded from the sample, the prevalence of adolescent OCD dropped to 1.83%.

An epidemiological survey of 1,032 Danish primary-school pupils using a self-report inventory of obsessive–compulsive symptomatology (LOI-CV), found that 4.1% of their sample obtained interference scores above the cutoff point (> 25), suggesting possible subclinical or clinical OCD. Of interest is the author's (Thomsen, 1993) cautionary note that many children tended to endorse numerous items on the questionnaire, although only 0.5–5% of the children reported high interference for these symptoms. This finding points to the potential for error when relying on cutoffs based on the presence–absence of obsessive–compulsive symptomatology, and to the need to consider interference as a defining criterion for classification.

When reviewing these studies, certain potential difficulties deserve comment. Diverging prevalence estimates may be attributable to differences in the criteria and measures employed. The use of a symptom inventory is likely to produce higher rates of reporting than a structured clinical interview with strict diagnostic criteria. This possibility is illustrated by the finding that approximately 95% of those scoring above the cutoff score in the first phase of the Flament et al. study (1988) did not meet criteria for OCD using a structured interview. Thus, comparisons of prevalence rates obtained by studies with diverse methodologies are quite difficult.

A somewhat different issue concerns the possibility of underreporting by individuals with OCD, since children and adolescents tend to be highly secretive and reluctant to admit or discuss their obsessive–compulsive symptoms (Clarizio, 1991; Wolff & Rapoport, 1988). In fact, Flament et al. (1988) noted that of their adolescents diagnosed with OCD, only 20% had sought treatment for OCD. Probable underreporting is further denoted by the finding that studies of the general population tend to obtain a higher estimated rate of OCD than those observing clinical populations. Valleni-Basile et al. (1994) propose that this discrepancy may have been exacerbated by beliefs in the clinical community of the low prevalence of OCD. Because of this, clinicians may not have systematically probed for the disorder and may have diagnosed these children with other disorders. The increased interest and burgeoning literature in the field of OCD have been accompanied by similar increases in the frequency of OCD diagnoses (Stoll, Tohen, & Baldessarini, 1992).

2.3. Onset

A large percentage of adult cases of the disorder are reported to originate in childhood (Rapoport et al., 1981). Onset of the disorder has been reported in children as young as 2 or 3 years of age, although the majority of cases appear to develop between the ages of 8 and 11 (Allsopp & Verduyn, 1990; Hanna, 1995; Hollingsworth et al., 1980; Last, Perrin, Hersen, & Kazdin, 1992; Rapoport, Swedo, & Leonard, 1992; Riddle et al., 1990; Toro et al., 1991). Flament et al. (1988), in their epidemiological study of nonreferred adolescents, reported a mean age of onset at 12.8 years, whereas age of onset for the largest consecutive sample of 70 clinic-referred children was somewhat lower (10.1 years; Rapoport et al., 1992).

Evidence regarding gender differences in age of onset is conflicting. Rapoport et al. (1992) reported that males tended to have earlier onset than females (a difference of 2.5 years), These findings were supported by Last and Strauss (1989), who found that boys reported a significantly earlier age of onset than girls (9.5 vs. 12.6 years). Conversely, other studies have reported either nonsignificant differences in ages of onset for boys and girls (Allsopp & Verduyn, 1990; Hanna, 1995) or an earlier age of onset for girls (Honjo et al., 1989; Riddle et al., 1990). Varying outcomes across studies make the discussion of gender differences in age of onset difficult and may point to difficulties inherent in reliance upon retrospectively recalled information.

Onset of the disorder has been reported to vary from very sudden and precipitous to a gradual emergence of symptoms over a few months (Allsopp & Verduyn, 1990; Flament et al., 1988; Hanna, 1995; Honjo et al., 1989; Rapoport, 1986a). In most cases, it is difficult to identify exact precipitating factors in an accurate fashion; however, Allsopp and Verduyn (1990) reported that they were able to retrospectively chronicle precipitating events for 18 of 44 (41%) cases of childhood OCD. These included a change of school, marked unhappiness in the school setting, and family disruption or disharmony. This study differs from others, which have reported that their subjects did not acknowledge the presence of any precipitating factors (Flament et al., 1988), and although emergence of obsessive–compulsive symptoms following stressful circumstances has been observed, difficulties associated with retrospective recall has led to scepticism. Prospective studies are needed.

2.4. Discontinuity with Normal Behavior

Certain ritualized behavior is common in childhood and has been considered part of the normal developmental process (Beiser, 1987; Leonard, Goldberger, Rapoport, Cheslow, & Swedo, 1990). Young children may evidence bathing, eating, and bedtime rituals or require things to be done "just so" in an attempt to exert some consistency or mastery over their environment. In older children, there may be ritualized play, with elaborate rules or prohibitions attached to activities (Leonard et al., 1990). Likewise, childhood superstitions (i.e., never walking under a ladder) mirror the content of obsessions or compulsions. The similarity of these behaviors to obsessive–compulsive symptoms has inspired the conceptualization of clinical OCD as an extreme example on a continuum from normal developmental rituals to pathological obsessions and compulsions.

To test the hypothesized relationship between OCD and an unusual level of superstitiousness or developmental rituals, Leonard et al. (1990) assessed and compared the frequency of childhood superstitions and developmental rituals in 38 consecutive cases of primary OCD and 22 control subjects (screened for psychopathology using a structured clinical interview). Each child and his or her parents completed a semistructured interview about superstitions and the child's developmental rituals. Non-significant differences between the OCD and the normal control groups were found in the frequency of childhood superstitions, with both groups reporting few current superstitions (mean = 2.1). Obsessive–compulsive children were rated by their parents as having had significantly more ritualized behaviors than their normal counterparts (70% vs. 27%), al-though when rituals resembling children's compulsive symptoms were excluded, overall means of ritualized behaviors for the patient and control groups did not differ.

Previous researchers had not observed exaggerated fastidiousness, superstitiousness, or increased normal childhood rituals among obsessive–compulsive youth (Rapoport, 1986a). Leonard et al. (1990) concluded that it was difficult to determine whether their unusual findings were the result of differential recall by parents in the two groups, whether some of the early ritualistic behaviors may have been short, subclinical bouts with the disorder, or whether these exaggerated childhood rituals might actually be markers for those at risk for the disorder and indicate continuity between childhood-onset OCD and normal rituals. Normal and compulsive rituals appear experientially dissimilar: Obsessive–compulsive behavior typ-ically presents much later in development and, whereas developmentally normal rituals tend to enhance socialization and increase the child's sense of mastery, obsessive–compulsive rituals are distressing and perceived as dystonic to the child.

2.5. Course of OCD

There is some suggestion that children with an "early onset" OCD (< 7 years of age) have symptoms that are more unusual than typical washing or checking rituals. These children may display symptoms such as blinking and breathing rituals or unusual obsessions (e.g., concerning yellow pencils) that are classified as "miscellaneous" obsessions and com-pulsions (Rettew, Swedo, Leonard, Lenane, & Rapoport, 1992). Early-onset OCD may also represent a variant of the disorder more closely related to Tourette's disorder (Rapoport et al., 1992). Despite phenomenological differ-ences, a significant relationship between the number or type of compulsions/ obsessions and age has not been consistently found (Rettew et al., 1992).

Gender may moderate symptom severity. For example, Hanna (1995) reported that symptom severity was influenced by an interaction between gender and age of onset, with boys with an early onset of the OCD (<

age 10), and girls with later onset, both displaying more severe forms of the disorder.

Children tend to display plasticity and overlap in terms of their particular symptoms at any given time (Thomsen, 1994a). Although a particular subtype may persist throughout the entire course of the disorder as the only symptom, children may alternatively display patterns of fading and emergence of various symptoms, and additionally, may at any given time exhibit symptoms spanning different categories of obsessions and compulsions (Hanna, 1995). Using a longitudinal design, Rettew et al. (1992) found, surprisingly, that none of their obsessive–compulsive sample (73 children) maintained the same symptom constellation from baseline to follow-up. For example, 4 patients (5%) developed washing rituals and contamination fears, 9 patients (12%) developed checking rituals, 7 (10%) developed repeating rituals, and 4 patients (5%) reported the emergence of aggressive obsessions. The appearance of new symptoms was all the more remarkable, given that subjects were receiving medication (clomipramine) in the interim between baseline and follow-up.

2.6. Comorbidity of OCD with Axis I Diagnoses

A wide range of Axis I diagnoses have been found to be comorbid with OCD in children and adolescents. Specifically, increased rates of depression, eating disorders, and other anxiety disorders seem to accompany OCD in children (Flament et al., 1988; Flament et al., 1990; Hanna, 1995; Honjo et al., 1989; Rapoport, 1986a; Swedo & Rapoport, 1990; Swedo, Rapoport, Leonard, et al., 1989; Toro et al., 1991; Valleni-Basile et al., 1994). In a nonreferred adolescent sample, 15 of 20 adolescents (75%) receiving a diagnosis of OCD had one or more other lifetime psychiatric diagnoses, whereas 10 (50%) had at least one other current diagnosis. Major depression was most frequent (5 cases), along with bulimia (3 cases), overanxious disorder (4 cases), and a history of clinical/subclinical panic attacks (4 cases; Flament et al., 1988).

Clinical samples have exhibited similar comorbidities. Swedo, Leonard, and Rapoport (1992) reported that a mere 26% of their sample had OCD as their only diagnosis. Associated diagnoses included depression (39%), anxiety disorders such as simple phobia (17%), overanxious disorder (16%), and separation anxiety (7%), developmental disabilities (24%), oppositional disorder (11%), and attention deficit disorder (10%).

A strong association between anxiety disorders and depression has been established in the child psychopathology literature, with a meaningful percentage of anxiety-disordered youth displaying affective problems (Brady & Kendall, 1992; Clark, Smith, Neighbors, Skerlec, & Randall, 1994).

Rates of comorbid depression reported for children with OCD, however, are lower than those of children with other anxiety disorders (e.g., panic disorder, overanxious disorder) or for obsessive–compulsive adults. Depression in adult cases of OCD has been found to be as high as 71% (Welner, Reich, & Robbins, 1976), and Rasmussen and Tsuang (1986) reported that 80% of adult OCD patients reported depressed mood. Of these, 74% reported secondary depression following social or occupational impairment due to their obsessive–compulsive symptoms. In contrast, comorbid depression has been identified in approximately 8–40% of OCD youth (Last et al., 1992; Rapoport, 1986a; Rapoport et al., 1992; Riddle et al., 1990; Swedo, Rapoport, Leonard, et al., 1992b; Toro et al., 1992).

Multiple anxiety disorders tend to co-occur with OCD, with 75% of one sample of obsessive–compulsive children demonstrating at least one additional anxiety disorder (Last et al., 1992). Overanxious disorder, simple phobia, and separation anxiety have been most frequently reported, with rates ranging from 7% (separation anxiety; Swedo, Rapoport, Leonard, et al., 1992) to 47% (simple phobia; Last et al., 1992). This overlap is significant, since the presence of multiple anxiety disorders may obscure the diagnostic picture—symptoms of OCD may be confused with overanxious ruminations or phobic avoidance. These complications point to the need for assessment of multiple disorders and careful differential diagnosis in the determination of OCD and associated disorders. We revisit this issue later in this chapter (section 3 on assessment).

A link between OCD and eating disorders, particularly anorexia nervosa, has been documented (Hsu, Kaye, & Weltzin, 1993). Persons with anorexia nervosa frequently display obsessive–compulsive symptoms unrelated to their preoccupations with food, and obsessive symptomatology has been indicated in 14% to 67% of anorexic patients (Piran, Kennedy, Garfinkel, & Owens, 1985; Rastam, Gillberg, & Gillberg, 1995). Moreover, many obsessive–compulsive patients frequently report a past history of anorexia nervosa (Fahy, Osacar, & Marks, 1993; Kasvikis, Tsakiris, Marks, Basoglu, & Noshirvani, 1986). Differences among OCD patients with and without an eating disorder have been reported. For example, Fahy et al. (1993) found an earlier age of onset in OCD patients with a history of anorexia nervosa.

A relationship between the nature of comorbid disorders and their temporal association to the onset of OCD has been suggested. In general, anxiety disorders and anorexia nervosa have tended to precede the occurrence of OCD, whereas affective disorders (major depression and dysthymic disorder) parallel or follow the development of OCD (Toro et al., 1991). These findings are consistent with the finding in adult studies that affective disruption in OCD sufferers may be related to impairment in functioning resulting from the time, distress, and avoidance dictated by obsessive–compulsive symptoms.

There are indications that childhood OCD may be inversely related to certain antisocial behaviors or conduct disorder. Flament et al. (1990) in their prospective 2–7 year study of 25 children and adolescents with OCD reported that only 8% of OCD children qualified for a lifetime diagnosis of conduct disorder versus 13% of controls. Similarly, none of the OCD sample received a diagnosis of drug abuse (vs. 22% of controls) and only 8% were alcohol abusers, as compared to 22% of the control group. These findings, however, do not preclude the possibility of comorbidity of OCD with identified conduct disorder. In fact, in a study of 15 adolescent girls with conduct disorder in a halfway house for delinquent girls, 16% were reported to be comorbid for OCD (Myers, Burket, Lyles, Stone, & Kemph, 1990).

2.6.1. Relationship to Tourette's Disorder

Obsessive–compulsive symptomatology tends to occur more frequently in Tourette's syndrome patients than in the general population, with up to one-third to one-half of adult (Pauls, Towbin, Leckman, Zahner, & Cohen, 1986; Pitman, Green, Jenike, & Mesulam, 1987) and child patients (Grad, Pelcovitz, Olson, Matthews, & Grad, 1987; Park, Como, Cui, & Kurlan, 1993; Pauls, 1992) with Tourette's also meeting diagnostic criteria for OCD. In addition, OCD has been linked to other tic orders, trichotillomania and Sydenham's chorea (Allen, Leonard, & Swedo, 1995; Swedo & Leonard, 1994). Several researchers have proposed that, taken together, the significant overlap and phenomenological similarities among these disorders point to an obsessive–compulsive spectrum whose defining feature is an inability to inhibit repetitive behaviors (Rapoport, 1994). Neurobiological dysfunction, either neuroanatomical or neurochemical in nature and involving dysfunction in the basal ganglia, has been implicated. Nevertheless, we consider the concept of an OCD spectrum to be of limited utility until the proposed mechanisms underlying these related disorders are clarified and the breadth and scope of the category are more clearly defined.

Support for the proposed relationship between Tourette's and OCD has come from several lines of evidence. The first of these are the aforementioned increased rates of OCD among children with Tourette's. Grad et al. (1987) compared rates of obsessive–compulsive symptomatology in 25 Tourette's syndrome children to 25 controls matched on age, gender, race, socioeconomic status and school achievement (ages 8–13). To differentiate tics from compulsions, acts were judged as compulsive only if they were complex (directed at undoing unwanted thoughts) and directed toward anxiety reduction. Results indicated that a greater proportion of the Tourette's group evidenced symptoms of OCD (28% of the sample), and although differences were not found between the two groups on a child self-report measure, analysis of parent/teacher reports indicated a relationship between Tourette's and the presence of obsessive–compulsive behaviors. The study further suggests that OCD continue to be considered a separate disorder rather than a secondary manifestation of Tourette's, since onset or termination of obsessive–compulsive symptoms did not seem to parallel the development of Tourette's.

Subsequent studies have proposed two potential subgroups of children with Tourette's, one that may be strongly associated with persistent obsessive–compulsive features and actually represent a variant of the disorder, and one that seems less related to OCD. A study by Park et al. (1993), retrospectively examining the charts of 101 children diagnosed with Tourette's disorder at initial assessment and at follow-up (mean of 1.6 years), noted that 50% of their sample could be diagnosed with OCD at baseline. At follow-up, 52% of this subsample continued to receive a diagnosis of OCD, whereas of the 50% who did not evidence OCD at baseline, only 8% subsequently developed the disorder.

Although a strength of these studies is the use of explicit criteria to determine OCD, their retrospective nature is problematic. The ability of the children, parents, or teachers to distinguish between the symptoms of OCD and Tourette's could not be determined, and it seems possible that significant overlap in reporting of the two disorders may have occurred. We further caution against strong conclusions based solely on Park et al. (1993) because of conspicuous methodological weaknesses, particularly their unfortunate use of different assessments at baseline and follow-up (neuropsychological testing vs. clinical judgment).

Reports of the presence of tics or Tourette's in OCD samples have noted an increased prevalence of these disorders in children with OCD (Riddle et al., 1990; Swedo, Rapoport, Cheslow, et al., 1989; Toro et al., 1991; Zohar et al., 1992). In the most extensive study of Tourette's in a childhood OCD sample, Leonard et al. (1992) assessed Tourette's symptoms and tics in 54 children with severe primary OCD participating in an National Institute of Mental Health (NIMH) treatment evaluation study of clomipramine. Obsessive–compulsive and Tourette's symptomatology was assessed 2–7 years posttreatment with an extensive battery including structured interviews, neurological evaluations, and child–clinician rating scales. Both at baseline and follow-up, approximately one-third of the sample received a diagnosis of current or chronic tics, whereas approximately 57–59% acknowledged lifetime histories of transient/chronic tics.

Lifetime or current Tourette's disorder was an exclusionary criterion at baseline; however, of the 32 patients who presented with a lifetime history of tics at follow-up, 8 (15% of the total sample) met criteria for Tourette's disorder. This high rate of Tourette's at follow-up seems particularly significant given the initial exclusionary criteria. The authors point out that although estimates of the prevalences of tic disorders and Tourette's in the general population have been plagued by methodological difficulties, rates of Tourette's disorder in their study are substantially higher than the published population prevalences of 0.3–0.4%. In addition, children receiving concurrent diagnoses of Tourette's and OCD were distinguished from the remainder of the sample by their male gender and earlier age of onset of OCD. Although the male predominance in Tourette's is well documented, an earlier age of OCD onset in those patients with concomitant Tourette's disorder has not been reported elsewhere. Whether this finding is related to the male predominance of this subsample, or whether this reflects a true difference in the subtypes of the disorder, remains unclear.

A third line of evidence for an OCD–Tourette's link concerns the rate of OCD in first-degree relatives of patients with Tourette's and related disorders (e.g., tic disorders; Lenane et al., 1992). When first-degree biological relatives of Tourette's patients with or without OCD are compared to adoptive relatives, the rate of OCD in biological family members (e.g., 19.0% and 26.7%) tends to be significantly higher than that of adoptive relatives and is substantially higher than the rate of the disorder in the general population (Pauls et al., 1986). A relationship between the presence of obsessive–compulsive symptoms in parents and the expression of OCD and Tourette's disorder has been suggested by the finding that children with Tourette's whose parents display important obsessive–compulsive symptomatology demonstrate significantly more obsessive–compulsive behaviors themselves, a later age of onset of Tourette's, and more complex tics than other children with Tourette's (DeGroot & Bornstein, 1994). Closer examination of familial patterns of OCD among persons with Tourette's and related disorders is needed for an identification of subtle parent–child interaction effects in the presentation of the disorder.

3. Family Characteristics of Children with OCD

3.1. Prevalence of Psychiatric Disorders among Family Members

Some controversy exists regarding the prevalence of OCD among first-degree relatives of obsessive–compulsive patients. Although some researchers have obtained significantly higher rates of the disorder in first-degree relatives compared to the general population (Rasmussen & Tsuang, 1986), others have found little or no difference between families of OCD patients and controls (e.g., McKeon & Murray, 1987). Despite these inconsistencies, there is mounting evidence for increased rates of obsessive compulsive disorder (and general psychiatric disorders) among family members of obsessive compulsive patients.

Adams (1973) described a series of 49 "obsessive" children seen over a period of 15 years. He reported a positive family history of obsessive compulsive symptoms in 71% of the children, whereas a family history of "other psychopathology" was noted in 55% of the patients. More recent reports also document a familial link in the disorder. Swedo, Rapoport, Leonard, et al. (1989), in their analyses of the NIMH sample of 70 obsessive–compulsive children, found a family history of OCD in 25% of the sample. This relationship was most prominent among father–son pairs (Swedo, Rapoport, Leonard, et al., 1989). In addition to increased rates of severe familial psychopathology among OCD probands, Hollingsworth et al. (1980) noted that a substantial number of severe medical illnesses were present in family members, including ulcerative colitis, duodenal ulcers, and cancer. Higher rates of medical illness among family members have not been replicated elsewhere, however.

Subsequent "bottom-up" studies have confirmed both the elevated rates of obsessive–compulsive disorder and tic disorders (Riddle et al., 1990), and psychiatric disorders such as affective illness and anxiety disorders in family members of OCD patients (Allsopp & Verduyn, 1990; Honjo et al., 1989; Pauls, Alsobrook, Goodman, & Rasmussen, 1995; Toro et al., 1991), as have "top-down" studies of the offspring of adults with OCD. In a study of OCD or agoraphobic adults, children of afflicted adults were seven times more likely to be diagnosed with an anxiety disorder than normal controls, and twice as likely to be diagnosed than those children whose parents suffered from other forms of psychopathology (Bernstein & Borchardt, 1991).

Several methodological issues have arisen from a review of these studies. Differences in sampling methods, as well as variations in the diagnostic criteria employed, may account for some of the variability among reports of familial incidence. Furthermore, the majority of these studies rely upon one or two informants (e.g., the child and one parent) to provide data on the entire family. This method of data collection has been found to underestimate the frequency of psychiatric disorder (Lenane et al., 1990).

Because of these criticisms, Lenane et al. (1990) initiated a study in which they assessed psychiatric diagnoses in all first-degree biological relatives of 46 children and adolescents with primary OCD. A total of 90 parents and 58 full siblings (ages 6 or older) were interviewed and compared to a group of parents of 34 conduct-disordered children. The researchers reported significantly higher rates of OCD among parents of obsessive–compulsive children, with 15 of the 90 parents (17%) receiving a diagnosis of OCD. Fathers were almost three times as likely to receive a diagnosis of OCD than mothers. In addition, fathers were more likely to receive a diagnosis of obsessive–compulsive personality (20%) than mothers (2%). Thirteen percent of the parents of obsessive–compulsive children were classified as having subclinical OCD. Five percent and 3% of siblings were diagnosed with OCD and subclinical OCD, respectively. When age correction for siblings was performed (since many siblings had not passed the age of risk), the rate of OCD or subclinical OCD rose to 35%.

In addition, 20 (45%) fathers and 30 (65%) mothers received an Axis I diagnosis other than OCD. Mood disorders, alcoholism, and anxiety disorders were the most prevalent. A strong relationship was found between the presence of an affective disorder and OCD in parents. Furthermore, 21 (36%) of the siblings had a non-OCD psychiatric diagnosis, and 45% of siblings ages 18 and over received a diagnosis of an affective disorder. These results indicate increased rates of psychological disorder among family members and are strengthened by the authors' generally sound methodology, in particular, their use of a structured diagnostic interview and a clinical comparison group. Nevertheless, absence of family interviewers blind to child's diagnosis may increase the possibility of bias, and the lack of a control group precludes a comparison of findings to the general population.

Not unlike a consideration of family factors in all forms of psychopathology, the relative contributions of genetic/familial versus environmental/learning factors have been compared in the development of OCD. High rates of familial psychopathology in general, and OCD and tic disorders in particular, have led some to hypothesize a nonspecific genetic link in the transmission of OCD and to interpret the rates of OCD among family members as representative of families that may be more "genetically loaded" for the expression of OCD (Lenane et al., 1990).

Lenane et al. (1990) argued against a simple modeling hypothesis of familial OCD in the transmission of the disorder. In comparing age of onset and primary symptoms of the probands to those of their afflicted family members, the researchers found no consistent patterns between parent and child symptoms, nor between older to younger siblings, which they interpreted as evidence against a modeling paradigm. We would propose, however, that this finding does not discount more general modeling effects of OCD or the possibility of social learning factors in the development of the disorder. Observational learning of parental anxiety has been implicated in childhood anxiety disorders (e.g., agoraphobia; see Silverman, 1987). What may be learned, rather than specific behaviors, are emotional reactions to ambiguous situations (Barrios & Hartmann, 1988). Thus, children whose parents display anxiety or avoidance to certain situations (e.g., possible contamination) may adopt this general behavioral style. In addition, the role of specific parental styles (e.g., overprotectiveness) has been proposed as a potential contributor to childhood psychopathology such as depression or anxiety (Barker, 1976; Kendall, 1992; McFarlane, 1987). What remains unclear are the family interactional variables that relate specifically to childhood OCD. We know precious little about the relative contributions of genetic and social learning factors to OCD, and discussions of this issue at present, are lacking a strong database.

3.2. Parental Personality Characteristics

The search for parental personality characteristics that might impact upon the development of OCD has its ties to psychoanalytic, behavioral, and biological/genetic models of the disorder. There have been suggestions that parents of OCD patients may be more likely to display traits of obsessive–compulsive personality, such as an overconcern with morality or cleanliness (Clark & Bolton, 1985b; Honjo et al., 1989; McKeon & Murray, 1987; Rasmussen & Tsuang, 1986), anxiety, and rigidity (Adams, 1972; Hoover & Insel, 1984). For example, Hoover and Insel (1984) described family members of 10 obsessive–compulsive patients and reported that they typically lived in somewhat isolated families that emphasized "attainment of cleanliness and perfection."

It has been speculated that parents of obsessive–compulsive youth may be strict and over-involved (Merkel, Pollard, Wiener, & Staebler, 1993) and have high expectations for their children (Hollingsworth et al., 1980). Clark and Bolton (1985b) compared the families of 12 OCD adolescents with 11 families of anxious, nonobsessive adolescents. No significant differences in parents' aspirations and expectations for their children were found between the two groups, although the obsessional adolescents perceived their parents as holding higher occupational standards for them, as compared to anxious adolescents. Actual parental expectations may play a less significant role in the maintenance of the disorder than children's perceptions of these expectations.

Taken together, the literature advances some interesting propositions concerning the interplay between parental disposition and psychopathology in the child, but unfortunately the studies are hindered by meth-

odological inconsistencies and limitations. The use of small subject samples in the majority of these studies limits the confidence we can place in
the data. Moreover, the lack of proper control groups prohibits comparison
to either normals or other psychiatric disorders and precludes discussion
of the specificity of the findings to OCD. The failure of many of these
studies to provide clear operational definitions of the constructs employed, and their reliance on unstandardized or subjective assessment
procedures may have led to wide discrepancies in their conclusions (Clark
& Bolton, 1985b).

4. Assessment of OCD

There are several methods of assessment for evaluating childhood
OCD, including structured clinical interviews, ratings and inventories,
and observational systems. Although most standardized measures of
OCD are recent developments and require further validation, they do
present researchers with an opportunity for systematic evaluation of
obsessive–compulsive symptomatology. Most of these measures were
standardized using DSM-III and DSM-III-R criteria. With the publication
of the DSM-IV (American Psychiatric Association, 1994), further validation
with DSM-IV criteria will be necessary.

4.1. Structured Interviews

Although none of the structured interviews available for the assessment of childhood OCD were developed specifically for this disorder,
many contain sections pertaining to obsessive–compulsive symptoms.
Structured or semistructured clinical interviews are frequently employed
both in research and clinical settings, in part because they reduce the
variance associated with clinical judgment, in part because they increase
comparability of diagnostic classification (Ollendick & Hersen, 1993), and
also because they permit the systematic evaluation of diverse problem
areas. Furthermore, because of their standardization, structured interviews are useful in comparing treatment and control groups for pre- and
posttreatment effects (Wolff & Wolff, 1991) and are open to direct evaluation of their psychometric properties. Most structured interviews offer
both parent and child sections, enabling the interviewer to obtain information about the child's difficulties from multiple informants. Children may
be reticent; however, interviews make possible the development of a
relationship between the child and interviewer (Kendall et al., 1992) and
permit clarification of ambiguous or unclear responses.

Several structured interviews have gained prominence in the literature: for example, the DICA (Herjanic & Reich, 1982), Children's Assessment Schedule (CAS; Hodges, 1983; rev. ed., 1986; 2nd rev. ed., 1990a; Hodges, Kline, Stern, Cytryn, & McKnew, 1982), Kiddie Schedule for Affective Disorders and Schizophrenia (K-SADS; Ambrosini, 1986; Puig-Antich & Chambers, 1978), Diagnostic Interview Schedule for Children (DISC; Costello, Edelbrock, Dulcan, Kalas, & Klaric, 1984; DISC-R; Shaffer et al., 1993; DISC 2.1; Fisher, Shaffer, Wicks, Piacentini, & Lapkin, 1990), and, more recently the Child and Adolescent Psychiatric Assessment (CAPA; Angold, Cox, Predergast, Rutter, & Simonoff, 1987). These interviews consist of a series of standardized questions permitting the assessment of a range of childhood psychopathology using DSM criteria, as well as multiple areas of functioning (e.g., school, home). Although acceptable reliabilities and validities for psychiatric diagnoses have been obtained with these interviews (DICA; Carlson, Kashani, Thomas, Vaidya, & Daniel, 1987; Vitiello, Malone, Buschle, Delaney, & Behar, 1990; CAS; Hodges, 1990; Hodges, Cools, & McKnew, 1989; Hodges et al., 1982; K-SADS; Apter, Orvaschel, Laseg, Moses, & Tyano, 1989; Carlson et al., 1987; Chambers et al., 1985; DISC [revised versions]; Fisher et al., 1993; Jensen et al., 1995; Schwab-Stone et al., 1993; Shaffer et al., 1983), they have tended to be weak in the assessment of childhood anxiety disorders. Retest reliabilities for anxiety disorders have often been low (e.g., CAS, $k = .72$; Hodges, Gordon, & Lennon, 1990; K-SADS, $k = .24$ [OCD $k = .23$]; Chambers et al., 1985; DISC 2.1, $k = .32-.50$; Jensen et al., 1995). Similarly, poor agreement among informants (i.e., parent and child) have been observed for anxiety diagnoses; for example, with the CAS ($r = .12-.26$, Hodges et al., 1990) and the K-SADS (ICC = .35; Apter et al., 1989). Although the CAPA has demonstrated promise in the assessment of anxiety and exhibited good retest reliability (e.g., $k = .74$ for Overanxious Disorder (OAD), $k = .64$ for any anxiety disorder; Angold & Costello, in press, further validation is encouraged for use in assessing childhood OCD.

The potential for misdiagnosis of OCD in children has been raised by Breslau (1987), who noted that one-third of children identified as having obsessions or compulsions were actually false positives. Similar figures were obtained for individual questions (e.g., "Do thoughts or pictures you don't like ever come into your head?"). To resolve this issue, Breslau proposed that interview items include a detailed description of the behavior, that concepts such as "unreasonable" or "senseless" be explained to the children through examples, and that training of interviewers target the clarification of vague, nonspecific answers.

In light of the difficulty in reliably assessing childhood anxiety through structured interviews, the Anxiety Disorders Interview Schedule for Children/Parents (ADIS-C/P) was developed specifically to diagnose anxiety disorders in children and differentiate these from other internalizing and externalizing problems (Silverman & Eisen, 1992). The ADIS-C/P consists of independent but comparable parent and child interviews, organized around DSM-III and DSM-III-R categories that enable the diagnostician to obtain information about the symptomatology, course, etiology, and interference of the problem behaviors.

Silverman and colleagues have reported good interrater and retest reliability for the ADIS C/P. In their initial evaluation, Silverman and Nelles (1988) administered the ADIS to 51 children (aged 6 to 18 years) and their mothers, and compared interviewer ratings with the ratings of an independent observer. Overall correlations for child and parent interviews were .98 and .93, respectively. Correlations for obsessions were .92 for child report and .98 for parent report, whereas the correlations for compulsions were .99 (child) and .99 (parent). Kappa coefficients for the classification of children as either "anxiety-disordered" or "other," were .85 for child reports, 1.0 for parent reports, and .46 for the combined version. Kappa coefficients, calculated for specific anxiety disorders in the child interview, ranged from .38 for overanxious disorder (child version) to 1.0 for several disorders including school phobia and simple phobia (child and composite versions). Due to low sample size, however, kappas could not be calculated for OCD diagnoses.

In a second study of 50 clinic-referred children, retest reliabilities over a 10- to 14-day period were calculated separately for diagnoses, symptom scores, and severity ratings (Silverman & Eisen, 1992). Overall kappas for diagnosis were .76, .67, and .75 for the child, parent, and composite scores, and .64 for OCD. When the authors separated the children into two groups based on their ages (6–11 years, 12–17 years), differences in the reliabilities for diagnoses and symptom scores emerged: Retest reliabilities for OCD symptom scores were significant for children in the older age group, but not for the younger children. Younger children had kappas of .18 (child interview) and −.06 (parent interviews), versus kappas of .73 (child interview) and .64 (parent interview) for the older children.

This finding is consistent with previous reports that the reliability of children's reports tends to improve as they increase in age (Edelbrock, Costello, Dulcan, Kalas, & Conover, 1985), and has been attributed to children's changing cognitive and language skills. The finding that parent reports also increase in reliability with the child's age is an interesting one and may need further consideration. Younger children may be more secretive about their obsessive–compulsive symptoms, or parents may confuse obsessive–compulsive behaviors with developmentally appropriate rituals, so that use of the ADIS-C/P with younger children would require additional clarification of obsessive–compulsive behaviors. Despite this limitation, the ADIS-C/P has been extensively used and has shown sensitivity to treatment effects, both in studies of anxiety-disordered youth (Kendall, 1994) and childhood OCD (Albano, Knox, & Barlow, 1995).

4.2. Rating Scales and Inventories

Self-report inventories are often used in the assessment of OCD—not as a means of diagnosis, but as a way of ascertaining the occurrence of obsessive–compulsive symptoms and their interference. Inventories are also useful for assessing changes in obsessive–compulsive behaviors over time (treatment effects) and provide supplementary information about the range of potential problematic behaviors (Wolff & Wolff, 1991).

4.2.1. The Leyton Obsessional Inventory—Child Version (LOI-CV)

The LOI-CV is a 44-item self-report instrument that has been systematically revised for use with children and adolescents. It measures subjective reports of obsessive–compulsive thoughts and behaviors (Berg, Rapoport, & Flament, 1986). Using a card-sort method, children indicate the presence or absence of specific obsessive–compulsive symptoms, including persistent thoughts, fear of dirt, and repetition. Items endorsed positively are presented again to obtain scores of resistance and interference.

Studies have indicated that the LOI-CV discriminates between obsessive–compulsive adolescents and normal controls (matched on age and IQ). Retest reliabilities (5-week period) were high, with intraclass correlations of .96, .97., and .94 for "Yes" scores, resistance, and interference, respectively (Berg et al., 1986).

The validity of the LOI-CV was evaluated with 19 patients in a clomipramine drug trial by comparing scores at Week 5 of placebo treatment with Week 5 of clomipramine treatment, and LOI-CV scores with changes on other measures of OCD. Correlations between the different measures were high ($r = .77$ to .89). Also, significant differences in scores on the LOI-CV were obtained between pre- and posttreatment, indicating that the LOI-CV is sensitive to change (Berg et al., 1986).

A survey-form of the Leyton Inventory has been developed using 20 items drawn from the original 44-item scale. In this version, the card-sort technique has been transformed into an inventory, and the rating of resistance has been dropped, as resistance was found to be less discriminating than interference (Berg, Whitaker, Davies, Flament, & Rapoport, 1988). The psychometric properties of the 20-item LOI-CV Survey Form are generally sound. The inventory demonstrated .81 internal reliability (Cronbach's alpha), with four factors (general obsessive, dirt-contamination, numbers-luck, and school) accounting for 47% of the variance. Particularly strong loadings for the general obsessive and dirt-contamination factors were obtained. Several items have been suggested as "red flags" and were likely to be checked by those with the highest scores on the inventory. Examples of these include "having to put things away at night in a special way" and "avoiding special numbers or words" (Berg et al., 1988).

The 20-item Leyton has been shown to possess adequate specificity and sensitivity. When an interference cutoff score of 25 or greater is used, sensitivity of the instrument is 75% and its specificity is 84% (Flament et al., 1988). If the criteria are changed to encompass respondents scoring 15 or above on "Yes" scores, sensitivity increases to 88% and the specificity becomes 77%. The Child Version of the Leyton thus serves as a good screening instrument, although additional use of a structured diagnostic interview may supplement its somewhat lower specificity and reduce the number of false positives.

4.2.2. The Yale–Brown Obsessive–Compulsive Scale (Y-BOCS)

The Y-BOCS is a rating scale developed to assess the severity of obsessive–compulsive symptoms in adults. The patient is asked to identify the presence of relevant obsessive–compulsive symptoms from a list of diverse obsessions and compulsions. Ten items in which the patient is asked to rate the severity of obsessions/compulsions on 5-point scales are subsequently presented (Goodman et al., 1989c). The amount of time spent, interference, distress, resistance, and control over symptoms are evaluated (Goodman et al., 1989b; Goodman et al., 1989c).

The adult version of the scale possesses good interrater and internal reliability. In addition, the Y-BOCS has demonstrated moderate correlations with two other established measures of OCD, the Clinical Global Impression (CGI) Obsessive–Compulsive Scale (Guy, 1976; $r = .74$) and the NIMH Global Obsessive–Compulsive Scale ($r = .67$) and is weakly correlated with measures of depression and anxiety in patients with minimal secondary symptoms. The Y-BOCS has also been found to be sensitive to treatment changes in symptoms; following drug treatment, Y-BOCS scores significantly decreased 20–25 % below baseline values (Goodman et al., 1989c).

By keeping items from the adult version, but altering wording to make it more easily understood, a version of the Y-BOCS has been developed for children (CY-BOCS; Johnston & March, 1992). As yet, no studies on the reliability and validity of the child version have been reported.

4.2.3. Maudsley Obsessive–Compulsive Inventory (MOCI)

The MOCI (Hodgson & Rachman, 1977), designed for use with adults, consists of 30 true–false items, providing a total score as well as scores on four subscales relating to checking, washing, doubting, and slowness. It has demonstrated good retest reliability and, due to its ease in administration and short time requirements, is highly practical to use. However, inaccurately low scores may be obtained by individuals who may show great impairment but manifest only one or two obsessions (Johnston & March, 1992). A version has not been developed for use with children, nor has the effectiveness of the current version of the MOCI been evaluated when applied to children. The only study to assess the sensitivity of the MOCI with an obsessive–compulsive adolescent sample (ages 14 to 17) found that the MOCI scores did not differentiate obsessional adolescents from a nonanxious control group (Clark & Bolton, 1985a).

4.2.4. Miscellaneous Other Rating Scales and Inventories

In addition to the commonly employed scales, other inventories and checklists have been developed for use in specific OCD research projects. Included among these are the OCD Impact Scale–Child (Piacentini, Jaffer, Liebowitz, & Gitow, 1992), and the Multidimensional Anxiety Scale for Children (MASC; March, 1994). Although these measures have shown promise in the assessment of OCD, research on their reliability and validity is lacking at this time and is strongly encouraged.

In summary, researchers and clinicians are encouraged to adopt a multimethod approach to the assessment of OCD in children. The use of both structured diagnostic interviews to establish a diagnosis and self-report inventories to assess specific symptoms of the disorder will enable the researcher to more fully evaluate the presentation of the disorder and to consider differences across measures. To date, parent and teacher measures specifically targeting OCD symptoms have not been developed; however, measures such as the Child Behavior Checklist (CBCL; Achenbach, 1991) that have demonstrated retest reliability, interparent agreement, and have been shown to possess construct, content, and criterion validity, may be employed to obtain both an indication of the child's general problem behaviors and symptoms. It is hoped that specific parent and teacher measures will be developed.

We note that direct behavioral observations are not typically included when assessing childhood OCD. Behavioral avoidance tasks (BATs), may be useful in obtaining direct measures of avoidance and anxiety and can serve as a measure of clinical change. Although standardized coding systems have not been published, Albano et al. (1995) have suggested a

BAT designed for OCD: levels of distress and resistance (amount of time prior to ritualizing) are assessed during imaginal exposure to specific, anxiety-provoking situations. Reliability and validity are currently being evaluated.

5. Theoretical Models of OCD

Cognitive-behavioral and neurobiological models have emerged as forerunners in etiological descriptions of OCD. Although traditionally viewed as separate (and opposing) conceptualizations, a recent trend suggests the integration of neurobiological and cognitive-behavioral tenets into a comprehensive model (e.g., Neural Network Modeling; Stein & Hollander, 1994; Barlow's Cognitive-Behavioral Biological model; Barlow, 1988). It should be noted that models of OCD and the supporting literature have been based almost exclusively on adults. It would seem misguided to overlook development in the expression of OCD and reflexively apply adult models to children, yet the absence of child research in these conceptual areas leaves adult models as the only available accounts of the disorder. This section therefore, will consider the adult literature, integrating, wherever appropriate, research on childhood OCD, and more generally, childhood anxiety.

5.1. Cognitive Models

The role of cognitive functioning in childhood anxiety disorders, and specifically OCD, has not been researched widely, although clinically, it has been recognized that cognitive features such as indecisiveness and overattentiveness to detail are an integral part of the disorder. More recently, evidence suggesting that OCD sufferers may differ qualitatively from their nonobsessive counterparts in cognitive functioning has emerged. Tallis (1995) proposed a tripartite system: studies investigating category formation, decision-making abilities, and the role of memory functioning in obsessive processes. In addition to these structural differences, researchers have focused on cognitive distortions in obsessive–compulsive individuals, particularly regarding appraisals of threat, personal responsibility, and anxiety.

5.1.1. Category Formation

Several authors have focused on obsessive–compulsive patients' organization of information, proposing that individuals with OCD are deficient in their ability to organize and integrate experience (Reed, 1968). Reed (1969) examined this hypothesis using a classification task in which subjects were required to identify only words that were "essential" to the initially presented target word. Twenty-five patients diagnosed with obsessive–compulsive personality disorder were compared with 25 psychiatric controls (other personality disorders) and 25 normal controls, matched on years of education. Although nonsignificant differences were found between the three groups in their performance on this task, when errors were analyzed to see if they were due to an overinclusive (too many alternatives accepted) or underinclusive (too few alternatives accepted) style, significant differences emerged. The obsessive–compulsive group was found to be significantly underinclusive, accepting fewer alternatives as essential to concepts than either of the two groups. The tendency for underinclusiveness has also been documented with nonverbal tasks (Reed, 1969). Obsessive–compulsive patients tend to be overly strict in their determination of class boundaries, in that they require a higher number of classes and allocate fewer members to each class.

The tendency toward overstructuring was supported by Persons and Foa's (1984) finding that obsessive–compulsive individuals required more piles in a task requiring them to sort both neutral and fear-related items. In addition, as compared to normal controls, patients required more time to sort the fearful items than the neutral items, suggesting that there may an exacerbation of a general tendency toward overcategorization when processing fear-related stimuli.

Recent attempts at replicating Persons and Foa's findings of overcategorization, however, have been unsuccessful (Jakes, 1992). Frost, Lahart, Dugas, and Sher (1988) employed Persons and Foa's card-sort task with students obtaining high (> 9) versus low (< 5) scores on the MOCI. Students identified as high compulsives did not use more categories than the compulsives, although, in accord with the Persons and Foa study, high compulsives took significantly longer to sort the fear cards than the neutral cards.

These findings raise questions about the generalizability of Persons and Foa's findings. As Tallis (1995) pointed out, the lack of a non-OCD, anxiety-disordered control group prevents a discussion of the specificity of the effects to OCD. Furthermore, the OCD group employed in the Persons and Foa study rated themselves as significantly more depressed than did control subjects. Since previous studies have shown a relationship between low mood and a tendency toward underinclusion, we cannot directly relate findings of underinclusion to obsessive–compulsive phenomena, or distinguish obsessive–compulsive from affective processes (Tallis, 1995).

5.1.2. Decision Making

Indecision and doubt have been documented clinically, and case reports have suggested that OCD patients experience a great deal of uncertainty and difficulty in making decisions. Tallis' (1995) review contended that "empirical investigations of obsessional indecision have failed to demonstrate its existence" (p. 31), and there is insufficient evidence to support the hypothesis that obsessive–compulsive patients require more time and information to reach a decision.

Researchers have attempted to empirically validate the self-reported indecision of obsessive–compulsive patients by employing signal detection or probability inference paradigms, and looking at the number of trials requested by the subjects prior to making a decision as a measure of indecisiveness (Milner, Beech, & Walker, 1971; Volans, 1976). One study (Sartory & Master, 1984) comparing obsessive patients with normal controls reported that the patients demonstrated significantly more uncertainty and doubt. Patients with obsessive–compulsive symptoms have been reported to require significantly more trials to make a decision than controls, but the relationship of this finding to indecisiveness is unclear, and methodological difficulties (e.g., increased rates of depression in the OCD group, poor matching of control groups) need attention.

5.1.3. Memory Impairments

Patients with OCD frequently appear to experience memory difficulties: They recount being unsure whether they performed a specific activity and report nagging feelings that "things aren't quite right." The chronic doubting that often accompanies ritualistic behavior has prompted researchers to examine the role of memory impairments in OCD. Specifically, although studies looking at short-term or long-term memory deficits in OCD patients have not found significant differences (Reed, 1977), it has been proposed that OCD patients experience deficits in memory for prior actions and poorer confidence about the quality of their remembering than controls.

To tap into memory for prior actions (Sher, Frost, & Otto, 1983), a group of undergraduate students previously separated into "checkers," "cleaners," and "noncheckers/noncleaners" on the basis of MOCI responses were asked to perform seven separate tasks, after which they were asked to describe as many tasks as they could recall. Those students identified as "checkers" displayed significantly more memory deficits in recalling past actions and remembered fewer of the performed tasks. Furthermore, they experienced difficulty in differentiating between real and imagined events. When "checkers" began to doubt their actions, they began to doubt the quality of their remembering and consistently underestimated their performance.

The original findings of Sher et al. (1983) have been replicated with nonclinical and clinical samples, and in both instances, subjects identified as checkers (vs. noncheckers) reported poorer recall for past actions (Sher, Mann, & Frost, 1984; Sher, Frost, Kushner, Crews, & Alexander, 1989). Moreover, these individuals obtained significantly lower memory quotients on the Weschler Memory Scale than noncheckers, although none of the other tests designed to identify memory deficits (e.g., digit span tests) differentiated the two groups. These findings, taken together, suggest that obsessive–compulsive symptoms (i.e., checking behaviors) are associated not with general memory impairments, but with relative difficulties on tasks requiring recall of prior behaviors. It has been proposed that it is as a result of this specific memory impairment that patients feel the need to return and check to alleviate their uncertainty.

Difficulty in distinguishing real from imagined events has been discussed in Johnson's theory of "reality monitoring" (Johnson, 1988; Johnson & Raye, 1981; Johnson, Raye, Foley, & Foley, 1981), which pertains to the circumstances under which memories of experiences might be confused with imagined memories. Although difficulty distinguishing real from imagined events has been proposed as a mechanism implicit in OCD patients' memory deficits, the evidence does not support reality-monitoring deficiencies in obsessive–compulsive individuals. Brown, Kosslyn, Breiter, Baer, and Jenike (1994) found, in a signal detection study of 28 patients with OCD (vs. 21 control subjects), that OCD subjects did not experience difficulty differentiating between a percept and a mental image, and that they were very aware of differences between what they had seen and what they had imagined. Although the authors note that their subjects had been undergoing drug treatment for the disorder, results suggest that the memory difficulties displayed by these individuals were not due to confusion about the source of the representations in memory (percepts rather than mental images). Instead, they propose that these impairments may be due to difficulties in using information stored in memory to guide behaviors (Brown et al., 1994).

5.1.4. Cognitive Distortions in OCD and Anxiety Disorders

In examining cognitive functioning in various childhood psychopathologies, an important distinction has been made between cognitive deficiencies and cognitive distortions (Kendall, 1985, 1991; Kendall & Mac-Donald, 1993). Cognitive deficiencies describe a lack of cognitive activity (e.g., problem solving, planning) in which such activity would be useful, and such deficiencies have been associated with externalizing behavior problems such as attention-deficit/hyperactivity disorder (ADHD). Cognitive distortions, on the other hand, refer to instances in which cognitive processing is occurring but in a distorted or "crooked" manner (e.g., exaggerated appraisals of threat). This distorted type of processing is more often linked to anxiety and affective disturbances. Although the role of cognitive functioning in childhood disorders has not been widely researched, there is evidence to suggest that the cognitive processing of anxious children is marked by cognitive distortions (Kendall & MacDonald, 1993). Distortions in obsessive–compulsive cognitions have been proposed although these do not appear to be exclusive to obsessive thinking, but may reflect more general anxious processing. It has been suggested that individuals with OCD misinterpret the demands of the environment and their own abilities to cope with these demands. Specifically, these individuals have been reported to display increased sensitivity to perceived threat in the environment, to experience an inflated sense of personal responsibility, to consistently overpredict their anxiety in anxiety-provoking situations, and to be hypervigilant for naturally occurring intrusive thoughts (Foa & Kozac, 1986; Foa & McNally, 1986; Kozac, Foa, & McCarthy, 1988).

Much cognitive theorizing about OCD is based on Lang's (1979) bioinformational conceptualization of fear, in which fear is represented as a memory network that includes information about the feared stimulus, information about behavioral responses, and interpretive information about the meaning of the stimulus and response factors. Foa and Kozac (1986) proposed that although normal and pathological fears involve stimulus and response components, fear structures in anxiety disorders are characterized either by high negative valences concerning the consequences of the stimuli, large fear responses and an elaborate fear structure, or strongly formed associations between representations of stimulus and response in the fear structure (Kozac et al., 1988). They suggest that heterogeneity of obsessive–compulsive symptoms is an indication of diversity in fear structures. Most obsessions and compulsions can be broken down into stimulus, response, and meaning; however, OCD is distinguished from other anxiety disorders by the wide range of stimulus and response associations present in the fear structure. Thus, an individual with contamination obsessions may fear personal harm from the contaminants and begin to associate a wide variety of situations with this fear, thus broadening the number of situations that can trigger rituals or passive avoidance.

Several cognitive impairments involving fear structures and evaluations of harm have been proposed. Obsessive–compulsive patients may experience difficulty in epistemological reasoning, distinguishing what is dangerous from what is safe, so that in the absence of evidence to the contrary, obsessive–compulsives assume that a situation is dangerous (Kozac et al., 1988). It has also been suggested that obsessive–compulsive individuals may display abnormalities in terms of threat appraisal, consistently overestimating the probability of occurrence of negative events and assigning a greater negative valence to the negative event (Kozac et al., 1988). McFall and Wollersheim (1979) have proposed that obsessive–compulsive individuals hold a number of unreasonable beliefs that impact upon the valence assigned to unpleasant events. These may include ideas that they must be perfectly competent to be worthwhile, that making mistakes or imperfection should result in punishment, and that certain thoughts or feelings are unacceptable and may lead to catastrophe (Kozac et al., 1988).

The hypersensitivity of obsessive–compulsive individuals to threat-related stimuli has received somewhat indirect support from studies of selective attention biases (Foa & McNally, 1986; Foa, Ilai, McCarthy, Shoyer, & Murdock, 1993; Lavy, Van Oppen, & Van den Hout, 1994). Using selective attention tasks such as the dichotic listening task (Foa & McNally, 1986) and the Stroop color-naming procedure (Lavy et al., 1994), studies have consistently reported that obsessive–compulsive individuals evidence delayed responding for specific, fear-related, negative or threatening words, compared to neutral or positive words. A discussion of overactive threat schemata in OCD is complicated by the fact that anxious individuals in general tend to show an attentional bias toward emotionally threatening stimuli. Biases in attention to as well as biases in memory for threatening stimuli have been demonstrated in adults with generalized anxiety disorder (GAD; Matthews & McLeod, 1985), specific phobia (Watts, McKenna, Sharrock, & Trezise, 1986), and post traumatic stress disorder (PTSD; Foa, Feske, Murdock, Kozac, & McCarthy, 1991; MacLeod & McLaughlin, 1995). Although fewer studies have investigated these processes in anxious children, research that has looked at differences in biased attention among anxiety-disordered and control children have obtained findings consistent with their adult counterparts, with anxious children displaying an attentional bias toward emotionally threatening words (Vasey, Daleiden, Williams, & Brown, 1995; Vasey, Elhag, & Daleiden, 1994). Thus, measures of response latencies comparing OCD groups with normal controls do little to clarify the schemata that distinguish OCD from other anxiety disorders.

In addition to misappraisals of threatening stimuli, anxious and obsessive–compulsive individuals may overpredict the level of anxiety that they will experience in feared situations. When anxiety patients (including OCD patients) in cognitive-behavioral treatment were asked to rate their predicted anxiety just before and after an *in vivo* exposure task, they were found to significantly overpredict the amount of anxiety that they would experience. This finding could not be accounted for by regression to the mean or by the tendency of patients to make high anxiety predictions (Arntz, Hildebrand, & Van Den Hout, 1994). Overestimates of anxiety may play a role in the avoidance seen in OCD and has implications for treatment, since subjects readjusted their appraisals following *in vivo* exposure. Treatment had an effect not only on the levels of fear experienced during the exposure, but also on the anxiety that the subjects predicted they would experience in the future.

Cognitive distortions proposed to be exclusive to OCD entail an inflated sense of responsibility and guilt (Rachman, 1993), and the psychological fusion of thoughts and actions, so that the line between reality and mental processes becomes more blurred. Salkovskis and colleagues have discussed the role of ideas of personal responsibility in the development of OCD, and have argued that it is this element in the appraisal of situations that distinguishes OCD from anxiety or depression (Rheaume, Ladouceur, Freeston, & Letarte, 1995; Salkovskis, 1989; Salkovskis & Kirk, 1989). Salkovskis' hypothesis has received partial support from the finding that when stimuli normally evoking anxiety and checking behaviors are presented in the presence of an experimenter, little or no checking behaviors are displayed by obsessive–compulsive subjects (Rachman & Hodgson, 1980; Roper & Rachman, 1975; Roper, Rachman, & Hodgson, 1973). The authors propose that checking decreases because, in the presence of the experimenter, responsibility is shared or shifted to the experimenter rather than the subject. Further support for the notion of distorted responsibility comes from a study conducted by Freeston, Ladouceur, Thibodeau, and Gagnon (1992), in which they factor-analyzed a questionnaire given to obsessive–compulsive subjects. Of the five factors identified on the questionnaire, only the factor labeled "evaluation," which included responsibility and guilt, was a significant predictor of compulsive behaviors, and was most highly correlated with avoidance responses.

Salkovskis has also introduced the importance of attempts at thought suppression in the development and maintenance of the disorder. The definition of OCD implies that individuals with the disorder actively attempt to suppress intrusive, distressing thoughts. Salkovskis suggests that paradoxically, these attempts at suppression may result in an enhancement of the unwanted thought (Salkovskis & Kirk, 1989). To address this hypothesis, Salkovskis and Campbell (1994) examined the effects of thought suppression on naturally occurring, personally relevant thoughts with 75 nonclinical subjects. Subjects were placed in one of five experimental conditions: thought suppression, mere mention control, and three suppression conditions with different distractors (general distraction instructions, general "don't distract" instructions, and an engaging task). The initial period was followed by a "think anything period," and thought frequency during both periods was measured with a counter. Results indicated that the suppression groups reported significantly more intrusive thoughts during both of the experimental periods, compared to the "mention only" control group. Distractors were effective in reducing the frequency of intrusive thoughts only when they involved an engaging task. Furthermore, the rate of intrusive thoughts was higher in all groups than indicated by self-reports prior to the experiment (four times in 10 minutes during the experiment versus 20 times in the past month). The authors suggest that self-monitoring as well as thought suppression may play a role in the maintenance of obsessive thinking (Salkovskis & Campbell, 1994).

5.2. Behavioral Models

Learning theorists have been concerned not with the content of obsessions, but have focused upon compulsive behavior, using the paradigm of avoidance learning to explain the development and maintenance of compulsive behavior. Although dated, the most-used model of avoidance learning employed in the description of OCD has been Mowrer's (1960) "two-factor theory." As applied to OCD, this theory proposes that the individual becomes conditioned to react with anxiety to innocuous stimuli through association with a painful or terrifying experience. An avoidance response (e.g., passive avoidance or compulsive ritualizing) reduces the anxiety. Subsequently, the maintenance of avoidance behavior is reinforced by reduction of the conditioned anxiety so that these behaviors become established and strengthened. Much of this theory is based upon animal models of avoidance learning, and direct evidence of its applicability to human OCD is lacking. A central criticism of this theory is the finding that most compulsive behavior arises without the occurrence of initial trauma or precipitating factors. In response to this criticism, Rachman and Hodgson (1980) proposed that anxiety is conditioned to certain cues associated with obsessions, which can be related back to cognitive theories of threat perception. Despite the lack of direct evidence for a learning model of OCD, it has proven useful and highly successful in its treatment applications (see section 6.1 for a review).

5.3. Neurobiological Models

Research on neurobiological links in OCD has been encouraged by two lines of evidence. The results of neuropharmacological studies have implicated the central nervous system (CNS) serotonergic system in obsessive–compulsive symptomatology, and the association of OCD to specific neuropsychological abnormalities has prompted investigators to speculate on the neuroanatomical basis of the disorder Other support comes from family/genetic studies of the disorder (Rasmussen, 1993; Section 3.1) reporting an increased prevalence of OCD and basal ganglia disorders among first-degree relatives of OCD patients.

5.3.1. Neuropharmacological Findings

Perhaps the most significant finding in recent pharmacological studies is the high selectivity in drug response of OCD. Potent serotonin reuptake inhibitors, such as clomipramine, fluoxetine, and fluvoxamine have been reported to be effective pharmacological treatments for OCD. These serotonin agonists are reported to lead to a 30–50% improvement in obsessive–compulsive symptoms. The importance of serotonin is further implicated by the finding that antidepressants possessing a similar structure to these compounds but less potent in their serotonin-inhibiting properties are not effective in reducing obsessive–compulsive symptomatology (Alessi & Bos, 1991; Jenike & Baer, 1988). Taken together, these findings have strengthened the hypothesis that obsessive–compulsive symptoms are believed to arise from an oversensitivity or overreactivity of specific CNS serotonergic pathways.

To demonstrate the antiobsessional properties of serotonin reuptake inhibitors, researchers have investigated the relationship between drug treatment effects and peripheral markers of serotonergic functioning. Flament, Rapoport, Murphy, Berg, and Lake (1987) reported that, compared to placebo, clomipramine was clinically effective and produced a marked decrease in platelet serotonin concentration. They obtained peripheral measures of serotonergic function (platelet serotonin concentration, monoamine activity, and plasma amine oxidase activity) from 29 child patients diagnosed with severe primary OCD and 31 control-group volunteers.

Self-report measures of obsessive–compulsive symptoms (e.g., the LOI-CV, NIMH-Obsessive–Compulsive Scale) were obtained at baseline and after 5 weeks of clomipramine in a double-blind placebo-controlled trial. Although differences in platelet serotonin levels were not found between patients and controls at baseline, significant negative correlations between platelet serotonin and measures of clinical severity at baseline were reported in the patient group. A decrease in platelet serotonin concentration, noted during treatment with clomipramine, was found to be closely related to self-reported improvement. Moreover, the authors reported a 10% decrease in monoamine oxidase (MAO) activity during clomipramine treatment, which was positively correlated with changes in symptoms. These findings parallel those with adults (Thoren et al., 1980), noting a positive correlation between clinical improvement and decreased concentrations of 5-hydroxyindoleacetic acid (5-HIAA), a serotonin metabolite. Differences in the concentration of 5-HIAA at baseline between patients with OCD and control subjects have not been found, however.

Although this evidence seems to point to the role of serotonergic mechanisms in OCD, questions pertaining to the nature of these effects remain. Although serotonin reuptake inhibition occurs within a few minutes of drug intake, the antiobsessional effects of these drugs develop only after several weeks of treatment (Goodman, Price, Rasmussen, Delgado, et al., 1989; Goodman, McDougle & Price, 1992), suggesting that a simple serotonergic uptake mechanism may not be the only factor involved (Lucey, 1994). Instead, clinical effects of these drugs may be dependent upon compensatory changes that occur following chronic uptake inhibition (Insel & Winslow, 1992). Numerous effects have been observed following long-term exposure to antidepressant medications, such as a decreased responsiveness of presynaptic firing and postsynaptic receptors in areas such as the neocortex (Peroutka & Snyder, 1981) and increases in the responsivity to serotonin in areas such as the hippocampus (Blier, de Montigny, & Chaput, 1987). From these findings, it has been proposed that OCD may be related to a disregulation of certain pathways, and that serotonin reuptake blockers may affect obsessive–compulsive symptoms by helping to offset these abnormalities (Piacentini, Jaffer, Gitow, et al., 1992).

A second, albeit disputed line of evidence for the serotonin hypothesis comes from studies demonstrating abnormal serotonin functioning in obsessive–compulsive patients. Although several studies have found no pretreatment differences in peripheral markers of serotonergic activity between obsessive–compulsive patients and controls (Flament et al., 1987; Hanna, Yuwiler, & Cantwell, 1991; Thoren et al., 1980), a few studies have reported differences (Swedo et al., 1992; Weizman et al., 1992). Insel, Mueller, Alterman, Linnoila, and Murphy (1985) compared 8 outpatients diagnosed with DSM-III OCD with 23 volunteers. Significantly higher rates of cerebrospinal 5-HIAA were found in the patient group than in the control group, which the authors proposed is an indicator of increased activity of the serotonin system. The authors did not, however, obtain significant differences in the numbers of platelet imipramine binding sites between patients and controls. Decreased platelet binding in obsessive–compulsive children was found by Weizman et al. (1992), in their study of 9 Tourette's syndrome children with obsessive–compulsive disorder. These children were compared to 8 children with untreated Tourette's, and 9 age- and gender-matched control children. The authors found that the density of imipramine binding sites in the patients with Tourette's and OCD was significantly lower when compared to patients with Tourette's only, as well as controls.

Findings from biochemical challenge studies represent a third line of evidence for the role of serotonin in OCD. Administration of the compound m-chlorophenylpiperazine (mCPP), a serotonin agonist, was found to worsen obsessive–compulsive symptomatology in certain OCD patients (Hollander et al., 1988; Zohar & Insel, 1987). This exacerbation of OCD symptoms was observed in obsessive–compulsive patients but not in normal controls. Furthermore, when patients were treated with clomipramine, they no longer displayed this behavioral overreactivity to mCPP (Zohar & Insel, 1987).

Despite these findings, the role of serotonin in the etiology of OCD remains in question. Inconsistent findings and lack of replication make a clear conclusion difficult. Studies of OCD-spectrum disorders (e.g., Tourette's disorder) have been unsuccessful in identifying genetic variations in serotonin receptors (Brett, Curtis, Robertson, & Gurling, 1995) and abnormal serotonin functioning and the increased sensitivity to challenge studies have not been supported consistently in the literature (Insel & Winslow, 1992). Furthermore, the effects of clomipramine are not restricted to the serotonergic system: Clomipramine has been found to act as a noradrenaline reuptake blocker (Flament et al., 1987; Insel et al., 1985; Insel & Winslow, 1992) as well as to possess a host of other neuropharmacological actions (Flament et al., 1987). Thus, although the serotonin hypothesis remains appealing, it has not been fully confirmed, nor can other explanatory mechanisms be excluded.

5.3.2. Neuroanatomical Findings

OCD has been associated with specific and nonspecific neuropsychological abnormalities. The very nature of the disorder, which involves unwanted and repetitive thoughts, has been taken as an indication of a neurological basis for the disorder. Neuropsychological theories, to be useful, should be able to address the mechanism by which seemingly inconsequential stimuli evoke the anxiety exhibited by OCD patients and explain why these concerns do not seem to attenuate following the performance of compulsive acts (Otto, 1992). Disruptions in certain brain areas modulating behavioral response and emotional processing have been implicated, and it has been hypothesized that frontal lobe and basal ganglia dysfunction might be involved in obsessive–compulsive symptoms. Preliminary confirmatory support has come from the findings of neuroimaging (Baxter et al., 1988; Swedo, Shapiro, Grady, et al., 1989) and neuropsychological assessment studies (Behar et al., 1984), as well as research on the relationship of OCD to various basal ganglia disorders. Taken together, these separate lines of inquiry have lent credence to the proposition of aberrant functioning in the frontal lobe and basal ganglia. It should be remembered that these findings are by no means conclusive, and studies obtaining no impairments in basal ganglia and frontal lobe functioning have also appeared in the literature (Boone, Ananth, Philpott, Kaur, & Djenderendjian, 1991).

A basic dysfunction of anxiety circuits may lead to overactive neural labeling of stimuli as dangerous or requiring attention, so that the organism becomes overly aroused and compensates with cognitive and motor responses. In addition, it is hypothesized that there might be a disconnection between sensory systems and motor–emotional systems, so that information concerning a completed act cannot reach motor systems. Compensatory mechanisms may thus persist in a repetitive and inappropriate manner (Otto, 1992).

The use of brain imaging techniques such as positron emission tomography (PET) has enabled researchers to compare brain metabolic activity in OCD patients with those of normal controls (Baxter et al., 1988; Swedo, Shapiro, Grady, et al., 1989). These studies have generally reported an increased rate of glucose metabolism in the orbital frontal cortex and in the caudate nucleus of OCD patients. Furthermore, studies of brain metabolism following treatment (e.g., with clomipramine) have found a normalization of brain functioning corresponding to a decrease in symptoms (Benkelfat, Nordahl, & Semple, 1990; Martinot, Allilaire, & Mazoyer, 1990). Following treatment, patients with hypermetabolism in the orbital frontal region and caudate nucleus were found to display decreases in metabolism toward more normal levels.

The association of OCD to several basal ganglia disorders lends further support to the role of basal ganglia dysfunction in the disorder. As previously noted, a strong relationship between OCD and Tourette's syndrome has been reported. OCD has also been reported to occur following head injury and in association with epilepsy (Kettl & Marks, 1986; Levin & Duchowny, 1991; Max et al., 1995). Swedo, Rapoport, Cheslow, et al. (1989) reported a high prevalence of obsessive–compulsive features among 23 patients with histories of Sydenham's chorea, a neurological disorder characterized by involuntary jerking movements of the arms and legs. These Sydenham's patients were compared to 14 patients with rheumatic fever on several measures of obsessive–compulsive symptomatology. Patients with Sydenham's chorea scored significantly higher on the obsessionality scales, and 5 of the 23 Sydenham's chorea patients (vs. none of the rheumatic fever subjects) obtained high interference scores on the LOI-CV.

These findings have been attributed to basal ganglia dysfunction, rather than more generalized dysfunction resulting from neurological trauma.

Finally, neuropsychological assessment studies have lent support to a hypothesis of cerebral dysfunction in certain patients with OCD, although once again, these findings are by no means consistent or conclusive. A full review of the literature on neuropsychological deficits in OCD is beyond the scope of this chapter; therefore a brief summary of the findings to date will be presented. In general, a number of studies have obtained performance on neuropsychological tests by OCD patients that are reflective of frontal lobe or caudate dysfunction (Flament et al., 1990). For example, Behar et al. (1984) administered a number of neuropsychological tests including Money's Road Map Test, Stylus Maze Learning task, Rey–Osterrieth Complex Figure Test, and tests of reaction time and two-flash threshold to 17 adolescents diagnosed with OCD. The performance of these adolescents was compared to that of 17 control subjects matched for age, gender, handedness, and IQ. Results indicated poorer performance by the OCD group on tests of frontal functioning (the Money Road Map Test, Stylus Maze learning task) and an immature approach toward the Rey–Osterrieth figure-copying task. These findings cannot be simply attributed to poor attention or an "obsessive style," since performance on tests of reaction time and two-flash threshold did not differ between the patient and control groups.

Findings of frontal lobe dysfunction have not been confirmed by all studies, as some researchers have observed no differences in tests of frontal lobe functioning among OCD and normal participants, but rather, have found that the patterns of deficits exhibited by patients with OCD might be more indicative of visuospatial or memory deficits. For example, Otto (1992) reviewed neuropsychological evidence for OCD and reported that several studies have indicated decreased performance on tests of visuospatial memory.

When reviewing studies of neurological abnormalities, one must remember that these are at best indirect evidence of possible dysfunction. Although the evidence seems promising, it cannot be taken as proof of a neurological basis for OCD. Insel and Winslow (1992) point out that findings of metabolic hyperactivity in one region of the brain might actually be a compensatory mechanism for regions of decreased activity that have not been identified through brain imaging studies, and may thus not be representative of dysfunction in the overactive region.

Furthermore, the finding of a neurological abnormality cannot be taken to represent a causal factor in the etiology of the disorder. There is little evidence to determine whether these brain dysfunctions are primary, causal factors or simply secondary effects of the disorder. Further research is required to clarify this issue and to integrate the findings of neurochemical and neuroanatomical dysfunction.

6. Treatment

Stanley and Turner (1995) point out that it was only three decades ago that OCD was considered virtually untreatable. Recent advances in the treatment of adult OCD have been made, primarily with behavioral and psychopharmacological therapies. These same treatments with children, closely modeling their adult counterparts, have also shown promise. This section reviews the status of cognitive-behavioral and pharmacological therapies in the treatment of childhood OCD.

Although not a central focus of this chapter, it is worth noting that family therapies have been reported to be useful adjuncts to treatment (Adams, 1985; Boyarsky, Perone, Lee, & Goodman, 1991; Swedo, Leonard, & Rapoport, 1992). Family functioning in childhood OCD is often disrupted (Thomsen, 1994b), and many children involve at least one parent in their rituals (Honjo et al., 1989; Hoover & Insel, 1984). Refusal to participate by the parents may lead to violent temper tantrums by the child, and limit setting may be further hindered by parental disagreement as to the best approach in the management of the problem (Bolton et al., 1983, Hoover & Insel, 1984). Because of this, involvement of the parents in behavioral treatment programs may be indicated. Insight-oriented psychotherapy typically has not been found to be helpful for children with OCD and will not be addressed.

6.1. Behavioral Therapy

For over 20 years, behavioral therapy has been employed with obsessive–compulsive adults. Typically, exposure and response prevention are conducted in a standardized, three-phase treatment program. The first phase is information gathering—data are obtained on the patient's particular symptoms and the treatment is tailored to his or her specific needs. The second phase—exposure and response prevention—is carried out both imaginally and *in vivo*. In addition, homework assignments are given to allow the patient to practice the learned skills between sessions. The final phase—maintenance—is designed to solidify and maintain treatment gains (e.g., Foa, 1991; Grayson, Foa, & Steketee, 1985).

Exposure involves placing the patient in situations that invoke anxiety or discomfort (De Silva & Rachman, 1992) and is based upon the principle that anxiety will gradually decrease following extended contact with the feared anxiety-provoking situation (Dar & Greist, 1992). The second component, response prevention, entails encouraging the patient not to carry out his or her compulsive behaviors during exposure to the feared situation (De Silva & Rachman, 1992). This facilitates adequate exposure to the situation by blocking the patient's rituals or avoidance (Dar & Greist, 1992). For example, a child with fears of contamination would be exposed to "contaminated" objects (e.g., handling newspapers, touching doorknobs) and encouraged to refrain from carrying out ritualistic behaviors such as repeated hand washing.

Exposure can involve either imaginal or real-life situations (*in vivo* exposure), and can be implemented either in a gradual fashion, or through flooding, which involves extended contact with the feared stimulus. Although flooding has been effective and cost-effective, graduated exposure has been recommended for use with children because of the high aversiveness and potential iatrogenic effects of flooding (Harris & Weibe, 1992).

In a review of the treatment outcome literature, Foa, Steketee, and Ozarow (1985) determined that 51% of adult patients receiving exposure/ response prevention were rated as symptom-free or much improved at posttreatment (70% or more reduction in symptoms), whereas 39% were moderately improved (31–69% reduction in symptoms), and 10% were considered treatment failures. Even with the inclusion of a high number of attritions/treatment refusals (30%), Stanley and Turner (1995) reported that 63% of OCD adults can be expected to respond favorably to exposure and response prevention.

Behavioral treatments with children have yet to be addressed systematically. More than 35 reports of behavioral interventions have been reported in the child OCD literature, but the majority are unsystematic, nonempirical case reports (Desmarais & Lavallee, 1988; Fine, 1973; Fisman & Walsh, 1994; Stanley, 1980; Willmuth, 1988) with only a few single case designs (Hollingsworth et al., 1980; Kearney & Silverman, 1990). Few studies have employed group designs to test for treatment versus comparison-group differences in obsessive–compulsive symptomatology (March, 1995).

A recent assessment of a standardized cognitive-behavioral treatment for children and adolescents was reported by Piacentini, Gitow, Jaffer, Graae, and Whitaker (1994). They examined the effectiveness of an outpatient treatment for children and adolescents with OCD using therapist-supervised exposure and response prevention. Three children (ages 9, 12, and 13) were assessed at pretreatment using a structured interview to confirm the presence of DSM-III-R OCD, and standardized measures including the CY-BOCS and the NIMH Global OCD Scale. Children underwent regular posttreatment evaluations for 1 year following completion of treatment. Treatment consisted of 10 two-hour sessions held once per week. In addition to exposure/response prevention, clients were taught coping strategies to manage anxiety during exposure (e.g., cognitive self-statements), and a contingency management program, in which children were systematically rewarded for completing in-session tasks was implemented. Homework assignments were assigned to enhance compliance with treatment. Finally, parents and other family members attended weekly family meetings over the course of therapy to educate the family about OCD and help the family develop more normalized patterns of family interaction. Two of the three cases showed marked improvement in obsessive–compulsive symptoms at posttreatment (as rated on self-report and therapist-report inventories), with gains maintained at 1-year follow-up. In the third case, only minimal improvement was found—the authors suggest that the patient's comorbid conditions and high level of associated family psychopathology may have contributed to difficulties in treatment.

To our knowledge, there are only two studies that have used a pre- and posttreatment design with obsessive–compulsive children. Kozac (1994) conducted a preliminary study of 10 children (ages 13 to 17 years) diagnosed with obsessive–compulsive disorder (DSM-III-R) criteria and treated with prolonged exposure and response prevention. Treatment duration ranged from 10 weekly 1.5-hour sessions to 15 daily 1.5-hour sessions. Based on pre- and posttreatment ratings on the Y-BOCS, 9 of the 10 patients were rated as clinically improved—a greater than two-thirds reduction in severity of their OCD symptoms. Average Y-BOCS reduction after treatment was 72%. Although the results of this study are promising, potential methodological limitations qualify the findings: The treatment was not standardized, and medication administration during treatment was uncontrolled, so that many patients may have continued receiving medication, including serotonin reuptake inhibitors, throughout treatment.

March, Mulle, and Herbel (1994) evaluated a manualized cognitive-behavioral treatment for childhood OCD. Participants consisted of 15 children ages 8 to 18 (10 females, 5 males), with a primary diagnosis of OCD, as determined by clinical interview (DSM-III-R) and the Y-BOCS checklist. In addition, clients were assessed using the NIMH Global Scale and the Clinical Global Impression Scale (CGI), with assessments conducted at pretreatment, posttreatment, and follow-up (mean follow-up 7.3 months). Treatment consisted of a 16-week therapy program composed of four phases: (1) psychoeducation; mapping the child's experience with OCD, including specific obsessions and compulsions, triggers, and consequences using a cartographic metaphor; (2) identification of areas in which the child has already had some success in resisting OCD and teaching the child to recognize this; (3) anxiety management training; (4) exposure/ response prevention. Unfortunately, in addition to the cognitive-behavioral treatment, all but one of the patients also received some form of medication for their obsessive–compulsive symptoms during treatment.

Repeated measures ANOVAs revealed treatment gains on the Y-BOCS, NIMH Global Scale, and CGI. These gains were maintained at follow-up. In general, 10 of the 15 patients experienced a greater than 50% reduction in Y-BOCS scores at follow-up; 6 patients were judged asymptomatic (NIMH Global scores of 2 or less) at posttreatment, and 9 were asymptomatic at follow-up. Only 3 of the 15 patients were considered treatment nonresponders (< a 30% improvement on either the Y-BOCS or NIMH scales).

Despite these promising findings, we (and the authors themselves) caution that several problematic factors must be considered. Despite the idea noted by the authors that their results were significantly higher than those typically obtained with medication alone, suggesting a contribution independent of medication, the concurrent treatment of clients with medication prohibits the discussion of the specific contribution of cognitive-behavioral therapy. The lack of a behavioral therapy–alone condition and the lack of a control group (e.g., waitlist control) is also problematic. Despite the shortcomings, the treatment proposed by March et al. (1994), and the effort to examine treatment outcome are important steps in a burgeoning field. Research is needed to specifically examine the efficacy of cognitive-behavioral treatment for obsessive–compulsive children. Cognitive treatment strategies, such as restructuring of cognitive self-statements (Piacentini et al., 1994), have been employed in the child treatment literature, but the distinct effects of cognitive therapy on obsessive–compulsive symptoms have not yet been demonstrated. An area in which cognitive therapy may be particularly helpful is addressing the thinking processes of the OCD child—challenging beliefs through discussion of inconsistencies, and providing alternative, rational explanations and submitting beliefs to reality testing through behavioral experimentation (Salkovskis, 1989; Warren & Zgourides, 1991). According to Kendall and McDonald (1993), a goal of cognitive therapies is to (1) identify the distortions and (2) aid the child in modifying the distorted thinking (Kendall et al., 1992). Cognitive therapy helps the child build a new perspective ("template"). Therapy corrects the child's habitual misinterpretations and provides alternate coping views (Kendall, 1993), challenges beliefs of personal responsibility for harm to others through normalizing interventions, reconstrues exaggerated beliefs about the probability and negative valence of feared events, and increases alternate coping skills (Sookman, Pinard, & Beauchemin,

1994). Although applicable, the effects of these interventions with children have not yet been systematically evaluated, nor have the additive effects of cognitive restructuring and exposure treatment been assessed.

6.2. Pharmacological Treatment

As with cognitive-behavioral treatments, the majority of outcome studies on pharmacological interventions have been conducted with adults. These studies suggest that antidepressants with specific serotonin (5-HT) uptake blocking effects can effectively treat obsessive–compulsive symptomatology. Of these, clomipramine has been researched widely; the efficacy of fluoxetine and fluvoxamine have also been examined. Although psychopharmacologic studies with obsessive–compulsive children have lagged behind those of adults, there is a growing body of evidence that supports the use of these medications with this population. A few recent reports suggest the efficacy of sertraline with adult OCD patients, and, although untested in a child population, there have been suggestions that sertraline may be effective and with relatively few side effects (Greist et al., 1995; Lydiard, 1994).

6.2.1. Clomipramine

Several studies with adults have demonstrated clomipramine to be superior to placebo in its antiobsessional effects (Mavissakalian, Turner, Michelson, & Jacob, 1985; Montgomery, 1980). Goodman et al. (1992) reported on a large multicenter trial of clomipramine involving over 500 primary OCD adult outpatients. The protocol consisted of a 2-week, single-blind placebo run-in, followed by random assignment to 10 weeks of double-blind treatment with either clomipramine or placebo. Clomipramine was found to be superior to placebo on all self-report measures of OCD, and reductions in symptoms appeared to represent clinically meaningful change. In addition to placebo comparison groups, clomipramine has been compared to other antidepressants (e.g., desipramine and zimelidine), and has consistently been found to be superior in its antiobsessional effects (Zohar & Insel, 1987).

Several studies with obsessive–compulsive youth have supported the use of clomipramine in the treatment of childhood onset OCD (DeVeaugh-Geiss et al., 1992; Flament et al., 1985; Rapoport, 1986b; Schreier, 1990; Wilens, Steingard, & Biederman, 1992). The first double-blind placebo-controlled trial of clomipramine with children (Flament et al., 1985) involved 19 children (ages 10–18) in an 11-week clomipramine–placebo crossover trial (1-week baseline evaluation followed by two 5-week periods of clomipramine and placebo treatment, administered in randomized order. In addition to medication, children were given individual supportive therapy. Assessments at pre- and posttreatment were conducted using a variety of assessment measures of obsessional symptoms, depression, and anxiety, including the LOI-CV, and NIMH Global Scale.

Clomipramine was effective in relieving obsessive–compulsive symptoms, and its effect appeared to be specific to OCD, since symptoms of anxiety and depression remained relatively unchanged during the study. Although there were no initial differences between placebo and drug on the rates of clinical change, subjects first given the drug were reported to quickly relapse when given the placebo. The authors state that it is unclear whether this is a true effect, or whether this reflects withdrawal symptoms following discontinuation of the active drug. Overall, although not all subjects improved with drug treatment, average improvement following treatment was a 40–60% decrease in symptoms on self-report measures. Patients typically reported that although symptoms were still present, they were decreased in intensity and interference. Interestingly, the authors noted that male subjects (who reported an earlier age of onset) tended to do better than female subjects. Furthermore, patients with rituals responded better than those with predominantly obsessional features.

Subsequent studies of children comparing clomipramine with other, less serotonergic-specific antidepressants, have found it to be superior in its antiobsessional properties (Leonard et al., 1991; Leonard, Swedo, Rapoport, Coffey, & Cheslow, 1988). Twenty-six children with primary OCD receiving long-term clomipramine treatment (mean length of treatment = 17.1 months) participated in an 8-month double-blind desipramine substitution. Children received clomipramine for the first 3 months of the study, after which they were assigned randomly to either a continued clomipramine group or a desipramine substitution group for 2 months. All subjects then received clomipramine for the final 3 months of the study. Whereas only 2 (18%) of the 11 subjects in the continued clomipramine group relapsed during the 2-month period, 8 (89%) of the 9 substituted subjects relapsed. This study not only suggests that clomipramine is superior to other antidepressants in its antiobsessional effects, but also documents the need for continued medication use for relapse prevention.

The high rate of relapse among patients taking clomipramine is a well-documented problem (Hollingsworth et al., 1980; Leonard et al., 1993; Pato, Zohar-Kadouch, Zohar, & Murphy, 1988), and buttresses the need for alternate treatments. Furthermore, recent reports of serious side effects from clomipramine, including paranoid ideation and aggressiveness (Alarcon, Johnson, & Lucas, 1991) and self-abusive behavior (Cruz, 1992), indicate that clomipramine may not be suitable for certain patients.

6.2.2. Fluoxetine

Fluoxetine, another 5-HT reuptake blocker, was first used as an anti-depressant (Piacentini, Jaffer, Gitow, et al., 1992). Although studied far less than clomipramine, it has shown potential as an effective antiobsessional drug. A handful of studies have demonstrated its effectiveness with adult patients (Fontaine & Chouinard, 1985; Jenike, Buttolph, Baer, Ricciardi, & Holland, 1989; Liebowitz, Hollander, Schneier, & Campeas, 1989; Tollefson et al., 1994).

Fewer studies have been published on the efficacy of fluoxetine with obsessive–compulsive children. Riddle et al. (1992) reported the results of a double-blind, placebo-controlled study with 14 children and adolescents. The double-blind crossover design consisted of an initial 8-week period on the first randomly assigned agent, followed by 12 weeks on the second agent. Obsessive–compulsive symptom severity was assessed using the CY-BOCS and the CGI's Obsessive–Compulsive Scale (OCS). Scores on the CY-BOCS decreased 44% following fluoxetine treatment, compared to 27% following placebo. Significant differences between the fluoxetine and placebo were also reported on the CGI-OCS.

Similarly, in a second outcome study, 4 of 8 adolescents with OCD treated with fluoxetine for a period of 8 weeks were rated as responders to the medication. Criteria for consideration as a "responder" were a reduction of at least 50% in the time spent on obsessions and compulsions and a substantial reduction in psychosocial impairment caused by obsessive–compulsive symptoms. An additional 2 patients had more "equivocal" responses, whereas the remaining 2 patients experienced difficulty in tolerating the medication and required cessation of the drug (Liebowitz, Hollander, Fairbanks, & Campeas, 1990). Recent replications of these studies have supported fluoxetine's efficacy in treating childhood OCD (Bouvard & Dugas, 1993; Geller, Biederman, Reed, Spencer, & Wilens, 1995).

There have been fewer reported side effects with fluoxetine than clomipramine. Common side effects such as nervousness, anxiety, and excitability have been noted in children receiving the drug (Riddle et al., 1990). In addition, reports of self-injurious behaviors in children have appeared. For example, King et al. (1991) noted the emergence or intensification of self-destructive behaviors in 6 of 42 children receiving fluoxetine for OCD, including severe suicidal ideation and self- mutilating behaviors.

6.2.3. Fluvoxamine

To our knowledge, there has been only one study of the efficacy of fluvoxamine with children and adolescents, although a handful of adult studies suggest that this drug might possess significant antiobsessional properties. Fluvoxamine has been found to be superior to placebo, with 45–60% of OCD patients responding favorably to the drug, and seems to lead to significant reductions in patients' obsessive–compulsive symptoms, although complete elimination of all obsessive–compulsive symptoms is not typically reported (Goodman, Price, Rasmussen, Delgado, et al., 1989a; Mattes, 1994; Price, Goodman, Charney, Rasmussen, & Heninger, 1987). Fluvoxamine (and more generally all of the selective serotonin reuptake inhibitors, or SSRIs), have also been effective in alleviating depressive symptoms in a large percentage of patients with comorbid depression (e.g., 50%; Goodman et al., 1989a), thus obscuring the specific effects of the drug on obsessive–compulsive symptomatology. Researchers have argued however, that despite the covariation of the drug's antiobsessional and antidysphoric effects, at least some of fluvoxamine's effects on obsessive–compulsive symptoms are independent of its antidepressant action (e.g., OCD drug response was unrelated to initial severity or presence of secondary depressive symptoms). This issue has not been addressed in the child literature.

Apter et al. (1994) compared the effects of fluvoxamine on OCD and depression in an 8-week, open-label trial with 20 adolescent inpatients, ages 13–18 years. Fourteen of the adolescents received a primary diagnosis of OCD; the remaining 6 were diagnosed with major depressive disorder. Symptoms were assessed using multiple measures, including the Y-BOCS and Children's Global Assessment Scale (CGAS; Shaffer et al., 1983). Fluvoxamine was effective in reducing obsessive–compulsive symptoms, as rated by the Y-BOCS, and was helpful in alleviating symptoms of depression. The results are confounded by the use of additional psychosocial interventions during the study period, so that the individual effects of fluvoxamine cannot be identified. A range of side effects was associated with use of fluvoxamine, including dermatitis, insomnia, anxiety, and more seriously, delirium and hallucinations (two cases).

7.   Conclusions

The study of childhood OCD is itself in its youth, and a great deal of research is required before conclusive statements concerning its presentation, etiology, and treatment can be made. Nevertheless, some observations about the current status of the field deserve mention.

• Although the literature on childhood OCD has expanded, much of it has concentrated on the epidemiological, phenomenological, and neurochemical aspects of the disorder. Gaps in the literature, particularly around psychosocial considerations and cognitive-behavioral interventions, are apparent. The complete absence of research on cognitive processes in childhood OCD is troubling: The field needs to pay greater attention to the role of developmental issues in information-processing models of child psychopathology. Differences between adults and children and developmental stages in childhood must be given greater consideration in cognitive theories. The direct application of cognitive-behavioral treatments to children with OCD, although based on theory and some clinical evidence, would be greatly enhanced by an understanding of the cognitive mechanisms involved in the disorder.

Cognitive distortions concerning the probability of harm, and one's responsibility for preventing it, entail both the ability to anticipate future outcomes and the development of a concept of self. In this regard, significant changes in the child's self-understanding (Damon & Hart, 1982) and anticipatory capabilities (Piaget & Inhelder, 1966) appear after about age 8 and must thus be considered in cognitive theories of OCD. Similarly, memory impairments hypothesized to underlie obsessive doubting in adults may not be appropriately translated to children because of differences in memory organization (Bjorklund, 1985). Finally, it seems likely that language development and ability for abstraction would play an important role in the development of distorted, obsessive schemata.

• To enable researchers and clinicians to evaluate the disorder and to communicate about research findings in a consistent manner, a reliable and systematic battery of assessments is needed. The number of standardized instruments for the assessment of childhood OCD is limited; nevertheless, we recommend that multiple measures of obsessive–compulsive symptomatology (e.g., structured diagnostic interviews, self-reports, direct behavioral observations, parent–teacher ratings) be employed. Further validation of the available measures (e.g., the CY-BOCS) is encouraged, and the development of parent questionnaires is recommended.

• Treatment studies employing group-comparison designs have been lacking. It is almost impossible to discuss the comparability of one treatment to another (or even to a waitlist control), as few studies and methodological limitations prevent informed conclusions. Admittedly, difficulties obtaining the participation of OCD children for research is an issue; notwithstanding, proper studies of the treatment childhood OCD are necessary to permit progress. Controlled studies of treatment effectiveness and eventual comparisons among various treatment approaches will provide the required information concerning the effectiveness of interventions and the interactive effects of treatment and specific client factors. Adequate baseline and follow-up data will be needed.

• Cognitive-behavioral therapies and pharmacological treatment may be highly compatible and complementary treatments. In addition, decision trees, such as the use of pharmacological treatment if behavioral or cognitive-behavioral therapy is unavailable or unsuccessful (Greist, 1992), seem wholly applicable to the treatment of OCD children.

• To enhance compliance with treatment and improve treatment outcome, we encourage flexibility in the application of treatments such as exposure–response prevention. Factors specific to OCD in children, such as a reluctance to discuss symptoms, opposition to giving up the compulsive behavior, and parental involvement in obsessive–compulsive symptom patterns, are best taken into consideration when treating children with the disorder.

8. References

Achenbach, T. M. (1991). *Manual for the Child Behavior Checklists/4-18 and 1991 profile.* Burlington: University of Vermont.

Adams, P. L. (1972). Family characteristics of obsessive children. *American Journal of Psychiatry, 128,* 1414–1417.

Adams, P. L. (1973). *Obsessive children: a sociopsychiatric study.* New York: Brunner/Mazel.

Adams, P. L. (1985). The obsessive child: A therapy update. *American Journal of Psychotherapy, 34,* 301–313.

Alarcon, R. D., Johnson, B. R., & Lucas, J. P. (1991). Paranoid and aggressive behavior in two obsessive–compulsive adolescents treated with clomipramine. *Journal of the American Academy of Child and Adolescent Psychiatry, 30,* 999–1002.

Albano, A. M., Knox, L. S., & Barlow, D. H. (1995). Obsessive–compulsive disorder. In A. R. Eisen, C. A. Kearney, & C. E. Schafer (Eds.), *Clinical handbook of anxiety disorders in children and adolescents* (pp. 282–316). Northvale, NJ: Jason Aronson.

Alessi, N., & Bos, T. (1991). Buspirone augmentation of fluoxetine in a depressed child with obsessive–compulsive disorder. *American Journal of Psychiatry, 148,* 1605–1606.

Allen, A. J., Leonard, H. L., & Swedo, S. E. (1995). Case study: A new infection-triggered, autoimmune subtype of pediatric OCD and Tourette's syndrome. *Journal of the American Academy of Child and Adolescent Psychiatry, 34,* 307–311.

Allsopp, M., & Verduyn, C. (1989). A follow-up of adolescents with obsessive–compulsive disorder. *British Journal of Psychiatry, 154,* 829–834.

Allsopp, M., & Verduyn, C. (1990). Adolescents with obsessive –compulsive disorder: A case note review of consecutive patients referred to a provincial regional adolescent psychiatry unit. *Journal of Adolescence, 13,* 157–169.

Ambrosini, P. J. (Ed.). (1986). *Schedule for Affective Disorders and Schizophrenia for School-Age Children (6–18 yrs.) (K-SADS-IIIR).* Unpublished manuscript.

American Psychiatric Association. (1994). *Diagnostic and Statistical Manual of Mental Disorders* (4th. ed., rev.). Washington, DC: Author.

Angold, A., Cox, A., Prendergast, M., Rutter, M., & Simonoff, E. (1987). *The Child and Adolescent Psychiatric Assessment (CAPA).* Unpublished manuscript, Duke University, Durham, North Carolina.

Angold, A., & Costello, E. J. (in press). A test–retest reliability study of child-reported psychiatric symptoms and diagnoses using the Child and Adolescent Psychiatric Assessment (CAPA-C).

Apter, A., Orvashel, H., Laseg, M., Moses, T., & Tyano, S. (1989). Psychometric properties of the K-SADS-P in an Israeli adolescent inpatient population. *American Journal of Child and Adolescent Psychiatry, 28,* 61–65.

Apter, A., Ratzoni, G., King, R. A., Weizman, A., Iancu, I., Ginder, M., & Riddle, M. A. (1994). Fluvoxamine open-label treatment of adolescent inpatients with obsessive–compulsive disorder or depression. *Journal of the American Academy of Child and Adolescent Psychiatry, 33,* 342–348.

Arntz, A., Hildebrand, M., & Van Den Hout, M. (1994). Overprediction of anxiety, and disconfirmatory processes in anxiety disorders. *Behaviour Research and Therapy, 32,* 709–722.

Barker, P. (1976). *Basic child psychiatry.* London: Crosby Lockwood.

Barlow, D. H. (1988). *Anxiety and its disorders.* New York: Guilford Press.

Barrios, B. A., & Hartmann, D. P. (1988). Fears and anxieties. In E. J. Mash & L. G. Terdal (Eds.), *Behavioral assessment of childhood disorders,* (2nd ed., pp. 196–264). New York: Guilford Press.

Baxter, L. R., Schwarz, J. W., Mazziotta, J. C., Phelps, M. E., Pahl, J. J., Guze, B. H., & Fairbanks, L. (1988). Cerebral glucose metabolic rates in nondepressed patients with obsessive–compulsive disorder. *American Journal of Psychiatry, 145,* 1560–1563.

Beech, (1974). *Obessional states.* London: Methuen.

Behar, D., Rapoport, J. L., Berg, C. J., Denckla, M. B., Mann, L., Cox, C., Fedio, P., Zahn, T., & Wolfman, M. G. (1984). Computerized tomography and neuropsychological test measures in adolescents with obsessive–compulsive disorder. *American Journal of Psychiatry, 141,* 363–369.

Beiser, H. R. (1987). Obsessive–compulsive disorder in children. *Psychiatric Journal of the University of Ottawa, 4,* 230–233.

Benkelfat, C., Nordahl, T. E., & Semple, W. E. (1990). Local cerebral glucose metabolic rates in obsessive–compulsive disorder: Patients treated with clomipramine. *Archives of General Psychiatry, 47,* 840–848.

Berg, C. J., Rapoport, J. L., & Flament, M. (1986). The Leyton Obessional Child Inventory–Child Version. *Journal of the American Academy of Child and Adolescent Psychiatry, 25,* 84–91.

Berg, C. J., Whitaker, A., Davies, M., Flament, M. F., & Rapoport, J. L. (1988). The survey form of the Leyton Obsessional Inventory–Child Version: Norms from an epidemiological study. *Journal of the American Academy of Child and Adolescent Psychiatry, 27,* 759–763.

Berman, L. (1942). Obsessive–compulsive neurosis in children. *Journal of Nervous and Mental Disease, 95,* 26–39.

Bernstein, G. A., & Borchardt, C. M. (1991). Anxiety disorders of childhood and adolescence: A critical review. *Journal of the American Academy of Child and Adolescent Psychiatry, 30,* 519–532.

Bjorklund, D. F. (1985). The role of conceptual knowledge in the development of organizations in children's memory. In C. J. Brainerd & M. Pressley (Eds.), *Basic processes in memory development.* (pp. 103–142). New York: Springer-Verlag.

Blier, P., deMontingy, C., & Chaput, Y. (1987). Modifications of the serotonin system by antidepressant treatments: Implications for the therapeutic response in major depression. *Journal of Clinical Psychopharmacology, 7,* 24S–35S.

Bolton, D., Collins, S., & Steinberg, D. (1983). The treatment of obsessive–compulsive disorder in adolescence. *British Journal of Psychiatry, 142,* 456–464.

Boone, K., Ananth, J., Philpott, L., Kaur, A., & Djenderendjian, A. (1991). Neuropsychological characteristics of nondepressed adults with obsessive–compulsive disorder. *Neuropsychiatry, Neuropsychology, and Behavioural Neurology, 4,* 96–109.

Bouvard, M., & Dugas, M. (1993). Fluoxetine in obsessive–compulsive disorder in adolescents. *International Clinical Psychopharmacology, 8*, 307–310.

Boyarsky, B. K., Perone, L. A., Lee, N. C., & Goodman, W. K. (1991). Current treatment approaches to obsessive–compulsive disorder. *Archives of Psychiatric Nursing, 5*, 299–306.

Brady, E. U., & Kendall, P. C. (1992). Comorbidity of anxiety and depression in children and adolescents. *Psychological Bulletin, 111*, 244–255.

Breslau, N. (1987). Inquiring about the bizarre: False positives in Diagnostic Interview Schedule for Children (DISC) ascertainment of obsessions, compulsions, and psychotic symptons. *Journal of the American Academy of Child and Adolescent Psychiatry, 26*, 639–644.

Brett, P. M., Curtis, D., Robertson, M. M., & Gurling, H. M. D. (1995). Exclusion of the 5-HT-sub(A) serotonin neuroreceptor and tryptophan oxygenase genes in a large British kindred multiply affected with Tourette's syndrome, chronic motor tics, and obsessive–compulsive disorder. *American Journal of Psychiatry, 152*, 437–440.

Brown, H. D., Kosslyn, S. M., Breiter, H. A., Baer, L., & Jenike, M. A. (1994). Can patients with obsessive–compulsive disorder discriminate between percepts and mental images? A signal detection analysis. *Journal of Abnormal Psychology, 103*, 445–454.

Carlson, G., Kashani, J., Thomas, M., Vaidya, A., & Daniel, A. (1987). Comparison of two structured interviews on a psychiatrically hospitalized population of children. *Journal of the American Academy of Child and Adolescent Psychiatry, 26*, 639–644.

Chambers, W. J., Puig-Antich, J., Hirsch, M., Paez, P., Ambrosini, P. J., Tabrizi, M. A., & Davies, M. (1985). The assessment of affective disorders in children and adolescents by semistructured interview. *Archives of General Psychiatry, 42*, 696–702.

Clarizio, H. F. (1991). Obsessive–compulsive disorder: The secretive syndrome. *Psychology in the Schools, 28*, 106–115.

Clark, D. B., & Bolton, D. (1985a). An investigation of two self-report measures of obsessional phenomena in obsessive–compulsive adolescents: Research note. *Journal of Child Psychology and Psychiatry, 26*, 429–437.

Clark, D. B., & Bolton, D. (1985b). Obsessive–compulsive adolescents and their parents: A psychometric study. *Journal of Child Psychology and Psychiatry, 26*, 267–276.

Clark, D. B., Smith, M. G., Neighbors, B. D., Skerlec, L. M., & Randall, J. (1994). Anxiety disorders in adolescence: Characteristics, prevalence and comorbidities. *Clinical Psychology Review, 14*, 113–137.

Costello, E. J. (1990). Child psychiatric epidemiology. In B. B. Lahey & A. E. Kazdin (Eds.), *Advances in clinical child psychology* (pp. 53–90). New York: Plenum Press.

Costello, A. J., Edelbrock, C. S., Dulcan, M. K., Kalaz, R. & Klaric, S. H. (1984). *Report on the NIMH Dianostic Interview Schedule for Children (DISC)*. Washington, DC: National Institute of Mental Health.

Cruz, R. (1992). Clomipramine side effects. *Journal of the American Academy of Child and Adolescent Psychiatry, 31*, 1168–1169.

Damon, W., & Hart, D. (1982). The development of self-understanding from infancy through adolescence. *Child Development, 53*, 841–864.

Dar, R., & Greist, J. (1992). Behavior therapy for obsessive–compulsive disorder. *Psychiatric Clinics of North America, 15*, 885–894.

DeGroot, C. M., & Bornstein, R. A. (1994). Obsessive characteristics in subjects with Tourette's syndrome are related to symptoms in their parents. *Comprehensive Psychiatry, 35*, 248–251.

Desmarais, P.-A., & Lavalle, Y.-J. (1988). Severe obsessive–compulsive syndrome in a 10 year old: A 3-year follow up. *Canadian Journal of Psychiatry, 33*, 405–408.

De Silva, P., & Rachman, S. (1992). *Obsessive–compulsive disorder: The facts*. New York: Oxford University Press.

DeVeaugh-Geiss, J., Moroz, G., Biederman, J., Cantwell, D., Fontaine, R., Greist, J. H., Reichler, R., Katz, R., & Landau, P. (1992). Clomipramine hydrochloride in childhood and adolescent obsessive–compulsive disorder—a multicenter trial. *Journal of the American Academy of Child and Adolescent Psychiatry, 31,* 45–49.

Edelbrock, C., Costello, A. J., Dulcan, M. K., Kalas, R., & Conover, N. C. (1985). Age differences in the reliability of the psychiatric interview of the child. *Child Development, 56,* 265–275.

Fahy, T. A., Osacar, A., & Marks, I. (1993). History of eating disorders in female patients with obsessive–compulsive disorder. *International Journal of Eating Disorders, 14,* 439–443.

Fine, S. (1973). Family therapy and a behavioral approach to childhood obsessive–compulsive neurosis. *Archives of General Psychiatry, 28,* 695–697.

Fisher, P. W., Shaffer, D., Piacentini, J. C., Lapkin, J., Kafantaris, V., Leonard, H., & Herzog, D. B. (1993). Sensitivity of the Diagnostic Interview Schedule for Children, 2nd Edition (DISC-2.1) for specific diagnses of children and adolescents. *Journal of the American Academy of Child and Adolescent Psychiatry, 32,* 666–673.

Fisher, P., Shaffer, D., Wicks, J., Piacentini, J., & Lapkin, J. (1990). *A User's Manual for the DISC-2.* New York: Division of Child Psychiatry, New York State Psychiatric Institute.

Fisman, S. N., & Walsh, L. (1994). Obsessive–compulsive disorder and fear of AIDS contamination in childhood. *Journal of the American Academy of Child and Adolescent Psychiatry, 33,* 349–353.

Flament, M. F., Koby, E., Rapoport, J. L., Berg, C. J., Zahn, T., Cox, C., Denckla, M., & Lenane, M. (1990). Obsessive–compulsive disorder: A prospective follow-up study. *Journal of Child Psychology and Psychiatry, 31,* 363–380.

Flament, M. F., Rapoport, J. L., Berg, C. J., Sceery, W., Kilts, C., Mellstrom, B., & Linnoila, M. (1985). Clomipramine treatment of childhood obsessive–compulsive disorder. *Archives of General Psychiatry, 42,* 977–983.

Flament, M. F., Rapoport, J. L., Murphy, D. L., Berg, C. J., & Lake, C. R. (1987). Biochemical changes during clomipramine treatment of childhood obsessive–compulsive disorder. *Archives of General Psychiatry, 44,* 219–225.

Flament, M. F., Whitaker, A., Rapoport, J. L., Davies, M., Berg, C. Z., Kalikow, K., Sceery, W., & Shaffer, D. (1988). Obsessive–compulsive disorder in adolescence: An epidemiological study. *Journal of the American Academy of Child and Adolescent Psychiatry, 27,* 764–771.

Foa, E. B. (1991). *Therapist manual for exposure treatment of obsessive–compulsives.* Philadelphia: Medical College of Pennsylvania.

Foa, E. B., Feske, U., Murdock, T. B., Kozac, M. J., & McCarthy, P. R. (1991). Processing of threat-related information in rape victims. *Journal of Abnormal Psychology, 100,* 156–162.

Foa, E. B., & Kozac, M. J. (1986). Emotional processing of fear: Exposure to corrective information. *Psychological Bulletin, 99,* 20–35.

Foa, E. B., Ilai, D., McCarthy, P. R., Shoyer, B., & Murdock, T. (1993). Information processing in obsessive–compulsive disorder. *Cognitive Therapy and Research, 17,* 173–189.

Foa, E. B., & McNally, R. J. (1986). Sensitivity to feared stimuli in obsessive–compulsives: A dichotic listening analysis. *Cognitive Therapy and Research, 10,* 477–485.

Foa, E. G., Steketee, G. S., & Ozarow, B. J. (1985). Behavior therapy with obsessive–compulsives: From theory to treatment. In M. Mavissakalian (Ed.), *Obsessive–compulsive disorders: Psychological and pharmacological treatments* (pp. 49–129). New York: Plenum Press.

Fontaine, R., & Chouinard, G. (1985). Fluoxetine in the treatment of obsessive–compulsive disorder. *Progress in Neuro-Psychopharmacology and Biological Psychiatry, 9,* 605–608.

Freeston, M. H., Ladouceur, R., Thibodeau, N., & Gagnon, F. (1992, June). *Intrusive thoughts, worry, and obsessions: Empirical and theoretical distinctions.* Communication presented at the World Congress of Cognitive Therapy, Toronto, Canada.

Frost, R., Lahart, C., Dugas, K., & Sher, K. (1988). Information processing among non-clinical compulsives. *Behaviour Research and Therapy, 26,* 275–277.

Geller, D. A., Biederman, J., Reed, E. D., Spencer, T., & Wilens, T. E. (1995). Similarities in response to fluoxetine in the treatment of children and adolescents with obsessive–compulsive disorder. *Journal of the American Academy of Child and Adolescent Psychiatry, 34,* 36–44.

Goodman, W. K., McDougle, C. J., & Price, L. H. (1992). Pharmacotherapy of obsessive–compulsive disorder. *Journal of Clinical Psychiatry, 53,* 29–37.

Goodman, W. K., Price, L. H., Rasmussen, S. A., Delgado, P. L., Heninger, G. R., & Charney, D. S. (1989a). Efficacy of fluvoxamine in obsessive–compulsive disorder. *Archives of General Psychiatry, 46,* 36–44.

Goodman, W. K., Price, L. H., Rasmussen, S. A., Mazure, C., Delgado, P., Heninger, G. R., & Charney, D. S. (1989b). The Yale–Brown obsessive–compulsive scale: II. Validity. *Archives of General Psychiatry, 46,* 1012–1016.

Goodman, W. K., Price, L. H., Rasmussen, S. A., Mazure, C., Fleischman, R. L., Hill, C. L., Heninger, G. R., & Charney, D. S., (1989c). The Yale-Brown obsessive–compulsive scale: I. Development, use and reliability. *Archives of General Psychiatry, 46,* 1006–1011.

Grad, L. R., Pelcovitz, D., Olson, M., Matthews, M., & Grad, G. J. (1987). Obsessive–compulsive symptomatology in children with Tourette's syndrome. *Journal of the American Academy of Child and Adolescent Psychiatry, 26,* 69–73.

Grayson, J. B., Foa, E. B., & Steketee, G. S., (1985). Obsessive–compulsive disorder. In M. Hersen & A. S. Bellack (Eds.), *Handbook of clinical behavior therapy with adults.* New York: Plenum Press.

Greist, J. H. (1992). An integrated approach to treatment of obsessive–compulsive disorder. *Journal of Clinical Psychiatry, 53,* 38–41.

Greist, J. H., Chouinard, G., Duboff, E., Halaris, A., Kim, S. W., Koran, L., Liebowitz, M., Lydiard, R. B., Rasmussen, S., White, K., & Sikes, C. (1995). Double-blind parallel comparison of three dosages of sertraline and placebo in outpatients with obsessive–compulsive disorder. *Archives of General Psychiatry, 52,* 289–295.

Guy, W. (1976). *ECDEU Assessment Manual for Psychopharmacology.* Washington, DC: U. S. Department of Health, Education, and Welfare.

Hanna, G. L. (1995). Demographic and clinical features of obsessive–compulsive disorder in children and adolescents. *Journal of the American Academy of Child and Adolescent Psychiatry, 34,* 19–27.

Hanna, G. L., Yuwiler, A., & Cantwell, D. P. (1991). Whole blood serotonin in juvenile obsessive–compulsive disorder. *Biological Psychiatry, 29,* 738–744.

Harris, C. V., & Wiebe, D. J. (1992). An analysis of response prevention and flooding procedures in the treatment of adolescent obsessive–compulsive disorder. *Journal of Behavior Therapy and Experimental Psychiatry, 23,* 107–115.

Herjanic, B., & Reich, W. (1982). Development of a structured psychiatric interview for children: Agreement between child and parent on individual symptoms. *Journal of Abnormal Child Psychology, 10,* 307–324.

Hodges, K. (1983; rev. ed., 1986; 2nd rev. ed., 1990). *Guidelines to aid in establishing interrater reliability with the Child Assessment Schedule.* Unpublished manuscript. Ypsilanti, MI: Eastern Michigan University.

Hodges, K. (1990). Depression and anxiety in children: A comparison of self-report questionnaires to clinical interview. *Psychological Assessment: A Journal of Consulting and Clinical Psychology, 2,* 376–381.

Hodges, K., Cools, J., & McKnew, D. (1989). Test–retest reliability of a clinical research interview for children: The Child Assessment Schedule (CAS). *Psychological Assessment: A Journal of Consulting and Clinical Psychology, 1,* 317–322.

Hodges, K., Gordon, Y., & Lennon, M. (1990). Parent–child agreement on symptoms assessed via a clinical research interview for children: The Child Assesment Schedule (CAS). *Journal of Child Psychology and Psychiatry, 31*, 427–436.

Hodges, K., Kline, J., Stern, L, Cytryn, L., & McKnew, D. (1982). The development of a child assessment interview for research and clinical use. *Journal of Abnormal Child Psychology, 10*, 173–189.

Hodgson, R., & Rachman, S. (1977). Obsessive–compulsive complaints. *Behavioural Research and Therapy, 15*, 389–395.

Hollander, E., Fay, M., Cohen, B., Campeas, R., Gorman, J. M., & Liebowitz, M. R. (1988). Serotonergic and noradrenergic sensitivity in obsessive–compulsive disorder: Behavioral findings. *American Journal of Psychiatry, 140*, 1015–1017.

Hollingsworth, C. E., Tanguay, P. E., Grossman, L., & Pabst, P. (1980). Long-term outcome of obsessive–compulsive disorder in childhood. *Journal of the American Academy of Child Psychiatry, 19*, 134–144.

Honjo, S., Hirano, C., Murase, S., Kaneko, T., Sugiyama, T., Ohtaka, K., Aoyama, T., Takei, Y., Inoko, K., & Wakabayashi, S. (1989). Obsessive–compulsive symptoms in childhood and adolescence. *Acta Psychiatrica Scandinavica, 80*, 83–91.

Hoover, C. F., & Insel, T. R. (1984). Families of origin in obsessive–compulsive disorder. *Journal of Nervous and Mental Disease, 172*, 207–215.

Hsu, L. G., Kaye, W., & Weltzin, T. (1993). Are the eating disorders related to obsessive–compulsive disorder? *International Journal of Eating Disorders, 14*, 305–318.

Insel, T. R., Mueller, E. A., Alterman, I., Linnoila, M., & Murphy, D. L. (1985). Obsessive–compulsive disorder and serotonin: Is there a connection? *Biological Psychiatry, 20*, 1174–1188.

Insel, T. R., & Winslow, J. T. (1992). Neurobiology of obsessive–compulsive disorder. *Psychiatric Clinics of North America, 15*, 813–823.

Insel, T. R., Zahn, T., & Murphy, D. L. (1985). Obsessive–compulsive disorder: An anxiety disorder? In A. H. Tuma & J. D. Maser (Eds.), *Anxiety and the anxiety disorders*. Hillsdale, NJ: Erlbaum.

Jakes, I. (1992). A cognitive investigation of obsessionality. Unpublished doctoral dissertation, London University.

Janet, P. (1903). *Les obsessions et la psychiasthenie*. Paris: Felix Arcan.

Jenike, M. A., & Baer, L. (1988). An open trial of buspirone in obsessive–compulsive disorder. *American Journal of Psychiatry, 145*, 1285–1286.

Jenike, M. A., Buttolph, L., Baer, L., Ricciardi, J., & Holland, A. (1989). Open trial of fluoxetine in obsessive–compulsive disorder. *American Journal of Psychiatry, 146*, 909–911.

Jensen, P., Roper, M., Fisher, P., Piacentini, J., Canino, G., Richters, J., Rubio-Stipec, M., Dulcan, M., Goodman, S., Davies, M., Rae, D., Shaffer, D., Bird, H., Lahey, B., & Schwab-Stone, M. (1995). Test–retest reliability of the Diagnostic Interview Schedule for Children (DISC 2.1): Parent, child, and combined algorithms. *Archives of General Psychiatry, 52*, 61–71.

Johnson, M. K. (1988). Discriminating the origin of information. In T. F. Oltmanns & B. A. Maher (Eds.), *Delusional beliefs* (pp. 34–65). New York: Wiley.

Johnson, M. K., & Raye, C. L. (1981). Reality monitoring. *Psychological Review, 88*, 67–85.

Johnson, M. K., Raye, C. L., Foley, H. J., & Foley, M. A. (1981). Cognitive operations and decision bias in reality monitoring. *American Jouranl of Psychology, 94*, 37–64.

Johnston, H. F., & March, J. S. (1992). Obsessive–compulsive disorder in children and adolescents. In W. M. Reynolds (Ed.), *Internalizing disorders in children and adolescents* (pp. 107–148). New York: Wiley.

Karno, M., Golding, J. M., Sorenson, S. B., & Burnam, M. A. (1988). The epidemiology of obsessive–compulsive disorder in five U. S. communities. *Archives of General Psychiatry*, *45*, 1094–1099.

Kasvikis, Y., Tsakiris, F., Marks, I., Basoglu, M., & Noshirvani, H. (1986). Past history of anorexia nervosa in women with obsessive–compulsive disorder. *International Journal of Eating Disorders*, *5*, 1069–1075.

Kearney, C. A., & Silverman, W. K. (1990). Treatment of an adolescent with obsessive–compulsive disorder by alternating response prevention and cognitive therapy: An empirical analysis. *Journal of Behavior Therapy and Experimental Psychiatry*, *21*, 39–47.

Kendall, P. C. (1985). Toward a cognitive-behavioral model of child psychopathology and a critique of related interventions. *Journal of Abnormal Psychology*, *13*, 357–372.

Kendall, P. C. (1991). Guiding theory for therapy with children and adolescents. In P. C. Kendall (Ed.), *Child and adolescent therapy: Cognitive-behavioral procedures* (pp. 3–22). New York: Guilford Press.

Kendall, P. C. (1992). Childhood coping: Avoding a lifetime of anxiety. *Behavioural Change, 9*, 1–8.

Kendall, P. C. (1993). Cognitive-behavioral therapies with youth: Guiding theory, current status, and emerging developments. *Journal of Consulting and Clinical Psychology*, *61*, 235–247.

Kendall, P. C. (1994). Treating anxiety disorders in children: Results of a randomized clinical trial. *Journal of Consulting and Clinical Psychology*, *62*, 100–110.

Kendall, P. C., Chansky, T. E., Kane, M. T., Kim, R. S., Kortlander, E., Ronan, K. R., Sessa, F. M., & Siqueland, L. (1992). *Anxiety disorders in youth: Cognitive-behavioral interventions*. Needham, MA: Allyn & Bacon.

Kendall, P. C., & MacDonald, J. P. (1993). Cognition in the psychopathology of youth and implications for treatment. In K. S. Dobson & P. C. Kendall (Eds.), *Psychopathology and cognition* (pp. 387–432). San Diego: Academic Press.

Kettl, P.A., & Marks, I. M. (1986). Neurological factors in obsessive–compulsive disorder: Two case reports and a review of the literature. *British Journal of Psychiatry*, *149*, 315–319.

King, R. A., Riddle, M. A., Chappell, P. B., Hardin, M. T., Anderson, G. M., Lombroso, P., & Scahill, L. (1991). Emergence of self-destuctive phenomena in children and adolescents during fluoxetine treatment. *Journal of the American Academy of Child and Adolescent Psychiatry*, *30*, 179–186.

Kozac, M. J. (1994). [Uncontrolled behavioral treatment of adolescent obsessive–compulsive disorder.] Unpublished raw data, Medical College of Pennsylvania, Philadelphia.

Kozac, M. J., Foa, E. B., & McCarthy, P. R. (1988). Obsessive–compulsive disorder. In C. G. Last & M. Hersen (Eds.), *Handbook of anxiety disorders* (pp. 87–108). New York: Pergamon Press.

Lang, P. J. (1979). A bioinformational theory of emotional imagery. *Psychophysiology, 16*, 495–512.

Last, C. G., Perrin, S., Hersen, M., & Kazdin, A. E. (1992). DSM-III-R anxiety disorders in children: Sociodemographic and clinical characteristics. *Journal of the American Academy of Child and Adolescent Psychiatry*, *31*, 1070–1076.

Last, C. G., & Strauss, C. C. (1989). Obsessive–compulsive disorder in childhood. *Journal of Anxiety Disorders, 3*, 295–302.

Lavy, E., Van Oppen, P., & Van Den Hout, M. (1994). Selective processing of emotional information in obsessive–compulsive disorder. *Behaviour Research and Therapy, 32*, 243–246.

Lenane, M. C., Swedo, S. E., Leonard, H., Pauls, D. L., Sceery, W., & Rapoport, J. L. (1990). Psychiatric disorders in first-degree relatives of children and adolescents with obsessive–compulsive disorder. *Journal of the American Academy of Child and Adolescent Psychiatry*, *29*, 407–412.

Lenane, M. C., Swedo, S. E., Rapoport, J. L., Leonard, H., Sceery, W., & Guroff, J. J. (1992). Rates of obsessive–compulsive disorder in first-degree relatives of patients with tricho-tillomania: A research note. *Journal of Child Psychiatry and Psychology, 33,* 925–933.

Leonard, H. L., Goldberger, E. L., Rapoport, J. L., Cheslow, D. L., & Swedo, S. E. (1990). Childhood rituals: Normal developmental or obsessive–compulsive symptoms? *Journal of the American Academy of Child and Adolescent Psychiatry, 29,* 17–23.

Leonard, H. L., Lenane, M. C., Swedo, S. E., Rettew, D. C., Gershon, E. S., & Rapoport, J. L. (1992). Tics and Tourette's disorder: a 2- to 7-year follow-up of 54 obsessive–compulsive children. *American Journal of Psychiatry, 149,* 1244–1251.

Leonard, H. L., Swedo, S. E., Lenane, M. C., Rettew, D. C., Cheslow, D. L., Hamburger, S. D., & Rapoport, J. L. (1991). A double-blind desipramine substitution during long-term clomipramine treatment in children and adolescents with obsessive–compulsive dis-order. *Archives of General Psychiatry, 48,* 922–927.

Leonard, H. L., Swedo, S. E., Lenane, M. C., Rettew, D. C., Hamburger, S. D., Bartho, J. J., & Rapoport, J. L. (1993). A 2- to 7-year follow-up study of 54 obsessive–compulsive children and adolescents. *Archives of General Psychiatry, 50,* 429–439.

Leonard, H., Swedo, S., Rapoport, J. L., Coffey, M., & Cheslow, D. (1988). Treatment of childhood obsessive–compulsive disorder with clomipramine and desmethylimipra-mine: A double-blind crossover comparison. *Psychopharmacology Bulletin, 24,* 93–95.

Levin, B., & Duchowny, M. (1991). Childhood obsessive–compulsive disorder and cingulate epilepsy. *Biological Psychiatry, 30,* 1049–1055.

Liebowitz, M. R., Hollander, E., Fairbanks, J., & Campeas, R. (1990). Fluoxetine for adoles-cents with obsessive–compulsive disorder. *American Journal of Psychiatry, 147,* 370–371.

Liebowitz, M. R., Hollander, E., Schneier, F., & Campeas, R., (1989). Fluoxetine treatment of obsessive–compulsive disorder: An open clinical trial. *Journal of Clinical Psychophar-macology, 9,* 423–427.

Lucey, J. V. (1994). BAP/SKB Young Psychopharmacologist Award: Toward a neuroendo-crinology of obsessive–compulsive disorder. *Journal of Psychopharmacology, 8,* 250–257.

Lydiard, R. B. (1994). Obsessive–compulsive disorder: a new perspective in diagnosis and treatment. IX World Congress of Psychiatry Symposium: The search for the ideal anti-depressant: How close are we? (1993, Rio de Janeiro, Brazil). *International Clinical Psycho-pharmacology, 9,* 33–37.

MacLeod, C., & McLaughlin, K. (1995). Implicit and explicit memory bias in anxiety: A conceptual replication. *Behaviour Research and Therapy, 33,* 1–14.

March, J. S. (1994). *Multidimensional Anxiety Scale for Children (MASC).* Tonawanda, NY: Multi-Health Systems.

March, J. S. (1995). Cognitive-behavioral psychotherapy for children and adolescents with obsessive–compulsive disorder: A review and recommendations for treatment. *Journal of the American Academy of Child and Adolescent Psychiatry, 34,* 7–18.

March, J. S., Mulle, K., & Herbel, B. (1994). Behavioral psychotherapy for children and adolescents with obsessive–compulsive disorder: An open trial of a new protocol-driven treatment package. *Journal of the American Academy of Child and Adolescent Psychiatry, 33,* 333–341.

Martinot, J. L., Allilaire, J. F., & Mazoyer, M. (1990). Obsessive–compulsive disorder: A clinical, neuropsychological and positron emission tomography study. *Acta Psychiatrica Scandinavica, 82,* 233–242.

Mathews, A., & MacLeod, C. (1985). Selective processing of threat cues in anxiety states. *Behaviour Research and Therapy, 23,* 563–569.

Mattes, J. A. (1994). Fluvoxamine in obsessive–compulsive nonresponders to clomipramine or fluoxetine. *American Journal of Psychiatry, 151,* 15–24.

Mavissakalian, M., Turner, S. M., Michelson, L., & Jacob, R. (1985). Tricyclic antidepressants in obsessive–compulsive disorder: Anti-obsessional or antidepressant agents? *American Journal of Psychiatry, 142,* 572–576.

Max, J. E., Smith, W. L., Lindgren, S. D., Robin, D. A., Mattheis, P. Stierwalt, J., & Morrisey, M. (1995). Case study: obsessive–compulsive disorder after severe traumatic brain injury in an adolescent. *Journal of the American Academy of Child and Adolescent Psychiatry, 34,* 45–49.

McFall, M. E., & Wollersheim, J. P. (1979). Obsessive–compulsive neurosis: A cognitive-behavioral formulation and approach to treatment. *Cognitive Therapy and Research, 3,* 333–348.

McFarlane, A. C. (1987). The relationship between patterns of family interaction and psychiatric disorder in children. *Australian and New Zealand Journal of Psychiatry, 21,* 383.

McKeon, P., & Murray, R. (1987). Familial aspects of obsessive–compulsive neurosis. *British Journal of Psychiatry, 151,* 528–534.

Merkel, W. T., Pollard, C. A., Wiener, R. L., & Staebler, C. R. (1993). Perceived parental characteristics of patients with obsessive–compulsive disorder, depression and panic disorder. *Child Psychiatry and Human Development, 24,* 49–57.

Milner, A., Beech, R., & Walker, V. (1971). Decision processes and obsessional behavior. *British Journal of Social and Clinical Psychology, 10,* 88–89.

Montgomery, S. A. (1980). Clomipramine in obsessional neurosis: A placebo controlled trial. *Pharmacological Medicine, 1,* 189–192.

Mowrer, O. H. (1960). *Learning theory and behavior.* New York: Wiley.

Murphy, D. L., Pickar, D., & Alterman, I. A. (1982). Methods for the quantitative assessment of depressive and manic behavior. In E. I. Burdock, A. Sudilovsky, & S. Gershon (Eds.), *The behavior of psychiatric patients* (pp 355–392). New York: Marcel Dekker.

Myers, W. C., Burket, R. C., Lyles, W. B., Stone L., & Kemph, B. (1990). DSM-III diagnoses and offenses in committed female juvenile delinquents. *Bulletin of the American Academy of Psychiatry and the Law, 18,* 47–54.

Ollendick, T., & Hersen, M. (1993). Child and adolescent behavioral asessment. In T. M. Ollendick & M. Hersen (Eds.), *Handbook of child and adolescent assessment* (pp. 3–14). Needham Heights, MA: Allyn & Bacon.

Otto, M. W. (1992). Normal and abnormal information processing: A neurobiological perspective on obsessive–compulsive disorder. *Psychiatric Clinics of North America, 15,* 825–848.

Park, S., Como, P. G., Cui, L., & Kurlan, R. (1993). The early course of the Tourette's syndrome clinical spectrum. *Neurology, 43,* 1712–1715.

Pato, M. T., Zohar-Kadouch, R., Zohar, J., & Murphy, D. L. (1988). Return of symptoms after discontinuation of clomipramine in patients with obsessive–compulsive disorder. *American Journal of Psychiatry, 145,* 1521–1525.

Pauls, D. L. (1992). The genetics of obsessive–compulsive disorder and Gilles de la Tourette's syndrome. *Psychiatric Clinics of North America, 15,* 759–766.

Pauls, D. L., Alsobrook, J. P., Goodman, W., & Rasmussen, S. (1995). A family study of obsessive–compulsive disorder. *American Journal of Psychiatry, 152,* 76–84.

Pauls, D. L., Towbin, K. E., Leckman, J. F., Zahner, G. E. P., & Cohen, D. J. (1986). Gilles de la Tourette's syndrome and obsessive–compulsive disorder. *Archives of General Psychiatry, 43,* 1180–1182.

Peroutka, S. J., & Snyder, S. H. (1981). Long-term antidepressant treatment decreases 3H-spiroperidol-labeled serotonin receptor binding. *Science, 210,* 88–90.

Persons, J. B., & Foa, E. B. (1984). Processing of fearful and neutral information by obsessive-compulsives. *Behaviour Research and Therapy, 22,* 259–265.

Piacentini, J., Gitow, A., Jaffer, M., Graae, F., & Whitaker, A. (1994). Outpatient behavioral treatment of child and adolescent obsessive–compulsive disorder. *Journal of Anxiety Disorders, 8,* 277–289.

Piacentini, J., Jaffer, M., Gitow, M., Graae, F., Davies, S. O., Del Bene, D., & Liebowitz, M. (1992). Psychopharmacologic treatment of child and adolescent obsessive–compulsive disorder. *Psychiatric Clinics of North America, 15,* 87–107.

Piacentini, J., Jaffer, M., Liebowitz, M., & Gitow, A. (1992). *Systematic assessment of impairment in youngsters with obsessive–compulsive disorder: The OCD Impact Scale.* Paper presented at the 26th Annual Meeting of the Association of the Advancement of Behavior Therapy, Boston, MA, November.

Piaget, J., & Inhelder, B. (1966). *The early growth of logic in the child.* New York: Harper & Row.

Piran, N., Kennedy, S., Garfinkel, P. E., & Owens, M. (1985). Affective disturbance in eating disorders. *Journal of Nervous and Mental Disease, 173,* 395–400.

Pitman, R. K., Green, R.C., Jenike, M. A., & Mesulam, M. M. (1987). Clinical comparison of Tourette's disorder and obsessive–compulsive disorder. 140th Annual Meeting of the American Psychiatric Association (1987, Chicago, Illinois). *American Journal of Psychiatry, 144,* 1166–1171.

Price, L. H., Goodman, W. K., Charney, D. S., Rasmussen, S. A., & Heninger, G. R. (1987). Treatment of severe obsessive–compulsive disorder with fluvoxamine. *American Journal of Psychiatry, 144,* 1059–1061.

Puig-Antich, J., & Chambers, W. (1978). *The Schedule for Affective Disorders and Schizophrenia for School-Aged Children (Kiddie-SADS).* New York: New York State Psychiatric Institute.

Rachman, S. (1993). Obsessions, responsibility and guilt. *Behaviour Research and Therapy, 31,* 149–154.

Rachman, S., & Hodgson, R. (1980). *Obsessions and compulsions.* Englewood Cliffs, NJ: Prentice-Hall.

Rapoport, J. L. (1986a). Childhood obsessive–compulsive disorder. *Journal of Child Psychology and Psychiatry, 27,* 289–295.

Rapoport, J. L. (1986b). Antidepressants in childhood atention deficit disorder and obsessive–compulsive disorder. *Psychosomatics, 27,* (Suppl. 11), 30–36.

Rapoport, J. L. (1994). Le "spectre obsessionnel–compulsif": Un concept utile?/"Obsessive–compulsive spectrum disorder": A useful concept? Special Issue: Lilly–Dista Symposium: Depression: From biology to pathology. *Encephale, 20,* 677–680.

Rapoport, J., Elkins, R., Langer, D. H. Sceery, W., Buchsbaum, M. S., Gillin, J. C., Murphy, D. L., Zahn, T. P., Lake, R., Ludlow, C., & Mendelson, W. (1981). Childhood obsessive–compulsive disorder. *American Journal of Psychiatry, 138,* 1545–1554.

Rapoport, J. L. Swedo, S. E., & Leonard, H. L. (1992). Childhood obsessive–compulsive disorder. *Journal of Clinical Psychiatry, 53,* 11–16.

Rasmussen, S. A. (1993). Genetic studies of obsessive–compulsive disorder. *Annals of Clinical Psychiatry, 5,* 241–247.

Rasmussen, S. A., & Tsuang, M. T. (1986). Clinical characteristics and family history in DSM-III obsessive–compulsive disorder. *American Journal of Psychiatry, 143,* 317–322.

Rastam, M., Gillberg, I.C., & Gillberg, C. (1995). Anorexia nervosa six years after onset: II. Comorbid psychiatric problems. *Comprehensive Psychiatry, 36,* 70–76.

Reed, G. F. (1968). Some formal qualties of obsessional thinking. *Psychiatrica Clinica, 1,* 382–392.

Reed, G. F. (1969). "Under-inclusion—A characteristic of obsessional personality disorder: II. *British Journal of Psychiatry, 115,* 787–790.

Reed, G. F. (1977). Obsessional personality disorder and remembering. *British Journal of Psychiatry, 130,* 177–183.

Rettew, D. C., Swedo, S. E., Leonard, H. L, Lenane, M. C., & Rapoport, J. L. (1992). Obsessions and compulsions across time in 79 children and adolescents with obsessive–

compulsive disorder. *Journal of the American Academy of Child and Adolescent Psychiatry, 31,* 1050–1056.

Rheaume, J., Ladouceur, R., Freeston, M. H., & Letarte, H. (1995). Inflated responsibility in obsessive–compulsive disorder: Validation of an operational definition. *Behaviour Research and Therapy, 33,* 159–169.

Riddle, M. A., Scahill, L., King, R. A., Hardin, M. T., Anderson, G. M., Ort, S. I., Smith, J. C., Leckman, J. F., & Cohen, D. J. (1992). Double-blind, crossover trial of fluoxetine and placebo in children and adolescents with obsessive–compulsive disorder. *Journal of the American Academy of Child and Adolescent Psychiatry, 31,* 1062–1069.

Riddle, M. A., Scahill, L., King, R., Hardin, M. T., Towbin, K. E., Ort, S. I., Leckman, J. F., & Cohen, D. J. (1990). Obsessive–compulsive disorder in children and adolescents. Phenomenology and family history. *Journal of the American Academy of Child and Adolescent Psychiatry, 29,* 766–772.

Roper, G., & Rachman, S. J. (1975). Obsessional–compulsive checking: Replication and development. *Behaviour Research and Therapy, 13,* 25–32.

Roper, G., Rachman, S. J., & Hodgson, R. (1973). An experiment on obsessional thinking. *Behaviour Research and Therapy, 11,* 271–277.

Salkovskis, P. M. (1989). Cognitive-behavioral factors and the persistence of intrusive thoughts in obsessional problems. *Behaviour Research and Therapy, 27,* 677–682.

Salkovskis, P. M., & Campbell, P. (1994). Thought suppression induces intrusion in naturally occurring negative intrusive thoughts. *Behavior Research and Therapy, 32,* 1–8.

Salkovskis, P. M., & Kirk, J. W. (1989). Obsessional problems. In K. Hawton, P. M. Salkovskis, J. W. Kirk & D. M. Clark (Eds.), *Cognitive-behavioural approaches to adult psychological disorder: A practical guide.* Oxford, UK: Oxford University Press.

Sartory, G., & Master, D. (1984). Contingent negative variation in obsessional–compulsive patients. *Biological Psychology, 18,* 253–267.

Schreier, H. A. (1990). OCD and tricyclics. *Journal of the American Academy of Child and Adolescent Psychiatry, 29,* 668–669.

Schwab-Stone, M., Fisher, P. W., Piacentini, J., Shaffer, D., Davies, M., & Briggs, M. (1993). The Diagnostic Interview Schedule for Children—Revised version (DISC-R): II. Test–retest reliability. *Journal of the American Academy of Child and Adolescent Psychiatry, 32,* 651–657.

Shaffer, D., Gould, M. S., Brosic, J., Ambrosini, P., Bird, H., & Aluwahlia, S. (1983). A children's global assessment scale (CGAS). *Archives of General Psychiatry, 40,* 1228–1234.

Shaffer, D., Schwab-Stone, M., Fisher, P. W., Cohen, P., Piacentini, J., Davies, M., Conners, C. K., & Regier, D. (1993). The Diagnostic Interview Schedule for Children—Revised version (DISC-R): I. Preparation, field testing, interrater reliability and acceptability. *Journal of the American Academy of Child and Adolescent Psychiatry, 32,* 643–650.

Sher, K. K., Frost, R., Kushner, M., Crews, T., & Alexander, J. (1989). Memory deficits in compulsive checkers: Replication and extension in a clinical sample. *Behaviour, Research and Therapy, 27,* 65–69.

Sher, K. K., Frost, R. O., & Otto, R. (1983). Cognitive deficits in compulsive checkers: An exploratory study. *Behaviour Research and Therapy, 21,* 357–364.

Sher, K. K., Mann, B., & Frost, R. O. (1984). Cognitive dysfunction in compulsive checkers: Further explorations. *Behaviour Research and Therapy, 22,* 493–502.

Silverman, W. K. (1987). Childhood anxiety disorders. Diagnostic issues, empirical support, and future research. *Journal of Child and Adolescent Psychotherapy, 4,* 121–126.

Silverman, W. K., & Eisen, A. R. (1992). Age differences in the reliability of parent and child reports of child anxious symptomatology using a structured interview. *Journal of the American Academy of Child and Adolescent Psychiatry, 31,* 117–124.

Silverman, W. K., & Nelles, W. B. (1988). The Anxiety Disorders Interview Schedule for Children. *Journal of the American Academy of Child and Adolescent Psychiatry, 27*, 772–778.

Sookman, D., Pinard, G., & Beauchemin, N. (1994). Multidimensional schematic restructuring treatment for obsessions: Theory and practice. *Journal of Cognitive Psychotherapy: An International Quarterly, 8*, 175–194.

Stanley, L. (1980). Treatment of ritualistic behavior in an eight-year-old girl by response prevention: A case report. *Journal of Child Psychology and Psychiatry, 21*, 85–90.

Stanley, M. A., & Turner, S. M. (1995). Current status of pharmacological and behavioral treatment of obsessive–compulsive disorder. *Behavior Therapy, 26*, 163–186.

Stein, D. J., & Hollander, E. (1994). A neural network approach to obsessive–compulsive disorder. *Journal of Mind and Behavior, 15*, 223–238.

Stoll, A. L., Tohen, M., & Baldessarini, R. J. (1992). Increasing frequency of the diagnosis of obsessive–compulsive disorder. *American Journal of Psychiatry, 149*, 638–640.

Swedo, S. E., & Leonard, H. L. (1994). Childhood movement disorders and obsessive–compulsive disorder. 146th Annual Meeting of the American Psychiatric Association Symposium: OCD: Comorbidity and management dilemmas (1993, San Francisco, CA). *Journal of Clinical Psychiatry, 55*, Suppl. 3), 32–37.

Swedo, S. E. Leonard, H. L., Kruesi, M. J. P., Rettew, D. C., Listwak, S. J., Berrettini, W., Stipetic, M., Hamburger, S., Gold, P.W., Potter, W. Z., & Rapoport, J. L. (1992). Cerebrospinal fluid neurochemistry in children and adolescents with obsessive–compulsive disorder. *Archives of General Psychiatry, 49*, 29–36.

Swedo, S. E., Leonard, H. L, & Rapoport, J. L. (1992). Childhood onset obsessive–compulsive disorder. *Psychiatric Clinics of North America, 15*, 767–775.

Swedo, S. E., & Rapoport, J. L. (1990). Obsessive–compulsive disorder in childhood. In M. Hersen & C. G. Last (Eds.), *Handbook of child and adult psychopathology: A longitudinal perspective* (pp. 211–219). New York: Pergamon Press.

Swedo, S. E., Rapoport, J. L., Cheslow, D. L., Leonard, H. L., Ayoub, E. M., Hosier, D. M., & Wald, E. R. (1989). High prevalence of obsessive–compulsive symptoms in patients with Sydenham's chorea. *American Journal of Psychiatry, 146*, 246–249.

Swedo, S. E., Rapoport, J. L., Leonard, H., Lenane, M., & Cheslow, D. (1989). Obsessive–compulsive disorder in children and adolescents: Clinical phenomenology of 70 consecutive cases. *Archives of General Psychiatry, 46*, 335–341.

Swedo, S. E., Schapiro, M. D., Grady, C. L., Cheslow, D. L., Leonard, H. L., Kumar, A., Friedland, R., Rapoport, S. I., & Rapoport, J. L. (1989). Cerebral glucose metabolism in childhood-onset obsessive–compulsive disorder. *Archives of General Psychiatry, 46*, 518–523.

Tallis, F. (1995). The characteristics of obsessional thinking: Difficulty demonstrating the obvious? *Clinical Psychology and Psychotherapy, 2*, 24–39.

Thomsen, P. H. (1993). Obsessive–compulsive disorder in children and adolescents: Self-reported obsessive–compulsive behavior in pupils in Denmark. *Acta Psychiatricia Scandinavica, 88*, 212–217.

Thomsen, P. H. (1994). Obsessive–compulsive disorder in children and adolescents: A 6- to 22-year follow-up study: Clinical descriptions of the course and continuity of obsessive–compulsive symptomatology. *European Child and Adolescent Psychiatry, 3*, 82–96.

Thomsen, P. H. (1994b). Obsessive–compulsive disorder in children and adolescents: A study of phenomenology and family functioning in 20 consecutive Danish cases. *European Child and Adolescent Psychiatry, 3*, 29–36.

Thoren, P., Asberg, M., Bertilsson, L., Mellstrom, B., Sjoqvist, F., & Traskman, L. (1980). Clorimipramine treatment of obsessive–compulsive disorder: II. Biochemical aspects. *Archives of General Psychiatry, 37*, 1289–1294.

Tollefson, G. D., Rampey, A. H., Potvin, J. H., Jenike, M. A., Rush, A. J., Dominguez, R. A., Koran, L. M., Shear, M. K., Goodman, W., & Genduso, L. A. (1994). A multicenter investigation of fixed-dose fluoxetine in the treatment of obsessive–compulsive disorder. *Archives of General Psychiatry, 51,* 559–567.

Toro, J., Cervera, M., Osejo, E., & Salamero, M. (1991). Obsessive–compulsive disorder in childhood and adolescence: A clinical study. *Journal of Child Psychology and Psychiatry, 33,* 1025–1037.

Valleni-Basile, L. A., Garrison, C. Z., Jackson, K. L., Waller, J. L, McKeown, R. E., Addy, C. L., & Cuffe, S. P. (1994). Frequency of obsessive–compulsive disorder in a community sample of young adolescents. *Journal of the American Academy of Child and Adolescent Psychiatry, 33,* 782–791.

Vasey, M. W., Daleiden, E. L., Williams, L. L., & Brown, L. M. (1995). Biased attention in childhood anxiety disorders: A preliminary study. *Journal of Abnormal Child Psychology, 23,* 267–279.

Vasey, M. W., Elhag, N., & Daleiden, E. L. 1994. Anxiety and the processing of emotionally threatening stimuli: Distinctive patterns of selective attention among high- and low-test anxious children. Unpublished manuscript.

Vitiello, B., Malone, R., Buschle, P. R., Delaney, M. A., & Behar, D. (1990). Reliability of DSM-III diagnoses of hospitalized children. *Hospital and Community Psychiatry, 41,* 63–67.

Volans, P. J. (1976). Styles of decision making and probability appraisal in selected obsessional and phobic patients. *British Journal of Social and Clinical Psychology, 15,* 305–317.

Wagner, K. D., & Sullivan, M. A. (1990). Fear of AIDS related to development of obsessive–compulsive disorder in a child. *Journal of the American Academy of Child and Adolescent Psychiatry, 30,* 740–742.

Warren, R. & Zgourides, G. D. (1991). *Anxiety disorders: A rational–emotive perspective.* New York: Pergamon Press.

Watts, F. N., McKenna, F. P., Sharrock, R., & Trezise, L. (1986). Colour naming of phobia related words. *British Journal of Psychology, 77,* 97–108.

Weizman, A., Mandel, A., Barber, Y., Weitz, R., Cohen, A., Mester, R., & Rehavi, M. (1992). Decreased platelet imipramine binding in Tourette syndrome children with obsessive–compulsive disorder. *Biological Psychiatry, 31,* 705–711.

Welner, A., Reich, T., & Robbins, E. (1976). Obsessive–compulsive neurosis: Record follow-up and family studies. *Comprehensive Psychiatry, 17,* 527–539.

Wilens, T. E., Steingard, R., & Biederman, J. (1992). Clomipramine for comorbid conditions. *Journal of the American Academy of Child and Adolescent Psychiatry, 31,* 171.

Willmuth, M. E. (1988). Cognitive-behavioral and insight-oriented psychotherapy of an eleven-year-old boy with obsessive–compulsive disorder. *American Journal of Psychotherapy, 42,* 472–478.

Wolff, R., & Rapoport, J. (1988). Behavioral treatment of childhood obsessive–compulsive disorder. *Behavior Modification, 12,* 252–266.

Wolff, R. P., & Wolff, L. S. (1991). Assessment and treatment of obsessive–compulsive disorder in children. *Behavior Modification, 15,* 372–393.

Zohar, J., & Insel, T. R. (1987). Obsessive–compulsive disorder: Psychobiological approaches to diagnosis, treatment and pathophysiology. *Biological Psychiatry, 22,* 667–687.

Zohar, A. H., Ratzoni, G., Pauls, D. L., Apter, A., Bleich, A., Kron, S., Rappaport, M., Weizman, A., & Cohen. D. J. (1992). An epidemiological study of obsessive–compulsive disorder and related disorders in Israeli adolescents. *Journal of the American Academy of Child and Adolescent Psychiatry, 31,* 1057–1061.

4

Advances in the Neuropsychological Bases of Child and Adolescent Psychopathology

Proposed Models, Findings, and Ongoing Issues

STEPHEN R. HOOPER
AND MICHAEL G. TRAMONTANA

1. Introduction

The past several decades have witnessed significant advances in the area of child neuropsychology. These advances have increased our knowledge base in developmental neuropsychology (e.g., Halperin, McKay, Matier, & Sharma, 1994; Molfese, 1995); pediatric neuropathology such as lead poisoning (Bellinger, 1995), cancers (Stehbens & Cool, 1994), childhood dementias (Shapiro & Klein, 1994), meningitis (Taylor, Schatschneider, & Rich, 1992), and traumatic brain injuries (Snow & Hooper, 1994); neurodevelopmental disorders such as learning disabilities (Feagans, Short, & Meltzer, 1991; Hooper & Willis, 1989; Rourke, 1985), mental retardation, and autism (Hooper, Boyd, Hynd, & Rubin, 1993); neuropsychological assessment strategies across the age range from infancy through adolescence (Aylward, 1993; Forster & Leckliter, 1995; Hooper, 1991; Korkman, 1995); and most important, treatment (Bakker, Licht, & Kappers, 1995; Korkman

STEPHEN R. HOOPER • Center for Development and Learning, University of North Carolina, Chapel Hill, North Carolina 27599.   MICHAEL G. TRAMONTANA • Division of Child and Adolescent Psychiatry, Vanderbilt University School of Medicine, Nashville, Tennessee 37212.

Advances in Clinical Child Psychology, Volume 19, edited by Thomas H. Ollendick and Ronald J. Prinz. Plenum Press, New York, 1997.

& Peltomaa, 1993; Newby, Recht, & Caldwell, 1993; Ylvisaker, Szekeres, & Hartwick, 1992).

Despite these noteworthy advances, the examination of the neuropsychological contributions to psychopathological behaviors observed during childhood and adolescence remains relatively new. Although such brain–behavior relationships have been hypothesized for well over 100 years, dating back to the observations of Hughlings Jackson (1879), who hypothesized that the emotional aspects of communication might be mediated by the right hemisphere, research evidence has appeared more slowly, particularly for children and adolescents. Although a number of mechanisms have been suggested whereby brain dysfunction may lead to psychopathology (e.g., direct effects, indirect effects, transactional effects), evidence as to their relative contributions is uncertain (Rutter, 1983; Tramontana & Hooper, in press). As a result, many questions remain to be examined.

This chapter provides a review of the advances in the study of the neuropsychological bases of child psychopathology. This chapter provides an overview of the cerebral asymmetry of emotion, with a particular focus on human laterality studies, and a brief discussion of several key neurobehavioral models that have been proposed to address the neurological–emotional interface. A major portion of this chapter deals with specific, representative neuropsychological findings in selected categories of child psychopathology. Finally, the chapter concludes with a discussion of several ongoing issues confronting this area.

2. Neurological Bases of Emotion

Definitional issues notwithstanding, there exist many different theoretical perspectives with respect to understanding emotional responses (Feyereisen, 1989). One group of theories explains emotions as bodily responses, with the affective system being independent of, and parallel to, the cognitive system (Zajonc & Marcus, 1984). For example, in the differential emotional theory, a set number of basic emotions are assumed to exist (e.g., anger, joy, fear), and these combine with each other and with cultural rules to form more complex emotional manifestations. Another group of theories, the cognitive theories, suggests that emotions can only result from some appraisal of the situation; that is, a cognitive process must take place before the bodily response can occur. As an example, in the cognition-arousal theory (Schachter & Singer, 1962), emotional experience depends on (1) physiological arousal and (2) the attribution of that arousal to an emotional source.

Regardless of the theoretical perspective taken, there are strong data implicating neurological and neuropsychological processes in the expression and reception of emotions. Furthermore, the neurological basis of emotional functioning in children and adolescents is compounded by issues pertinent to development, brain plasticity, and the presence of other kinds of neurodevelopmental and/or acquired phenomena (e.g., brain injuries, learning disabilities). Whereas, other sources can be reviewed for in-depth discussions pertaining to the neuroanatomical and neurochemical basis of emotion (e.g., Joseph, 1990; Kennard, Emslie, & Weinberg, 1989), this section focuses on key findings from the human laterality studies.

2.1. Human Laterality Studies and Emotions: An Overview

Over two decades ago, Heilman, Scholes, and Watson (1975) reported that a lesion in the right hemisphere in a region homologous to Wernicke's area resulted in the inability to comprehend the affective components of language; however, the ability to understand the propositional meaning was not impaired. Similarly, Ross and Mesulam (1979) described two patients who had lesions in the right hemisphere in the area homologous to Broca's area. They noted that these patients were able to use propositional speech, although neither had the ability to impart affective qualities to their speech nor could they use their limbs, face, or body movements to convey emotions and affect. As can be surmised from these case reports, over the past several decades, evidence relating to the cerebral asymmetry of emotion has been advanced. Although considerable debate is ongoing with respect to many of these findings, it is now clear that the neurological contribution to normal as well as aberrant emotional functioning cannot be overlooked or underestimated.

Perhaps one of the least debated findings is the involvement of the frontal lobe in emotional expression and regulation. For example, Kolb and Milner (1981a, 1981b) found frontal lobe lesions to impair both voluntary and spontaneous facial expressions. The linkage to frontal lobe functioning also has been made in infants during the first year of life. In a series of well-controlled studies examining brain electrophysiological (EEG) patterns during the presentation of emotion-eliciting stimuli, Davidson and colleagues (see Davidson, 1994, for a review) found no evidence of parietal asymmetry between happy and sad stimuli; however, frontal asymmetries did emerge, and they discriminated between the stimuli, with greater relative left-sided activation elicited in response to the happy stimuli compared to the sad stimuli. Furthermore, Davidson and colleagues reported that when the separate contributions of the left and right frontal regions were examined, it was the left hemisphere that changed more than the right between conditions. These findings replicated the findings by these investigators with an adult population (Davidson, Schwartz, Saron, Bennett, & Goleman, 1979), and were later extended even further downward to newborns (Fox & Davidson, 1988).

Davidson (1984) proposed that these frontal asymmetries were uniquely associated with the dimensions of approach and avoidance. Davidson argued that positive emotions that are accompanied by approach should be associated with left frontal activation, whereas negative emotions accompanied by withdrawal should be associated with right frontal activation. Schaffer, O'Connor, Shafer, and Prupis (1983) also found that adults scoring high on the Beck Depression Inventory show decreased left frontal activation during rest compared to nondepressed controls. In general, these investigators suggested that the frontal region is most likely associated with three major features of emotion: the motor components, the organization of the multisystem response pattern that constitutes emotion, and the ability to inhibit or regulate emotion (Bell & Fox, 1994).

These investigators also suggested that right frontal activation during resting baseline may indicate a specific vulnerability to experience certain negative emotional states (e.g., depression), whereas those with left frontal activation may be more able to quickly terminate their reactions and invoke a variety of adaptive coping strategies via the self-monitoring of responses (Kopp, 1989). Tomarken, Davidson, and Henriques (1990) noted that greater right frontal activation during rest was correlated with increased intensity of self-reported fear in response to films designed to elicit negative affect. Davidson and Fox (1989) also found that among 10-month-old infants, those with resting right frontal activation were more likely to cry in response to brief maternal separation than were infants showing left frontal activation during rest. Those who continued to react to the distress may show an underlying pattern of cerebral activation, and this activation may be an early marker for psychological adjustment issues. Furthermore, Dawson (1993) reported evidence suggesting that the infant's parenting environment, specifically parental depression, may contribute to shaping patterns of frontal activation asymmetries and subsequently generalize to other social interactional patterns. This has been hypothesized to be secondary to the infants receiving excessive stimulation of brain regions associated with negative emotions, and reduced stimulation of brain regions associated with positive emotions. This differential pattern of brain stimulation also is believed to be occurring during a sensitive neurodevelopmental period for brain regions associated with the development of emotional modulation.

Although the expression of emotions appears to be related to differential activation of right and left frontal regions, the perception of emotional stimuli seems to be more accurate when the stimuli are presented in such a way as to first reach the right hemisphere, and this seems to hold for positive or negative emotions (Bryden & Levy, 1983; Davidson & Fox, 1989). These findings would be consistent with the specialization of the right hemisphere in most individuals to engage in simultaneous processing, thus taking advantage of the integrative and holistic properties of the right hemisphere. In particular, the parietal regions appear critical to these emotional reception processes (Bryden, 1982; Etcoff, 1986), although it has been suggested that the perception of emotional information may be independent of the more general visual–perceptual processing attributes typically ascribed to this hemisphere (Blonder, Bowers, & Heilman, 1991).

In summary, the human laterality studies suggest that the reception of emotional stimuli appears to be mediated largely by the posterior regions of the right hemisphere, regardless of the content of the emotional message. The bulk of evidence also seems to indicate that the expression of emotions appears to be differentially distributed between the right and left frontal regions, with the left hemisphere being the primary modulator of approach types of emotions (e.g., happiness) and the right hemisphere being the primary modulator of avoidance types of emotion (e.g., sadness). Although these findings will continue to require ongoing investigation, it is important to note that these findings appear to be robust across age—extending downward to the newborn state and upward into adulthood. This developmental perspective should hold many implications for the emergence of psychopathology.

3. Neuropsychological Models of Psychopathology

Given this brief overview of the current status of cerebral asymmetry for emotional expression and reception, an array of neurological positions and models have been advanced to explain the presence of psychopathology during childhood and adolescence. For example, Gainotti (1989) has presented a theoretical model examining the neurobiological basis of emotion and psychopathology. Within this theoretical perspective, psychopathology is believed to originate from neuroanatomical, neurophysiological, and/or neuroendocrine dysfunction via acquired and/or neurodevelopmental etiological mechanisms. This is consistent with the work of Gray (1982), Tucker (1989), and Kinsbourne (1989), who addressed this issue directly via proposed activation/release models, particularly with respect to internalizing disorders. More recently, neuropsychological factors also have been implicated directly in the manifestation of psychopathology in children and adolescents, particularly internalizing disorders (Rourke, 1989). The models of Gray, Tucker, Kinsbourne, and Rourke are briefly presented in this regard because of their robust nature and/or their potential application to children and adolescents.

3.1. Gray's Model

Gray (1982) provides one of the most well-rounded neurobiological models for understanding anxiety and fear. This model has been applied not only to the manifestation of anxiety symptoms, but it also has been applied to anxiety disorders and normal variations in personality characteristics (e.g., anxiousness). It is based on data largely arising from experimental findings with animals that include pharmacological efforts, environmental studies (i.e., the effects of infantile stress on adult behaviors), and genetic investigations (i.e., selective breeding to create reactive and nonreactive genotypes). In general, these separate lines of investigation have produced a convergence of data for Gray to hypothesize a separate subsystem in the brain for mediating anxiety.

In addition to these three lines of research, Gray noted that two behavioral systems were intimately tied to these functions: the behavioral inhibition system and the fight–flight system. The behavioral inhibition system mediates the reaction of an organism to anxiety-producing stimuli, such as signs of punishment, nonreward, and novel situations, as well as the responses to these stimuli (i.e., behavioral inhibition, hypervigilance, increased arousal). This behavioral system has been intimately linked to Papez's (1937) circuit or the limbic system, which has been implicated in the elaboration of emotional experiences, with particular emphasis on the septohippocampal neural connections.

More specifically, damage to the septal area or to the hippocampal formation, which maintains bidirectional connections with the septum, creates reactions that mirror behavioral inhibition. In fact, it has been hypothesized that antianxiolytic drugs create their effects by impacting upon this neural system, although these effects have been deemed indirect (Gray & Rawlins, 1986). This neural system also involves noradrenergic neurons in the locus coeruleus—which assist in the determination of the behavioral output of the behavioral inhibition system, serotonergic neurons in the raphe nuclei—which assist in determining the behavioral inhibition output and the neuronal projections that interconnect these various cell groups. Activity in these fibers is increased by anxiety-type stimulation and stress, and begin to provide further neural clarification of anxiety manifestations.

The second behavioral system, the fight–flight system, mediates an organism's response (e.g., striking, biting, jumping, hissing, defensive posturing in laboratory animals) to stimuli associated with unconditioned pain or nonreward. It is a motivation system designed to suppress feelings of anxiety and to protect the organism. The major neural components of this system are the amygdala, ventromedial hypothalamus, and the midbrain central gray.

Taken together, these two behavioral systems and their corresponding neural networks purportedly interact to account for nearly all of the manifestations of anxiety, and perhaps treatment responses, that can be seen in animals and humans. Given the neurotransmitters involved in the neuronal systems, evidence also has emerged to implicate effects on the developing brain and subsequent responses to anxiety-producing stimuli. In general, Gray's model involves the behavioral aspects of anxiety, the cognitive aspects of anxiety via the information-processing activities of the septohippocampal system, and the autonomic signs of anxiety via connections into the spinal cord. Although a scientifically robust model, the application of this model to humans, particularly children and adolescents, will require further investigation.

3.2. Tucker's Model

Along with Gray's model, Tucker's (1989) model of emotional functioning and its application to psychopathology is one of the more robust models derived to date. Although many models deal with cortical to subcortical, anterior to posterior cortex, and left hemisphere to right hemisphere relationships, the Tucker model proposes these relationships as well as the involvement of neurophysiological control mechanisms. Tucker and Frederick (1986) noted that these interconnections influence not only emotional behaviors, but also the quality of these behaviors. For example, the disruption of the thalamus has potential impact on emotions and behavior by impairing the thalamocortical projections, and the exact nature of these types of interconnections require further exploration.

Tucker and Williamson (1984) speculated that the underlying cognitive functional systems of the right hemisphere provide control mechanisms for the perceptual arousal system. As attention is regulated by these systems, an individual's emotional responsivity on the "depression–elation" and/or hypervigilance dimensions is determined. Disruption of these regulatory systems likely will contribute to variability in an individual's emotional tone and responsiveness. In contrast, although not without some involvement in the generation of emotion, the left hemisphere apparently maintains cognitive homeostasis via its language specialization and propositional qualities. Furthermore, Tucker and Williamson asserted that

these hemispheric asymmetries likely are related to asymmetries of pharmacological systems (i.e., left hemisphere being more cholinergic and
dopaminergic and the right being more noradrenergic), and that these
neurotransmitter systems must be included in any model of emotional
functioning.

This model holds promise with respect to increasing our understanding of normal and abnormal emotional functioning. The complexity of this
model via its involvement of a multitude of neurobiological systems (i.e.,
cortical, subcortical, neurotransmitters) contributes to its robust nature
and would seem to lend itself nicely to developmental psychopathology.
However, its application to children and adolescents remains unknown at
this time, although efforts to apply a developmental perspective have been
advanced (Tucker, 1991). In particular, the discussion of neurotransmitters
in the evolution of emotional function and dysfunction, and their interrelationships with cortical and subcortical regions, necessitates the study of
children with anxiety symptoms and anxiety disorders over a longitudinal
course.

3.3. Kinsbourne's Model

Another model to be considered also will require further substantia-
tion, particularly with respect to its application to children. Kinsbourne
and Bemporad (1984) and, more recently, Kinsbourne (1989) presented a
model of emotional control in which they proposed emotions to be "inter-
polated at strategic points in the basic blueprint of cognitive activity" (pp.
248–249). Using an approach–avoidance paradigm, Kinsbourne attributed approach behaviors to activation of the left hemisphere, whereas
avoidance behaviors were attributed to the right. Furthermore, he attributed the ongoing behavior of the individual to the activity of selected
regions in the left hemisphere and orientation to interruptions of this
activity to the right hemisphere.

According to Kinsbourne's model, the left frontal cortex tends to be
responsible for formulating plans, whereas the left posterior cortex maintains the information necessary for the outcome of the plans. During such
actions, the left hemisphere inhibits any emotional responsiveness that
might be propagated by the right. However, if the posterior regions of the
left hemisphere do not contain the necessary information to complete the
plan, or if there is any other kind of interruption, then the left hemisphere
activity can be superseded by the right hemisphere. In general, this model
suggests that the left hemisphere tends to be more responsible for action
control than emotional control, with the converse being true for the right
hemisphere. In addition, Kinsbourne asserted that the limbic system is

likely involved in the reorganization of the reception and expression of a variety of emotions following a lesion or, perhaps, a neurodevelopmental impairment. This model appears to have significant promise, but it is clear that additional work must be done, especially in its application to children and adolescents.

3.4. Rourke's Nonverbal Learning Disability Model

Although Rourke (1989) has popularized the nonverbal learning disability model, early descriptions by Johnson and Myklebust (1971) over two decades ago provided preliminary descriptions of these children. They stated that children with this disorder typically were unable to comprehend the significance of many aspects of the environment, could not pretend and anticipate, and failed to learn and appreciate the implications of actions such as gestures, facial expressions, caresses, and other elements of emotion. Johnson and Myklebust noted that this disorder constituted a fundamental distortion of the total perceptual experience of the child. They labeled this a *social perception disability*, and Myklebust (1975) later coined the term *nonverbal learning disability*. Although this linkage to brain damage/dysfunction had been emergent in the adult literature (e.g., Ross & Mesulam, 1979), it remained for Denckla (1983) to make the comparison of these children to adults with right hemisphere involvement. She described this group of children as experiencing a social (emotional) learning disability.

Unlike the activation/release models proffered by Gray (1982), Tucker (1989), and Kinsbourne (1989), Rourke (1989) has proposed a model that is psychometrically as opposed to neurologically derived. It is based on selected aspects of a neuropsychologically based learning disability subtype model, and on a theory of differential hemispheric functioning advanced by Goldberg and Costa (1981). With respect to the latter, relying primarily on data and speculative evidence derived from adult samples, Goldberg and Costa asserted that the right hemisphere is relatively more specialized for intermodal integration, whereas the left hemisphere is more specialized for intramodal integration. Neuroanatomically, these investigators postulated that intramodal integration may be related to a higher ratio of gray matter (i.e., neuronal mass and short nonmyelinated fibers) to white matter (i.e., long myelinated fibers) characteristic of the left hemisphere, whereas intermodal integration may be related to the lower ratio characteristic of the right hemisphere.

Rourke extended this model by applying a developmental perspective and, given his previous findings with respect to learning disability subtypes (e.g., see Rourke, 1985), extended it to account for nonverbal learning disabilities. Rourke hypothesized that involvement of the white matter of the right hemisphere (i.e., lesioned, excised, or dysfunctional white matter) interacts with developmental parameters, resulting in nonverbal learning disabilities. He reasoned that although a significant lesion in the right hemisphere may be sufficient to produce a nonverbal learning disability, it is the destruction of white matter (i.e., matter associated with intermodal functions) that is necessary to produce these types of learning disabilities. Furthermore, it is important to note that the white matter fibers are an integral part of the three principal neural axes: commissural fibers (right-to-left interhemispheric connections), association fibers (anterior-to-posterior intrahemispheric connections), and projection fibers (superior-to-inferior connections). Generally, the nonverbal learning disability syndrome would be expected to develop under any circumstance that interferes significantly with the functioning of right hemispheric functional systems or with access to those systems (e.g., agenesis of the corpus callosum). Functionally, the characteristics of such an individual, which Rourke noted should be observable by approximately ages 7 to 9 years (Rourke, Young, & Leenaars, 1989), implicate neuropsychological, academic, and social-emotional/adaptive domains.

Neuropsychologically, individuals with nonverbal learning disabilities tend to present a distinct profile of strengths and weaknesses. Relative strengths include auditory perception, simple motor functions, and intact rote verbal learning. Selective auditory attention, phonological skills, and auditory–verbal memory also appear intact. Neuropsychological deficits include bilateral tactile-perception problems and motor difficulties that usually are more marked on the left than on the right side of the body, visual–spatial organization problems, and nonverbal problem-solving difficulties. Paralinguistic aspects of language also are impaired (e.g., prosody, pragmatics).

Academically, these individuals evidence adequate word decoding and spelling, with most spelling errors reflecting good phonetic equivalents. Graphomotor skills eventually appear age-appropriate but are delayed early in development. Marked academic deficits tend to be manifested in mechanical arithmetic, mathematical reasoning, and reading comprehension. Academic subject areas, such as science, also tend to be impaired, largely due to reading comprehension deficiencies and deficits in nonverbal problem solving.

Perhaps one of the most interesting aspects associated with this syndrome is that there appears to be a strong relationship with social–emotional and adaptive behavior deficits. These individuals present great difficulty adapting to novel situations and manifest poor social perception and judgment. These difficulties, in turn, result in poor social-interaction skills. There appears to be a marked tendency for these individuals to engage in social withdrawal and social isolation as age increases and, consequently, they tend to be at risk for internalized forms of psychopathology such as depression and anxiety. In fact, Rourke et al. (1989) and Bigler (1989) noted the increased risk that these individuals have for clinical depression and suicide. Earlier work by Potter and Rourke (1985), and more recently by Fuerst, Fisk, and Rourke (1990), also suggest the possible linkage of this model to children with anxiety disorders.

Rourke proposed this model as an approximation of a developmental neuropsychological model for nonverbal learning disabilities. Given its neuropsychological base, this model is noteworthy, particularly as it may contribute to conceptualizations of differential diagnosis and, perhaps, to issues of severity. One of the major contributions of this model is the conjecture that social–emotional disturbances, particularly internalizing types of disorders (e.g., anxiety, depression), typically are associated with this neuropsychological pattern. Although ongoing examination of these hypotheses is required, this model provides the opportunity to study the interaction between neurological and neuropsychological interactions as they may be contributing, directly and/or indirectly, to manifestations of internalizing forms of psychopathology.

4.   Findings in Selected Categories of Child Psychopathology

This section provides a review of neurodiagnostic findings in major categories of child psychopathology. Included here are findings pertaining to childhood schizophrenia, pervasive developmental disorders, attention-deficit/hyperactivity disorder, conduct disorders, depression, anxiety disorders, and Tourette syndrome. With this we will return to the question of specificity, that is, the extent to which different patterns of brain dysfunction are associated with specific types of psychopathology.

4.1.   Schizophrenia

Netley, Lockyer, and Greenbaum (1975) postulated that neurological involvement is a necessary antecedent for the development of childhood schizophrenia, and Bloom (1993) has postulated that the appearance of schizophrenia is related to neurodevelopmental deviation in cortical neurons. Although overall IQ reportedly falls within the average range (Russell, Bott, & Sammons, 1989), children within this category have been found to show a greater frequency of soft neurological signs (Hertzig & Walker, 1975; Owens & Johnstone, 1980), abnormal EEGs (Netley et al., 1975), histories of perinatal complications (Torrey, Hersh, & McCabe, 1975) and, when compared to other psychiatric subjects, they tend to show a greater degree of generalized cognitive impairment (Carter, Alpert, & Stewart, 1982).

A great deal of attention has been given to identifying the early developmental precursors of schizophrenia in high-risk populations, such as the offspring of schizophrenic parents. These children have been found to show a greater frequency of nonspecific neurological signs (Erlenmeyer-Kimling et al., 1982; Marcus, Hans, Mednick, Schulsinger, & Michelson, 1985), although some investigators have cited mild dyscoordination and hyperactivity as occurring most frequently (Rieder & Nichols, 1979). Furthermore, Fish (1977) reported three specific types of neurological abnormality that distinguished infants at risk for schizophrenia: abnormally quiet state; visual–motor problems, particularly on bimanual tasks; and decreased vestibular responsiveness.

For the most part, the evidence regarding specific neuropsychological features in childhood schizophrenia has been inconclusive. Whereas one study found that childhood schizophrenics differed from other psychiatric controls specifically in terms of Performance IQ (Carter et al., 1982), another study found that it was Verbal IQ that distinguished children at risk for schizophrenia from normal controls (Gruzelier, Mednick, & Schulsinger, 1979). More recently, however, frontal lobe involvement—specifically dorsolateral prefrontal cortex—has been postulated as contributing to the behavioral manifestations typically seen in childhood-onset schizophrenia (Park & Holzman, 1992; Ross, Radant, & Hommer, 1993). For example, the developmental sequence for smooth pursuit tracking abilities parallels neurointegrative development, particularly frontal lobe developmental patterns, and eye tracking abnormalities have been found in adolescents at risk for schizophrenia (Pavlidus, 1980). This supposition is important not only for its clear connection to the behavioral manifestations, such as illogical thinking, loose associations, and impaired attention, but it also could be traced to aberrant frontal myelination patterns during childhood and adolescence.

Relatedly, similar to the sparse neuropsychological evidence suggesting profile specificity, no clear localizing patterns have been found with respect to neurostructural and electrophysiological findings. One recent positron emission tomography (PET) study did show striking posterior right parietal hypometabolism in 11 unmedicated childhood-onset schizophrenics; however, these findings also were suspected as being related to the attentional deficiencies seen in these children (Gordon et al., in press).

4.2. Pervasive Developmental Disorders: Autistic Disorder

Of all of the pervasive developmental disorders, one of the most studied is autistic disorder or autism. Autism is a behavioral syndrome characterized by impairment in reciprocal social interactions, poor communication abilities, and a pronounced restriction of interests and activities. It is distinct from mental retardation, although the majority of children with autism carry a concurrent diagnosis of mental retardation (Folstein & Rutter, 1987). It is also distinct from a number of other childhood disorders, including schizophrenia (Green et al., 1984) and developmental receptive language disorder (Lincoln, Courchesne, Kilman, Elmasian, & Allen, 1988).

A variety of etiological processes for autism have been proposed, but none has gained widespread acceptance to date. However, regardless of the specific anomaly or etiology that is hypothesized, the general consensus is that some form of brain impairment is involved (Damasio & Maurer, 1978). Children with autism tend to have a significant prenatal or perinatal history and show a high rate of soft neurological signs (Jones & Prior, 1985). Garreau, Barthelemy, Sauvage, Leddet, and LeLord (1984) further noted that the presence of neurological impairment was associated with an earlier onset of autistic features. An increased incidence of seizure disorders has been found in this population, particularly with increasing age, with approximately 25–30% of children with autism developing seizures by adulthood (Deykin & MacMahon, 1979). However, this finding may be applicable mainly to cases with IQs below 70 (Bartak & Rutter, 1976).

A number of brain imaging studies have documented the presence of structural abnormalities in autism, although the precise findings have varied greatly. Some of these have identified left hemisphere defects and, in some cases, bilateral defects, particularly involving frontal and temporal regions (Gillberg & Svendsen, 1983; Maurer & Damasio, 1982). Findings suggestive of reversed asymmetry have been noted as well (e.g., Hier, LeMay, & Rosenberger, 1979). Other findings have included anomalies involving various subcortical structures, such as the basal ganglia (Jacobson, LeCouter, Howlin, & Rutter, 1988), brainstem (Gaffney, Kuperman, Tsai, & Minchin, 1988), and cerebellar regions (Courchesne, Yeung-Courchesne, Press, Hesselink, & Jernigan, 1988; Gaffney, Tsai, Kuperman, & Minchin, 1987). There also have been studies in which structural abnormalities were identified, but no specific localizable pattern emerged (e.g., Balottin et al., 1989; Caparulo et al., 1981). Other studies have found no structural abnormalities of any kind (e.g., Harcherik et al., 1985; Prior, Tress, Hoffman, & Boldt, 1984).

Electroencephalographic (EEG) abnormalities also have been identified, with a prevalence rate of 40–50% in one study (Tsai, Tsai, & August, 1985). The abnormalities generally have been varied, although a pattern consisting of excessive slow-wave activity and decreased alpha bilaterally has been reported (Cantor, Thatcher, Hrybyk, & Kaye, 1986). Small (1975) suggested that the presence of a normal EEG is associated with a higher IQ and a more favorable developmental course. Auditory and visual evoked potentials (EP) also have been observed to be impaired, with auditory processing capabilities evidently more impaired than visual processing (Courchesne, Lincoln, Kilman, & Galambos, 1985; DeMyer, Hingtgen, & Jackson, 1981). Moreover, Courchesne, Lincoln, Yeung-Courchesne, Elmasian, and Grillon (1989) have identified two endogenous components of EP, Nc and P3b, that appear to be associated with abnormal neural responses involving general cognition and attention to important external information.

Other assorted neurobiological findings have been reported. Using PET, Rumsey, Rapoport, and Sceery (1985) found diffusely elevated glucose utilization but no clear focal abnormalities among an adult sample. Coleman, Romano, Lapham, and Simon (1985) found no consistent differences in a postmortem cell count of selected left hemispheric regions between an adult with autism and a control subject. However, Bauman and Kemper (1985) found anatomical differences involving the forebrain and cerebellum in a postmortem comparison of a 29-year-old autistic man with that of a normal 25-year-old. The investigators suggested that the cerebellar abnormalities were of unknown etiology but probably were acquired early in development, possibly at or before 30-weeks gestation.

From a neuropsychological perspective, children with autism have been described as having poor motor imitation abilities (Jones & Prior, 1985); disproportionate impairment in sequential processing abilities (Tanguay, 1984); unusually narrow attention focus and problems shifting their attentional sets (Rumsey, Andreasen, & Rapoport, 1986); a variety of memory problems, including difficulties remembering noncontextualized information (Ameli, Courchesne, Lincoln, Kaufman, & Grillon, 1988) as well as the exceptional rote recall seen in many autistic savants (Lucci, Fein, Holevas, & Kaplan, 1988); deficits in language pragmatics (Dewey & Everard, 1974) and dysprosodies (Baltaxe & Simmons, 1983); nonverbal communication deficiencies, such as facial expression (Rumsey et al., 1986); general problem solving difficulties (Szatmari, Offord, Siegel, Finlayson, & Tuff, 1990); and academic achievement deficits (Minshew, Goldstein, Taylor, & Siegel, 1994). As a group, IQ scores tend to be significantly lower than normals but comparatively higher than children with mental retardation (Kagan, 1981). The neurocognitive profiles of children with autism also can be rather varied when compared to children with mental retardation (Fein, Waterhouse, Lucci, & Snyder, 1985), although a pattern indicative of better visual–perceptual abilities than language abilities typically has been asserted (e.g., Lincoln et al., 1988). Furthermore, Lincoln et al. suggested that this verbal-performance pattern may be less associated with autism than differences between rote and abstract reasoning, which may be especially salient in children with this disorder. In addition, the degree of language impairment appears to be strongly predictive of the child's prognosis (Wing, 1971). Although related to childhood language disorders, the communication deficits in children with autism are qualitatively different from those seen in developmental dysphasia or acquired aphasia (Arnold & Schwartz, 1983).

Additionally, many of the neuropsychological studies have been directed toward investigating the presence of lateralized deficits. The findings have included a reversal of ear advantage for speech sounds (i.e., left ear rather than right) on dichotic listening tasks (Blackstock, 1978; James & Barry, 1983; Prior & Bradshaw, 1979); increase prevalence rates of left and mixed handedness of about 20% and 34%, respectively (Soper et al., 1986); and performance profiles on neuropsychological test batteries suggestive of predominantly left hemispheric dysfunction (Appelbaum, Egel, Koegel, & Imhoff, 1979; Dawson, 1983; Hoffman & Prior, 1982). In a study by Dawson, Finley, Phillips, and Galpert (1986), there was evidence of an atypical pattern of hemispheric specialization, with about 70% of the sample showing right hemispheric dominance for speech. However, the investigators noted that many of the children exhibited bilateral rather than unilateral dysfunction, and they also speculated that the dysfunction might involve subcortical as well as cortical levels. This interpretation is consistent with the findings in some of the brain imaging studies reported earlier.

Overall, the research on autism provides a variable picture with respect to neurobiological and neuropsychological features. With the exception of aberrations in language development and communication skills, there is little agreement as to the neurodevelopmental features that are necessarily characteristic of this disorder. Some children with autism show significant anomalies in brain structure, whereas others do not. The same is true with respect to their neurophysiological and neuropsychological presentation. Although some children show evidence of lateralized dysfunction involving the left cerebral hemisphere, this by no means is a definitive characteristic of the syndrome (Fein, Humes, Kaplan, Lucci, & Waterhouse, 1984). However, although the precise mechanisms remain unclear, there probably is not another category of child psychopathology for which the evidence of a neurobiological foundation is more compelling than in the case of autism and, perhaps, other pervasive developmental disorders (e.g., Asperger's syndrome).

4.3. Attention-Deficit/Hyperactivity Disorder (ADHD)

This is another syndrome in which an organic etiology is commonly assumed, although the precise mechanisms are far from clear. Earlier thinking linked ADHD with minimal brain dysfunction (MBD) because of the purported behavioral similarities between children with ADHD and those with documented brain damage (Strauss & Lehtinen, 1947). However, problems in documenting the presence of underlying brain dysfunction (e.g., Rutter, 1983; Taylor, 1983) led to a more descriptive approach in conceptualizing the disorder. Children with ADHD have been characterized as showing inattention, impulsivity , and overactivity (Douglas, 1980, 1983); a deficit in self-directed instruction (Kendall & Broswell, 1985); poor self-regulation of arousal, particularly in meeting environmental demands (Douglas, 1983); and deficiencies in rule-governed behavior (Barkley, 1981a, 1981b).

There have been numerous debates over diagnostic criteria, issues of heterogeneity, and whether ADHD is truly distinguishable from other forms of disruptive behavior problems. Nonetheless, it has been one of the most commonly diagnosed child psychiatric disorders (Mattison et al., 1986). The current diagnostic criteria listed in the fourth edition of the *Diagnostic and Statistical Manual of Mental Disorders* (DSM-IV, American Psychiatric Association, 1994) recognizes three subtypes of ADHD: predominantly inattentive; predominantly hyperactive–impulsive; as well as a combined subtype.

There have been a number of theories regarding the neurological basis of ADHD (Riccio, Hynd, Cohen, & Gonzalez, 1993). To date, the evidence is strongest with respect to implicating frontal lobe dysfunction in the increased distractibility and impulsive orienting reactions to irrelevant stimuli often seen in children with ADHD (Passler, Isaac, & Hynd, 1986; Stuss & Benton, 1984; Zambelli, Stamm, Maitinsky, & Loiselle, 1977). Various specific patterns of localization have been proposed, including frontal regions anterior and medial to the precentral motor cortex (Mattes, 1980), as well as frontolimbic pathways (Lou, Henriksen, & Bruhn, 1984; Newlin & Tramontana, 1980).

There has been a clustering of findings specifically implicating right frontal dysfunction. Voeller and Heilman (1988) found ADHD children to be markedly deficient on a task of motor persistence, a deficit ordinarily associated with right frontal lobe impairment. In a subsequent study (Voeller, Alexander, Carter, & Heilman, 1989), the motor persistence of children with ADHD improved significantly with the administration of methylphenidate. Similarly, in a study of regional cerebral blood flow (Lou et al., 1984), children with ADHD exhibited lower perfusion rates in the region of the caudate, an anterior subcortical structure known to be involved in the motor regulatory system. Metabolic levels normalized with the administration of methylphenidate, and then declined as the medication wore off. A subsequent study by Lou, Henriksen, Bruhn, Borner, and Nielsen (1989) replicated the earlier findings, but pinpointed the right striatal region as specifically deficient in children with ADHD. As before, the administration of methylphenidate resulted in a normalization of metabolic activity. Some investigators have even shown gender differences, in brain metabolic activity, with females manifesting reduced global brain metabolism on PET (Ernst et al., 1994).

From a different perspective, Hynd, Semrud-Clikeman, Lorys, Novey, and Eliopulos (1990) found that ADHD children did not demonstrate the typical right frontal asymmetry on magnetic resonance imaging (MRI) found in normal controls. The finding lacked specificity, however, in that both ADHD and dyslexic cases had significantly smaller right frontal widths when compared to normal control children. Nonetheless, the right frontal region and left planum have been deemed highly predictive of group membership of children with dyslexia or attention deficits (Semrud-Clikeman et al., in press). Additional morphometric analyses have yielded findings suggesting smaller anterior and posterior regions (Semrud-Clikeman et al., 1994) of the corpus callosum in children with ADHD when compared to normal controls.

Barkley, Grodzinsky, and Du Paul (1992) have reviewed a total of 22 neuropsychological studies of frontal lobe functioning in children with attention deficit disorder, with and without hyperactivity. Tests of response inhibition were found to discriminate hyperactive cases from normals, although many measures presumed to assess frontal lobe dysfunction were not reliably sensitive to deficits in either ADD group. Numerous inconsistencies were noted, many of which were seen as due to methodological differences across studies.

4.4. Conduct Disorders

Research in this broad category of child psychopathology has been beset with a number of problems. First, as a diagnosis, it pertains to a very heterogeneous range of disturbances in which the manifestation of socially unacceptable behavior is the primary common feature. Second, the bulk of research has focused on adolescents, particularly the juvenile offender. If one excludes children with ADHD, little is known with respect to the neurological and neuropsychological features of conduct disorders manifested at early ages. Third, youngsters with conduct disorders have a higher risk for accidental head injury (Lewis & Shanok, 1977; Lewis, Pincus, & Glaser, 1979; Pincus & Tucker, 1978); thus, although neurological abnormalities may be seen on examination, they may be the product—not the cause—of the initial conduct disorder. This problem obviously is compounded by the emphasis on studying older as opposed to younger conduct-disordered subjects. With these limitations in mind, the findings for this general category of psychopathology are summarized here.

A number of studies have reported abnormal neurological findings in youngsters with conduct disorders (Elliott, 1982; Korhonen & Sillanpaa, 1976; Krynicki, 1978; Woods & Eby, 1982). Electrophysiological studies (Coble et al., 1984; Elliott, 1982; Krynicki, 1978; Luchins, 1983) have found EEG sleep abnormalities, specifically in the expression of slow-wave (delta) activity (Coble et al., 1984); seizure activity that may contribute to recurrent and unprovoked rage attacks (Elliott, 1982); and in some cases, frontal lobe paroxysmal activity, particularly in conduct-disordered adolescents with a significant history of assaultive behavior (Krynicki, 1978). The later finding bears some relationship to the work of Woods and Eby (1982) and Pontius and Ruttiger (1976), who postulated a delay in the development of normal inhibitory mechanisms (i.e., frontal lobe functions) in repetitively aggressive youngsters.

Children with conduct disorders have been reported to show a higher incidence of episodes of disturbed consciousness and, as already noted, to suffer more head injuries than other children (see Lewis & Shanok, 1977; Lewis et al., 1979; Pincus & Tucker, 1978). However, they have not been found to differ from normal controls in terms of perinatal problems, except for more frequently being small for gestational age (McGee, Silva, & Williams, 1984). These findings further serve to suggest that the neurological features in some of these children may postdate the initial onset of their conduct disorders.

Conduct-disordered youngsters have been found to have a high rate of learning disabilities (Cannon & Compton, 1980; Robbins, Beck, Pries, Jacobs, & Smith, 1983; Zinkus & Gottlieb, 1978), as well as more generalized problems with language performance (Funk & Ruppert, 1984; Stellern, Marlowe, Jacobs, & Cossairt, 1985; Wardell & Yeudall, 1980). This appears to apply to both nonincarcerated (Robbins et al., 1983) as well as incarcerated (Cannon & Compton, 1980) populations. These findings suggest that the presence of cognitive impairments, perhaps particularly of a verbal nature, places the youngster at risk for acting out impulsively when placed in frustrating or provocative social situations. The degree of impulsivity *per se* is unrelated to either the type or the number of crimes committed by delinquent youth (Oas, 1985). Rather, it may be that the presence of faulty capacities in verbal reasoning and judgment, along with impulsivity, are the necessary ingredients in the production of chronic antisocial conduct. Thus, although unrelated to the degree of impulsivity, the presence of at least a 15-point inferiority in Verbal IQ versus Performance IQ on the Wechsler Intelligence Scale for Children—Revised (WISC-R) was found to be predictive of recidivism in adjudicated white delinquent boys (Haynes & Bensch, 1981).

Some studies have examined the relative effects of language and executive function deficits. Linz, Hooper, Hynd, Isaac, and Gibson (1990) selected 20 adolescents meeting DSM-III criteria for conduct disorder from a juvenile evaluation center and compared them to 20 normal adolescents on nine Lurian tasks measuring behaviors attributed to frontal lobe functioning. Differences were obtained on the verbal conflict and verbal retroactive inhibition tasks, although these disappeared when controlling for receptive vocabulary. Cole, Usher, and Cargo (1993) examined the relationship between cognitive factors and risk for disruptive behavior disorders in a sample of 82 preschoolers. Verbal, visuospatial, and executive function abilities were examined in terms of their relationship with labeling emotions and behavioral control. Difficulties in both verbal and visuospatial processes were associated with a higher risk for behavioral difficulties. Additionally, whereas verbal abilities contributed to the prediction of emotion-labeling accuracy, executive functions were predictive of behavioral control. The latter study was noteworthy also for the examination of behavioral risk in a younger sample.

Further investigations into the pattern of neuropsychological deficits in conduct disorders have produced mixed results. Berman and Siegal (1976) found that delinquents performed more poorly than normal controls on virtually every task of the Halstead–Reitan Battery. Whereas prominent deficits were observed in tasks requiring verbal mediation, concept formation, and perceptual organization, only minimal difficulties were found in memory and gross motor coordination. Brickman, McManus, Grapentine, and Alessi (1984) found that more violent youth tended to show more impairment on the Luria–Nebraska Neuropsychological Battery (LNNB) than their nonviolent counterparts, with Expressive Speech and Memory being the distinguishing summary scales. This was true with respect to both male and female offenders. These findings were similar to the results of earlier studies with delinquent populations by Lewis, Shanok, and Pincus (1982) and Voorhees (1981), and generally consistent with more recent results by Warr-Leeper, Wright, and Mack (1994) using antisocial boys carrying the diagnoses of oppositional defiant disorder or conduct disorder. Hooper and Brown (1995) showed language problems to be prominent in a well-defined sample of children and adolescents with aggressive assaultive conduct disorders. These findings were robust even when controlling for a large number of variables including history of abuse, documented drug and alcohol abuse, extended hospitalizations, special education needs, ADHD, and a variety of demographic variables. However, in controlling for the presence of psychosis and a history of neurological disorder, Tarter, Hagedus, Alterman, and Katz-Garris (1983) failed to find differences in neuropsychological, intellectual, and psychoeducational performance across groups of adolescent offenders differing with respect to their type of offense (i.e., violent, nonviolent, sexual).

The previously noted problems limit the generalizations that one can make with respect to this category of child psychopathology. It is probably fair to say that, as a group, youngsters with conduct disorders, especially those with aggressive assaultive tendencies, have more limited verbal abilities and a heightened rate of neurological signs (these, however, may arise secondarily as consequences of their behavior disorders). With the possible exception of cases with prominent histories of repetitive, assaultive behavior, the specific role of neurological factors in conduct disorders remains unclear.

4.5. Depression

MacAuslan (1975) reported that children with depression have an increased frequency of neurological soft signs when compared to normal controls. Furthermore, Shaffer et al. (1985) noted that adolescents with early soft signs were more likely to have a psychiatric disorder characterized by symptoms such as anxiety, withdrawal, and depression. Additionally, social isolation rather than aggression is more likely to be a persistent problem in children with physical disabilities secondary to brain damage (see Breslau & Marshall, 1985) and, although debated (Szatmari et al., 1990), internalizing rather than externalizing symptoms have been found to be more clearly tied to neuropsychological impairment in psychiatrically hospitalized boys (Tramontana, Hooper, & Nardolillo, 1988). Also, apart from gross social disinhibition, depression was the only psychiatric symptom that bore a specific relationship to lesion localization in the series of studies on head injury conducted by Rutter (1983). Thus, depression appears to be an important feature of the brain-impaired child, perhaps especially in terms of long-range outcomes.

Much of the neuropsychological investigation into childhood depression has focused specifically on the question of lateralization of dysfunction. Research demonstrating the specialized role of right cerebral hemisphere in the reception of human emotion and affective cues, along with reports of right hemispheric dysfunction (Tucker, 1980) and decreased lateral prefrontal cortex metabolism (Baxter, Schwartz, & Phelps, 1989) in adults suffering from depression, prompted inquiries into the existence of such relationships in children. A number of studies have reported impaired nonverbal abilities relative to verbal abilities in children with depression.

For example, Kaslow, Rehm, and Siegel (1984) found that higher scores on the Children's Depression Inventory (CDI) were associated with poor performance on the WISC-R subtests of Block Design, Coding, and Digit Span in a mixed group of childhood depressives. No significant relationships were found for WISC-R Vocabulary or the Trail Making Test of the Halstead–Reitan Battery. Blumberg and Izard (1985) found a similar pattern of results using the Peabody Picture Vocabulary Test and WISC-R Block Design, with the CDI again serving as the index of depression. In both studies, girls were found to perform more poorly than boys on Block Design. Children of bipolar probands likewise have been found to show a disproportionate inferiority in Performance IQ relative to Verbal IQ when compared to normal controls (Decina et al., 1983). However, the fact that left-handedness was overrepresented in their sample of children at risk for affective disorder would tend to argue against an inference of right hemispheric dysfunction. More generally, the findings in the preceding studies constitute very weak evidence of lateralized right hemispheric dysfunction. The obtained pattern of results simply may reflect the differential sensitivity of performance measures to the effects of depressed concentration and motor speed, and lethargic organization and planning.

Several studies have reported improvements on neuropsychological measures suggestive of both right hemispheric and frontal lobe dysfunction subsequent to treatment with antidepressant medication (Brumback, Staton, & Wilson, 1980; Staton, Wilson, & Brumback, 1981; Wilson & Staton, 1984). Specifically, Staton et al. (1981) found that remission of melancholic symptoms was associated with improved performance on WISC-R Similarities, Comprehension, Block Design, and Coding, as well as on the Matching Familiar Figures Test, the Category Test of the Halstead–Reitan Battery, and the Visual Reception Subtest of the Illinois Test of Psycholinguistic Abilities. Although the localizing significance of this pattern of results is uncertain, two children in the study reportedly had a mild left-sided motor deficits that also seemed to improve subsequent to antidepressant treatment. The latter finding, if replicated, would constitute more convincing evidence of improvement in lateralized dysfunction.

A number of electrophysiological studies have been reported as well. Rochford, Weinapple, and Goldstein (1981) found greater EEG variance in the right hemisphere than in the left in a heterogeneous group of depressed adolescents. This pattern was distinct from that of normal controls, who demonstrated about equal hemispheric variance, and from adolescents with paranoid symptomatology, who exhibited greater variance in the left hemisphere. However, Knott, Waters, Lapierre, and Gray (1985) found no evidence of specific hemispheric abnormalities in a comparison of EEG patterns and auditory-evoked potentials in matched pairs of siblings discordant for affective disorder. They did find that the bipolar group spent less time in EEG alpha, suggesting a hyperarousal of the nervous system in this form of affective disorder. EEG abnormalities in rapid-eye-movement (REM) sleep latencies also have been described in depressed adolescents, although this finding has not been documented in prepubescent children (Mendlewicz, Hoffman, Kerkhofs, & Linkowski, 1984).

Sackeim, Decina, and Malitz (1982) reviewed much of the earlier literature pertaining to functional brain asymmetry and affective disorders. They concluded that affective disorders, particularly unipolar depression, tend to be associated with right hemispheric cognitive dysfunction and/or electrophysiological overactivation. In contrast, bipolar patients may evidence right- or left-sided hemispheric hyperactivation, depending on whether the individual is experiencing a depressive (right hemisphere) or manic (left hemisphere) episode. These assertions will require further validation with child and adolescent subjects. Although adult patients with depression reportedly have shown reduced volume of the putamen nuclei (Husain et al., 1991), decreased glucose metabolic activity in the frontal lobes and basal ganglia (Baxter et al., 1989; Buchsbaum, Wu, & DeLisi, 1986), and decreased metabolic activity in the cingulate and thalamus, particularly in bipolar patients (Baxter et al., 1989), such findings have yet to be found in children or adolescents. Botteron, Vannier, Geller, Todd, and Lee (1995) recently presented preliminary MRI findings on a small sample of children and adolescents with mania. These findings suggested the presence of ventricular abnormalities, with temporal horn enlargement or asymmetry, and some subcortical hyperintensities; however, these findings clearly will require replication with larger samples.

Another perspective comes from the model of nonverbal learning disability of Rourke and associates noted earlier, and its relationship to internalizing forms of psychopathology. Rather than lateralized dysfunction, per se, nonverbal learning disabilities are seen as more directly related to the extent of white matter disruption present. Lateralized findings may be explained, however, owing to the higher ratio of white matter to gray matter in the right versus left hemisphere (Rourke, 1987), and the general increase of this ratio from the period of late childhood through adolescence (Jernigan, Trauner, & Hesselink, 1991).

4.6. Anxiety Disorders

The relationship between anxiety and neuropsychological factors is complex. Much of the discussion of anxiety within the context of neuropsychological functioning has dealt with the disruptive effects it may exert on formal test performance. Thus, anxiety may be viewed as a source of interference contributing to false-positive diagnosis or invalid inferences of neuropsychological deficit, especially in situations with high base rates of psychiatric disorder (Tramontana, 1983).

Alternatively, anxiety may arise as a secondary reaction in situations in which a child's deficits are challenged or brought to the fore (Tramontana & Hooper, 1989). For example, a language-impaired child may react with avoidance or withdrawal in situations requiring spoken communication. In this case, the anxiety is symptomatic of a breakdown in the child's ability to cope effectively with his or her deficits. The child's actual performance may suffer from disruptive or distracting emotional reactions. Worse yet, the underlying deficits may become compounded in time if the child's anxiety leads to a chronic avoidance of appropriate learning and stimulation experiences.

Efforts specifically designed to assess the impact of anxiety on specific neurocognitive functions in children and adolescents are only beginning to be discussed. For example, Benjamin, Costello, and Warren (1990) reported that teachers rated children with anxiety disorders as having increased school dysfunction, suggesting the possible presence of an increased rate of learning disabilities in their children. In a more detailed study, Frost, Moffitt, and McGee (1989) examined members of a birth cohort at age 13. Individuals were grouped into a single-disorder group, a multiple-disorder group, and a no-disorder group, and they were assessed for psychopathology and neuropsychological dysfunction. As might have been expected, the multiple-disorder group showed the highest rate of neuropsychological dysfunction and performed significantly worse than the no-disorder group across verbal, visuospatial, verbal memory, and visual–motor neuropsychological parameters. More specifically, these investigators found their anxiety-disorder group to perform significantly worse than the no-disorder group on the visual–motor integration factor. There were no other neuropsychological differences noted between the anxiety-disorder group and the other groups.

The identification of neuropsychological patterns in children and adolescents with anxiety disorders is only beginning to be pursued, with available neuropsychological findings relating only to several of the anxiety disorders: obsessive–compulsive disorder and post-traumatic stress disorder. Additional emergent neuropsychological findings on other anxiety disorders also will be mentioned.

4.6.1. Obsessive–Compulsive Disorder

Studies investigating the neuropsychological correlates of child and adolescent obsessive–compulsive disorder have presented mixed findings. Kaufman (1979) reported lower WISC-R Performance IQ in patients with obsessive–compulsive disorder when compared to matched controls. Kaufman observed that many of these patients exhibited cognitive rigidity in their problem solving, and that their incessant need to check and recheck their efforts interfered with the efficiency of their performance and, ultimately, with their obtained scores on timed tests (i.e., subtests on the WISC-R Performance Scale). Furthermore, Rapoport, Elkins, and Langer (1981) observed that these children failed to demonstrate the expected right ear advantage on a dichotic listening task and, although visual–perceptual abilities were largely intact, they demonstrated impairment in planning and efficiently evaluating their behavior. Consistent with the adult literature (e.g., Flor-Henry, 1979), Rapoport interpreted these findings as implicating frontal and dominant hemispheric functions.

More recent studies have implicated frontal lobe involvement and basal ganglia dysfunction (Behar et al., 1984; Cox, Fedio, & Rapoport, 1989), whereas other studies have generated findings showing visual–spatial deficits and left hemibody signs suggestive of possible right hemisphere involvement (Behar et al., 1984; Cox et al., 1989). In particular, Behar et al. (1984) demonstrated significantly higher ventricular-brain ratios and a greater frequency of age-inappropriate synkinesias in their patients when compared to a matched control group. Memory, reaction time, and decision time did not differ from their normal counterparts (Behar et al., 1984). Furthermore, neuropsychological findings indicative of subtle deficits in visual–spatial abilities and visual memory, with intact verbal memory, attention, intelligence, and frontal lobe abilities, have been documented in adults (Boone, Ananth, Philpott, Kaur, & Djenderedjian, 1991). Another study has raised concerns for planning and organizational abilities of children with obsessive–compulsive disorder, and has made suggestions of linkages to trichotillomania (Rettew et al., 1991). These assertions also will require further study.

Obsessive–compulsive disorder has been linked to neurological dysfunction in adults, primarily implicating EEG abnormalities over the temporal lobes—consistent with temporal lobe epilepsy (Jenike, 1984; Jenike & Brotman, 1984), and disturbances in the interconnections of the basal ganglia, thalamus, and orbitofrontal and anterior cingulate cortex (Alarcon, Libb, & Boll, 1994; Modell, Mountz, Curtis, & Gredens, 1989; Wise & Rapoport, 1989). There also were findings suggestive of possible right hemispheric dysfunction (visual–spatial deficits; left hemibody signs), larger ventricular-brain ratios on computerized tomography (CT), and a greater frequency of age-inappropriate synkinesias when compared to matched controls. These neuroanatomical associations remain to be examined in children with obsessive–compulsive disorder.

4.6.2. Post-Traumatic Stress Disorder

Post-traumatic stress disorder (PTSD) is an especially noteworthy area of emerging interest. As in other areas, much of the neuropsychological investigation to date has been specifically with adults. One study, for example, compared the attention and memory performance of military personnel with and without PTSD (Vasterling, Root, Brailey, Uddo, & Sutker, 1994). Those with PTSD were impaired on tasks of attention and mental control, especially when a visual component was involved. Poor organization on a constructional task and a greater susceptibility to proactive interference in verbal learning also were noted. The findings were seen as consistent with neurobiological models of PTSD emphasizing the role of hyperarousal and frontal-subcortical systems. Other findings have specifically related extreme stress with damage to the hippocampus and with associated deficits in memory function. Bremner et al. (1995) found that Vietnam combat veterans had a statistically significant 8% smaller right hippocampal volume on MRI relative to a matched comparison group. Deficits in short-term verbal memory were also noted. Similarly, Shiffer, Teicher, and Papanicolaou (1995) reported significant left-dominant auditory evoked potential asymmetry for neutral memories in patients with a history of childhood traumas; however, this dominant asymmetry shifted to the right during the unpleasant memory. Normal control subjects did not show such a shift on either task.

Taken together, the implication is that some of the memory disturbances seen in PTSD result from experientially induced structural changes are not merely the product of defensive processes. This is an exciting line of inquiry that we hope will be extended to victims of child abuse and trauma as well.

4.6.3. Other Anxiety Disorders

To date, there have been precious few other studies conducted to examine the neuropsychological functioning of children and/or adolescents with various types of anxiety disorder or manifesting selective types of anxious symptoms. For example, there have been no efforts in the pediatric literature devoted to examining neuropsychological and/or neurobiological issues in social phobias, simple phobias, separation anxiety, panic disorder, or avoidant disorder. Furthermore, although some initial neurocognitive correlates have been advanced for children and adolescents with elective mutism, largely involving speech and language deficits, the relatively small prevalence of this disorder has hindered group investigations of these claims (Hooper & Linz, 1992). At present, one study has been done with children and adolescents with conversion disorder, and emergent information is available on panic disorder.

Regan and LaBarbera (1984) presented case study evidence indicating a strong lateralization of symptoms in conversion disorders in hospitalized child and adolescent patients. Interestingly, this is in direct opposition to the adult literature in which symptoms are typically manifested on the nondominant side of the body. Regan and LaBarbera speculated that there may be a developmental component in the manifestation of conversion phenomena. In the adult, the nondominant or right hemisphere has been recognized as the primary mediator of emotional content that, in turn, determines somatic manifestations. In the child, these functions may still be mediated, in part, by the dominant hemisphere, and consequently the conversion symptoms may be associated with the dominant side of the body.

With respect to panic disorder, neurologically based theories have been emergent (e.g., George & Ballenger, 1992), largely implicating the right parahippocampal region and related biological findings (e.g., those implicating neuroendocrine and sleep-related abnormalities; Roy-Byme, Mellman, & Uhde, 1988); however, none of these conjectures has been applied to children. Neuropsychological findings suggesting selective memory deficits (Norton, Schaefer, Cox, Dorward, & Wozney, 1988), and problems with visual learning, visual recall, and verbal recall (Lucas, Telch, & Bigler, 1991) have been documented with adult panic disorder patients, and these findings hold much promise for the understanding the panic problems seen in children and adolescents.

4.7. Tourette's Syndrome

Unlike many conditions, such as cerebral palsy, Tourette's syndrome usually occurs in individuals who seem to be within normal limits neurologically, and who have evidenced no signs of motor dysfunction (Bruun, 1988). Although a specific etiology of this disorder has yet to be uncovered, current thinking suggests that it is a neurological disorder (Devinsky, 1983), with a major neurophysiological component (Glaze, Frost, & Jankovic, 1983). Others have suggested that Tourette's syndrome is dominated by a neurochemical disturbance that impacts cortical and subcortical functioning.

For example, Comings (1990) cited evidence suggesting that many of the behaviors exhibited by individuals with Tourette's syndrome can be explained by abnormalities in the dopaminergic pathways. The model by Comings (1990) involves dopaminergic neuron sites in the midbrain and the associated ventral tegmental and substantia nigra regions. These neuron sites fuel ascending pathways to the anterior cingulate gyrus, various limbic structures, and selected nuclei of the thalamus (Iversen & Alpert, 1982). Descending pathways to the locus coeruleus also are in operation (Deutch, Goldstein, & Roth, 1986). In particular, connecting pathways located in the right frontal regions have been hypothesized to be responsible for the disinhibitory features characteristic of this disorder, whereas the presence of motor and vocal tics potentially implicates hypersensitivity of pathways to the limbic system and subcortical components (e.g., basal ganglia). Many of these neuroanatomical structures (e.g., basal ganglia, substantia nigra) have been implicated in other movement disorders, such as Parkinson's disease, Huntington's disease, and tardive dyskinesia. Other neurotransmitters have been implicated (e.g., serotonin), but the pathophysiology of these mechanisms remains less clear.

With respect to neurostructural findings, Leckman and Cohen (1988) noted that CT scan procedures have not proven useful with this population—a finding echoed by others (Harcherick et al., 1985). Several other investigators, however, have documented abnormal computed axial tomography (CAT) scan findings in their samples. Caparulo et al. (1981) noted that approximately 38% of their patients had abnormal CT scans, but none showed localizing or lateralizing findings. Kjaer, Boris, and Hansen (1986) presented a case report of a female patient with Tourette's syndrome who had a large porencephalic cyst located in the right temporal–parietal region with concomitant involvement of the basal ganglia and thalamic structures. In an adult population, PET has revealed evidence of hypermetabolism in the frontal and temporal regions. Hypermetabolism also was noted in the cingulate gyrus and inferior corpus striatum, both of which contain dopamine neurons (Chase et al., 1984). Only one postmortem case has been reported (Singer, Tune, Butler, Zaczek, & Coyle, 1982), and no abnormalities were described.

Shapiro, Shapiro, Bruun, and Sweet (1978), and others (Volkmar et al., 1984) described approximately a 40% rate of EEG abnormalities (i.e., increased slow wave and posterior spikes) and nonlocalizing neurological signs in a small number of individuals with tic disorder. Generally, these investigators indicated that the EEG abnormalities were not diagnostic of Tourette's syndrome, although Comings (1990) argued that selected EEG patterns might be useful in distinguishing the child with Tourette's syndrome who is evidencing explosive temper outbursts.

At present, no consistent pattern of neuropsychological deficits has emerged that characterizes this disorder. Whereas some investigators have identified specific neurocognitive impediments (e.g., Ferrari, Matthews, & Barabas, 1984; Incagnoli & Kane, 1983), others have suggested a more heterogeneous clinical profile. For example, Ferrari et al. (1984) found that many of the individuals in their sample evidenced visual–spatial and visual–motor deficits, and other cognitive abilities were relatively intact (e.g., language). More recent studies of larger and more rigorously defined samples have suggested that the majority of children with Tourette's syndrome fall within normal limits on neuropsychological testing, with only a small percentage of children showing neuropsychological impairment (Bornstein, 1990). In fact, Yeates and Bornstein (1992) presented evidence suggesting that the presence of neuropsychological deficits in children with Tourette's syndrome may be related more to the influence of comorbid psychiatric conditions (e.g., obsessive–compulsive disorder, ADHD) than to any direct effects of Tourette's syndrome.

5. Ongoing Issues and Concerns

As can be seen, from the human laterality studies, proposed models, and categorical findings to date, much has been learned about the neurological basis of child psychopathology; however, several ongoing issues continue to persist for clinicians and researchers in this area of interest.

First, it would seem that the field continues to be plagued by changing definitions in diagnostic categories, such as in autism and attention-deficit/hyperactivity disorder. Although striving for more precision in diagnosis is laudable, the changes create enormous problems when trying to compare across studies. Relatedly, studies addressing dimensional classification systems (e.g., internalized, externalized) might prove useful as well, and few studies have utilized this strategy when examining neuropsychological correlates and characteristics. Some notable examples do exist, however, and these should be applauded (e.g., McBurnett et al., 1993).

Second, the plethora of assessment issues inherent in the field of neuropsychology, especially developmental neuropsychology, manifests itself in the domain of child psychopathology. Although neuropsychological assessment appears to have key relevance to increasing our understanding of a psychiatric population, as well as the developmental unfolding of emotional reception and expression, the varied assessment technologies contribute to measurement issues and subsequent comparison problems across studies.

The application of newer assessment models, such as the factor-based models of attention (Mirsky et al., 1991) and executive functioning (Welsh & Pennington, 1988), also set the stage for understanding how the sub-components of these multidimensional constructs will be manifested in different forms of psychopathology. For example, Rumsey (1992) has hypothesized the differential manifestation of attentional components in autistic disorder using the Mirsky model of attention. As may be self-evident from this example, these assessment models will contribute to more precise hypothesis testing with a child psychiatric population, and they may implicate different kinds of clinical intervention based on selected findings.

Third, it remains paramount for a developmental perspective to be maintained when examining the interface between neuropsychology and psychopathology. The studies by Davidson and colleagues (Davidson, 1994) and Dawson (1994) are exemplary here. Dawson's studies are especially noteworthy in that she has raised questions invoking a developmental transactional model for brain functioning and emotional responsivity, and her work begs the question of specific types of intervention that might be clinically relevant at an early age with respect to possibly mediating the emergence of psychopathology at a later age. Much of the available work does not invoke a developmental perspective, however, and the field would benefit from increased activities in this vein. In fact, the interface between neuropsychology and child psychopathology will require better integration between developmental literature, neurological/neuropsychological science, and child psychopathology.

6. Conclusions

This chapter has provided an overview of many of the advances that have emerged over the past several decades with respect to the neuropsychology of child psychopathology. A brief overview of trends and findings from the human laterality studies was provided, and discussion pertaining to a number of proposed neuropsychologically based models was provided. Neurobiological findings pertinent to specific diagnostic categories of child psychopathology also were presented in detail.

At present, it would seem that there are indeed strong neurological contributions to the expression and reception of emotions. Although the precise mechanisms involved remain open for continued debate, it does seem that the current literature would support the premise that posterior regions of the right hemisphere remain primary for the reception of emotional material, whereas the expression of emotions appears to be differentially modulated by frontal regions, that is, approach-type emotions being modulated by the left hemisphere and avoidance-type emotions being modulated by the right hemisphere. Additionally, these findings appear to be present in the newborn, and they may be modifiable by environmental conditions. Furthermore, a variety of neuropsychological models have been proposed to date, with notable contributions coming from Gray (1982), Tucker (1989), Kinsbourne (1989), and Rourke (1989).

Finally, although it is abundantly clear that the presence of psychopathology heightens the risk and/or presence of brain dysfunction (Rutter, 1983), there appears to be little evidence of specificity in the type or pattern of brain dysfunction associated with different categories of child psychopathology. For example, we saw evidence suggestive of left hemispheric dysfunction in disorders as dissimilar as autism and conduct disorder; frontal lobe dysfunction was reported in one study or another for almost all of the categories of disturbance considered. With the neurodiagnostic findings overlapping to such an extent, these hardly could be used to provide a satisfactory explanation for the different forms of psychopathology manifested. Ongoing issues related to neuropsychological measurement, methodological constraints, and inconsistencies in the use of diagnostic terminology and criteria obviously could continue to impact here.

Overall, the neuropsychology of child psychopathology continues to represent an important and challenging aspect of the broader field of child neuropsychology. It is a complex area of investigation for the researcher and clinician alike, as there are many confounding factors that can obscure the study of brain–behavior relationships in child psychopathology. We hope our discussion of some of the advances to date has given the reader an appreciation for the importance and enormous complexity of this topic.

ACKNOWLEDGMENTS

This chapter was completed with support from grants from Maternal Child Health (MCJ-379154-02-0) and the Administration of Developmental Disabilities (90DD0207) awarded to the Center for Development and Learning.

7. References

Alarcon, R. D., Libb, J. W., & Boll, T. J. (1994). Neuropsychological testing in obsessive–compulsive disorder. A clinical review. *Journal of Neuropsychiatry and Clinical Neurosciences, 6,* 217–228.
Ameli, R., Courchesne, E., Lincoln, A., Kaufman, A., & Grillon, C. (1988). Visual memory

processes in high-functioning individuals with autism. *Journal of Autism and Developmental Disorders, 18,* 601–615.

American Psychiatric Association (1994). *Diagnostic and statistical manual of mental disorders (4th ed.).* Washington, DC: Author.

Applebaum, E., Egel, A. L., Koegel, R. L., & Imhoff, B. (1979). Measuring musical abilities of autistic children. *Journal of Autism and Developmental Disorders, 9,* 279–285.

Arnold, G., & Schwartz, S. (1983). Hemispheric lateralization of language in autistic and aphasic children. *Journal of Autism and Developmental Disorders, 13,* 129–139.

Aylward, G. P. (1993). Update on early developmental neuropsychological assessment: The Early Neuropsychological Optimality Rating Scales. In M. G. Tramontana & S. R. Hooper (Eds.), *Advances in child neuropsychology* (Vol. 2, pp. 172–200). New York: Springer-Verlag.

Bakker, D. J., Licht, R., & Kappers, E. J. (1995). Hemispheric stimulation techniques in children with dyslexia. In M. G. Tramontana & S. R. Hooper (Eds.), *Advances in child neuropsychology* (Vol. 3, pp. 144–177). New York: Springer-Verlag.

Balottin, U., Bejor, M., Cecchini, A., Martelli, A., Palazzi, S., & Lanzi, G. (1989). Infantile autism and computerized tomography brain-scan findings: Specific versus nonspecific abnormalities. *Journal of Autism and Developmental Disorders, 19,* 109–117.

Baltaxe, C. A. M., & Simmons, J. Q. (1983). Communication deficits in the adolescent and adult autistic. *Journal of Speech and Hearing Disorders, 40,* 439–458.

Barkley, R. (1981a). Hyperactivity. In E. G. Mash & L. G. Terdal (Eds.), *Behavioral assessment of childhood disorders* (pp. 127–184). New York: Guilford Press.

Barkley, R. (1981b). *Hyperactive children: A handbook for diagnosis and treatment.* New York: Guilford Press.

Barkley, R. A., Grodzinsky, G., & Du Paul, G. J. (1992). Frontal lobe functions in attention deficit disorder with and without hyperactivity: A review and research report. *Journal of Abnormal Child Psychology, 20,* 163–188.

Bartak, L., & Rutter, M. (1976). Differences between mentally retarded and normally intelligent autistic children. *Journal of Autism and Childhood Schizophrenia, 6,* 109–122.

Bauman, M., & Kemper, T. (1985). Histoanatomic observations of the brain in early infantile autism. *Neurology, 35,* 866–874.

Baxter, L. R., Schwartz, J. M. J., & Phelps, M. E. (1989). Reduction of prefrontal cortex glucose metabolism common to three types of depression. *Archives of General Psychiatry, 46,* 243–250.

Behar, D., Rapoport, J. L., Berg, C. J., Denckla, M. B., Mann, L., Cox, C., Fedio, P., Zahn, T., & Wolfman, M. G. (1984). Computerized tomography and neurological test measures in adolescents with obsessive–compulsive disorder. *American Journal of Psychiatry, 14,* 363–369.

Bell, M. A., & Fox, N. A. (1994). Brain development over the first year of life: Relations between electroencephalographic frequency and coherence and cognitive and affective behaviors. In G. Dawson & K. W. Fischer (Eds.), *Human behavior and the developing brain* (pp. 314–345). New York: Guilford Press.

Bellinger, D. (1995). Lead and neuropsychological function in children: Progress and problems in establishing brain–behavior relationships. In M. G. Tramontana & S. R. Hooper (Eds.), *Advances in child neuropsychology* (Vol. 3, pp. 12–47). New York: Springer-Verlag.

Benjamin, R., Costello, E. J., & Warren, M. (1990). Anxiety disorder in a pediatric sample. *Journal of Anxiety Disorders, 4,* 293–316.

Berman, A., & Siegal, A. (1976). Adaptive and learning skills in juvenile delinquents: A neuropsychological analysis. *Journal of Learning Disabilities, 9,* 583–590.

Bigler, E. D. (1989). On the neuropsychology of suicide. *Journal of Learning Disabilities, 22,* 180–185.

Blackstock, E. (1978). Cerebral asymmetry and the development of early infantile autism. *Journal of Autism and Childhood Schizophrenia, 8,* 339–353.

Blonder, L. X., Bowers, D., & Heilman, K. M. (1991). The role of the right hemisphere on emotional communication. *Brain, 114,* 1115–1127.

Bloom, F. E. (1993). Advancing a neurodevelopmental origin for schizophrenia. *Archives of General Psychiatry, 50,* 224–227.

Blumberg, S., & Izard, C. (1985). Affective and cognitive characteristics of depression in 10- and 11-year-old children. *Journal of Personality and Social Psychology, 49,* 194–202. (Abstract)

Boone, K. B., Ananth, J., Philpott, L., Kaur, J.,& Djenderedjian, A. (1991). Neuropsychological characteristics of nondepressed adults with obsessive–compulsive disorder. *Neuropsychiatry, Neuropsychology, and Behavioral Neurology, 4,* 96–109.

Bornstein, R. A. (1990). Neuropsychological performance in children with Tourette's syndrome. *Psychiatry Research, 33,* 73–81.

Botteron, K. N., Vannier, M. W., Geller, B., Todd, R. D., & Lee, B. C. P. (1995). Preliminary study of magnetic resonance imaging characteristics in 8- to 16-year-olds with mania. *Journal of the American Academy of Child and Adolescent Psychiatry, 34,* 742–749.

Bremner, J. D., Randall, P., Scott, T. M., Broneu, R. A., Seibyl, J. P., Southwick, S. M., Delaney, R. C., McCarthy, G., Charney, D. S., & Innis, R. B. (1995). MRI-based measurement of hippocampal volume in patients with combat-related posttraumatic stress disorder. *American Journal of Psychiatry, 152,* 973–981.

Breslau, N., & Marshall, I. A. (1985). Psychological disturbance in children with physical disabilities: Continuity and change in a 5-year follow-up. *Journal of Abnormal Child Psychology, 13,* 199–216.

Brickman, A., McManus, M., Grapetine, W., & Alessi, N. (1984). Neuropsychological assessment of seriously delinquent adolescents. *Journal of the American Academy of Child Psychiatry, 23,* 453–457.

Brumback, R. A., Staton, R. D., & Wilson, H. (1980). Neuropsychological study of children during and after remission of endogenous depressive episodes. *Perceptual and Motor Skills, 50,* 1163–1167.

Bruun, R. D. (1988). The natural history of Tourette's syndrome. In D. J. Cohen, R. D. Bruun, & J. F. Leckman (Eds.), *Tourette's syndrome and tic disorders: Clinical understanding and treatment* (pp. 21–39). New York: Wiley.

Bryden, M. P. (1982). *Laterality: Functional asymmetry in the intact brain.* New York: Academic Press.

Bryden, M. P., & Lev, R. G. (1983). Right-hemispheric involvement in the perception and expression of emotion in normal humans. In K. M. Heilman & P. Satz (Eds.), *Neuropsychology of human emotion* (pp. 6–44). New York: Guilford Press.

Buchsbaum, M. S., Wu, J., & DeLisi, L. E. (1986). Frontal cortex and basal ganglia metabolic rates assessed by positron emission tomography with [^{18}F]2-deoxyglucose in affective illness. *Journal of Affective Disorders, 10,* 137–152.

Cannon, I., & Compton, C. (1980). School dysfunction in the adolescent. *Pediatric Clinics of North America, 27,* 79–96.

Cantor, D., Thatcher, R., Hrybyk, M., & Kaye, H. (1986). Computerized EEG analyses of autistic children. *Journal of Autism and Developmental Disorders, 16,* 169–187.

Caparulo, B. K., Cohen, D. J., Rothman, S. L., Young, G., Katz, J., Shaywitz, S., & Shaywitz, B. (1981). Computed tomographic brain scanning in children with developmental neuropsychiatric disorders. *Journal of the American Academy of Child Psychiatry, 20,* 338–357.

Carter, L., Alpert, M., & Stewart, S. (1982). Schizophrenic children's utilization of images and words in performance of cognitive tasks. *Journal of Autism and Developmental Disorders, 12,* 279–293.

Chase, T. M., Foster, N. L., Fedro, P., Brooks, R., Mansi, L., Dessier, R., & DiChiro, G. (1984). Gilles de la Tourette syndrome: Studies with the fluorine-18 label fluorodeoxyglucose positron emission topographic method. *Annals of Neurology*, 15, 175.

Coble, P., Taska, L., Kupfer, D., Kazdin, A., Unis, A., & French, N. (1984). EEG sleep "abnormalities" in preadolescent boys with a diagnosis of conduct disorder. *Journal of the American Academy of Child Psychiatry*, 23, 438–447.

Cohen, D. J., Caparulo, B., & Shaywitz, B. (1976). Primary childhood aphasia and childhood autism: Clinical, biological, and conceptual observations. *Journal of the American Academy of Child Psychiatry*, 15, 604–645.

Cole, P. M., Usher, B. A., & Cargo, A. P. (1993). Cognitive risk and its association with risk for disruptive behavior disorder in preschoolers. *Journal of Clinical Child Psychology*, 22, 154–164.

Coleman, P., Romano, J., Lapham, L., & Simon, W. (1985). Cell counts in cerebral cortex of an autistic patient. *Journal of Autism and Developmental Disorders*, 15, 245–255.

Comings, D. E. (1990). *Tourette syndrome and human behavior*. Duarte, CA: Hope Press.

Courchesne, E., Lincoln, A., Kilman, B., & Galambos, R. (1985). Event-related brain potential correlates of the processing of novel visual and auditory information in autism. *Journal of Autism and Developmental Disorders*, 15, 55–76.

Courchesne, E., Lincoln, A. J., Yeung-Courchesne, R., Elmasian, R., & Grillon, C. (1989). Pathophysiologic findings in a nonretarded autism and receptive developmental language disorder. *Journal of Autism and Developmental Disorders*, 19, 1–17.

Courchesne, E., Yeung-Courchesne, R., Press, G. A., Hesselink, J. R., & Jernigan, T. L. (1988). Hypoplasia of cerebellar vernal lobules VI and VII in autism. *New England Journal of Medicine*, 318, 1349–1354.

Cox, C. S., Fedio, P., & Rapoport, J. L. (1989). Neuropsychological testing of obsessive–compulsive adolescents. In J. L. Rapoport (Ed.), *Obsessive–compulsive disorder in children and adolescents* (pp. 73–86). Washington, DC: American Psychiatric Association Press.

Damasio, A. R., & Maurer, R. G. (1978). A neurological model for childhood autism. *Archives of Neurology*, 35, 777–786.

Davidson, R. J. (1984). Affect, cognition and hemispheric specialization. In C. E. Izard, J. Kagan, & R. Zajonc (Eds.), *Emotions, cognition and behavior* (pp. 320–365). New York: Cambridge University Press.

Davidson, R. J. (1994). Temperament, affective style, and frontal lobe asymmetry. In G. Dawson & K. W. Fischer (Eds.), *Human behavior and the developing brain* (pp. 518–536). New York: Guilford Press.

Davidson, R. J., & Fox, N. A. (1982). Asymmetrical brain activity discriminates between positive versus negative affective stimuli in human infants. *Science*, 218, 1235–1237.

Davidson, R. J., & Fox, N. A. (1989). Frontal brain asymmetry predicts infants' response to maternal separation. *Journal of Abnormal Psychology*, 98, 127–131.

Davidson, R. J., Schwartz, G. E., Saron, C., Bennett, J., & Goleman, D. J. (1979). Frontal versus parietal EEG asymmetry during positive and negative affect. *Psychophysiology*, 16, 202–203.

Dawson, G. (1994). Development of emotional expression and emotion regulation in infancy. Contributions of the frontal lobe. In G. Dawson & K. W. Fischer (Eds.), *Human behavior and the developing brain* (pp. 346–379). New York: Guilford Press.

Dawson, G. (1983). Lateralized brain dysfunction in autism: Evidence from the Halstead–Reitan Neuropsychological Battery. *Journal of Autism and Developmental Disorders*, 13, 269–286.

Dawson, G., Finley, C., Phillips, S., & Galpert, L. (1986). Hemispheric specialization and the language abilities of autistic children. *Child Development*, 57, 1440–1453.

Decina, P., Kestenbaum, C., Farber, S., Kron, L., Gargan, M., Sackeim, H., & Fieve, R. (1983). Clinical and psychological assessment of children of bipolar probands. *American Journal of Psychiatry, 140,* 548–553.

DeMyer, M., Hingtgen, J., & Jackson, R. (1981). Infantile autism reviewed: A decade of research. *Schizophrenia Bulletin, 7,* 388–451.

Denckla, M. B. (1983). The neuropsychology of social–emotional learning disabilities. *Archives of Neurology, 40,* 461–462.

Deutch, A. Y., Goldstein, M., & Roth, R. H. (1986). Activation of the locus coeruleus induced by stimulation of the ventral segmental area. *Brain Research, 363,* 307–314.

Devinsky, O. (1983). Neuroanatomy of Gilles de la Tourette's syndrome. *Archives of Neurology, 40,* 508–514.

Dewey, M. A., & Evard, M. P. (1974). The near-normal autistic adolescent. *Journal of Autism and Developmental Disorders, 4,* 348–356.

Deykin, E., & MacMahon, B. (1979). The incidence of seizures among children with autistic symptoms. *American Journal of Psychiatry, 136,* 1310–1312.

Douglas, V. (1980). Higher mental processes in hyperactive children: Implications for training. In R. Knights & D. Bakker (Eds.), *Treatment of hyperactive and learning disordered children* (pp. 65–92). Baltimore: University Park Press.

Douglas, V. (1983). Attention and cognitive problems. In M. Rutter (Ed.), *Developmental neuropsychiatry* (pp. 280–329). New York: Guilford Press.

Elliott, F. A. (1982). Neurological findings in adult minimal brain dysfunction and the dyscontrol syndrome. *Journal of Nervous and Mental Disease, 170,* 680–687.

Erlenmeyer-Kimling, L., Cornblatt, B., Friedman, D., Marcuse, Y., Rutschmann, J., Simmens, S., & Deni, S. (1982). Neurological, electrophysiological, and attentional deviations in children at risk for schizophrenia. In F. Henn & H. Nasrallah (Eds.), *Schizophrenia as a brain disease* (pp. 61–98). New York: Oxford University Press.

Ernst, M., Liebenauer, L. L., King, C., Fitzgerald, G. A., Cohen, R. M., & Zametkin, A. J. (1994). Reduced brain metabolism in hyperactive girls. *Journal of the American Academy of Child and Adolescent Psychiatry, 33,* 858–868.

Etcoff, N. L. (1986). The neuropsychology of emotional expression. In G. Goldstein & R. E. Tarter (Eds.), *Advances in clinical neuropsychology* (Vol. 3, pp. 127–179). New York: Plenum Press.

Feagans, L. V., Short, E. J., & Meltzer, L. J. (Eds.). (1991). *Subtypes of learning disabilities. Theoretical perspectives and research.* Hillsdale, NJ: Erlbaum.

Fein, D., Humes, M., Kaplan, E., Lucci, D., L Waterhouse, L. (1984). The question of left hemisphere dysfunction in infantile autism. *Psychological Bulletin, 95,* 258–281.

Fein, D., Waterhouse, L., Lucci, D., & Snyder, D. (1985). Cognitive subtypes in developmentally disabled children: A pilot study. *Journal of Autism and Developmental Disorders, 15,* 77–95.

Ferrari, M., Matthews, W. S., & Barabas, G. (1984). Children with Tourette syndrome: Results of psychological tests given prior to drug treatment. *Journal of Developmental and Behavioral Pediatrics, 5,* 116–119.

Feyereisen, P. (1989). Theories of emotions and neuropsychological research. In F. Boller & J. Grafman (Eds.), *Handbook of neuropsychology, Volume 3* (pp. 271–281). New York: Elsevier Science Publishers.

Fish, B. (1977). Neurologic antecedents of schizophrenia in children. *Archives of General Psychiatry, 34,* 592–597.

Flor-Henry, P. (1979). On certain aspects of the localization of the cerebral systems regulating and determining emotion. *Biological Psychiatry, 14,* 677–698.

Folstein, S. E., & Rutter, M. (1987). Autism: Familial aggregation and genetic implications.

In E. Schopler & G. Mesibov (Eds.), *Neurobiological issue in autism* (pp. 83–105) New York: Plenum Press.

Forster, A. A., & Leckliter, I. N. (1995). Advances in neuropsychological constructs: Interpreting factor analytic research from a model of working memory. In M. G. Tramontana & S. R. Hooper (Eds.), *Advances in child neuropsychology* (Vol. 3, pp. 117–143). New York: Springer-Verlag.

Fox, N. A., & Davidson, R. J. (1988). Patterns of brain electrical activity during facial signs of emotion in 10-month-old infants. *Developmental Psychology, 24,* 230–236.

Frost, L. A., Moffitt, T. E., & McGee, R. (1989). Neuropsychological correlates of psychopathology in an unselected cohort of young adolescents. *Journal of Abnormal Psychology, 98,* 307–313.

Fuerst, D. R., Fisk, J. L., & Rourke, B. P. (1990). Psychosocial functioning of learning-disabled children: Relations between WISC Verbal IQ–Performance IQ discrepancies and personality subtypes. *Journal of Consulting and Clinical Psychology, 58,* 657–660.

Funk, J. B., & Ruppert, E. (1984). Language disorders and behavioral problems in preschool children. *Journal of Developmental and Behavioral Pediatrics, 5,* 357–360.

Gaffney, G. R., Kuperman, S., Tsai, L.Y., & Minchin, S. (1988). Morphological evidence for brainstem involvement in infantile autism. *Biological Psychiatry, 24,* 578–586.

Gaffney, G. R., Tsai, L. Y., Kuperman, S., & Minchin, S. (1987). Cerebellar structure in autism. *American Journal of Diseases of Childhood, 141,* 1330–1332.

Gainotti, G. (1989). Features of emotional behavior relevant to neurobiology and theories of emotions. In G. Gainotti & C. Caltagirone (Eds.), *Emotions and the dual brain* (pp. 9–27). New York: Springer-Verlag.

Garreau, B., Barthelemy, C., Sauvage, D., Leddet, I., & LeLord, G. (1984). A comparison of autistic syndromes with and without associated neurological problems. *Journal of Autism and Developmental Disorders, 14,* 105–111.

George, M. S., & Ballenger, J.C. (1992). The neuroanatomy of panic disorder: The emerging role of right parahippocampal region. *Journal of Anxiety Disorders, 6,* 181–188.

Gillberg, C., & Svendsen, P. (1983). Childhood psychosis and computed tomographic brain scan findings. *Journal of Autism and Developmental Disorders, 13,* 19–32.

Glaze, D. G., Frost, J. D., & Jankovic, J. (1983). Gilles de la Tourette syndrome: Disorder of arousal. *Neurology, 33,* 586–592.

Goldberg, E., & Costa, L. D. (1981). Hemisphere differences in the acquisition and use of descriptive systems. *Brain and Language, 14,* 144–173.

Gordon, C. T., Casanova, M., Zametkin, A., Zahn, T., Hong, W., & Rapoport, J. L. (in press). Childhood-onset schizophrenia: Neurobiological characterization and pharmacologic response: NIMH studies in progress. *Schizophrenia Bulletin.*

Gray, J. A. (1982). *The neuropsychology of anxiety: An enquiry into the functions of the septo-hippocampal system.* Oxford: Oxford University Press.

Gray, J. A., & Rawlins, J. N. P. (1986). Comparator and buffer memory: An attempt to integrate two models of hippocampal function. In R. L. Isaacson & K. H. Pribram (Eds.), *The hippocampus* (Vol. 4, pp. 159–201). New York: Plenum Press.

Green, W., Campbell, M., Hardesty, A., Grega, D., Gadron-Gayol, M., Shell, J., & Erlenmeyer-Kimling, L. (1984). A comparison of schizophrenic and autistic children. *Journal of the American Academy of Child Psychiatry, 23,* 399–409.

Gruzelier, J., Mednick, S., & Schulsinger, F. (1979). Lateralized impairments in the WISC profiles of children at genetic risk for psychopathology. In J. Gruzelier & P. Flor-Henry (Eds.), *Hemisphere asymmetries of function in psychopathology* (pp. 105–110). Amsterdam: Elsevier/North-Holland.

Halperin, J. M., McKay, K. E., Matier, K., & Sharma, V. (1994). Attention, response inhibition, and activity level in children: Developmental neuropsychological perspectives. In M. G. Tramontana & S. R. Hooper (Eds.), *Advances in child neuropsychology* (Vol. 2, pp. 1–54). New York: Springer & Verlag.

Harcherik, D. F., Cohen, D. J., Ort, S., Paul, R., Shaywitz, B. A., Volkmar, F. R., Rothman, S. L. G., & Leckman, J. F. (1985). Computed tomographic brain scanning in four neuropsychiatric disorders of childhood. *American Journal of Psychiatry, 142,* 731–734.

Haynes, J., & Bensch, M. (1981). The P > V sign on the WISC-R and recidivism in delinquents. *Journal of Consulting and Clinical Psychology, 49,* 480–481.

Heilman, K. M., Scholes, R., & Watson, R. T. (1975). Auditory affective agnosia: Disturbed comprehension of affective speech. *Journal of Neurology, Neurosurgery, and Psychiatry, 38,* 69–72.

Hertzig, M. E., & Walter, H. A. (1975). Symptom formation as an expression of disordered information processing in schizophrenic children. *Journal of Autism and Childhood Schizophrenia, 5,* 13–24.

Hier, D. B., LeMay, M., & Rosenberger, P. B. (1979). Autism and unfavorable left–right asymmetries of the brain. *Journal of Autism and Developmental Disorders, 9,* 153–159.

Hoffman, W. L., & Prior, M. R. (1982). Neuropsychological dimensions of autism in children: A test of the hemispheric dysfunction hypothesis. *Journal of Clinical Neuropsychology, 41,* 27–41.

Hooper, S. R. (1991). Neuropsychological assessment of the preschool child. In B. Bracken (Ed.), *Psychoeducational assessment of the preschool child* (2nd ed, pp. 465–485.) Boston: Allyn & Bacon.

Hooper, S. R., Boyd, T. A., Hynd, G. W., & Rubin, J. (1993). Definitional issues and neurobiological foundations of selected severe neurodevelopmental disorders. *Archives of Clinical Neuropsychology, 8,* 297–307.

Hooper, S. R., & Brown, T. (1995). *Neuropsychological functioning of children and adolescents with conduct disorder and aggressive-assaultive features.* Manuscript in submission.

Hooper, S. R., & Linz, T. D. (1992). Elective mutism. In S. R. Hooper, G. W. Hynd, & R. E. Mattison Eds.), *Child psychopathology: Diagnostic criteria and clinical assessment* (pp. 409–459). Hillsdale, NJ: Erlbaum.

Hooper, S. R., & Willis, W. G. (1989). *Learning disability subtyping: Neuropsychological foundations, conceptual models, and issues in clinical differentiation.* New York: Springer-Verlag.

Husain, M. M., McDonald, W. M., Doraiswamy, M., et al. (1991). A magnetic resonance imaging study of putamen nuclei in major depression. *Psychiatry Resident: Neuroimaging, 40,* 95–99.

Hynd, G. W., Semrud-Clikeman, M., Lorys, A., Novey, E. S., & Eliopulos, D. (1990). Brain morphology in developmental dyslexia and attention deficit disorder/hyperactivity. *Archives of Neurology, 47,* 919–926.

Incagnoli, T., & Kane, R. (1983). Developmental perspective of the Gilles de la Tourette syndrome. *Perceptual and Motor Skills, 57,* 1271–1281.

Iversen, S. D., & Alpert, J. E. (1982). Functional organization of the dopamine system in normal and abnormal behavior. In A. J. Friedhoff & T. N. Chase (Eds.), *Gilles de la Tourette syndrome* (pp. 69–76). New York: Raven Press.

Jackson, H. J. (1879). On affections of speech from disease of the brain. *Brain, 2,* 202.

Jacobson, R., LeCouteur, A., Howlin, P., & Rutter, M. (1988). Selective subcortical abnormalities in autism. *Psychological Medicine, 18,* 39–48.

James, A. L., & Barry, R. J. (1983). Developmental effects in the cerebral lateralization of autistic, retarded and normal children. *Journal of Autism and Developmental Disorders, 13,* 43–56.

Jenike, M. A. (1984). Obsessive–compulsive disorder: A question of a neurologic lesion. *Comprehensive Psychiatry, 25,* 298–304.

Jenike, M. A., & Brotman, A. W. (1984). The EEG in obsessive–compulsive disorder. *Journal of Clinical Psychiatry, 45,* 122–124.

Jernigan, T. L., Trauner, D. A., & Hesselink, J. R. (1991). Maturation of human cerebrum observed *in vivo* during adolescence. *Brain, 114,* 2037–2049.

Johnson, D. J., & Myklebust, H. R. (1971). *Learning disabilities.* New York: Grune & Stratton.

Jones, V., & Prior, M. (1985). Motor imitation abilities and neurological signs in autistic children. *Journal of Autism and Developmental Disorders, 15,* 37–46.

Joseph, R. (1990). *Neuropsychology, neuropsychiatry, and behavioral neurology.* New York: Plenum Press.

Kagan, V. E. (1981). Nonprocess autism in children: A comparative etiopathogenic study. *Soviet Neurology and Psychiatry, 14,* 25–30.

Kaslow, N., Rehm, L., & Siegel, A. (1984). Social-cognitive and cognitive correlates of depression in children. *Journal of Abnormal Child Psychology, 12,* 605–620.

Kaufman, A. S. (1979). *Intelligent testing with the WISC-R.* New York: Wiley.

Kendall, P., & Broswell, L. (1985). *Cognitive-behavioral therapy for impulsive children.* New York: Guilford Press.

Kennard, B. D., Emslie, G. J., & Weinberg, W. A. (1989). Mood, affect, and their disorders in children and adolescents. In S. J. Segalowitz & I. Rapin (Eds.), *Handbook of neuropsychology: Vol. 7. Child neuropsychology* (pp. 331–355). New York: Elsevier Science Publishers.

Kinsbourne, M. (1989). A model of adaptive behavior related to cerebral participation in emotional control. In G. Gainotti & C. Caltagirone (Eds.), *Emotions and the dual brain* (pp. 248–260). New York: Springer-Verlag.

Kinsbourne, M., & Bemporad, B. (1984). Lateralization of emotion: A model and the evidence. In N. Fox, & R. J. Davidson (Eds.), *The psychobiology of affective development* (pp. 259–291). Hillsdale, NJ: Erlbaum.

Kjaer, M., Boris, P., & Hansen, L. G. (1986). Abnormal CT scan in a patient with Gilles de la Tourette syndrome. *Neuroradiology, 28,* 362–363.

Knott, V., Waters, B., Lapierre, Y., & Gray, R. (1985). Neurophysiological correlates of sibling pairs discordant for bipolar affective disorder. *American Journal of Psychiatry, 142,* 248–250.

Kolb, B., & Milner, B. (1981a). Performance of complex arm and facial movements after focal brain lesions. *Neuropsychologia, 17,* 491–503.

Kolb, B., & Milner, B. (1981b). Observations on spontaneous facial expression after focal cerebral excisions and after intracarotid injection of sodium amytal. *Neuropsychologia, 19,* 505–514.

Kopp, C. B. (1989). Regulation of distress and negative emotions: A developmental view. *Developmental Psychology, 25,* 343–354.

Korhonen, T., & Sillanpaa, M. (1976). MBD-like behavior and neuropsychological performances. *Acta Paedopsychiatrica, 42,* 75–87.

Korkman, M. (1995). A test-profile approach in analyzing cognitive disorders in children: Experiences of the NEPSY. In M. G. Tramontana & S. R. Hooper (Eds.), *Advances in child neuropsychology,* (Vol. 3, pp. 84–116). New York: Springer-Verlag.

Korkman, M., & Peltomaa, A. K. (1993). Preventive treatment of dyslexia by a preschool training program for children with language impairments. *Journal of Clinical Child Psychology, 22,* 277–287.

Krynicki, V. E. (1978). Cerebral dysfunction in repetitively assaultive adolescents. *Journal of Nervous and Mental Disease, 166,* 59–67.

Leckman, J. F., & Cohen, D. J. (1988). Descriptive and diagnostic classification of tic disorders. In D. J. Cohen, R. D. Bruun, & J. F. Leckman (Eds.), *Tourette's syndrome and tic disorders: Clinical understanding and treatment* (pp. 3–19). New York: Wiley.

Lewis, D., Pincus, J., & Glaser, G. (1979). Violent juvenile delinquents: Psychiatric, neurological, psychological, and abuse factors. *Journal of the American Academy of Child Psychiatry, 18*, 307–319.

Lewis, D., & Shanok, S. (1977). Medical histories of delinquent and nondelinquent children: An epidemiological study. *American Journal of Psychiatry, 134*, 1020–1025.

Lewis, D., Shanok, S., & Pincus, J. (1982). A comparison of the neuropsychiatric status of female and male incarcerated delinquents: Some evidence of sex and race bias. *Journal of the American Academy of Child Psychiatry, 21*, 190–196.

Lincoln, A. J., Courchesne, E., Kilman, B. A., Elmasian, R., & Allen, M. (1988). A study of intellectual abilities in high-functioning people with autism. *Journal of Autism and Developmental Disorders, 18*, 505–524.

Linz, T. D., Hooper, S. R., Hynd, G. W., Isaac, W., & Gibson, R. (1990). Frontal lobe functioning in conduct disordered juveniles: Preliminary findings. *Archives of Clinical Neuropsychology, 5*, 411–416.

Lou, H. C., Henriksen, L., & Bruhn, P. (1984). Focal cerebral hypoperfusion in children with dysphasia and/or attention deficit disorder. *Archives of Neurology, 41*, 825–829.

Lou, H. C., Henriksen, L., Bruhn, P., Borner, H., & Nielsen, J. (1989). Striatal dysfunction in attention deficit and hyperkinetic disorder. *Archives of Neurology, 46*, 48–52.

Luchins, D. (1983). Carbamazepine for the violent psychiatric patient. *Lancet, 1*, 766.

Lucci, D., Fein, D., Lolevas, A., & Kaplan, E. (1988). Paul: A musically gifted autistic boy. In L. K. Obler & D. Fein (Eds.), *The exceptional brain: Neuropsychology of talent and special abilities* (pp. 310–324). New York: Guilford Press.

Lucas, J. A., Telch, M. J., & Bigler, E. D. (1991). Memory functioning in panic disorder. A neuropsychological perspective. *Journal of Anxiety Disorders, 5*, 1–20.

MacAuslan, A. (1975). Physical signs in association with depressive illness in childhood. *Child-Care-Health-Development, 1*, 225–232.

Marcus, J., Hans, S., Mednick, S., Schulsinger, F., & Michelson, N. (1985). Neurological dysfunctioning in offspring of schizophrenics in Israel and Denmark: A replication analysis. *Archives of General Psychiatry, 42*, 753–761.

Mattes, J. A. (1980). The role of frontal lobe dysfunction in childhood hyperkinesis. *Comprehensive Psychiatry, 21*, 358–369.

Mattison, R., Humphrey, F., Kales, S., Handford, H., Finkenbinder, R., & Hernit, R. (1986). Psychiatric background and diagnoses of children evaluated for special class placement. *Journal of the American Academy of Child Psychiatry, 25*, 514–520.

Maurer, R. G., & Damasio, A. R. (1982). Childhood autism from the point of view of behavioral neurology. *Journal of Autism and Developmental Disorders, 12*, 195–205.

McBurnett, K., Harris, S. M., Swanson, J. M., Pfiffner, L. J., Tamm, L., & Freeland, D. (1993). Neuropsychological and psychophysiological differentiation of inattention/overactivity and aggression/defiance symptom groups. *Journal of Clinical Child Psychology, 22*, 165–171.

McGee, R., Silva, P. A., & Williams, S. M. (1984). Perinatal, neurological, environmental and developmental characteristics of seven-year-old children with stable behavioral problems. *Journal of Child Psychology and Psychiatry and Allied Disciplines, 25*, 573–586.

Mendlewicz, J., Hoffman, G., Kerkhofs, M., & Linkowski, P. (1984). EEG and neuroendocrine parameters in pubertal and adolescent depressed children: A case report study. *Journal of Affective Disorders, 6*, 265–272.

Minshew, N. J., Goldstein, G., Taylor, H. G., & Siegel, D. J. (1994). Academic achievement in high functioning autistic individuals. *Journal of Clinical and Experimental Neuropsychology*, *16*, 261–270.

Mirsky, A., Antony, B., Duncan, C., Ahearn, M., & Kellam, S. (1991). Analysis of the elements of attention: A neuropsychological approach. *Neuropsychology Review*, *2*, 109–145.

Modell, J. G., Mountz, J. M., Curtis, G. C., & Greden, J. G. (1989). Neurophysiological dysfunction in basal ganglia/limbic striatal and thalamocortical circuits as a pathogenic mechanism of obsessive–compulsive disorder. *Journal of Neuropsychiatry and Clinical Neuroscience*, *1*, 27–36.

Molfese, D. L. (1995). Electrophysiological responses obtained during infancy and their relation to later language development: Further findings. In M. G. Tramontana & S. R. Hooper (Eds.), *Advances in child neuropsychology* (Vol. 3, pp. 1–11). New York: Springer-Verlag.

Myklebust, H. R. (1975). Nonverbal learning disabilities: Assessment and intervention. In H. R. Myklebust (Ed.), *Progress in learning disabilities* (Vol. 3, pp. 85–121). New York: Grune & Stratton.

Netley, C., Lockyer, L., & Greenbaum, G. H. (1975). Parental characteristics in relation to diagnosis and neurological status in childhood psychosis. *British Journal of Psychiatry*, *127*, 440–444.

Newby, R. F., Recht, D., & Daldwell, J. (1994). Empirically tested interventions for subtypes of reading disabilities. In M. G. Tramontana & S. R. Hooper (Eds.), *Advances in child neuropsychology* (Vol. 2, pp. 201–232). New York: Springer-Verlag.

Newlin, D. B., & Tramontana, M. G. (1980). Neuropsychological findings in a hyperactive adolescent with subcortical brain pathology. *Clinical Neuropsychology*, *2*, 178–183.

Norton, G. R., Schaefer, E., Cox, B. J., Dorward, J., & Wozney, K. (1988). Selective memory effects in nonclinical panickers. *Journal of Anxiety Disorders*, *2*, 169–177.

Oas, P. (1985). Impulsivity and delinquent behavior among incarcerated adolescents. *Journal of Clinical Psychology*, *41*, 422–424.

Owens, D., & Johnstone, E. (1980). The disabilities of chronic schizophrenia—Their nature and the factors contributing to their development. *British Journal of Psychiatry*, *136*, 384–395.

Papez, J. W. (1937). A proposed mechanism of emotion. *Archives of Neurology and Psychiatry*, *38*, 725–743.

Park, S., & Holzman, P. S. (1992). Schizophrenics show spatial working memory deficits. *Archives of General Psychiatry*, *49*, 975–982.

Passler, M., Isaac, W., & Hynd, G. W. (1986). Neuropsychological development of behavior attributed to frontal lobe functioning in children. *Developmental Neuropsychology*, *1*, 349–370.

Pavlidus, G. T. (1980). Eye movements in reading and beyond. *Nursing Mirror*, *150*, 22–26.

Pincus, J., & Tucker, G. (1978). Violence in children and adults. *Journal of the American Academy of Child Psychiatry*, *17*, 277–288.

Pontius, A., & Ruttiger, K. (1976). Frontal lobe system maturational lag in juvenile delinquents shown in narrative test. *Adolescence*, *11*, 509–518.

Porter, J., & Rourke, B. P. (1985). Socioemotional functioning of learning-disabled children: A subtypal analysis of personality patterns. In B. P. Rourke (Ed.), *Neuropsychology of learning disabilities: Essentials of subtype analysis* (pp. 257–279). New York: Guilford Press.

Prior, M. R., & Bradshaw, J. (1979). Hemisphere functioning in autistic children. *Cortex*, *15*, 73–81.

Prior, M. R., Tress, B., Hoffman, W. L., & Boldt, D. (1984). Computed tomographic study of children with classic autism. *Archives of Neurology*, *41*, 482–484.

Rapoport, J., Elkins, R., & Langer, D. (1981). Childhood obsessive–compulsive disorder. *American Journal of Psychiatry*, *138*, 1545–1554.

172   STEPHEN R. HOOPER AND MICHAEL G. TRAMONTANA

Regan, J., & LaBarbera, J. D. (1984). Lateralization of conversion symptoms in children and adolescents. *American Journal of Psychiatry, 14,* 1279–1280.

Rettew, D. C., Cheslow, D. L., Rapoport, J. L., Leonard, H. L., Lenane, M. C., Black, B., & Swedo, S. (1991). Neuropsychological test performance in trichotillomania: A further link with obsessive–compulsive disorder. *Journal of Anxiety Disorders, 5,* 225–235.

Riccio, C. A., Hynd, G. W., Cohen, M. J., & Gonzalez, J. J. (1993). Neurological basis of attention-deficit hyperactivity disorder. *Exceptional Children, 60,* 118–124.

Rieder, R. O., & Nichols, P. L. (1979). Offspring of schizophrenics. III. Hyperactivity and neurological soft signs. *Archives of General Psychiatry, 36,* 665–674.

Robbins, D. M., Beck, J. C., Pries, R., Jacobs, D., & Smith, C. (1983). Learning disability and neuropsychological impairment in adjudicated, unincarcerated male delinquents. *Journal of the American Academy of Child Psychiatry, 22,* 40–46.

Rochford, J., Weinapple, M., & Goldstein. L. (1981). The quantitative hemispheric EEG in adolescent psychiatric patients with depressive or paranoid symptomatology. *Biological Psychiatry, 16,* 47–54.

Ross, E. D., & Mesulam, M. M. (1979). Dominant language functions of the right hemisphere? Prosody and emotional gesturing. *Archives of Neurology, 36,* 144.

Ross, R., Radant, A. D., & Hammer, D. W. (1993). A developmental study of smooth pursuit eye movements in normal children from 7 to 15 years of age. *Journal of the American Academy of Child and Adolescent Psychiatry, 32,* 783–791.

Rourke, B. P. (Ed.). (1985). *Neuropsychology of learning disabilities: Essentials of subtype analysis.* New York: Guilford Press.

Rourke, B. P. (1989). *Nonverbal learning disabilities: The syndrome and the model.* New York: Guilford Press.

Rourke, B. P., Young, G. C., & Leenaars, A. A. (1988). A childhood learning disability that predisposes those afflicted to adolescent and adult depression and suicide risk. *Journal of Learning Disabilities, 22,* 169–175.

Roy-Byrne, P. P., Mellman, T. A., & Uhde, T. W. (1988). Biologic findings in panic disorder: Neuroendocrine and sleep-related abnormalities. *Journal of Anxiety Disorders, 2,* 17–29.

Rumsey, J. M. (1992). Neuropsychological studies of high-level autism. In E. Schopler & G. B. Mesibov (Eds.), *High-functioning individuals with autism* (pp. 41–64). New York: Plenum Press.

Rumsey, J. M., Andreasen, N. C., & Rapoport, J. L. (1986). Thought, language, communication, and affective flattening in autistic adults. *Archives of General Psychiatry, 43,* 771–777.

Rumsey, J. M., Rapoport, J. L., & Sceery, W. R. (1985). Autistic children as adults: Psychiatric, social and behavioral outcomes. *Journal of the American Academy of Child Psychiatry, 24,* 465–473.

Russell, A. T., Bott, L., & Sammons, C. (1989). The phenomenology of schizophrenia occurring in childhood. *Journal of the American Academy of Child and Adolescent Psychiatry, 28,* 399–407.

Rutter, M. (1983). Issues of prospects in developmental neuropsychiatry. In M. Rutter (Ed.), *Developmental neuropsychiatry* (pp. 577–598). New York: Guilford Press.

Sackeim, H. A., Decina, P., & Malitz, S. (1982). Functional brain asymmetry and affective disorders. *Adolescent Psychiatry, 10,* 320–335.

Schacter, S., & Singer, J. (1962). Cognitive, social, and physiological determinants of emotional state. *Psychological Review, 69,* 379–399.

Schiffer, F., Teicher, M. H., & Papanicolaou, A. C. (1995). Evoked potential evidence for right brain activity during the recall of traumatic memories. *Journal of Neuropsychiatry and Clinical Neurosciences, 7,* 169–175.

Semrud-Clikeman, M., Filipek, P. A., Biederman, J., Steingard, R., Kennedy, D., Renshaw, P.,

& Bekken, K. (1994). Attention-deficit hyperactivity disorder: Magnetic resonance imaging morphometric analysis of the corpus callosum. *Journal of the American Academy of Child and Adolescent Psychiatry, 333*, 875–881.

Semrud-Clikeman, M., Hooper, S. R., Hynd, G. W., Hem, K., Presley, R., & Watson, T. (in press). Prediction of group membership in developmental dyslexia, attention-deficit hyperactivity disorder, and normal controls using brain morphometric analysis of magnetic resonance imaging. *Archives of Clinical Neuropsychology*.

Shaffer, D. (1978). "Soft" neurological signs and later psychiatric disorder—A review. *Journal of Child Psychology and Psychiatry, 19*, 63–65.

Shaffer, D., O'Connor, P. A., Shafer, S. Q., & Prupis, S. (1983). Neurological "soft signs": Their origins and significance for behavior. In M. Rutter (Ed.), *Developmental neuropsychiatry* (pp. 144–163). New York: Guilford Press.

Shaffer, D., Schonfeld, I., O'Connor, P.A., Stokman, C., Trautman, P., Shafer, S., & Ng, S. (1985). Neurological soft signs. *Archives of General Psychiatry, 42*, 342–351.

Shapiro, A. K., Shapiro, E., Bruun, R. D., & Sweet, R. D. (1978). *Gilles de la Tourette syndrome.* New York: Raven Press.

Shapiro, E. G., & Klein, K. (1994). Dementia in childhood: Issues in neuropsychological assessment with application to the natural history and treatment of degenerative storage diseases. In M. G. Tramontana & S. R. Hooper (eds.), *Advances in child neuropsychology* (Vol. 2, pp. 119–171). New York: Springer-Verlag.

Shapiro, T., Burkes, L., Petti, T. A., & Ranz, J. (1978). Consistency of "nonfocal" neurological signs. *Journal of the American Academy of Child Psychiatry, 17*, 70–78.

Singer, H. S., Tune, L. E., Butler, I. J., Zaczek, R., & Coyle, J. T. (1982). Clinical symptomatology, CSF neurotransmitter metabolites, and serum haloperidol levels in Tourette syndrome. In A. J. Friedhoff & T. N. Chase (Eds.), *Gilles de la Tourette syndrome* (pp. 177–183). New York: Raven Press.

Small, J. (1975). EEG and neurophysiological studies of early infantile autism. *Biological Psychiatry, 10*, 385–397.

Snow, J. H., & Hooper, S. R. (1994). Pediatric traumatic brain injury. Thousand Oaks, CA: Sage.

Soper, H., Satz, P., Orsini, D., Henry, R., Mvi, J., & Schulman, M. (1986). Handedness patterns of autism suggest subtypes. *Journal of Autism and Developmental Disorders, 16*, 155–167.

Staton, R. D., Wilson, H., & Brumback, R. A. (1981). Cognitive improvement associated with tricyclic antidepressant treatment of childhood major depressive illness. *Perceptual and Motor Skills, 53*, 219–234.

Stehbens, J. A., & Cool, V. A. (1994). Neuropsychological sequelae of childhood cancers. In M. G. Tramontana & S. R. Hooper (Eds.), *Advances in child neuropsychology* (Vol. 2, pp. 55–84). New York: Springer-Verlag.

Stellern, J., Marlowe, M., Jacobs, J., & Cossairt, A. (1985). Neuropsychological significance of right hemisphere cognitive mode in behavior disorders. *Behavioral Disorders, 10*, 113–124.

Strauss, A., & Lehtinen, L. (1947). *Psychopathology and education of the brain-injured child.* New York: Grune & Stratton.

Stuss, D., & Benson, D. (1984). Neuropsychological studies of the frontal lobes. *Psychological Bulletin, 95*, 3–28.

Szatmari, P., Offord, D. R., Siegel, L. S., Finlayson, M. A. J., & Tuff, L. (1990). The clinical significance of neurocognitive impairments among children with psychiatric disorders: Diagnosis and situational specificity. *Journal of Child Psychology, Psychiatry, and Allied Disciplines, 31*, 287–299.

Tanguay, P. (1984). Toward a new classification of serious psychopathology in children. *Journal of the American Academy of Child Psychiatry, 23*, 273–384.

Tarter, R. E., Hegedus, A. M., Alterman, A. I., & Katz-Garris, L. (1983). Cognitive capacities of juvenile violent, nonviolent, and sexual offenders. *Journal of Nervous and Mental Disease*, *171*, 564–567.

Taylor, H. G. (1983). MBD: Meanings and misconceptions. *Journal of Clinical Neuropsychology*, *5*, 271–287.

Taylor, H. G., Schatschneider, C., & Rich, D. (1992). Sequelae of haemophilus influenzae meningitis: Implications for the study of brain disease and development. In M. G. Tramontana & S. R. Hooper (Eds.), *Advances in child neuropsychology* (Vol. 1, pp. 50–108). New York: Springer-Verlag.

Tomarken, A. J., Davidson, R. J., & Henriques, J. B. (1990). Resting frontal brain asymmetry predicts affective responses to films. *Journal of Personality and Social Psychology*, *59*, 791–801.

Torrey, E. F., Hersh, S. P., & McCabe, K. D. (1975). Early childhood psychosis and bleeding during pregnancy: A prospective study of gravid women and their offspring. *Journal of Autism and Childhood Schizophrenia*, *5*, 287–297.

Tramontana, M. G. (1983). Neuropsychological evaluation of children and adolescents with psychopathological disorders. In C. J. Golden & P. J. Vincente (Eds.), *Foundations of clinical neuropsychology* (pp. 309–340). New York: Plenum Press.

Tramontana, M. G., & Hooper, S. R. (1989). Neuropsychology of child psychopathology. In C. R. Reynolds & E. Fletcher-Janzen (Eds.), *Handbook of clinical child neuropsychology* (pp. 87–106). New York: Plenum Press.

Tramontana, M. G., & Hooper, S. R. (in press). Neuropsychology of child psychopathology. In C. R. Reynolds & E. Fletcher-Janzen (Eds.), *Handbook of clinical child neuropsychology* (2nd ed.) New York: Plenum Press.

Tramontana, M. G., Hooper, S. R., & Nardolillo, E. M. (1988). Behavioral manifestations of neuropsychological impairment in children with psychiatric disorders. *Archives of Clinical Neuropsychology*, *3*, 369–374.

Tsai, L., Tsai, M., & August, G. (1985). Brief Report: Implications of EEG diagnosis in the subclassification of infantile autism. *Journal of Autism and Developmental Disorders*, *15*, 339–344.

Tucker, D. M. (1991). Development of emotion and cortical networks. In M. Gunnar & C. Nelson (Eds.), *Minnesota symposium on child development: Developmental neuroscience*. New York: Oxford University Press.

Tucker, D. M. (1980). Lateral brain function, emotion, and conceptualization. *Psychological Bulletin*, *89*, 19–46.

Tucker, D. M. (1989). Neural substrates of thought and affective disorders. In G. Gainotti & C. Caltagirone (Eds.), *Emotions and the dual brain* (pp. 225–234). New York: Springer-Verlag.

Tucker, D. M., & Frederick, S. L. (1986). Emotion and brain lateralization. In H. Wagner & T. Manstead (Eds.), *Handbook of psychophysiology: Emotion and social behaviour*. New York: Wiley.

Tucker, D. M., & Williamson, P. A. (1984). Asymmetric neural control systems in human self-regulation. *Psychological Review*, *91*, 185–215.

Vasterling, J. J., Rost, L., Brailey, K., Uddo, M., & Sutker, P. B. (1994, February). *Attention and memory performances in post-traumatic stress disorder.* Paper presented at the 22nd Annual Meeting of the International Neuropsychological Society, Cincinnati, OH.

Voeller, K. K. S., Alexander, A. W., Carter, R. L., & Heilman, K. (1989). Motor impersistence in children with attention-deficit hyperactivity disorder decreases in response to treatment with methylphenidate. *Neurology*, *39*, 276.

Voeller, K. K. S., & Heilman, K. (1988). Attention deficit disorder in children: A neglect syndrome? *Neurology*, *38*, 806–808.

Volkmar F. R., Leckman, J. F., Detlor, J., Harcherick, D. F., Pritchard, J. W., Shaywitz, B. A., & Cohen, D. J. (1984). EEG abnormalities in Tourette syndrome. *Journal of the American Academy of Child Psychiatry, 23,* 352–353.

Voorhees, J. (1981). Neuropsychological differences between juvenile delinquents and functional adolescents. *Adolescence, 16,* 57–66.

Wardell, D., & Yeudall, L. (1980). A multidimensional approach to criminal disorders. The assessment of impulsivity and its relation to crime. *Advances in Behavioral Research and Therapy, 2,* 159–177.

Warr-Leeper, G., Wright, N. A., & Mack, A. (1994). Language disabilities of antisocial boys in residential treatment. *Behavioral Disorders, 19,* 159–169.

Welsh, M. C., & Pennington, B. F. (1988). Assessing frontal lobe functioning in children: Views from developmental psychology. *Developmental Neuropsychology, 4,* 199–230.

Wilson, H., & Staton, R. D. (1984). Neuropsychological changes in children associated with tricyclic antidepressant therapy. *International Journal of Neuroscience, 24,* 307–312.

Wing, L. (1971). Perceptual and language development in autistic children: A comparative study. In M. Rutter (Ed.), *Infantile autism: Concepts, characteristics, and treatment* (pp. 173–197). London: Churchill Livingstone.

Wise, S. P., & Rapoport, J. L. (1989). Obsessive–compulsive disorder: Is it basal ganglia dysfunction? In J. L. Rapoport (Ed.), *Obsessive–compulsive disorder in children and adolescents* (pp. 327–344). Washington, DC. American Psychiatric Association Press.

Woods, B. T., & Eby, M. D. (1982). Excessive mirror movements and aggression. *Biological Psychiatry, 17,* 23–32.

Yeates, K. O., & Bornstein, R. A. (February, 1992). *Attention deficit disorder and neuropsychological functioning in children with Tourette's syndrome.* Paper presented at the 20th Annual Meeting of the International Neuropsychological Society, San Diego, CA.

Ylvisaker, M., Szekeres, S. F., & Hartwick, P. (1992). Cognitive rehabilitation following traumatic brain injury in children. In M. G. Tramontana & S. R. Hooper (Eds.), *Advances in child neuropsychology* (Vol. 1, pp. 168–218). New York: Springer-Verlag.

Zajonc, R. B., & Marcus, H. (1984). Affect and cognition: The hard interface. In C. E. Izard, J. Kagan, & R. B. Zajonc (Eds.), *Emotion, cognition, and behavior* (pp. 73–102). Cambridge, UK: Cambridge University Press.

Zambelli, A. J., Stamm, J. S., Maitinsky, S., & Loiselle, D. L. (1977). Auditory evoked potentials and selective attention in formerly hyperactive adolescent boys. *American Journal of Psychiatry, 134,* 742–747.

Zinkus, P. W., & Gottlieb, M. I. (1978). Learning disabilities and juvenile delinquency. *Clinical Pediatrics, 17,* 775–780.

5

Understanding and Treating Child and Adolescent Sexual Offenders

JUDITH V. BECKER AND JOHN A. HUNTER, JR.

1. Introduction

Sexual abuse and sexual assault continue to be major social problems in our society. Finkelhor and colleagues (1990) reported on the prevalence of sexual abuse in a national survey of adult men and women. Twenty-seven percent of all females and 16% of males surveyed reported that they had been sexually abused prior to age 18. Pithers and colleagues (1995) note that sexual abuse has both emotional and financial consequences. The majority of females seeking outpatient mental health services report a history of sexual abuse at some point in their lives (Frontline, 1988). In terms of the financial costs to society, Pithers et al. (1993) reported that in the state of Vermont, the annual cost of responding to child sexual abuse can be estimated at $42 million.

Historically, it was believed that those responsible for sexual abuse and assault in our society were adult males. Recent data indicate that sexual abuse and assault are perpetrated by adult females as well as males, by female adolescents as well as juvenile males. Abel, Mittelman, and Becker (1985) found that of more than 400 adult sex offenders interviewed, 58% reported the onset of their deviant sexual interest patterns prior to age 18. Reports indicate that juveniles are responsible for 20% of reported rapes, and as many as 30% of cases of child sexual abuse may be perpetrated by juveniles (Brown, Flanagan, & McLeon, 1984; Fehrenbach, Smith, Monastersky, & Deisher, 1986).

JUDITH V. BECKER AND JOHN A. HUNTER, JR. • Department of Psychology, University of Arizona, Tucson, Arizona 85721.

Advances in Clinical Child Psychology, Volume 19, edited by Thomas H. Ollendick and Ronald J. Prinz. Plenum Press, New York, 1997.

In the last 13 years, there has been a tremendous growth in programs to treat juvenile offenders in the United States. In 1982, only 20 programs had been identified nationally that treated juvenile offenders; however, the Safer Society Program reported that as of 1993 there were more than 800 specialized treatment programs for juvenile sex offenders (National Adolescent Perpetrator Network, 1993). In 1986, a National Task Force on Juvenile Sex Offending was created. The purpose of the Task Force was to suggest standards for assessing and treating juvenile sex offenders. The Task Force issued its first report in 1988, and a revised report was published in 1993 (National Adolescent Perpetrator Network, 1993). Both of these reports are recommended reading for those interested in further information about juvenile offenders. Due to the relative paucity of scientific literature on adolescent offenders, the Task Force, rather than creating standards, presented their findings as "assumptions" upon which assessments and treatment are based.

Although there has been a tremendous increase in available clinical services for juvenile sex offenders, research for the most part has not kept up. Becker, Harris, and Sales (1993) conducted a literature review to identify relevant studies. They conducted a 10-year search on both Med Line and Psych List, and identified 73 articles. Of those articles identified, 59% defined characteristics of juvenile sex offenders, 31.5% discussed treatment issues, and 10% related to miscellaneous issues (e.g., mothers of sex offenders). There is only one controlled therapy outcome study reported in the literature, and of those articles that discussed characteristics, only a small percentage utilized control or comparison groups. Clearly, the field is in need of more empirical research.

This chapter will focus on what has been reported in the literature relative to the characteristics of juvenile sexual offenders, "motivators" for sexually abusive and aggressive behavior, assessment of juvenile sex offenders, and treatment issues and modalities. Since the majority of the published literature focuses on juvenile male sex offenders, so also will this chapter.

2. Characteristics

Juvenile sex offenders show many of the same typyes of sexually abusive behaviors as do offending adults. They may "fondle" either male or female victims, penetrate their victims, or engage in nontouching behaviors including voyeurism or exhibitionism. Fehrenbach et al. (1993) reported on a sample of 305 juvenile sex offenders. The most common offense was fondling (59%), followed by rape (23%), exhibitionism (11%), and other noncontact offenses (7%).

Certain characteristics have been identified as prevalent among juvenile sex offenders, including skills deficits (Awad & Saunders, 1989; Katz, 1990); a history of nonsexual delinquency (Becker, Kaplan, Cunningham-Rathner, & Kavoussi, 1986); poor academic performance and learning problems (Awad & Saunders, 1989); other mental health problems, including depression (Becker, Kaplan, Tenke, & Tartaglini, 1991); and lack of proper sex education (Kaplan, Becker, & Cunningham-Rathner, 1988).

The aforementioned characteristics are not necessarily unique to juvenile sex offenders. For those studies that have utilized comparison groups of nonsexual delinquents, frequently no differences are found (Ford & Linney, 1995; Lewis, Shankok, & Pincus, 1979; Tarter et al., 1983). Ford and Linney (1995) compared juvenile sexual offenders, status offenders, and violent nonsexual offenders on a variety of characteristics including social skills, interpersonal relationships, and self-concept. These authors reported that the comparison groups did not differ in assertiveness, self-concept, or family-history variables. Differences were found in sexual and physical abuse, and parental use of violence. Juvenile sex offenders experienced more abuse and violence than the other groups.

The family environment has also been implicated in reports on juvenile sex offenders. Family instability, frequent violence, and high rates of disorganization have been reported (Awad & Saunders, 1989; Smith & Israel, 1987). Blaske, Bouduin, Henggeler, and Mann (1989) report that the families of both sex offenders and violent nonsexual offenders are found to have little positive communication and considerable negative communication.

3. Etiology and Motivators

Although researchers have proposed a number of theories to explain the etiology of sexually inappropriate behavior, to date there is no generally accepted theory regarding juvenile sexual offending. A number of factors have received empirical and clinical attention in the literature, including maltreatment experiences, exposure to pornography, substance abuse, and exposure to aggressive role models (Hunter & Becker, 1994).

Physical abuse has been reported in 25–50% of sampled sex offenders, and a history of sexual abuse has been found in 40–80% of juvenile sex offenders (Kahn & Chambers, 1991; Ryan, Lane, Davis, & Isaac, 1987; Smith, 1988). The rate of abuse can vary based on how sexual abuse is defined (e.g., fondling vs. penetration). It is also important to note that adolescent males often have difficulty in disclosing and describing their own histories of abuse, and in some cases, it is not until a therapeutic relationship has been formed that they feel secure enough to discuss their own abuse.

Although clearly not all juvenile sexual offenders have been sexually abused, a compelling question arises: Why do some sexually abused males go on to engage in acts of sexual abuse or aggression? Recently Hunter and Figueredo (1995) shed some light on that issue. They used structural equation modeling to delineate the relationship between a history of sexual victimization, the family-support variable, and personality and adjustment in the prediction of patterns of sexual perpetration.

In the study, 235 juvenile males (average age 14.7) served as participants. Five categories of youth were evaluated on a host of variables. The five groups were (1) juvenile child molesters with a history of sexual victimization, (2) juveniiles who had been sexually abused but had no history of sexual perpetration, (3) juveniles with a history of sexual victimization but no history of sexual perpetration, (4) a psychiatric control group, and (5) a normal control group. Four variables were identified as predictors of the perpetrator classification category: (1) the younger the juvenile at the time of victimization; (2) the greater number of incidents of abuse the youth had experienced; (3) the longer the period of time to disclosure of the sexual abuse; and (4) the level of perceived family support postrevelation of abuse. These authors report that their findings are consistent with developmental theory, in that the earlier and more frequent the occurrence of trauma during early developmental periods, the greater and more lasting the disruption to development of the child.

Another recently published study has also implicated maltreatment experience in sexual aggression in juvenile males. Kobayashi, Sales, Becker, Figueredo, and Kaplan (1995) utilized structural equation modeling to test a theoretical model that included child physical and sexual abuse, bonding to parents, and perceived parental deviance. These authors found that being physically abused by the father and sexually abused by a male increased sexual aggressiveness. Bonding to the mother was found to decrease the level of sexual aggressiveness. These authors reported that their results supported two causal processes: (1) a social learning process, and (2) a child–parent attachment, or social bonding, process. An ethological perspective was also seen as being consistent with the study results.

Although alcohol and drugs have been implicated in the commission of violent, nonsexual crimes, the relationship between substance abuse and juvenile sex offenders has not been well established. Lightfoot and

Barbaree (1993), in their review of the literature on the topic, report that between 3.4% and 72% of juvenile sex offenders were under the influence of alcohol or drugs at the time of the offense.

Becker and Stein (1991) report that 61% of their sample of juvenile sex offenders admitted to alcohol consumption; however, 49% reported that alcohol had no effect on their sexual arousal. A significant statistical relationship was found between alcohol use and the number of victims that the juvenile had. These authors also report that 39% of the sample reported using drugs. No statistically significant relationship was found between drug usage and number of victims. Lightfoot and Barbaree (1993) have called for the utilization of valid and reliable alcohol- and drug-screening assessment instruments for this population. They have also stated that the important question to be answered is, "Is substance use a risk factor for offending, independent of the presence of a substance abuse or dependence?" (p. 218). We agree with these authors on both issues.

What, if any, role does pornography play in either the initiation of sexual offending in juvenile offenders or the maintenance of the behavior? Becker and Stein (1991) surveyed their sample of juvenile sex offenders as to the type of sexually explicit material they used most often (the word "pornography" was not used, since it is seen as a pejorative term). Magazines were the most frequently used form of sexually explicit material (35%), followed by videotapes (26%). Nine percent of the sample reported not using sexually explicit material. No statistical relationship was found between use of sexually explicit materials and number of victims.

Ford and Linney (1995) reported that 42% of a sample of juvenile sex offenders reported exposure to hard-core, sexually explicit magazines compared to 29% of violent nonsexual offenders and status offenders. Furthermore, the juvenile sex offenders were exposed at younger ages (5 to 8 years).

There is an extreme paucity of research on the impact that sexually violent material has on the development of deviant arousal patterns. Further research is needed to elucidate what, if any, role it plays. Perhaps sexually violent material serves as a reinforcer, given that individuals seek out material that they are attracted to. Further research is needed to answer these questions.

4. Comorbid Psychological Problems

A number of researchers have reported on the presence of other psychological and psychiatric problems in a juvenile sex offender population. Lewis and colleagues (1979), in a comparison study of juvenile males incarcerated for violent sexual assaults and those incarcerated for violent nonsexual acts, found that both groups had a significant prevalence of other psychiatric symptoms including depression, auditory hallucinations, paranoia, and thought disorders.

Kavoussi, Kaplan, and Becker (1988) conducted structured psychiatric interviews with a sample of adolescent sex offenders seen on an outpatient basis. Results of that study indicated that conduct disorder was the most common diagnosis (48%). There was a higher prevalence of conduct disorder in those adolescents who had raped (75%) compared to those who had molested children (38%). Twenty percent of the adolescents had some symptoms of adjustment disorder with depressed mood. Nineteen percent of the adolescents had no DSM diagnosis. Attention deficit disorder with hyperactivity was also reported in the histories of juvenile sex offenders (Kavoussi et al., 1988).

A possible reason for the lack of major psychiatric problems in the Kavoussi et al. study is that the participants in this study were outpatients, whereas the participants described by Lewis were incarcerated juvenile males. Since the more violent pathological juveniles are incarcerated, this may explain the difference, due to the fact that the more disturbed adolescents are placed in residential care.

Becker et al. (1991) systematically assessed depressive symptomatology in an adolescent sex offender population. In the study, 256 juvenile sex offenders who were evaluated as outpatients were administered the Beck Depression Inventory (BDI). Participants were categorized as to whether they had ever been the victim of sexual abuse, physical abuse, or both. The mean BDI score for all participants was 14.3 (SD 11.5), which falls within the mild depression range. Those participants who themselves had an abuse history had a mean score of 15 compared to a score of 10 for the unabused participants. For the juvenile offenders who had an abuse history, 35.8% were undepressed, 15% mildly depressed, 20% moderately depressed, and 29.2% severely depressed.

Kaplan et al. (1984) utilized the BDI to assess depressive symptomatology in a range of 398 junior- and senior-high-school students. In comparing the scores of the juvenile sex offenders to Kaplan's sample, the scores of the juvenile sex offenders were twice that of those reported by Kaplan.

The results of this study indicate that juvenile sex offenders have a higher level of depressive symptomatology than that found in a random sample of juveniles. These findings underscore the need to evaluate juvenile sex offenders for depression, particularly those youth who have a history of either physical or sexual abuse, and to address this issue as part of a comprehensive treatment plan.

These findings underscore the need to conduct comprehensive psychological evaluations of the juvenile sex offenders who present for assessment to ensure that comprehensive treatment plans are developed.

5. Juvenile Female Sexual Offenders

Very few scientific articles have addressed the topic of juvenile female sexual offenders. Fehrenbach and Monastersky (1988) have described the characteristics of 28 female juvenile sexual offenders at an outpatient clinic. The sample was described as having molested children of both genders; however, more of them had female victims. The majority of victims were acquaintances of the juveniles, and frequently the victimization occurred during the context of baby-sitting. Fifty percent of the female offenders reported a history of sexual abuse, and 20% had been physically abused.

Hunter et al. (1993) have reported on 10 severely psychosexually and emotionally disturbed female offenders who were in residential treatment. The majority of the youth had prior histories of maltreatment. The majority of these girls had been sexually abused by multiple perpetrators. Sixty percent of their sexual abusers were female.

Recently, Matthews, Hunter, and Vuz (in press) compared data on 67 juvenile female sexual offenders with 70 juvenile male sexual offenders. The average age of the juvenile females was 14.3 years, with a range from 11 to 18. The juvenile males ranged in age from 11 to 17, with an average age of 14.7. These youth were compared on the following variables: history of maltreatment, characteristics of sexual perpetration, and developmental and psychiatric characteristics. Whereas 77.6% of the juvenile females had a history of sexual abuse, 44.3% of the juvenile males had a history of sexual abuse.

The females were abused at younger ages, 64% prior to age 5, compared to 25.8% of the males prior to age 5. The juvenile females also had more perpetrators ($\bar{X}$ = 4.5 for juvenile females) than the juvenile males ($\bar{X}$ = 1.4). Physical abuse was prevalent in the histories of 60% of the juvenile females compared to 44.9% of the males.

A comparison of psychiatric/developmental characteristics revealed that almost equal number of juvenile male and female offenders had received prior mental health treatment (71.6% female and 75.4% male), had suicidal ideation or attempted suicide (43.9% female and 42% male), and had run away (33.3% female and 29% male). More of the juvenile females (25.4%) abused alcohol or drugs than did the males (14.3%). However, more of the males (44.9%) had learning disabilities than did the females (23.4%).

A comparison of their perpetration characteristics revealed that a greater percentage of the juvenile males (54.5%) penetrated their victims than did the juvenile females (26.9%). The juvenile female offenders had more victims ($\bar{X}$ = 2.3) than did the juvenile males ($\bar{X}$ = 1.8). The females also committed more offenses against their victims ($\bar{X}$ = 16.9) than did the juvenile males ($\bar{X}$ = 6.4).

Matthews et al. (in press) concluded that juvenile male and female offenders are a heterogenous group, and empirically validated typologies should be developed for both groups. They also recommended that given many of the youth's prior histories of maltreatment experiences, therapy should focus on how "repetitive developmental trauma" impacted on both emotional and psychosexual development. Given their history of maltreatment, these youth have difficulty with emotional intimacy and, consequently, the therapeutic relationship may be fraught with distancing and projections on the part of the youth. Therapists are advised to be sensitive to both transference and countertransference issues when working with this population.

6. Assessment

In order to develop a comprehensive treatment plan for the youthful sexual offender and his or her family, it is imperative that a comprehensive assessment of the youth and his or her family be completed. The evaluator should obtain and review the following records: (1) victim statement, (2) juvenile court records, (3) mental health records, and (4) school records. A comprehensive assessment includes a clinical interview, psychometric assessment, and when warranted, phallometric assessment.

Prior to beginning the clinical interview, it is important to inform the youth, who may be referred by the juvenile court or be on probation, about the limits of confidentiality. If a waiver of confidentiality has been signed, it is helpful to remind the youth and family that a report will be generated and sent to the appropriate official or agency. Since the majority of youth will either deny that they committed a sexual offense or minimize the extent of their inappropirate sexual behavior, the evaluator should be sensitive to factors that motivate such behaviors. Frequently youth are embarrassed, ashamed, and/or fearful of the potential consequences of full disclosure. Parents frequently experience similar emotions.

The following sample dialogue illustrates how the initial interview might be conducted: "Hello Jim, I'm Dr. _____. What is your understanding as to why we are meeting today?" If the youth accurately identifies the reason for the evaluation, reinforce him or her by stating,

"Yes, that is also my understanding." Not surprisingly, many youth are brought for evaluation and treatment without being fully informed as to why they are being evaluated. In such cases, it is advisable to provide the youth with a thorough explanation of why the evaluation is occurring and what the evaluation will consist of.

The evaluator should tell the youth that he or she is not going to pass moral judgment on the juvenile, but rather is there to determine in what areas the juvenile is skilled and has strengths and in which areas remediation is necessary. It is also helpful to inform the youth that the evaluator has had experience in conducting such evaluations, and he or she will not be shocked or negatively affected by the youth's disclosure. Facial expressions and body language on the part of the evaluator should be monitored throughout the evaluation. Youth are inclined not to divulge information if they feel they are being negatively appraised.

Once the introductions have been made, the purpose of the interview explained, the limits of confidentiality determined, and consent obtained, the evaluator then proceeds to collect information. A psychosexual evaluation is comprehensive and covers what most good clinical interviews cover, including developmental history, social and medical history, family functioning, academic history, alcohol and drug abuse, psychological/ psychiatric problems, and a mental status exam. An in-depth sexual history is taken. The manner in which questions are asked can impact on how much information the youth discloses. Rather than inquiring as to whether the youth has or has not engaged in specific sexual behavior, the evaluator asks "How old were you when _____?" Relevant information to be obtained includes age of first sexual knowledge, first crush, first kiss, first sexual touch; age at which puberty was entered; age at first masturbation, frequency of masturbation; age of first exposure to sexually explicit material; types and frequency of use of sexually explicit material; number of sexual partners, ages, gender of sexual partners, and types of sexual acts engaged in with sexual partners. Inquiries are also made as to the relationship of the sexual "partner" to the youth, as well as who initiated the sexual behavior and how the youth felt about the sexual interaction.

Experience indicates that adolescent males in particular have difficulty discussing their own past histories of victimization. Consequently, when an evaluator asks, "Have you been sexually abused?," some will initially answer "No," even though they have. An evaluator's use of the term "sexual partner" or the phrase "sexual experiences you have had," enables the youth to discuss an abusive experience without having to label himself a victim.

A similar interview format can be used to obtain information regarding a range of paraphiliac interests and behaviors. For example, an evaluator may ask questions such as "How old were you the first time you had thoughts about peeking into a window or room to see people disrobing or engaged in sexual acts?" "How old were you the first time you peeked?" "How old were you the first time you exposed your genitals to a person who had not asked to see them?" "How old were you the first time you forced sex on someone?" "How old were you the first time you dressed in women's undergarments?" Since research (Abel, Becker, Cunningham-Rathner, Mittleman, & Rouleau, 1988) with adults has indicated that people with sexual behavior problems usually participate in more than one category of inappropriate sexual behavior, it is important to question the youth about all categories of paraphiliac behavior. Since juveniles are reluctant to volunteer such inforamtion, the clinician must inquire; otherwise, important information about other categories of sexual interest may be missed.

Other relevant information to obtain is how the youth selected the victim. Specifically, is he attracted to a certain body type or gender, or is it that the youth looked for someone who was vulnerable. It is important to ascertain the *modus operandi*. Some youth will manipulate their victims into being sexual with them; others may bribe them, verbally or physically coerce or, in some cases, utilize excessive physical force or restrain their victims. Again, it is important for the evaluator to verify the offender's statement. This is underscored by a study conducted by Becker and Hunter (1993), in which 118 adolescent sex offenders were questioned as to their use of aggression during the sexual offense and the type of sexual behavior engaged in, and compared to the referral source's report. Although 42% of the adolescent offenders reported that no violence was used in the commission of the sexual offense, referral source reports indicated that only 8% had not used violence in the commission of the sexual offense. Although 25% of the adolescents reported using physical violence, referral source reports indicated that 61% had actually used physical violence. Discrepancies were also found in the self-reports of the types of sexual abuse or assault committed. Whereas 15% reported having vaginally penetrated their victims, referral sources reported that 18% had. Likewise, although 22% reported having anally penetrated their victims, referral sources reported that 26% had.

The nature of the youth's sexual fantasies are also important to assess. In many cases, sexual fantasies serve as a rehearsal for the actual behavior in which the youth will engage. Therefore, it is useful to obtain information on what percent of the youth's sexual fantasies involve males versus females, the age range of the persons the youth fantasizes about, the type of sexual activity engaged in, the amount of coercion or force used as part of the sexual act, and finally, whether there have been any changes in the themes or sexual fantasies over time. In some cases, there is an escalation in the amount of physical force or violence used as fantasy themes.

A number of psychometric instruments have been utilized by clinicians and clinical researchers in evaluating youthful offenders. The following is not meant to be a comprehensive list but is reflective of domains to be assessed and what, if any, data has been published relative to these instruments.

6.1. The Adolescent Cognition Scale

This instrument is a 32-item forced-choice inventory that the adolescent must either endorse or reject (true or false). A sum score is derived, reflecting the total number of cognitive distortions endorsed. The reliability and discriminate utility of this instrument was evaluated (Hunter, Becker, Kaplan, & Goodwin, 1991). To assess the test–retest reliability, the instrument was administered to 37 adolescent sex offenders on consecutive days. Only 17 of the 32 items were significantly positively correlated between first- and second-test administration. To assess the discriminative utility of the instrument, scores were compared between matched samples of adolescents who had committed sexual offenses and adolescents who had no known history of sexual offense. The instrument did not discriminate between the two groups. Hypothesized reasons for the failure to discriminate include the following: (1) The sex-offending youth may have given the socially desirable response as opposed to how they really viewed each situation presented; (2) adolescent sex offenders may not as yet have developed the cognitive distortions characteristic of adult sex offenders; (3) the presence of cognitive distortion, in and of itself, is not sufficient to lead to sexual offending behavior. The authors are currently working to revise the scale.

6.2. The Adolescent Sexual Interest Cardsort (ASIC)

This inventory is a 64-item self-report measure of sexual interest and is basically a revision of a scale development by Abel (1979) for adult sexual offenders. The inventory consists of sexual vignettes, which the adolescent is requested to rate on a 5-point scale, indicating whether he is aroused by thoughts of engaging in the specific sexual behavior described. Recently Hunter, Becker, and Kaplan (1995) evaluated both the test–retest reliability and concurrent validity of the instrument. Reliability was assessed by administering the instrument to 32 adolescent sex offenders on consecutive days. Sixty of the 64 items produced statistically significant correlations.

Evaluation of the concurrent validity consisted of correlating the self-related interest (ASIC) with phallometrically measured (see section 6.4 on phallometry) arousal of each of 14 common sexual-stimulus categories. Statistically significant correlations between responses to the ASIC and phallometric responses were found for only 4 of the 14 categories. Only 2 of the categories (consensual sex with a same-age female and voyeurism) produced means in the positive direction on the ASIC. It was hypothesized that dissimulation affected the outcome and, as with adult offenders, caution is urged in relying on the self-reports of sexual offenders.

6.3. The Multiphasic Sex Inventory

This instrument was developed by Nichols and Molinder (1984) to assess a wide range of psychosexual characteristics. This instrument includes scales that identify individuals who feel sexually insecure and inadequate, measures the extent of "normal" sexual interests and drives, and identifies individuals who are preoccupied with sexual matters. The scales assess cognitive distortions and immaturity. The Sexual History Scale encompasses sexual-deviancy development, gender-orientation development, and gender-identity devleopment. We are unaware of any published data on the reliability and validity of this instrument with a juvenile sex offender population.

It is also recommended that assessment of intellectual and personality functioning be conducted. Since some youth are dyslexic or have reading difficulty, it is important to assess their reading ability prior to presenting them with a battery of assessment instruments to complete.

There is a dearth of psychometrically sound assessment instruments specific to the juvenile sex offender population. Instrument development for this population is greatly encouraged.

6.4. Phallometric Assessment

Penile plethysmography is one form of assessing physiological sexual arousal. The procedure consists of the presentation of sexual stimuli (audiotapes, slides, videos) while penile tumescence is measured via a penile transducer. Although a substantial body of literature exists on the use of this form of assessment with adults (Murphy & Barbaree, 1994), there is scant research on the utility of phallometric assessment with adolescent sexual offenders. This form of assessment can be useful and appropriate for some adolescent offenders when used in a manner consistent with guidelines recommended by the Association for the Treatment of

Sexual Abusers (1991) and the National Task Force on Juvenile Sexual Offending (National Adolescent Perpetrator Network, 1993). It is recommended that assessment should only be performed with the full consent of the adolescent, parent(s), and the agency that referred the adolescent. Use of this form of assessment with prepubertal youth is not recommended.

The authors have conducted a series of studies on the use of phallometric assessment with adolescent offenders, and the results of those studies are summarized (Becker, Hunter, Stein, & Kaplan, 1989; Becker, Hunter, Goodwin, Kaplan, & Martinez, 1992; Becker, Kaplan, & Tenke, 1992; Hunter & Becker, 1994). In general, the data indicate that the relationship between phallometric arousal and certain clinical characteristics appears weaker in an adolescent population than in an adult population (Hunter & Becker, 1994).

6.5. Assessment of Children with Sexual Behavior Problems

Pithers et al. (1995) have described a comprehensive assessment protocol for children with sexual behavior problems and their caregivers. A thorough intake interview should be conducted. Berliner, Manois, and Monastersky (1986) have developed such protocols. Inventories that can be utilized include behavioral rating scales, the Child Sexual Behavior Inventory (Friedrich et al., 1992), and measures of anxiety and self-competence. Some parents or caregivers may have characteristics that could serve to moderate or exacerbate behaviors of children. It is important to assess them. A comprehensive clinical interview is recommended, including taking a sexual history, as well as gathering information about history of maltreatment, substance abuse, and criminal history. Assessment instruments to consider using include the Family Environment Scale (Moos & Moos, 1981), Brief Symptom Inventory (Derogatis, 1991), and measures of social support, depression, and anxiety.

The assessment and treatment of prepubescent children who present with sexual behavior problems is a relatively new area of study and, to date, there are no published controlled therapy outcome studies with the population.

7. Treatment: An Overview

Although there is a considerable body of literature on the treatment of adult sex offenders, there are few controlled outcome studies on the effectiveness of treatment for children with sexual behavior problems and adolescent sex offenders. In part, the lack of controlled outcome studies relates to the ethics of randomly assigning known offenders who may represent a danger to the public safety to a "waitlist control group" or to a "no-treatment control group." Also, some of the uncontrolled studies have been fraught with methodological problems. (For those readers interested in reviews and critiques of the existing literature on adult sex offenders, they are referred to Becker, 1994; Furby, Weinott, & Blackshaw, 1989; Marshall, Jones, Ward, et al., 1991; Marshall & Pithers, 1994.)

In many ways, the development of treatment programs for juvenile sex offenders has incorporated modifications of elements of treatment strategies used for adult offenders. The development of a treatment plan for the juvenile sex offender and his family follows from a comprehensive evaluation. Treatment plans should be individualized, and clinicians are warned against the "one size fits all" philosophy. In general, treatment for juvenile sex offenders can be categorized as to the philosophy of the treatment providers and the form of intervention used. Most programs utilize some or all of the following interventions: psychoeducational, cognitive-behavioral, family therapy, and relapse prevention. Some programs also use pharmacological treatments as an adjunct. The clinician must be cognizant of the safety of the community in making a determination as to whether a particular youth can receive outpatient treatment, or whether residential treatment is recommended. If a youthful offender is to be treated in the community, it is imperative that there are individuals to provide appropriate support, supervision, and monitoring of the child's behavior while in the community. If parents are in denial as to the fact that their child committed a sexual offense, they may not be motivated to see that the child attends therapy sessions, or they may decline participation in family therapy.

At present, the National Center for Child Abuse and Neglect has funded two demonstration projects to evaluate the efficacy of various treatments for children with sexual behavior problems. Pithers et al. (1995) describe one program in Vermont under the direction of R. S. Gray. In this program, children and their parents meet separately in groups for 1 hour and then meet together for a half hour. Group activities are highly structured. The treatment is 32 weeks in duration and covers the following topics: establishing safety rules; accountability for behavior; recognition, management, and expression of emotions; empowerment; healthy sexual development; cognitive distortions; victim empathy; grief work; personal victimization issues; decision making; "clarification scrapbook," and relapse prevention. There is also the establishment of a presentation team and a graduation ritual. This program is ongoing, and data analysis has not been completed.

7.1. Treating Adolescent Sex Offenders

The first step in treatment includes having the juvenile accept responsibility for his or her behavior. There are many reasons why the juvenile does not accept responsibility for his or her behavior, including shame, embarrassment, and fear of consequences. Often the manner in which juveniles are approached about their behavior can impact on their behavior. For example, a parent may approach the juvenile and state, "The police just called and said that there is an allegation that you abused Sallie. You didn't do that, did you?" Conversely, the parent might say, "If you abused her, I'm going to throw you out of the house." These types of statements made by parents make it difficult for juveniles to disclose their behavior. Also, when attorneys have been appointed to defend juveniles, they may have been told by the attorney not to speak about the case to anyone. There are a number of methods that can be used to confront denial and facilitate accountability on the part of juveniles. Educating juveniles about what treatment can offer or in terms of competency development, specifically learning how to develop and sustain healthy relationships with peers, can also help in persuading them to discuss problem areas. If juveniles are placed in ongoing treatment groups with other juveniles who have accepted responsibility for their behavior, this affords them an opportunity to see that they are not alone. It also allows the "admitters" to inform the "deniers" that they were in the same place and understand why it is difficult to "own up" to their behavior.

A primary goal of treatment is to prevent further victimization from occurring and to arrest the development of further psychosexual problems. Other treatment goals include increasing the social competence in order that juveniles can develop functional, age-appropriate relationships with their peers. The following treatment model developed by the authors includes as treatment components the following:

1. *Values Clarification*: To provide clarification of sexual values as they are relevant to the cessation of destructive and exploitative sexual relationships, and to promote healthy and age-appropriate relationships.
2. *Cognitive Restructuring*: To assist adolescents in understanding the thoughts, feelings, and events that contributed to their sexual acting out, and to correct distortions in thinking pertinent to their tendency to minimize, rationalize, or project blame onto others.
3. *Empathy Training*: To provide adolescents with instructions and experiential practice designed to enhance their capacity to empathize with others.

4. *Education in Human Sexuality*: To provide a basic understanding of human sexuality and relationship functioning, with the goal of promoting healthy, consensual, age-appropriate relationships within the context of a relationship, and when they are at an age to be responsible for those relationships.
5. *Anger Management*: To assist adolescents in identifying stimuli and situations in which they have responded with anger or physical and verbal aggression as opposed to appropriate verbal communication of feelings. Youth are taught how to manage anger impulses.
6. *Impulse Control*: Adolescents are assisted in acquiring skills related to the development of improved sexual impulse control, and the ability to interrupt deviant sexual thoughts that lead to heightened sexual arousal and eventual acting out.
7. *Education as to What the Processes of the Behavior Were*: Adolescents are provided with an understanding of the nature of adolescent sexual perpetration, including its causes and treatment.
8. *Assistance with Academics*: Academic achievement and success is crucial for adolescents to function in our society. It is important to provide special education instruction and support to youth who are learning-disabled and emotionally troubled, and who cannot function in a regular education environment.
9. *Basic Vocational and Living Skills*: Assistance is provided to those adolescents who are chronologically of an age at which they will be living independently.
10. *Family Therapy*: To ensure that the family system is a functional one, family therapy is provided.

A variety of treatment modalities are utilized with juvenile offenders, including individual therapy, group therapy, and family therapy. The treatment model is utilized on both an outpatient and inpatient basis. The basic philosophy of treatment is that juveniles are given an opportunity to change their behavior. For those juveniles who have been allowed to remain in the community to receive treatment, it is important that adequate supervision of the juveniles be available and utilized in the community setting. Juveniles who are placed in a residential facility are those for whom either adequate supervision is not available in the community or who represent too great a risk to public safety to remain in the community. Although to date there is not available an empirically derived risk assessment instrument, the authors use the following in determining the level of care necessary for any juvenile:

1. *Arrests*: The greater the number of previous arrests, the more likely residential treatment is required.

2. *Number of Victims*: The more victims, the greater the need for residential treatment.

3. *Level of Psychopathy*: To the degree that juveniles have a history of conduct-disordered behavior beginning at an early age, in which people have been exploited and the rights of others not valued, the greater the need for residential placement.

4. *Distortions in Thinking Patterns*: The greater the number and intensity of cognitive distortions, the greater the risk to society.

5. *Types of Offense*: If the offense was premeditated, involved force, and penetration was effected, the more likely residential treatment is required.

6. *Degree of Compulsivity and Arousal*: When there is a compulsive quality to the behavior and excessive sexual arousal to paraphiliac behavior, residential placement is recommended. Compliance with treatment interventions can be a problem for both the juvenile offender and his or her family. Methods use to facilitate compliance include ensuring that both the juvenilie and parent(s) have a thorough understanding of why treatment has been recommended. This involves describing to both the juvenile and parent(s) the potential benefits of complying with treatment. It is critical that an adversary position not be taken with the parent(s). The clinician should work with the parent(s) to assist in helping the child accomplish and maintain therapeutic gains.

A further issue relates to ensuring that a continuum of care is in place. Children in residential placement should be transitioned back to their community and families in a manner, and at a pace, that ensures both success to the youth and community safety.

7.2. Treatment Outcome and Recidivism

There is only one controlled treatment outcome study on juvenile sex offenders that appears in the professional literature. Blaske et al. (1989) compared multisystemic therapy with individual therapy. Juveniles were followed on average for 37 months. Although 75% of the youth who received individual therapy were recidivists, only 12.5% of those who received the multisystemic therapy reoffended.

Kahn and Chambers (1991) conducted a retrospective follow-up on 221 juvenile sex offenders treated in 10 programs in the state of Washington. Two of the programs were institution-based correctional programs and both were outpatient programs. Juveniles were followed on average for 20 months. Whereas the sexual recidivism rate was low (7.5%), the overall recidivism rate (nonsexual offenders) was high (44.8%).

Schram, Milloy, and Rowe (1991) reported on the results of an extended follow-up of 197 of the juveniles on which Kahn and Chambers reported. The rate of sexual reoffense continued to remain low, with 12.2% having been arrested for a sex offense and a 10% conviction rate.

Becker (1990) provided follow-up data on 80 juvenile sex offenders who were treated on an outpatient basis and followed, in many cases, up to 2 years. Recidivism data were determined by interviewing the youth, families, and referral sources. Eight percent of the youth had sexually reoffended.

Bremer (1992) reported on the sexual recidivism of residentially treated juvenile sex offenders. Six percent were convicted for nonsexual offenses.

Although the results of these studies provide reason for optimism, more research is needed. The only controlled treatment outcome study had a small sample size. Furthermore, longer follow-ups are needed. Questions to be answered include the following: What are the behaviors of these youth when they reach adulthood? What percentage become parents? Do they maintain control of their behavior, or do they abuse their own children?

8. Conclusions and Recommendations

Existing literature indicates that juvenile sexual offenders are a heterogenous population. Although we lack an empirically derived theory to explain the etiologies of their inappropriate behaviors, it is clear from our clinical experience that there is not one causative factor, but multiple pathways. Although existing research indicates that treated juvenile sex offenders evidence relatively low recidivism rates, large-scale, well-controlled treatment outcome studies comparing differential therapeutic approaches with long-term follow-ups are lacking.

The following clinical and research agenda is proposed for the future:

1. The development of empirical typologies for female offenders, male offenders, incest versus nonincest offenders, and for those who molest individuals of one gender as opposed to both.
2. Theory development and evaluation.
3. The development of forensically sound and defensible specific assessment instruments for juvenile sex offenders.
4. Controlled treatment outcome studies with long-term follow-ups.

5. Every community should have available a continuum of services for juvenile offenders, which would include specialized group homes, therapeutic foster care, residential treatment centers, and community-based treatment for both juveniles and their families.

9. References

Abel, G. G., Becker, J. V., Cunningham-Rathner, J., Mittelman, J., & Rouleau, J. (1988). Multiple paraphiliac diagnoses among sex offenders. *Bulletin of the American Academy of Psychiatry and Law*, 16, 153–168.

Abel, G. G., Mittelman, M. S., & Becker, J. V. (1985). Sexual offenders: Results of assessment and recommendations for treatment in clinical criminology. In M. H. Ben-Aron, S. J. Hucker, & C. D. Webster (Eds.), *The assessment and treatment of criminal behavior* (pp. 191–205). Toronto: M&M Graphic.

Association for the Treatment of Sexual Abusers. (1993). *The ATSA Practitioner's Handbook*. Lake Oswego, OR: Association for the Treatment of Sexual Abusers.

Awad, G. A., & Saunders, E. (1989). Adolescent child molesters: Clinical observations. *Child Psychiatry and Human Development*, 19, 195–206.

Becker, J. V. (1990). Treating adolescent sexual offenders. *Professional Psychology: Research and Practice*. 21(5), 362–365.

Becker, J. V. (1994). Offenders: Characteristics and treatment. *The Future of Children*, 4, 176–197.

Becker, J. V., Harris, C. D., & Sales, B. D. (1993). Juveniles who commit sex offenses: A critical review of research in sexual aggression. In G. C. N. Hall, R. Hirschman, & J. Graham, et al. (Eds.), *Issues in etiology and assessment, treatment, and policy*. Washington, DC: Taylor & Francis.

Becker, J. V., & Hunter, J. A. (July, 1993). Aggressive sex offenders. *Child and Adolescent Psychiatric Clinics of North America: Sexual and Gender Identity Disorders*, 2(3), 477–487. Philadelphia: W. B. Saunders.

Becker, J. V., Hunter, J. A., Goodwin, D., Kaplan, M., & Martinez, D. (1992). Test–retest reliability of audiotaped phallometric stimuli with adolescent sexual offenders. *Annals of Sex Research*, 5, 45–51.

Becker, J. V., Hunter, J. A., Stein, R., & Kaplan, M. (1989). Factors associated with erection in adolescent sex offenders. *Journal of Psychopathology and Behavioral Assessment*, 2, 353–362.

Becker, J. V., Kaplan, M. S., Cunningham-Rathner, J., & Kavoussi, R. (1986). Characteristics of adolescent incest sexual perpetrators: Preliminary findings. *Journal of Family Violence*, 1, 85–97.

Becker, J. V., Kaplan, M. S., & Tenke, C. E. (1992). The relationship of abuse history, denial, and erectile response profiles of adolescent sexual perpetrators. *Behavior Therapy*, 23, 87–97.

Becker, J. V., Kaplan, M. S., Tenke, C. E., et al. (1991). The incidence of depressive symptomatology in juvenile sex offenders with a history of abuse. *Child Abuse and Neglect*, 15, 531–536.

Becker, J. V., & Stein, R. M. (1991). Is sexual erotica associated with sexual deviance in adolescent males? *International Journal of Law and Psychiatry*, 14, 85–95.

Berliner, L., Manois, L., & Monastersky, C. (1986). *Child sexual behavior disturbance: An assessment and treatment model*. Seattle: Sexual Assault Center & University of Washington.

Blaske, D., Bouduin, C., Henggeler, S., & Mann, B. (1989). Individual, family, and peer characteristics of adolescent sex offenders and assaultive offenders. *Developmental Psychology*, 25, 846–855.

196 JUDITH V. BECKER AND JOHN A. HUNTER, JR.

Bourdin, C. M., Henggeler, S. W., Blaske, D. M., & Stein, R. J. (1990). Multisystemic treatment of adolescent sexual offenders. *International Journal of Offender Therapy and Comparative Criminology, 34*, 105–114.

Bremer, J. F. (1992). Serious juvenile sex offenders: Treatment and long-term follow-up. *Psychiatric Annals, 22*, 326–332.

Brown, F., Flannagan, T., & McLeon, M. (Eds.). (1984). *Sourcebook of criminal justice statistics.* Washington, DC: Bureau of Justice Statistics.

Derogatis, L. R., (1991). Brief symptom inventory. *Clinical Psychometric Research.*

Fehrenbach, P. A., & Monastersky, C. (1988). Characteristics of female adolescent sexual offenders. *American Journal of Orthopsychiatry, 58*, 148–151.

Fehrenbach, P. A., Smith, W., Monastersky, C., & Deisher, R. W. (1986). Adolescent sexual offenders: Offender and offense characteristics. *American Journal of Orthopsychiatry, 56*, 225–233.

Finkelhor, D., Hotaling, G. T., Lewis, F. T., et al. (1990). Sexual abuse in a national survey of adult men and women: Prevalence, characteristics, and risk factors. *Child Abuse and Neglect, 14*, 19–28.

Ford, M. E., & Linney, J. A. (1995). Comparative analysis of juvenile sexual offenders, violent homosexual offenders, and status offenders. *Journal of Interpersonal Violence, 10*, 56–70.

Friedrich, W. N., Grambsch, P., Damon, L., et al. (1992). Child Sexual Behavior Inventory: Normative and clinical comparisons. *Psychological Assessment, 4*, 303–311.

Frontline: The Vermont Treatment Program for Sexual Aggressors (1988). Wellington, NZ: Television New Zealand.

Furby, L., Weinrott, J., & Blackshaw, L. (1989). Sex offender recidivism: A review. *Psychological Bulletin, 105*, 3–30.

Gray, A. S., & Pithers, W. D. (1993). Relapse prevention with sexually aggressive adolescents and children: Expanding treatment and supervision. In H. E. Barbaree, S. Hudson, & W. Marshall (Eds.), *The juvenile sex offender* (pp. 289–319). New York: Guilford Press.

Hunter, J. A., & Becker, J. V. (1994). The role of deviant sexual arousal in juvenile sexual offending: Etiology, evaluation, and treatment. *Criminal Justice and Behavior, 21*, 132–149.

Hunter, J. A., Becker, J. V., Goodwin, D. W., & Kaplan, M. S. (1995). The Adolescent Sexual Interest Card Sort: Test–retest reliability and concurrent validity in relation to phallometric assessment. *Archives of Sexual Behavior, 24*, 555–561.

Hunter, J. A., Becker, J. V., Kaplan, M. S. & Goodwin, D. W. (1991). The reliability and discriminative utility of the adolescent cognition scale for juvenile sexual offenders. *Annals of Sex Research, 4*, 281–286.

Hunter, J. A., & Figueredo, A. J. (1995). *The role of sexual victimization in the etiology of juvenile perpetrates of child molestation.* Unpublished manuscript.

Hunter, J. A., Lexier, L. J., Goodwin, D. W., Browne, P. A., & Dennis, C. (1993). Psychosexual, attitudinal, and developmental characteristics of juvenile female sexual perpetrators in a residential treatment setting. *Journal of Child and Family Studies, 2*(4), 317–326.

Kaemingk, K. L., Koselka, M., Becker, J. V., & Kaplan, M. S. (1995). Age and adolescent sexual offender arousal. *Sexual Abuse: A Journal of Research and Treatment, 1*, 249–257.

Kahn, T. J., & Chambers, H. J. (1991). Assessing reoffense risk with juvenile sexual offenders. *Child Welfare, 19*, 333–345.

Kaplan, M., Becker, J. V., & Cunningham-Rathner, J. (1988). Characteristics of parents of adolescent incest perpetrators: Preliminary findings. *Journal of Family Violence, 3*, 183–191.

Kaplan, S., Hong, G., & Weinhold, C. (1984). Epidemiology of depressive sympomatology in adolescents. *Journal of the Academy of Child Psychiatry, 23*, 91–98.

Katz, R. (1990). Psychological adjustment in adolescent child molesters. *Child Abuse and Neglect, 14*, 567–575.

Kavoussi, R. J., Kaplan, M., & Becker, J. V. (1988). Psychiatric diagnoses in adolescent sex offenders. *Journal of American Academy of Child Adolescent Psychiatry, 27*, 241–243.

Kobayashi, J., Sales, B. D., Becker, J. V., Figueredo, A. J., & Kaplan, M. S. (1995). Perceived parental deviance, parental–child bonding, child abuse, and child sexual aggression. *Sexual Abuse: A Journal of Research and Treatment, 7*(1), 25–44.

Lewis, D. O., Shankok, S. S., & Pincus, J. H. (1979). Juvenile male sexual assaulters. *American Journal of Psychiatry, 136*, 1194–1196.

Lightfoot, L. O., & Barbaree, H. E. (1993). The relationship between substance use and abuse and sexual offending in adolescents. In H. E. Barbaree, W. L. Marshall, & S. W. Hudson (Eds.), *The juvenile sex offender* (pp. 203–204). New York: Guilford Press.

Marshall, W., Jones, R., Ward, T., et al. (1991). Treatment outcome with sex offenders. *Clinical Psychology Review, 11*, 465–485. (On page 467, the authors cite five studies that concluded that the likelihood of reoffense among released offenders with more than one prior conviction was significantly greater than first offenders.)

Marshall, W., & Pithers, W. (1994). A reconsideration of treatment outcome with sex offenders. *Criminal Justice and Behavior, 21*, 10–27.

Matthews, R., Hunter, J. A., & Vuz, J. (in press). Juvenile female sexual offenders: Clinical characteristics and treatment issues. *Journal of Interpersonal Violence.*

Moos, R. H., & Moos, B. (1981). *Revised Family Environment Scale.* Palo Alto, CA: Consulting Psychologists Press.

Murphy, W. D., & Barbaree, H. E. (1994). Assessments of sex offenders by measures of erectile response: Psychometric properties and decision making. Brandon, VT: Safer Society Press.

National Adolescent Perpetrator Network. (1993). The revised report from the National Task Force on Juvenile Sexual Offending. *Juvenile and Family Court Journal, 44*, 1–120.

Nichols, H. R., & Molinder, I. (1984). *Multiphasic Sex Inventory*, 437 Bowes Drive, Tacoma, Washington.

Pithers, W. D., Becker, J. V., Kafka, M., Morenz, B., Schlank, A., & Leombruno, T. (1995). Children with sexual behavior problems, adolescent sexual abusers, and adult sex offenders: Assessment and treatment. *American Psychiatric Press Review of Psychiatry, 14*, 779–819.

Pithers, W. D., Johnson, L., Elliott, A., et al. (1993). *The Vermont Integrated Action Plan for the Prevention of Child Sexual Abuse: Transforming Vermont into the first abuse-free state.* Waterbury: Vermont Department of Corrections.

Ryan, G., Lane, S., Davis, J., & Isaac, C. (1987). Juvenile sex offenders: Development and correction. *Child Abuse and Neglect, 11*, 385–395.

Schram, D. D., Milloy, C. D., & Rowe, W. E. (1991). *Juvenile sex offenders: A follow-up study of reoffense behavior.* Unpublished manuscript.

Smith, H., & Israel, E. (1987). Sibling incest: A study of the dynamics of 25 cases. *Child Abuse and Neglect, 11*, 101–108.

Smith, W. R. (1988). Delinquency and abuse among juvenile sexual offenders. *Journal of International Violence, 3*, 400–411.

Tarter, R., Hegedus, A., Alterman, A., & Katz-Garris, I. (1983). Cognitive capacities of juvenile, non-violent and sexual offenders. *Journal of Nervous and Mental Disease, 171*, 564–567.

6 Adolescent Substance Abuse and Family Therapy Outcome
A Review of Randomized Trials

HOLLY B. WALDRON

1. Introduction

Family therapy as a treatment for substance abuse was embraced in community mental health agencies and other clinical settings in the 1970s and came to be viewed as a viable treatment alternative for many at-risk populations, including adolescents (Coleman & Davis, 1978; Kaufman & Kaufman, 1992). In the clinical literature, the importance of family-based interventions for substance abuse has remained widely accepted (Craig, 1993), and family therapy is frequently implemented with adolescent abusers (cf. Selekman & Todd, 1991). As in the broader family therapy literature, however, treatment approaches have been derived primarily from theories of family functioning and clinical experience, rather independently from research (Bry, 1988), and with little attention to systematic evaluation.

In the last decade, however, considerable advances have been made in researching the effectiveness of family treatments for alcohol- and substance-use problems generally and adolescent substance abuse in particular (cf. Liddle & Dakof, 1995). Much of the impetus for family therapy outcome research with adolescents can be attributed to the pivotal work of Stanton, Todd, and their colleagues (1982), who conducted the first systematic treatment outcome study of family therapy and found dramatic reductions in drug use by adult heroin addicts following a brief (10 sessions) phase of family therapy, and to the work of José Szapocznik and his

HOLLY B. WALDRON • Department of Psychology, University of New Mexico, Albuquerque, New Mexico 87131.

Advances in Clinical Child Psychology, Volume 19, edited by Thomas H. Ollendick and Ronald J. Prinz. Plenum Press, New York, 1997.

colleagues, who demonstrated the effectiveness of family therapy with adolescents in the first controlled studies (Scopetta, King, Szapocznik, & Tillman, 1979; Szapocznik, Kurtines, Foote, Perez-Vidal, & Hervis, 1983, 1986). Since these early investigations, nearly a dozen randomized trials of family therapy outcome have been completed or are underway.

This chapter is intended to provide a comprehensive review of family therapy outcome research on adolescent substance abusers, focusing on controlled, comparative studies and considering the context of the broader adolescent substance abuse literature. The chapter is divided into four main sections. The first section focuses on the key conceptual issues of defining and measuring adolescent substance abuse. The second briefly summarizes the major conceptual models underlying family therapy research. The third section presents a review of studies of the effectiveness of family-based treatments. The fourth section summarizes the findings, discusses factors in the substance abuse and family therapy literatures that may mediate outcome, and explores the implications for future research.

2. Conceptualizing Adolescent Substance Abuse

2.1. Experimental versus Problem Use

The prevailing view of adolescent substance abuse is that initiation and maintenance of use derive from a broad spectrum of interacting influences. A host of factors has been identified that influence substance use, ranging from factors associated with the broad social context (e.g., laws and norms favorable toward substance use and drug availability) to individual and interpersonal factors (e.g., physiological responsivity to drugs, parent–child bonding; cf. Hawkins, Catalano, & Miller, 1992), with some evidence suggesting that use is determined more by sheer number of risk factors present than by the presence of any particular factor (Bry, McKeon, & Pandina, 1982; McGee & Newcomb, 1992).

In an attempt to integrate the numerous and, at times, seemingly disparate theories of the determinants of substance use, Flay and Petraitis developed the theory of triadic influence as a comprehensive, overarching macromodel (Flay & Petraitis, 1994; Petraitis, Flay, & Miller, 1995). This model organizes causal factors into levels ranging from very proximal, to distal, to ultimate and describes three streams of influence that flow through the levels: (1) cultural–environmental factors that influence attitudes, (2) social situation–contextual factors that influence social learning and normative beliefs, and (3) intrapersonal factors that influence self-efficacy.

Although the triadic influence model provides a valuable integration of substance-use theories and research findings, the process by which adolescents who engage in experimentation develop serious abuse patterns remains poorly understood (Dishion, Patterson, & Reid, 1988). Before substance use becomes problematic, adolescents pass through a stage during which they are not committed to continuing use and have not integrated substance use as a regular part of life (Clayton, 1992). National survey data show that experimentation with drugs, as a class of behavior, is normative (Johnston, Bachman, & O'Malley, 1991). The majority of adolescents who experiment with hard drugs do not become addicted (Shedler & Block, 1990), and most adolescents appear to "mature out" of problem use with a sharp decrease in illicit drug use and heavy drinking as they transition to adulthood (Kouzis & Labouvie, 1992; Raveis & Kandel, 1987). Some theorists have even argued that, to a degree, drug use has developmental and adaptational utility for adolescents. Labouvie (1986) and Shedler and Block (1990), for example, have suggested that drug use may serve as a signal of independence from parents and identification with peers, or as opposition to, or deviation from, societal norms and values, both of which could be viewed as normal exploration of identity issues.

Although theorists generally agree that adolescent substance use is multidimensional, there is considerable ambiguity regarding what constitutes problem substance use (Bailey, 1989; Hughes, Power, & Francis, 1992). Research suggests that use of substances during the teen years can interfere with crucial developmental tasks, such as prosocial identity formation, interpersonal and educational skill acquisition, and family and work responsibility assumption (Baumrind, 1985; Bentler, 1992). Moreover, habitual or heavy use has been conceptualized as part of a broader problem-behavior cluster, associated with juvenile delinquency, poor school performance, precocious sexual activity, and other deviant or unconventional behaviors (Donovan & Jessor, 1985; Elliott, Huizinga, & Ageton, 1985; Newcomb & Felix-Ortiz, 1992). In one sense, any level of substance use by adolescents could precipitate problems by increasing the likelihood of arrest for substance-related offenses and increasing adolescents' exposure to risky situations such as driving while intoxicated, engaging in sexual behavior that increases risk for AIDS, and engaging in violent exchanges (Farrell, Danish, & Howard, 1992; FeCaces, Stinson, & Hartford, 1991). However, Baumrind (1985) argued that drug abuse should be defined empirically, using frequency and problem consequences as determinants.

One area of study that may hold promise for understanding the process by which nonproblem experimental use becomes problematic is research on the developmental trajectory associated with initiation of use. Typically, adolescents who become abusers follow a relatively invariant sequence for drug use, beginning with alcohol and/or cigarette use, followed by marijuana, and then other hard drugs. This progression from "soft" to "hard" drug use, the "gateway" phenomenon (Kandel, 1975), has been confirmed in a number of studies (Andrews, Hops, Ary, Lichtenstein, & Tildesley, 1991; Kandel, Yamaguchi, & Chen, 1992; Welte & Barnes, 1985). Moreover, Ellickson, Hays, and Bell (1992) found that *weekly* alcohol use followed marijuana use and preceded use of all other illicit drugs, and that weekly smoking formed a distinct stage between initial use of pills and other hard drugs. So although dysfunctional use of drugs can be generally characterized by increasing quantities and varieties of drugs used (Kandel, 1982), the issue of defining problem substance use may involve not only identifying the types and number of substances adolescents have used, and the quantity and frequency of use, but also the sequencing or patterning of use. As Dishion et al. (1988) noted, different models may be required to explain experimental drug use, patterned use, and the movement into regular use considered indicative of substance abuse.

Unfortunately, as can be seen in the section on treatment outcome studies, issues related to defining adolescent substance abuse have been virtually ignored by family researchers. The vast majority of family therapy studies has been characterized by wide variations in subject sampling strategies and wide-ranging substance use at intake among participating adolescents. Such methodological problems may represent primary sources for inconsistency of findings and noncomparability across studies.

2.2. Assessment of Substance Use

Most instruments measuring adolescent substance use are still in the developmental stages, and their effectiveness for problem identification is largely unknown. The majority of approaches to assessment has been adapted from those used with adults, and measures have not been evaluated for their reliability and validity with adolescent populations. Unlike adults, adolescents display less physical dependence, have fewer physical and neurological problems related to use, use less overall but use larger amounts at one time, are developmentally more varied, and have an increased likelihood of certain negative social consequences, given their position of dependence and lower status in family and social systems (Barnes, 1984; White & Labouvie, 1989). Whereas a sizable portion of adults may be characterized by heavy drinking and smoking, with no other drug use, such a pattern of use is rare among adolescents. Also, given the smaller body size and weaker tolerance of many youth, adolescents can experience dangerous effects at a lower level of use than adults. Because adolescent use could differ significantly from patterns of adult use, an adolescent could be using substances problematically but bear little or no resemblance to an adult with a substance-use problem when assessed with adapted adult measures. Thus, the need for adolescent-specific assessment is apparent. The lack of availability of appropriate, psychometrically sound measures of substance-adolescent use and abuse has contributed to insufficient standardization of assessment tools across studies and an overreliance on "home grown" instruments that limit the degree to which treatment effectiveness comparisons can be made.

Almost all measures of substance use focus on some type of direct self-report of frequency (e.g., how many days per month use occurred) and intensity (e.g., number of drinks consumed) of use. An obvious goal for treatment is to reduce frequency and/or intensity, if not to zero use, then to a less harmful or risky level, and to increase the proportion of abstinent days. However, as Liddle and Dakof (1995b) note, many paper-and-pencil instruments measuring use of alcohol, tobacco, and other drugs are scaled in such a way that precludes detailed assessment of high use, with the highest category of use often limited (e.g., three times or more per week). As a result, such instruments could fail to detect reductions in use among very heavy users following intervention. Moreover, such instruments fail to capture quantity of alcohol use with the degree of precision that would allow calculation of peak blood alcohol concentration, potentially important as an indicator of dangerous of even life-threatening alcohol use.

An alternative method is the timeline follow-back procedure (cf. Sobell & Sobell, 1992), a structured interview technique that samples a specific time period, using a monthly calendar and memory anchor points to reconstruct daily consumption during the period of interest. A number of studies have compared the methods, including quantity/frequency measures and timeline follow-back, finding generally similar estimates, although Grant, Tonigan, and Miller (1995) found lower estimates of use for paper-and-pencil quantity/frequency measures compared to more detailed interview methods. In principle, the timeline follow-back may offer the most sensitive assessment for adolescents, having the advantage of assessing the widely variable drinking patterns that often characterize teen drinking, and that might not be modeled adequately by the averaging approaches (Leccese & Waldron, 1994). For example, adolescents may drink in association with specific, sporadic events, such as homecoming weekends, finding someone to buy alcohol for them, or having money, such that their drinking is driven by irregular external factors, more so than for adults. Relying on gross quantity/frequency indicators of use, especially for adolescents, may tend to obscure important patterns of use.

Brook, Whiteman, and Gordon (1982), for example, found that family factors related more powerfully to stage of substance use than to frequency of use. Also, using latent growth modeling to detect similarities and differences in developmental trajectories for substance use, Duncan, Duncan, and Hops (1994) found that family cohesion may be more central in delaying escalation of cigarette use than escalation of other substances. With a more detailed and precise assessment of quantity, frequency, and patterning of use, researchers may be able to evaluate the effectiveness and efficacy of family therapies in more sensitive or meaningful ways. For example, forestalling adolescents' progression through the drug-use sequence or initiating their return back through the gateway may reflect treatment effectiveness better than overall amount or frequency of use. Just as family-interaction researchers have found that sequential analyses of behavior provide patterning information about communication exchanges between family members that rates of behavior do not provide, so timeline follow-back sequencing of drug use over a period of time may provide a rich source of outcome data unavailable with gross frequency/intensity measures.

Adult studies have shown that direct self-report measures have high sensitivity in detecting substance-use problems and compare favorably to biomedical measures such as blood and urine tests (National Institute on Alcohol Abuse and Alcoholism, 1990). Even adolescent self-report of substance use, often held suspect because of the increased potential for distortion, given the negative repercussions youth may encounter when reporting on their own use, is more accurate than once thought (Needle, McCubbin, Lorence, & Hochhauser, 1983). However, biomedical markers can be valuable for corroborating self-report. When multiple measures, such as self-report, urinalyses, and collateral reports attained by interviewing parents or peers, converge to give the same results, there is greater confidence in the validity of measures. Another useful aspect of biomedical tests is the potential for a "bogus pipeline" effect, creating the impression that there is an accurate check on self-report and thereby increasing honesty in descriptions of one's substance use (Miller, Westerberg, & Waldron, 1995).

2.3. Other Dimensions of Substance Use Assessment

Several interview instruments have been designed specifically to determine whether an individual meets currently established criteria for disorders of substance abuse and substance dependence according to a specific taxonomic system. Diagnosis, as a binary (present vs. absent) process, represents a gross indicator of problem use with limited utility as an outcome measure in treatment research. As a treatment issue, however, adolescents whose use is prolonged and heavy without periods of abstinence must be assessed for dependence, since physiological withdrawal may require specific medical or psychological interventions (Stanton, Todd, & Associates, 1982).

To the extent that substance abuse is multiply determined and associated with diverse problem behaviors presumably generated by common causes, broad, multidimensional assessment is vital (Henggeler et al., 1991; Maisto & Conners, 1990). Newcomb and Bentler (1989) maintained that any focus on substance use, in isolation from the associated antecedents, concurrent events, or consequences constituting the more general problem-behavior syndrome of which substance abuse is a part, will be distorted. Specific instruments are available or are under development for adolescents to measure other aspects of substance use, such as negative consequences of substance use, positive and negative expectancies associated with use, and readiness for change, as well as adolescent functioning in other domains of behavior (Leccese & Waldron, 1994). Evaluation of these aspects of substance use may provide insights for researchers as to potential mechanisms of change.

Again, however, most treatment outcome research has relied on self-report of drug use, with little attention to problem consequences or other behavioral domains related to abuse. Variation in responding to treatment, even among youth with uniformly heavy use patterns, may be associated with the consequences of substance use, the contexts within which it occurs, the functions that the use serves in the adolescent's life, and the co-occurrence of other problem behaviors.

3. Theoretical and Conceptual Bases of Family Therapy Models

3.1. Family Factors Associated with Adolescent Substance Use

Theories focusing on etiology and antecedents of adolescent substance use have long recognized family factors as an important influence in the development and maintenance of sutstance abuse (cf. Hawkins et al., 1992; Kaufman & Kaufman, 1992). General findings have included the influence of parent and sibling use (Brook, Whiteman, Gordon, & Brook, 1988; Dishion et al., 1988), parent attitudes toward use (Barnes & Welte, 1986), parenting practices (Baumrind, 1991; Shedler & Block, 1990), poor communication and parent–adolescent conflict (Hops, Tildesley, Lichtenstein, Ary, & Sherman, 1990; Thompson & Wilsnack, 1987), parent–child bonding (Elliott et al., 1985; Penning & Barnes, 1982), and patterns of parental overinvolvement–underinvolvement (Kaufman & Kaufman, 1992).

Family factors are likely interdependent and bidirectional. For example, Dishion et al. (1988) found that parental drug use had both a direct effect, believed to result from modeling and opportunities for use, and an indirect effect, resulting from impaired parental control when parents were under the influence of drugs or alcohol. Similarly, findings of increased stress, increased conflict, highly charged negative affect, lack of openness, and poor cohesion in families, as well as the tendency of adolescents to seek support in relationships outside the family, may all have reciprocal influence. One model suggests that adolescents may not directly imitate their parents' use of specific drugs, but they may be exposed to observing that drug use is one method of coping with psychological stress (Kandel, Kessler, & Margulies, 1978). Effective problem solving may, in turn, attenuate drug use by providing an alternative for coping with stressful life events and family disturbance. Examining another aspect of influence, Duncan and his colleagues (1994) found the largest effects of family cohesion on adolescent substance use occurring in middle and later adolescence. Taking their results, together with other research (Dishion et al., 1988; Patterson, Reid, & Dishion, 1992), they suggested that variation in family influence may be curvilinear over time, with a low point in early adolescence when peer influences peak. Such research begins to tease apart the complex interactions among family variables associated with substance abuse and holds promise for much-needed model development for adolescent substance abuse.

In light of the substantial research literature emphasizing the importance of family variables for understanding adolescent substance abuse, it is surprising that family therapy researchers have not focused more effort on the role of the family in the development and maintenance of abuse or, with rare exceptions (e.g., Henggeler et al., 1991; Liddle et al., 1995), on integrating more of the findings from the literature into their treatment models. But, as Alexander, Holtzworth-Munroe, and Jameson (1994) point out, family therapies have traditionally been derived primarily from theory and clinical experience, with research serving more to clarify and justify treatment models rather than to develop new models prospectively. The theoretical perspectives taken most often in adolescent treatment studies involving family therapy have been family systems approaches, although several studies of behavioral or social learning approaches and multisystemic or ecological approaches have also been conducted.

3.2. Family Systems Models

Family systems perspectives, stemming from general systems theory (von Bertalanffy, 1948), view the family as a basic social system consisting of the individual members of the family and the processes (e.g., rules for behaving, roles, repeated sequences of behaviors) that characterize the relationships among members, all reciprocally interdependent. Family systems develop communication patterns and repeated behavioral sequences to regulate family members and maintain equilibrium (i.e., homeostasis). Families may differ along a variety of dimensions characterizing the system, including how the subsystems are organized for relationship functioning; how diffuse or rigid the boundaries are between individuals, subsystems, or the family and extrafamilial systems; or how power is distributed in the subsystems (Haley, 1976; Minuchin, 1974).

Problems such as substance abuse are conceptualized as maladaptive behaviors expressed by one or more family members, but reflecting dysfunction in the system as a whole. The behavior is believed to serve an important function in the family, allowing the family to cope with internal or external stressors, or maintain other processes that have become established in the organization of the system (Stanton, Todd, & Associates, 1982). For example, the attention required to cope with substance abuse in one family member may allow the family to avoid conflict in the marital dyad that could threaten the integrity of the family or reflect the family's inability to cope with the transition of the abuser from childhood into adolescence.

Treatment is aimed at restructuring the interactional patterns associated with the abuse, theoretically making the abuse unnecessary in the maintenance of system functioning. Techniques include: (1) forming a therapeutic relationship (i.e., joining) in which the therapist can elicit the recurring behavioral sequences (i.e., enactment), interrupting and destabilizing the dysfunctional behavioral exchanges; (2) helping family members understand the interrelatedness of their behaviors and see the symptomatic behavior in a way consistent with family change (e.g., reframing); and (3) restructuring or shifting family interaction patterns and establishing new behaviors (e.g., manipulating seating arrangements to fortify a weak parental dyad, establishing rules of communicating, and solving problems that preclude triangulation or conflict avoidance; cf. Stanton, Todd, & Associates, 1982; Szapocznik et al., 1983).

3.3. Behavioral Family Models

Behavioral family therapy models have relied primarily on operant and social learning theories to understand the behavior of an individual in the context of the family. Behaviors such as substance use are viewed as patterns of responses, learned in the context of social interactions (e.g., observing parents, siblings, peers, or other models in the media) and established as a result of the contingencies in the environment (Akers, Krohn, Lanza-Kaduce, & Radosevich, 1979). Consequences that follow behaviors associated with substance use serve to increase (reinforcement) or decrease (punishment) the probability that the behavior will occur again. Substance abuse, then, is determined at least in part by the family-related consequences of the behaviors and the antecedents that indicate the consequences that are in effect (Bry, 1988).

For treatment, emphasis is on contingency management aimed to increase prosocial behavior (e.g., reinforcing behaviors incompatible with substance use, such as involvement in academic and extracurricular activities) and reduce substance use (e.g., punishing behaviors, such as violating curfew with loss of privileges). Techniques such as problem-solving skills or other coping skills training are commonly implemented to provide families with a behavioral repertoire that will allow them to resolve problems independently (Fleischman, Horne, & Arthur, 1983). The increased positive interactions families experience when putting such skills to use are presumed to reinforce the likelihood that the new behaviors will become established patterns.

3.4. Ecological Models

Multisystemic treatments are based on the recognition that substance use and other related problem behaviors derive commonly from many sources of influence and occur in the context of multiple systems (Henggeler et al., 1991). Treatment is directed toward assessing these multiple influences and intervening so that change is supported throughout all the systems affecting the problem behavior, including the intrapersonal system of the individual adolescent, the interpersonal systems of the family and peers, and the extrapersonal systems of the school and the community.

Multisystemic family therapy typically includes sessions or parts of sessions held conjointly with the adolescent and other family members, but may also include individual sessions targeted on decision making, emotion regulation, or other intrapersonal factors that may be influencing substance use. Actual techniques implemented during treatment are generally drawn from other family models, including family systems and behavioral perspectives, and from intervention approaches within the general psychotherapy literature. Therapists work to evaluate factors in the youth's and family's ecological environment that may be contributing to identified problems and plan treatment to include individual and family work within the context of traditional therapy as well as meet with staff in other systems as needed to implement interventions at the broader levels.

4. Treatment Outcome Studies

4.1. Inclusion Criteria

One of the most significant developments in the area of family treatment of adolescent substance abuse in the last 10 years has been the appearance of controlled trials examining the efficacy of family therapy. To identify empirical outcome studies for this review, a computerized literature search was conducted, reference lists of published articles were reviewed, letters of inquiry were sent out to researchers in the family therapy and substance abuse fields, and, in some cases, authors were contacted directly. Studies were included if they (1) focused on adolescent substance use, (2) evaluated the effectiveness of at least one family-based treatment condition and one or more comparison conditions for adolescent substance use (although a number of studies compared two family therapy approaches), and (3) involved random assignment to treatment conditions. As a result, 13 studies were identified, most of which were recently reviewed by Liddle and Dakof (1995b) and included in a meta-analysis by Stanton and Shadish (in press). All the studies were generally well designed, with clearly articulated interventions, specific criteria for evaluating effectiveness, and appropriate statistical procedures for data analysis. Tables 1 and 2 summarize major characteristics of the studies and overall findings.

4.2. Family Systems Studies

Despite wide application and reporting of use of family therapy in treatment settings, until 1989, the only systematic research using randomized assignment to treatment conditions had been conducted at the University of Miami by Szapocznik and his colleagues (Szapocznik et al., 1983, 1986). Szapocznik et al. (1983) compared the effectiveness of two treatment modalities, conjoint family therapy and one-person family therapy, to evaluate whether family-therapy outcome varies on the basis of who participates in the sessions. Both therapy approaches were primarily structural systems therapies, with the one-person intervention aimed at effecting change at the family level while working only with the adolescent substance abuser. Of the 62 families presenting for treatment, 37 families, who completed at least four therapy sessions and the pre- and posttreatment assessments, were included in the data analysis, and 24 families, who returned for assessment 6–12 months after treatment, were included in a follow-up analysis.

TABLE 1

Study Characteristics of Randomized Trials Evaluating Family Therapy for Adolescent Substance Abuse

Study	Nature of substance use	N	Patient age, gender, race/ethnicity	Nonfamily comparison group(s)	Therapists	Length of Tx	Tx manual	Tx adherence ratings
Szapocznik, Kurtines, Foote, Perez-Vidal, & Hervis, 1983	Unclear: "drug-using adolescents"	35	12–20 yrs., M = 17 78% male 100% Hispanic (84% Cuban American)	No	N = 5 All Master's degrees 3–23 yrs. experience	4–12 sessions	No	No
Szapocznik, Kurtines, Foote, Perez-Vidal, & Hervis, 1986	Moderate-heavy: 80% primary marijuana (47% daily use), some alcohol, barbituate use	35	M = 17 yrs % gender not reported 100% Hispanic (77% Cuban American)	No	N = 5 All Master's degrees M = 8.5 yrs. experience	4–15 sessions	No	No
Szapocznik, Perez-Vidal, Brickman, Foote, Santisteban, Hervis, & Kurtines, 1988	Moderate-heavy: 83% marijuana (47% several times weekly), 80% cocaine, 7% nonusers	108	12–21 yrs. 67% male 100% Hispanic (82% Cuban American)	No	N = 1 Ph.D. 15 yrs. experience	Not reported	No	Yes
Santisteban, Szapocznik, Perez-Vidal, Kurtines, Murray, & LaPierriere, 1995	Unclear: exhibited "behavioral correlates of drug use"	193	12–18 yrs., M = 15.6 70% male 100% Hispanic (54% Cuban American)	No	N = 11 6 M.D., 6 Ph.D., 1 Master's degree	Not reported	Yes	Yes

Study	N	Sample	Drug use		Therapist	Duration		
Joanning, Thomas, Quinn, & Mullen, 1992	134	11–20 yrs., M = 15.4 60% male 68% Anglo, 29% Hispanic, 3% African-American	Unclear: nonaddicted alcohol and illicit drug users, 39% substance-related offense	Yes	N = 7 All Master's degrees 5+ yrs. experience	7–15 sessions	Yes	No
Friedman, 1989	135	14–21 yrs., M = 17.9 % gender not reported 89% Anglo 11% other	Heavy: 88% alcohol (average use 9x/month), 87% marijuana (average use 26x/month), 52% amphetamines, 28% cocaine	No	N = 6 4–17 yrs. experience	24 weeks	Yes	Yes
Lewis, Piercy, Sprenkle, & Trepper, 1990	136	12–22 yrs., M = 16 81% male 96% Anglo 3% African-American 1% Hispanic	Unclear: regular users with 35% using marijuana in past month	Yes	Not reported	12 sessions	No	No
Azrin, Donohue, Besalel, Kogan, & Acierno, 1994	26	M = 16 yrs. 77% male 79% Anglo, 19% African-American	Moderate-heavy: 96% marijuana, 35% cocaine, 31% LSD	Yes	Not reported	15 sessions	No	Yes
Krinsley, 1991	29	12–15 yrs., M = 14 66% male 82% Anglo, 18% African-American or Hispanic	Light: "at risk for dropping out," x = 5 days of use in past 3 months	Yes	N not reported All Master's degrees with 1 Ph.D.	Varied, x = 8 sessions	Yes	Yes

(continued)

TABLE 1
(Continued)

Study	Nature of substance use	N	Patient age, gender, race/ethnicity	Nonfamily comparison group(s)	Therapists	Length of Tx	Tx manual	Tx adherence ratings
Scopetta, King, Szapocznik, & Tillman, 1979	Moderate-heavy: 82% primary marijuana or tranquilizers (average use several times weekly), 39% polydrug use	33	$M = 17.2$ 64% male 100% Hispanic	No	$N = 8$ 6 Master's degrees 2 Bachelor's degrees	Varied; 3–20 sessions, $x = 12$	No	No
Henggeler, Borduin, Melton, Mann, Smith, Hall, Cone, & Fucci, 1991	Unclear: Study 1—100% recent arrest for substance-related offense; Study 2—some alcohol, marijuana	1: 200 2: 47	1: $M = 14.4$ yrs. 67% male 70% Anglo, 30% African-American 2: $M = 15$ yrs. 72% male 68% Anglo, 29% Hispanic, 3% African-American	1: Yes 2: Yes	All Master's degrees 1: $N = 12$ 2: $N = 3$ $M = 1.5$ yrs. experience	1: 24–28 hours 2: $x = 36$ hours ($SD = 34$)	1: No 2: No	1: No 2: No
Liddle, Daykof, Parker, Diamond, Barrett, & Garcia, 1995	Heavy: 51% daily marijuana, alcohol use plus hard drugs; 49% marijuana, alcohol use on average 3–4x/ week	151	13–18 yrs., $M = 15.9$ 80% male 51% Anglo, 18% African-American, 15% Hispanic, 6% Asian, 10% other	Yes	N not reported 80% Master's degrees, 20% Ph.D.	14–16 sessions	Yes	No

TABLE 2
Summary of Treatment Outcome Study Findings

Study	Treatment groups (*n*)	Substance use outcome measure(s)	Assessment point	Findings
Szapocznik, Kurtines, Foote, Perez-Vidal, & Hervis, 1983	Strategic structural family therapy (FT) (*n* = 18) vs. One-person strategic structural FT (*n* = 19)	Self-report of frequency of drug use	Posttreatment (*n* = 37) 6–12 month follow-up (*n* = 24)	Reduced substance use and improved psychiatric and family functioning in both conditions. No differences between tx conditions. Slightly greater reductions in substance use in one-person tx.
Szapocznik, Kurtines, Foote, Perez-Vidal, & Hervis, 1986	Strategic structural FT (*n* = 17) vs. One-person strategic structural FT (*n* = 18)	Self-report of frequency of drug use	Posttreatment (*n* = 35) 6–12 month follow-up (*n* = 20)	Reduced substance use, improved psychiatric and family functioning in both conditions. No differences between tx conditions. Slightly greater improvement in family functioning in one-person FT.
Szapocznik, Perez-Vidal, Brickman, Foote, Santisteban, Hervis, & Kurtines, 1988	Strategic structural FT plus engagement intervention (*n* = 56) vs. Strategic structural FT (*n* = 52)	Self-report of frequency of drug use Rate of patient engagement and retention in tx	Posttreatment	Greater retention of drug-abusing patients in FT plus intensive engagement (93%) than in FT alone (47%).

(*continued*)

TABLE 2
(Continued)

Study	Treatment groups (*n*)	Substance use outcome measure(s)	Assessment point	Findings
Santisteban, Szapocznik, Perez-Vidal, Kurtines, Murray, & LaPerriere, 1995	Strategic structural FT plus engagement intervention (*n* = 52) vs. Strategic structural FT (*n* = 67) vs. Adolescent group therapy (*n* = 74)	Rate of client engagement and retention in tx	Posttreatment	Greater retention of drug-abusing patients in FT plus intensive engagement (81%) than in FT alone (60%). Greater retention for non-Cuban Hispanics (97%) than for Cuban Hispanics (64%).
Joanning, Thomas, Quinn, & Mullen, 1992	Structural-strategic FT (*n* = 40) vs. Adolescent group theapy (*n* = 52) vs. Family drug education (*n* = 42)	Number of abstainers (self- and other report) Random urinalyses	Posttreatment	Significantly more abstainers in family therapy (54%) than either of the two comparison conditions (28% and 16% for family education and group, respectively). No pre–post differences in family functioning for any condition.
Friedman, 1989	Functional FT (*n* = 85) vs. Parent training group (*n* = 50)	Self-report of frequency of drug use Drug use severity score	9-month follow-up	Reduced substance use, improved psychiatric and family functioning in both conditions. No differences between tx conditions.
Lewis, Piercy, Sprenkle, & Trepper, 1990	Purdue Brief FT (*n* = 44) vs. Family drug education (*n* = 40)	Self-report of frequency of drug use Drug use severity score Random urinalyses	Posttreatment	Reduced substance use in family therapy, but not education group.

Study	Conditions	Measure	Assessment Point	Results
Azrin, Donohue, Besalel, Kogan, & Acierno, 1994	Behavioral FT (n = 15) vs. Adolescent group therapy (n = 11)	Number of abstainers (self- and other report) Random urinalyses	Posttreatment	Greater reductions in substance use, improved psychiatric functioning, and better school performance for family therapy condition than supportive group.
Krinsley, 1991	Behavioral FT plus school intervention (n = 12) vs. School intervention only (n = 17)	Number of days of use reported using timeline follow-back over a continuous 12-month period	Continuous reporting for 7–10 month follow-up	Greater reductions in substance use and better school performance for family therapy plus school intervention compared to family therapy alone, with differences even greater at follow-up.
Scopetta, King, Szapocznik, & Tillman, 1979	Structural family therapy (FT) plus multisystem intervention vs. Structural FT	Self-report of frequency of drug use	Posttreatment	Reduced substance use (57% abstinent) and improved psychiatric and family functioning in both conditions. No differences between tx conditions.
Henggeler, Borduin, Melton, Mann, Smith, Hall, Cone, & Fucci, 1991	1: Multisystems FT vs. Individual therapy 2: Multisystems FT vs. Juvenile probation monitoring	1: Arrest for substance-related offense 2: Self-report of frequency of alcohol and marijuana use	1: 4-year follow-up 2: Posttreatment	1: Significantly fewer substance-related arrests in family therapy compared to individual therapy condition. 2: Reduced substance use in family therapy only.
Liddle, Dakof, Parker, Diamond, Barrett, & Garcia, 1995	Multidimensional FT vs. Adolescent group therapy	Self-report of frequency of substance use	Posttreatment 6-month follow-up 12-month follow-up	Greater reductions in substance use for family therapy than either family education or group. Family therapy and group therapy both showed reductions in substance use.

A self-report of frequency of substance use was obtained for adolescents, using the substance-abuse score from the Psychiatric Status Schedule (Spitzer, Endicott, Fleiss, & Cohen, 1970). Other outcome measures included other aspects of adolescent psychiatric functioning, parents' perception of the adolescents' problems, family members' perceptions of the family environment, and ratings of family functioning completed by a trained research associate. Families in both intervention conditions showed significant improvement at the end of therapy. Moreover, compared to conjoint therapy, one-person family therapy led to slightly greater improvement in the areas of drug abuse and psychiatric functioning at follow-up. There were no differences between groups on family ratings.

Szapocznik et al. (1986) replicated their 1983 study with a second sample of Hispanic families ($n = 35$). The study was virtually identical to the first, although the number of sessions allowed was extended from 12 to 15. Once again, both conditions were associated with significant improvements in functioning from pretreatment, and the one-person condition was more successful in sustaining improved family functioning at follow-up.

The studies had several limitations, including small sample sizes, high attrition, inadequate substance-use measurement, and the absence of a nonfamily comparison condition. Also, in the first study, the authors reported a significant difference in number of sessions between the two conditions, with all adolescents in the one-person condition receiving at least 8 sessions and almost a third of the families in the conjoint condition receiving only 4–7 sessions. Thus, the slightly better outcome for the one-person condition could be due to the increased amount of therapy for these youth. Also, because the enhancements to outcome that appear at follow-up are for different measures in each of the two studies, the extent and nature of the improvement for one-person therapy are unclear. Another concern is the exclusive focus on Cuban Hispanics, limiting generalizability. The role ethnicity may have played in responses to treatment is not known.

Recognizing the problem of engaging drug abusers and their families in treatment, Szapocznik and his colleagues turned their research efforts toward evaluating ways to enhance patient retention in treatment. In one study, Szapocznik et al. (1988) compared their family systems therapy in combination with an intensive engagement intervention to family systems therapy alone (with engagement as usual). Although therapists in both conditions were allowed to make as many contacts with families as needed within a 3-week period until the family presented for admission, therapists in the engagement-as-usual family therapy condition were allowed only to express concern to the family, ask limited questions, and handle administrative aspects of treatment initiation. Therapists in the intensive engagement condition could provide support, begin alliance building, reframe, negotiate, and even employ restructuring interventions either over the phone or in person with members of the family as deemed appropriate. The results were quite pronounced: 93% of the substance abusers and their families in the intensive engagement condition completed intake, compared to 47% of the engagement-as-usual group. Once engaged in treatment, there were no further attrition differences between the groups.

In the second study evaluating treatment engagement, Santisteban et al. (1996) recruited an even larger and more multicultural Hispanic sample, using more stringent criteria for successful engagement and including two control conditions: family therapy employing usual engagement techniques and an adolescent group therapy condition. They replicated the findings of the first study, and even with stricter criteria for treatment engagement, they found 81% of the substance abusers and their families in the intensive engagement condition completing intake, compared to 60% in the comparison conditions. Moreover, they found that ethnicity was associated with a differential engagement rate in the intensive condition: 97% of the non-Cuban Hispanics in the intensive condition were engaged versus 64% of the Cuban Hispanics, allowing them to explore further the role of ethnicity in family therapy process. Although Santisteban and his colleagues did not measure substance use as an indicator of outcome, they argue that no benefit from treatment can be derived unless the patients participate in treatment.

Still another evaluation of the effectiveness of the engagement and treatment components of the structural strategic family systems therapy is currently underway. This project was undertaken by Joan Koss, working with Mexican American and families of Mexican descent with drug-abusing youth in the southwestern region of the country (Koss & Baca, in press). The design is a replication of Santisteban et al. (1996) with patients randomly assigned to one of three conditions: family therapy, intensive engagement; family therapy, usual engagement; or adolescent group therapy. Family therapists have been trained using the treatment manuals developed for the Miami projects and adapted for use with a Mexican American population. Adherence is strictly monitored and maintained. Treatment outcome is measured across a broad spectrum of domains, including rates of engagement and retention, a comprehensive substance-use assessment using standardized instruments and urinalyses, structured interviews and questionnaires measuring psychiatric functioning, and multiple measures of family functioning, including observations of family interactions.

Preliminary results from the first 80 subjects (of a projected total of 135 subjects retained) suggest that all intervention conditions are associated with reductions in symptoms of conduct disorder, attention deficit, oppositional defiance, depression, and anxiety. Moreover, the family treatments appear more effective than group therapy in reducing symptoms of obsessive–compulsive disorder, and in improving several areas of family functioning. No data are yet available for substance-use outcome and, of course, no conclusions can be drawn until analysis of the full data set is completed. Nevertheless, the study addresses several weaknesses in previous research by including a nonfamily comparison condition, as Santisteban et al. did, establishing tightly controlled treatment conditions and evaluation procedures, and relying on careful measurement using psychometrically sound methods.

Joanning, Thomas, Quinn, and Mullen (1992) examined a family systems intervention, similar to the family therapy approach evaluated by Szapocznik et al. (1983, 1986) and integrating aspects of both structural and strategic approaches (Stanton, Todd, & Associates, 1982). They compared family therapy to two comparison conditions: a family drug-education intervention and adolescent group therapy. The family drug education condition consisted of formal presentation and films providing information on substance use and abuse, without focusing specifically on families' personal concerns. The group treatment was a process-oriented intervention. Assessments were conducted prior to treatment, at the end of treatment, and at a 6-month follow-up. Adolescent drug use and problem behavior were measured "using a decision tree based upon urinalyses, a drug involvement survey, videotaped family assessment interviews, therapist evaluations, school records, and legal involvement" (p. 349). Multiple measures of family functioning were also obtained.

The results at posttreatment revealed that family therapy was most effective in decreasing problem behaviors and drug use, with 54% of youth in family therapy abstinent, compared to 29% in the family education condition and 17% in group therapy condition. The three groups did not differ on changes in family functioning and, in fact, there were no pre–post changes on measures of family functioning, even in the family systems condition. As in other family therapy studies, adolescents represented a wide range of substance users, with no systematic assessment of use except to exclude physiologically addicted (presumably the most serious) users. Moreover, outcome measurement of use relied heavily on judgments made by parents, therapists, and other professionals. Other limitations included an overrepresentation of single-parent families in the group therapy condition and a massive attrition rate due to regional unemployment that precluded any meaningful follow-up assessment.

In two other investigations, the family therapies evaluated were integrative models, comprised of elements of both systems and behavioral approaches. Friedman (1989) compared the effectiveness of functional family therapy (Barton & Alexander, 1981) to a parenting skills group intervention. As a systemic model, functional family therapy is based on the assumption that family members and their behaviors are mutually interdependent, and that the meaning of behavior resides in the context of relationships. Early in therapy, intervention is aimed at lowering family resistance and creating a collaborative context in which long-term change can occur. Behavior change is then instituted, using a systemic analysis of the relational intimacy–distancing functions of behaviors in the family to guide the application of behavior therapy techniques. In this way, the model represents an integration of family systems and behavioral therapy approaches. The parenting group, a behaviorally oriented skills training program, focused on teaching parents to use contingency management, communication skills, and assertiveness skills. Outcome was measured only at a 9-month follow-up point, and substance use was measured using a self-report instrument and an index of severity, derived from the self-reported frequency of use and severity of drug use. Other domains of assessment included self-esteem and other areas of psychological functioning, and several family functioning measures.

At follow-up, both groups found significant reductions in substance use of more than 50%, with improvements in other areas of functioning as well. Although no differences were found between the two therapy modalities on any dimensions, 93% of the families in family therapy engaged in treatment, compared to only 67% of the parenting group families. In a reanalysis that included treatment dropouts as failures, Stanton and Shadish (in press) reported that a significant difference between the two groups emerged, underscoring the importance of considering differential attrition in conducting treatment outcome research. In addition to attrition, the study was limited, in that adolescents in both conditions received some individual therapy as needed, determined by the therapists. Although there were no differences between conditions with respect to number of individual sessions, this additional treatment could have obscured differences between the two groups. Moreover, as in other trials, no comprehensive assessment of substance use was conducted at intake or following treatment.

Lewis, Piercy, Sprenkle, and Trepper (1990) also evaluated an integrative family therapy model, comparing Purdue Brief Family Therapy, to a didactic, family-oriented parenting skills intervention similar to Friedman's parent group and an educational intervention that included all family members. The majority of the adolescents had been mandated to treatment through the juvenile justice system. Lewis et al. described their family condition as drawing from treatments such as the functional family therapy model and structural strategic systems therapy model, shown to be effective with other problem youth (Barton & Alexander, 1981) and drug-abusing adults (Stanton, Todd, & Associates, 1982). Substance use was assessed using a self-report frequency measure, an index of severity of use, and the categorization of adolescents into soft (i.e., tobacco, alcohol, or marijuana) and hard (i.e., all other illicit drugs) drug-use groups. Both interventions were found to significantly reduce drug use. However, a greater percentage of youth receiving family therapy decreased their use, compared to the parenting group intervention. The information Lewis et al. provided about adolescents' substance use at intake and treatment attrition was limited, and the reliability and validity of their substance-use outcome measures were not addressed. Moreover, they did not report any follow-up data.

4.3. *Behavioral Family Studies*

Azrin, Donohue, Besalel, Kogan, and Acierno (1994) compared behavioral family therapy to a process-oriented, nondirective (supportive) adolescent group therapy intervention. Group sessions were 2 hours long, scheduled weekly, and parents attended the sessions once per month. The behavioral family intervention consisted of hourly individual sessions held conjointly with the adolescent and his or her parents. Therapists employed modeling, rehearsal, and self-monitoring techniques with families and gave written homework assignments to be reviewed and during sessions. Principal procedures included (1) stimulus control, working to increase time spent in safe versus risky situations; (2) urge control, to interrupt internal stimuli that were precursors to drug use and substitute other internal and external stimuli; and (3) social control/contracting to emphasize parental assistance in providing safe (vs. risky) activities. In addition, there were secondary procedures focusing on specific skills such as anger management and problem solving.

With respect to outcome measures, reports were obtained from subjects and their parents at each session regarding type and frequency of drug use, school attendance, employment, institutionalization, and arrests for the period since the previous session. Urine samples were also obtained at each session. One sample per month underwent broad-screen assay for all commonly used drugs. All others were analyzed for the specific drugs that had been detected on any of the broad-screen analyses, including the pretreatment analysis. Similar to the decision tree used by Joanning et al. (1992), drug use was considered to have occurred in a given month if a positive report of use at any time during the month was obtained via urinalysis, self-report, or parental report.

Compared to the supportive group intervention, behavioral family therapy produced greater reductions in substance use. In the month preceding treatment, all youth had used some drugs. In the group condition, 91% of youths continued to use drugs in all but the fourth month, when it went down to about 85%. In the behavioral family condition, 73% used drugs the first month, decreasing irregularly to 27% usage during the sixth month, for an overall reduction of 73% in the number of youth using drugs. Mean number of days per month of drug use was initially about seven for both groups. In the family condition, use decreased to about 2 days per month by the second month and remained at that level, while in the group condition it increased to and remained at about 9 days per month. Reported alcohol use decreased by about 50% for family therapy and increased by about 50% for group therapy. Significantly better outcomes were also found for school attendance, depression, and parent satisfaction with youth.

Although Azrin et al. (1994) did not use standardized measures of substance use, they provided a more complete description of patients' drug use before and after treatment than many family therapy studies. However, their sample size was quite small, they provided little information on patient attrition, and no follow-up measures were obtained.

In another behavioral family therapy evaluation, Krinsley (1991) examined the impact of a school-based behavioral family therapy intervention compared to a school-based intervention-only condition. The school-based condition was a preexisting early intervention/prevention program conducted by teacher "sponsors" for adolescents identified by school staff as at risk for dropping out of school. The program lasted throughout the school year. The main focus of family therapy was on communication and problem-solving skills, and on positive contingency management. Booster sessions were provided to families for an average of 8 months. Treatment adherence ratings were used to ensure that the therapy conformed with the manual.

Outcome measures included school performance; adolescent drug use, measured using timeline follow-back procedures (Sobell & Sobell, 1992); and family relationship measures. Because of the small sample size and the high incidence of nonuse, nonparametric tests were used to examine substance-use frequency. The results showed that, relative to pretreatment, students who participated in family therapy raised their grade point averages, whereas students in the school-based program lowered their averages. Regarding substance use, students in the family-plus-school condition showed greater reductions that students in the school intervention alone during the 15 months following treatment. The differences between groups appeared even greater over time, underscoring the importance of conducting follow-up assessments.

Like the Azrin et al. (1994) study, Krinsley (1991) examined a very small sample of adolescents and their families. Unlike the majority of family therapy studies, however, their study had several strengths, including careful substance-use assessment using a standardized procedure, use of a treatment manual with ratings of treatment integrity, and follow-up measurement.

4.4. Ecological Family Therapy Studies

In an early study, Scopetta et al. (1979) investigated whether family interventions need to be ecologically focused, or whether intervention within the conjoint family context is sufficient. They compared a multisystems intervention, operationalized as family therapy in combination with at least two other direct interventions with other systems outside the family (e.g., school, juvenile justice), to a family therapy–alone condition in which only interventions occurring in the therapist's office and within the conjoint mode were allowed. Although there were no differences between the two family-based treatments, both interventions were characterized by marked reductions in substance use from pre- to posttreatment, with 57% abstinence at the end of treatment. The authors acknowledged that the administration of the treatment was not tightly controlled, and the two groups may not have been distinctly different from one another. Alternatively, family therapy may have been sufficiently powerful that the effect of an add-on component would have to be large to be detected.

Using a more complex ecological intervention, Henggeler et al. (1991) conducted two studies, comparing multisystemic family therapy to individual therapy in the first study and to a treatment-as-usual juvenile-probation supervision intervention in the second. According to Henggeler and his colleagues, multisystemic family therapy has much in common with the structural family therapy approaches studied by Lewis et al. (1990) and Szapocznik et al. (1988), but is distinct from these approaches in the view that individuals are "nested within a complex of interconnected systems that encompass individual, family, and extrafamilial (peer, school, neighborhood) factors" (Henggeler et al., 1991, p. 43) and in its treatment of dysfunction in other systems as needed.

Outcome was determined on the basis of arrests for a substance-related offenses in Study 1 and using self-report questions concerning frequency of alcohol and marijuana use during the previous 3 months from a self-report delinquency scale for Study 2. As had been found in treating delinquents, multisystemic family therapy produced significantly better outcomes at posttest. In Study 1, fewer youth who received family therapy were subsequently arrested for substance-related offenses (4%), compared to youth who received individual therapy (16%) and to treatment refusers (17%). Similarly, adolescents in Study 2 who received family therapy used less alcohol and marijuana after treatment was completed, compared to youth receiving juvenile probation supervision. Because the main focus of these studies was on juvenile delinquency, however, the sample included both users and nonusers, and the measurement of substance use was imprecise. Moreover, no other measures of adolescent or family functioning were reported, and no follow-up assessment was conducted.

Evaluating an ecological treatment developed specifically for adolescent substance abusers, Liddle et al. (1995) compared a multisystemic, multidimensional family therapy to two alternative treatments: adolescent group therapy and a family education group. The family intervention included sessions with individual adolescents, focusing on issues such as self-efficacy and decision-making skills, sessions with parents, focusing on parents' negative thinking patterns and parenting styles, and interactions with extrafamilial systems as needed. The family education group was guided by family systems theory, and used presentations, discussions, and exercises to develop parenting skills and restructure the family with a united parental subsystem. The adolescent group intervention focused primarily on the development of coping skills.

Outcome measures included treatment retention, a variety of substance-use indicators (e.g., self-report of frequency of use, number of drugs used, urinalyses), school performance, and adolescent acting-out behaviors (e.g., anger control, aggression, impulsivity). With respect to attrition, significantly more patients were retained in treatment in the multidimension family therapy condition (73%) than in group therapy (52%). All three conditions were associated with reduced substance use, with greatest and most consistent improvement in the family therapy condition, in which youth decreased their use from daily to about once a week for alcohol and marijuana, with 30% abstinent. Group therapy participants also showed gradual decline in drug use from pretreatment to follow-up, not apparent at posttreatment, and the authors suggested that the effect may have resulted from the delay between adolescents putting newly acquired skills into use and deriving benefit from implementing them.

5. Summary of Findings and Recommendations

5.1. Substance Use Outcomes

Taken together, the results of randomized clinical trials provide ample evidence that family therapy is an effective treatment for adolescent substance abusers. The findings suggest that more drug-abusing patients enter and participate in family treatment that in other treatments (e.g., Friedman, 1989; Joanning et al., 1992, Liddle et al., 1995), and some family therapy approaches lead to better engagement and retention than other family approaches (e.g., Santisteban et al., 1996; Szapocznik et al., 1988). Although a number of studies provided only limited information about numbers of patients entering and continuing in treatment (e.g., Azrin et al., 1994; Lewis et al., 1990), only one study (Henggeler et al., 1991) reported finding no differences between family therapy and a nonfamily intervention.

Every study demonstrated significant reductions in substance use from pre- to posttreatment. In seven of eight studies comparing family therapy to a nonfamily-based intervention, youth receiving family therapy showed greater reductions in substance use than those receiving adolescent group therapy (Joanning et al., 1992; Azrin et al., 1994; Liddle et al., 1995; Koss & Baca, 1995), family education (Joanning et al., 1992; Liddle et al., 1995); and individual therapy, individual tracking through schools, or juvenile justice systems (Henggeler et al., 1991; Krinsley, 1991). When compared to parenting skills training programs, family therapy fared better in one study (Lewis et al., 1990), but no differences were found in Friedman's (1989) study when dropouts were excluded from analysis. The only other instances in which no differences emerged between treatment conditions were in studies comparing two family therapy interventions to one another (Szapocznik et al., 1983, 1986, Scopetta et al., 1979). See Stanton and Shadish (in press) for effect sizes in their meta-analysis of family therapy outcome studies.

The consistency of support for family therapy interventions is remarkable, given the problems, limitations, and widely varying theoretical models, designs, approaches to measurement, and other methodological issues. The studies focused on different populations (e.g., heavy abusers, juvenile delinquents, high-risk middle-school students), and most of the studies appeared to include quite heterogeneous samples, ranging from heavy (daily) users of marijuana and alcohol, with frequent use of hard drugs and many associated problem consequences to nonusers. Substance use at intake was often not well specified, and detailed and comprehensive assessment of substance use was rare. Typically, studies omitted information about the psychometric properties of assessment instruments used. Studies were also hampered by small sample sizes (Szapocznik et al., 1983, 1986; Azrin et al., 1994; Krinsley, 1991), confounds such as amount of therapy received (Szapocznik et al., 1983; Joanning et al., 1992), systematic differences between groups (Joanning et al., 1992), and failure to assess change immediately following treatment (Friedman, 1989). At least half of the studies did not include follow-up assessment, a critical limitation, given that several studies conducting follow-up assessments found that patterns of substance-use reductions changed over time (Krinsley, 1991; Liddle et al., 1995; Szapocznik et al., 1983, 1986), and different conclusions could be drawn about treatment effectiveness on the basis of point in time of measurement.

Moreover, differential attrition across conditions may have created confounds in interpreting the results of the outcome studies. One the one hand, as Stanton and Shadish (in press) astutely observed, the enhanced rate of engagement and retention in family therapy conditions denotes a strength of family interventions with adolescent substance abusers, since attrition is associated with resistance to treatment and a continuation of substance-use problems (Epstein, McCrady, Miller, & Steinberg, 1994; Snow, Tebes, & Arthur, 1992). On the other hand, treatments with higher engagement and retention rates may include a higher proportion of severe abusers, and greater success in retention may increase the burden for those treatments to demonstrate greater therapeutic effectiveness. Thus, findings of support for family therapy may be conservative estimates of the effectiveness of this treatment modality.

To address the issue of attrition, more effort needs to be exerted to follow treatment dropouts. In treatment studies of adult substance abusers, in which subjects are often without employment or permanent addresses, an 80% follow-up rate is considered a minimum acceptable rate, and in a recent meta-analysis of outcome studies, Miller et al. (1995) reported that 57% of all controlled trials in the alcohol field had accounted for 85% of cases and higher. Within the family therapy field, however, follow-up rates have often been poorer. Family researchers need to apply more rigorous efforts toward obtaining follow-up data, especially with families who fail to engage or terminate treatment prematurely, to examine the relationship between treatment outcome and attrition more systematically.

Another area for improvement in family research is in measuring substance use before and after treatment. While many studies were conducted some time ago, the assessment literature has advanced in many important ways in the past few years, and a variety of standardized, psychometrically sound assessment methods are now available. Although Stanton and Shadish (in press) found no differences in outcome comparing studies using urinalysis as a measure of substance use to those using only self-report measures, there is evidence that biological indicators may improve the accuracy of self-report. Also, more sensitive, specific information about the patterning of use may tell us about the role the family plays in the progression of use and provide clues for developing better family interventions.

5.2. Outcomes for Other Areas of Functioning

The evidence for the effectiveness of family therapy in reducing problem behaviors and improving functioning in other areas is less clear than for substance use. The majority of studies found significant improvements across treatment conditions from pre- to posttreatment. However, in only two studies (Azrin et al., 1994, Krinsley, 1991), both evaluating behavioral family interventions, were family-based treatments superior to alternative interventions in effecting change in other areas (e.g., reduced depression and problem behaviors, improved school performance).

No studies addressed issues associated with dual diagnosis, an area in critical need of attention, since research clearly indicates that individuals with substance-use disorders commonly have associated psychiatric diagnoses, including depression, anxiety disorders, attention deficit and conduct disorders (Gold & Slaby, 1991). The relationship between substance abuse and other comorbid disorders includes a range of possibilities, including other disorders developing as a consequence of substance abuse or vice versa, other disorders altering the course of substance abuse or vice versa, or, consistent with a general deviance perspective, disorders originating from common factors (Bukstein, Brent, & Kaminer, 1989). Some research has revealed differential dropout rates in substance abusers with dual diagnosis of mood versus conduct disorder, so comorbid conditions may play a role in the course of treatment as well.

In the area of family functioning, improvements were reported for nonfamily-based treatments and family therapy alike, with no findings of significant differences between groups. These results are similar to marital therapy outcomes with adult alcoholics, which have failed to show consistent improvements in relationship functioning following treatment, even when drinking has been reduced (McCrady et al., 1986; O'Farrell, Cutter, & Floyd, 1985). The absence of family change in combination with reductions in substance use calls into question the basic assumptions in family theories regarding the importance of family interactions in the development and maintenance of substance-use problems. However, measures of family functioning were almost exclusively self-report paper-and-pencil measures, and direct observations of families were rare (Liddle et al., 1995; Szapocznik et al., 1983). In keeping with the emphasis on the role of family interactions in traditional family research, an obvious next step is to add observational methods to self-report measures, evaluating family functioning from multiple vantage points. As Liddle and Dakof (1995b) have implied, without assessments of family interactions to examine the relationship between family functioning and reductions in substance use, vital mediators of change may go undetected.

5.3. Family Therapy Process

Despite the evidence provided that family therapy is superior to other interventions for adolescent abusers, none of the studies reviewed reported examining therapy process variables that may have been associated with change. Within the broader family therapy literature, therapy process and outcome research has shown great promise in isolating therapist, client, and interactional mediators of outcome (Alexander et al., 1994) and the equivocal findings in the clinical trials for adolescent substance abusers highlight the need for incorporating a process perspective in this area of endeavor as well. For example, Friedman (1989) found no differences between family therapy and parent training, and Joanning et al. (1992) and Liddle et al. (1995) found that the differences between family therapy and family education conditions did not appear as large as those between family therapy and adolescent group therapy. Studies evaluating family therapy, parenting skills training, and family education groups all found some degree of reduction in substance use from pre- to posttreatment. One explanation for the unilateral success of these treatments is that they are all designed to impact entire family systems rather than just the individual user (Lewis et al., 1990), but measures of therapy process will likely be essential in identifying components of the interventions associated with changes in adolescents' drug use.

Relatedly, no clear pattern emerged for the superiority of one treatment model over another. As Table 1 reflects, few studies indicated use of a treatment manual, and fewer still used actual adherence ratings to ensure that the components described were actually being delivered. Possibly, no differences on the basis of theoretical model were found because, despite what techniques and procedures family therapy researchers say are being implemented, family therapists engaged in essentially the same behaviors across models. Alternatively, therapists may have been true to their models, but the effects of common factors present across all family interventions, such as therapist neutrality with families and/or family expectancies, may have been critical mediators of change. In general, studies provided very limited information about therapist characteristics or other design aspects, such as whether therapists delivered only one type of treatment or operated across therapeutic modalities such that greater competence in one modality could have affected outcome. One improvement in this research, in addition to obtaining measures of therapist and client variables, would be the inclusion of more diverse comparison conditions. However, the problem of adolescent substance use is sufficiently severe that many comparison conditions (e.g., no-treatment, attention placebo) are generally deemed inappropriate for ethical reasons (Stanton & Shadish, in press).

One area of study that may hold promise, especially in understanding the process of engagement in treatment, is family resistance–motivation. Creating a motivational context for change represents a major phase of treatment, presumed to produce higher engagement and retention rates in the functional family therapy model (Alexander & Parsons, 1982). Within the substance abuse literature, a general point of agreement is that lack of motivation for change represents a significant treatment obstacle (Miller et al., 1995). Miller and his colleagues have developed a motivational enhancement approach that has been shown effective as an add-on to traditional treatments and as a stand-alone brief intervention (Miller & Rollnick, 1991). The central feature of motivational enhancement therapy, like the motivational phase of functional family therapy, is the nonblaming, nonjudgmental stance taken by the therapist. This focus is wholly consistent with Stanton and Shadish's observation that a nonconfrontational, nonblaming perspective appears to be essential in the treatment of families with substance-abusing members, and this component of therapy process merits close examination in future studies.

Therapy process may also shed light on the importance of extrafamilial interventions. Thus far, no clear evidence has been presented that multisystemic, ecological interventions are more effective than other family therapy interventions. If the primary mechanisms of change are within the family, then multisystemic intervention may be unnecessary and unwarranted, given the extra costs. Together with family interaction research, studies examining the relationship between family therapy process and outcome may be essential to identify key mechanisms of change. Several investigators have recently completed family therapy process studies with adolescent substance abusers or have work underway (e.g., Diamond & Liddle, 1996; Waldron, 1994), but considerably more effort should be devoted to this area to take the next step in evaluating the effectiveness of family therapy interventions.

5.4. Adolescent Gender, Ethnicity, and Development Phase

Although a substantially higher proportion of adult substance abusers are male, and research on the heritability of substance abuse and dependence reveals differences for adult males and females, relatively equal numbers of adolescent girls and boys abuse alcohol and other drugs. These and other differences found in the adult and adolescent substance-use literatures argue simultaneously for increasing research focus on the role of gender and development in understanding adolescent abuse and developing treatment models that take into account these central issues. It seems intuitively obvious that an 11-year-old, entering the early phase of adolescent, may drink for different reasons and may experience different consequences that an 18-year-old in late adolescence, preparing to leave home. In developmental studies, McGee and Newcomb (1992) and Duncan et al. (1994) have found that patterns of use and family functioning vary as a function of developmental stage, implying the need for different models for treating youth across the adolescent period. With respect to gender, different models may also be needed, with girls' substance abuse perhaps best understood in the context of factors such as reasons for using, negative and positive consequences, and expectancies related to use, or family relationships. Although these issues have been severely neglected in the family therapy literature, Liddle and his colleagues (1995) have attempted to create a developmentally sensitive model for family therapy with adolescent substance abusers. Future research should focus on examining the components of such models, evaluating the importance of the developmental and gender-specific intervention for outcome.

Considerably more attention has been given to examining the influence of ethnicity on patterns of interactions in families with substance-abusing adolescents (Waldron, 1992) and on family therapy process and outcome (Koss & Baca, in press; Santisteban et al., 1996; Szapocznik et al., 1988; Waldron, 1994). However, broad-based, culturally sensitive intervention models have not yet been developed.

5.5. Conclusions

The appearance of well-designed clinical trials evaluating family therapy interventions in recent years represents a major advance in the treatment of adolescent substance abuse. The studies have invariably demonstrated that family therapy leads to decreased substance use and, when compared to alternative, nonfamily interventions, family therapy appears to emerge as the superior treatment. However, the mechanisms associated with treatment effectiveness have not been examined, and a failure to find differences on family functioning variables between modalities challenges traditional views such as family interaction perspectives on the role of the family in problem substance use. Family researchers need to channel more efforts into prospective model building, incorporating empirical work from the broader substance abuse literature and relying on more comprehensive, detailed measurement of use. Moreover, family therapy process research is urgently needed to focus more directly on the influence of the family and interactions between the therapist and the family on adolescent substance use.

6. References

Alexander, J. F., Holtzworth-Munroe, A., & Jameson, P. (1994). The process and outcome of marital and family therapy: Research review and evaluation. In S. L. Garfield & A. E. Bergin (Eds.), *Handbook of psychotherapy and behavior change* (4th ed., pp. 595–630). New York: Wiley.

Alexander, J. F., & Parsons, B. V. (1982). *Functional family therapy*. Moneterey, CA: Brooks/Cole.

Akers, R. L., Krohn, M. D., Lanza Kaduce, L., & Radosevich, M. (1979). Social learning and deviant behavior: A specific test of a general theory. *American Sociology Review, 44*, 636–655.

Andrews, J. A., Hops, H., Ary, D., Lichtenstein, E., & Tildesley, E. (1991). The construction, validation and use of a Guttman scale of adolescent substance use: An investigation of family relationships. *Journal of Drug Issues, 21*, 557–572.

Azrin, N. H., Donohue, B., Besalel, V. A., Kogan, E. S., & Acierno, R. (1994). Youth drug abuse treatment: A controlled outcome study. *Journal of Child and Adolescent Substance Abuse, 3*, 1–16.

Bailey, G. W. (1989). Current perspectives on substance use in youth. *Journal of the American Academy of Child and Adolescent Psychiatry, 28* 151–162.

Barnes, G. M. (1984). Adolescent alcohol abuse and other problem behaviors: Their relationships and common parental influences. *Journal of Youth and Adolescence, 13*, 329–348.

Barnes, G. M., & Welte, J. W. (1986). Patterns and predictors of alcohol use among 7–12th grade students in New York State. *Journal of Studies on Alcohol, 71*, 59–69.

Barton, C., & Alexander, J. F. (1981). Functional family therapy. In A. S. Gurman & D. P. Kniskern (Eds.), *Handbook of family therapy* (pp. 403–443). New York: Brunner/Mazel.

Baumrind, D. (1985). Familial antecedents of adolescent drug use: A developmental perspective. In C. L. Jones & R. J. Battjes (Eds.), *Etiology of drug abuse: Implications for prevention* (pp. 13–44). National Institute on Drug Abuse Research Monograph 56. Rockville, MD: Department of Health and Human Service.

Baumrind, D. (1991). The influence of parenting style on adolescent competence and substance use. *Journal of Early Adolescence, 11*, 56–95.

Bentler, P. M. (1992). Etiologies and consequences of adolescent drug use: Implications for prevention. *Journal of Addictive Diseases, 11*, 47–61.

Brook, J. S., Whiteman, M., & Gordon, A. S. (1982). Qualitative and quantitative aspects of adolescent drug use: Interplay of personality, family, and peer correlates. *Psychological Reports, 51*, 1151–1163.

Brook, J. S., Whiteman, M., Gordon, A. S., & Brook, D. W. (1988). The role of older brothers in younger brother's drug use viewed in the context of parent and peer influences. *Journal of Genetic Psychology, 151*, 59–75.

Bry, B. H. (1988). Family-based approaches to reducing adolescent substance use: Theories, techniques and findings. In E. R. Rahdert & J. Grabowski (Eds.), *Adolescent drug abuse: Analyses of treatment research* (pp. 39–68). National Institute on Drug Abuse Research Monograph 77. Rockville, MD: Department of Health and Human Services.

Bry, B. H., & Krinsley, K. E. (1992). Booster sessions and long-term effects of behavioral family therapy on adolescent substance use and school performance. *Journal of Behavior Therapy and Experimental Psychiatry, 23*, 183–189.

Bry, B. H., McKeon, P., & Pandina, R. J. (1982). Extent of drug use as a function of number of risk factors. *Journal of Abnormal Psychology, 91*, 273–279.

Bukstein, O. G., Brent, D. A., & Kaminer, Y. (1989). Comorbidity of substance abuse and other psychiatric disorders in adolescents. *American Journal of Psychiatry, 146*, 1131–1141.

Clayton, R. R. (1992). Transitions in drug use: Risk and protective factors. In M. Glantz & R.

Pickens (Eds.), *Vulnerability to drug abuse* (pp. 15–51). Washington, DC: American Psychological Association Press.

Coleman, S. B., & Davis, D. T. (1978). Family therapy and drug abuse: A national survey. *Family Process, 17*, 21–29.

Craig, R. J. (1993). Contemporary trends in substance abuse. *Professional Psychology: Research and Practice, 24*, 182–189.

Diamond, G., & Liddle, H. A. (1996). Resolving a therapeutic impasse between parents and adolescents in multidimensional family therapy. *Journal of Consulting and Clinical Psychology, 64*, 481–488.

Dishion, T. J., Patterson, G. R., & Reid, J. R. (1988). Parent and peer factors associated with drug sampling in early adolescence: Implications for treatment. In E. R. Rahdert & J. Grabowski (Eds.), *Adolescent drug abuse: Analyses of treatment research* (pp. 69–93). National Institute on Drug Abuse Research Monograph 77. Rockville, MD: Department of Health and Human Services.

Donovan, J. E., & Jessor, R. (1985). Structure of problem behavior in adolescence and young adulthood. *Journal of Consulting and Clinical Psychology, 56*, 890–904.

Duncan, T. E., Duncan, S. C., & Hops, H. (1994). The effects of family cohesiveness and peer encouragement on the development of adolescent alcohol use: A cohort-sequential approach to the analysis of longitudinal data. *Journal of Studies on Alcohol, 55*, 588–599.

Ellickson, P. L., Hays, R. D., & Bell, R. M. (1992). Stepping through the drug use sequence: Longitudinal scalogram analysis of initiation and regular use. *Journal of Abnormal Psychology, 101*, 441–451.

Elliott, D. S., Huizinga, D., & Ageton, S. S. (1985). *Explaining delinquency and drug use.* Beverly Hills, CA: Sage.

Epstein, E. E., McCrady, B. S., Miller, K. J., & Steinberg, M. N. (1994). Attrition from conjoining alcoholism treatment: Do dropouts differ from completers? *Journal of Substance Abuse, 6*, 249–265.

Farrell, A. D., Danish, S. J., & Howard, C. W. (1992). Relationship between drug use and other problem behaviors in urban adolescents. *Journal of Consulting and Clinical Psychology, 60*, 705–712.

FeCaces, M., Stinson, F. S., & Hartford, T. C. (1991). Alcohol use and physically risky behavior among adolescents. *Alcohol Health and Research World, 15*, 228–233.

Flay, B. R., & Petraitis, J. (1994). The theory of triadic influence: A new theory of health behavior with implications for preventive interventions. *Advances in Medical Sociology, 4*, 19–44.

Fleischman, M. J., Horne, A. M., & Arthur, J. L. (1983). *Troubled families: A treatment program.* Champaign, IL: Research Press.

Friedman, A. S. (1989). Family therapy vs. parent groups: Effects on adolescent drug abusers. *American Journal of Family Therapy, 17*, 335–347.

Gold, M. S., & Slaby, A. E. (Eds.). (1991). *Dual diagnosis in substance abuse.* New York: Marcel Dekker.

Grant, K. A., Tonigan, J. S., & Miller, W. R. (1995). Comparison of three alcohol consumption measures: A concurrent validity study. *Journal of Studies on Alcohol, 56*, 168–172.

Haley, J. (1976). *Problem-solving therapy.* San Francisco: Jossey-Bass.

Hansen, W. B., Graham, J. W., Sobel, J. L., Shelton, D. R., Flay, B. R., & Johnson, C. A. (1987). The consistency of peer and parent influences on tobacco, alcohol, and marijuana use among young adolescents. *Journal of Behavioral Medicine, 10*, 559–579.

Hawkins, J. D., Catalano, R. F., & Miller, J. Y. (1992). Risk and protective factors for alcohol and other drug problems in adolescence and early adulthood: Implications for substance abuse prevention. *Psychological Bulletin, 112*, 64–105.

Henggeler, S.W., Borduin, C. M., Melton, G. B., Mann, B. J., Smith, L. A., Hall, J. A., Cone, L., & Fucci, B. R. (1991). Effects of multisystemic therapy on drug use and abuse in serious juvenile offenders: A progress report from two outcome studies. *Family Dynamics of Addition Quarterly, 1,* 40–51.

Hops, H., Tildesley, E., Lichtenstein, E., Ary, D., & Sherman, L. (1990). Parent–adolescent problem-solving interactions and drug use. *American Journal of Drug and Alcohol Abuse, 16,* 239–258.

Hughes, S. O., Power, T. G., & Francis, D. J. (1992). Defining patterns of drinking in adolescence: A cluster analytic approach. *Journal of Studies on Alcohol, 53,* 40–47.

Joanning, H., Thomas, F., Quinn, W., & Mullen, R. (1992). Treating adolescent drug abuse: A comparison of family systems therapy, group therapy, and family drug education. *Journal of Marital and Family Therapy, 18,* 345–356.

Johnston, L. D., Bachman, J. G., & O'Malley, P. M. (1991). *Monitoring the future: Questionnaire responses from the nation's high school seniors 1990.* Ann Arbor: Institute for Social Research, University of Michigan.

Kandel, D. B. (1975). Stages in adolescent involvement in drug use. *Science, 190,* 912–914.

Kandel, D. B. (1982). Epidemiological and psychosocial perspectives on adolescent drug use. *Journal of American Academic Clinical Psychiatry, 21,* 328–347.

Kandel, D. B., Kessler, R. C., & Margulies, R. S. (1978). Antecedents of adolescent initiation into stages of drug use: A developmental analysis. *Journal of Youth and Adolescence, 7,* 13–40.

Kandel, D. B., Yamaguchi, K., & Chen, K. (1992). Stages of progression in drug involvement from adolescence to adulthood: Further evidence for the gateway theory. *Journal of Studies on Alcohol, 53,* 447–457.

Kaufman, E., & Kaufmann, P. (1992). *Family therapy of drug and alcohol abuse* (2nd ed.). Needham Heights, MA: Allyn & Bacon.

Koss, J. G., & Baca, L. (in press). A new group therapy for Hispanic adolescents: A fourth life-space. *Journal of Clinical Child Psychology.*

Kouzis, A. C., & Labouvie, E. W. (1992). Use intensity, functional elaboration, and contextual constraint as facets of adolescent alcohol and marijuana use. *Psychology of Addictive Behaviors, 6,* 188–195.

Krinsley, K. E. (1991). Behavioral family therapy for adolescent school problems: School performance effects and generalization to substance use (Doctoral dissertation, Rutgers University). *Dissertation Abstracts International, 52,* 1725b.

Labouvie, E. W. (1986). The coping function of adolescent alcohol and drug use. In R. K. Silbereisen, K. Eyferth, & G. Rudinger (Eds.), *Development as action in context: Problem behavior and normal youth development* (pp. 229–240). New York: Springer-Verlag.

Leccese, M., & Waldron, H. B. (1994). Assessing adolescent substance abuse: A critique of current measurement instruments. *Journal of Substance Abuse Treatment, 11,* 553–563.

Lewis, R. A., Piercy, F. P., Sprenkle, D. H., & Trepper, T. S. (1990). Family-based interventions for helping drug-abusing adolescents. *Journal of Adolescent Research, 5,* 82–95.

Liddle, H. A., & Dakof, G. A. (1995a). Family-based treatment for adolescent drug use: State of the science. In E. R. Rahdert & D. J. Czechowicz (Eds.), *Adolescent drug abuse: Clinical assessment and therapeutic interventions* (pp. 218–254). National Institute on Drug Abuse Research Monograph 156. Rockville, MD: Department of Health and Human Services.

Liddle, H. A., & Dakof, G. A. (1995b). Efficacy of family therapy for drug abuse: Promising but not definitive. *Journal of Marital and Family Therapy, 21,* 511–544.

Liddle, H. A., Dakof, G. A., Parker, K., Barrett, K., Diamond, G. S., Garcia, R., & Palmer, R. (1995). *Multidimensional family therapy of adolescent substance abuse.* Manuscript submitted for publication.

Maisto, S. A., & Conners, G. J. (1990). Clinical diagnostic techniques and assessment tools in alcohol research. *Alcohol Health and Research World*, *14*, 232–238.

McCrady, B. S., Noel, N. E., Abrams, D. B., Stout, R. L., Newlson, H. F., & Hay, W. M. (1986). Comparative effectiveness of three types of spouse involvement in outpatient behavioral alcoholism treatment. *Journal of Studies on Alcohol*, *47*, 459– 467.

McGee, L., & Newcomb, M. D. (1992). General deviance syndrome: Expanded hierarchical evaluations at four ages from early adolescence to adulthood. *Journal of Consulting and Clinical Psychology*, *60*, 766–776.

Miller, W. R., Brown, J. M., Simpson, T. L., Handmaker, N. S., Bien, T. H., Luckie, L. F., Montgomery, H. A., Hester, R. K., & Tonigan, J. S. (1995). What works? A methodological analysis of the alcohol treatment outcome literature. In R. K. Hester & W. R. Miller (Eds.), *Handbook of alcoholism treatment approaches: Effective alternatives* (2nd ed., pp. 12–44). Boston: Allyn & Bacon.

Miller, W. R., & Rollnick, S. (1991). *Motivational interviewing*. New York: Guilford Press.

Miller, W. R., Westerberg, V., & Waldron, H. B. (1995). Evaluating alcohol problems in adults and adolescents. In R. K. Hester & W. R. Miller (Eds.), *Handbook of alcoholism treatment approaches: Effective alternatives* (2nd ed., pp. 17–53). Boston: Allyn & Bacon.

Minuchin, S. (1974). *Families and family therapy*. Cambridge, MA: Harvard University Press.

National Institute on Alcohol Abuse and Alcoholism. (1990). *Alcohol and health: Seventh special report to the U.S. Congress*. Rockville, MD: Department of Health and Human Services.

Needle, R., McCubbin, H., Lorence, J., & Hockhauser, M. (1983). Reliability and validity of adolescent self-reported drug use in a family-based study: A methodological report. *International Journal of Addiction*, *18*, 901–912.

Newcomb, M. D., & Bentler, P. M. (1989). Substance use and abuse among children and teenagers. *American Psychologist*, *44*, 242–248.

Newcomb, M. D., & Felix-Ortiz, M. (1992). Multiple protective and risk factors for drug use and abuse: Cross-sectional and prospective findings. *Journal of Personality and Social Psychology*, *63*, 280–296.

O'Farrell, T. J., Cutter, H. S. G., & Floyd, F. J. (1985). Evaluating behavioral marital therapy for male alcoholics: Effects on marital adjustment and communication from before to after treatment. *Behavior Therapy*, *16*, 147–167.

O'Farrell, T. J. & Maisto, S. A. (1987). The utility of self-report and biological measures of alcohol consumption in alcoholism treatment outcome studies. *Advances in Behavior Research and Therapy*, *9*, 91–125.

Penning, M., & Barnes, G. E. (1982). Adolescent marijuana use: A review. *International Journal of Addictions*, *17*, 749–791.

Petraitis, J., & Flay, B. R., & Miller, T. Q. (1995). Reviewing theories of adolescent substance use: Organizing pieces in the puzzle. *Psychological Bulletin*, *117*, 67–86.

Patterson, G. R., Reid, J. B., & Dishion, T. J. (1992). *Antisocial boys*. Eugene, OR: Castalia.

Raveis, V. H., & Kandel, D. B. (1987). Changes in drug behavior from middle to late twenties: Initiation, persistence, and cessation of use. *American Journal of Public Health*, *77*, 607–611.

Santisteban, D. A., Szapocznik, J., Perez-Vidal, A., Kurtines, W. M., Murray, E. J., & LaPerriere, A. (1996). Efficacy of interventions for engaging youth/families into treatment and some factors that may contribute to differential effectiveness. *Journal of Family Psychology*, *10*, 35–44.

Scopetta, M. A., King, O. E., Szapocznik, J., & Tillman, W. (1979). *Ecological structural family therapy with Cuban immigrant families*. Report to the National Institute on Drug Abuse, Grant No. H81DA 01696.

Selekman, M. D., & Todd, T. C. (1991). *Family therapy approaches with adolescent substance abusers*. Needham Heights, MA: Allyn & Bacon.

Shedler, J., & Block, J. (1990). Adolescent drug use and psychological health: A longitudinal inquiry. *American Psychologist, 45,* 612–630.

Snow, D. L., Tebes, J. K., & Arthur, M. W. (1992). Panel attrition and external validity in adolescent substance use research. *Journal of Consulting and Clinical Psychology, 60,* 804–807.

Sobell, L. C., & Sobell, M. B. (1992). Timeline follow-back: A technique for assessing self-reported alcohol consumption. In R. Z. Litten & J. P. Allen (Eds.), *Measuring alcohol consumption: Psychosocial and biochemical methods* (pp. 41–72). Totowa, NJ: Humana Press.

Spitzer, R. L., Endicott, J., Fleiss, J. L., & Cohen, J. G. (1970). The psychiatric status schedule: A technique for evaluating psychopathology and impairment in role functioning. *Archives of General Psychiatry, 23,* 41–55.

Stanton, M. D., & Shadish, W. R. (in press). Outcome, attrition, and family/marital treatment for drug abuse: A meta-analysis and review of the controlled, comparative studies. *Psychological Bulletin.*

Stanton, M. D., Todd, T.C., & Associates. (1982). *The family therapy of drug abuse and addiction.* New York: Guilford Press.

Szapocznik, J., Kurtines, W. M., Foote, F. H., Perez-Vidal, A., & Hervis, O. (1983). Conjoint versus one-person family therapy: Some evidence for the effectiveness of conducting family therapy through one person. *Journal of Consulting and Clinical Psychology, 51,* 889–899.

Szapocznik, J., Kurtines, W. M., Foote, F. H., Perez-Vidal, A., & Hervis, O. (1986). Conjoint versus one-person family therapy: Further evidence for the effectiveness of conducting family therapy through one person with drug-abusing adolescents. *Journal of Consulting and Clinical Psychology, 54,* 395–397.

Szapocznik, J., Perez-Vidal, A., Brickman, A. L., Foote, F. H., Santisteban, D., Hervis, O, & Kurtines, W. M. (1988). Engaging adolescent drug abusers and their families in treatment: A strategic structural systems approach. *Journal of Consulting and Clinical Psychology, 56,* 552–557.

Thompson, K. M., & Wilsnack, R. W. (1987). Parental influence on adolescent drinking: Modeling, attitudes, or conflict? *Youth and Society, 19,* 22–43.

von Bertalanffy, L. (1948). *General systems theory: Foundation, development, applications.* New York: Braziller.

Waldron, H. B. (1992). *Families of alcohol-abusing adolescents.* National Institute on Alcohol Abuse and Alcoholism, Grant No. R01 AA08718.

Waldron, H. B. (1994). *Drug abuse treatments for adolescents.* National Institute on Drug Abuse, Grant No. R01 DA09422.

Welte, J. W., & Barnes, G. M. (1985). Alcohol: The gateway to other drug use among secondary-school students, *Journal of Youth and Adolescence, 14,* 487–498.

White, H. R., & Labouvie, E. W. (1989). Toward the assessment of adolescent problem drinking. *Journal of Studies on Alcohol, 50,* 30–37.

7

Children of Lesbian and Gay Parents

CHARLOTTE J. PATTERSON

1. Introduction

What kinds of home environments are best able to support children's psychological adjustment and growth? This question has long held a central place in the field of research on child development. Researchers in the United States have often assumed that the most favorable home environments are provided by white, middle-class, two-parent families, in which the father is paid to work outside the home but the mother is not. Although rarely stated explicitly, it has most often been assumed that both parents in such families are heterosexual.

Given that smaller numbers of American families fit the traditionally normative pattern (Hernandez, 1988; Laosa, 1988) today than in earlier years, it is not surprising that researchers have increasingly challenged implicit or explicit criticism of home environments that differ from it by virtue of race, ethnicity, income, household composition, and/or maternal employment (Harrison, Wilson, Pine, Chan, & Buriel, 1990; Hetherington & Arasteh, 1988; Hoffman, 1984; McLoyd, 1990; Spencer, Brookins, & Allen, 1985). Together with the authors of cross-cultural and historical studies (Cole, 1988; Elder, 1986; Rogoff, 1990), these researchers have emphasized the variety of pathways through which healthy psychological development can take place, and the diversity of home environments that can support such development.

In this chapter, I describe recent research from the social sciences on the personal and social development of children with lesbian and gay parents. Beginning with estimates of the numbers of such children, I then

CHARLOTTE J. PATTERSON • Department of Psychology, University of Virginia, Charlottesville, Virginia 22903.

Advances in Clinical Child Psychology, Volume 19, edited by Thomas H. Ollendick and Ronald J. Prinz. Plenum Press, New York, 1997.

outline sociocultural, theoretical, and legal reasons that justify attention to their development. With this material as background, I then review research evidence on sexual identity, personal development, and social relationships among children of lesbian and gay parents. I first describe research on children of divorced lesbian and gay parents; I then examine research on children born to or adopted by lesbian mothers, describing in some detail the findings from my own Bay Area Families Study. In the final section, I draw a number of conclusions from the results of research to date and offer suggestions for future work.

2. Perspectives on Lesbian and Gay Parents and Their Children

Interest in children of lesbian and gay parents has emerged from a number of directions (Allen & Demo, 1995; Laird, 1993; Patterson, 1992). For lesbians and gay men, especially those who may be parents themselves, or who may be considering parenthood, it is valuable to learn about issues and challenges that are common to lesbian and gay parents and their children. Information about the psychosocial development of children with gay or lesbian parents may also be of interest to clinical psychologists and others who are concerned with processes of coping with prejudice, discrimination, and oppression.

In addition to those just mentioned, there are at least three other perspectives from which interest in children of lesbians and/or gay men has emerged. First, the phenomenon of openly gay or lesbian parents bearing and/or raising children represents a sociocultural innovation that is unique to the present historical era; as such, it raises questions about the impact of cultural change on children. Second, from the standpoint of psychological theory, children of lesbian or gay parents pose a number of significant questions for existing theories of psychosocial development. Finally, both in adjudication of child-custody disputes and in administration of adoption and foster-care policies, the legal system in the United States has frequently operated under strong assumptions about difficulties faced by children of lesbians and gay men, and there are important questions about the veridicality of such assumptions. Before reviewing the results of empirical research, I briefly discuss key issues from each of these three perspectives.

2.1. Social and Cultural Issues

Although same-sex attractions and sexual activities have undoubtedly existed throughout history, the emergence of large numbers of openly self-identified gay men and lesbians is a recent phenomenon. Although the beginnings of homophile organizations date to the 1950s and even earlier (D'Emilio, 1983; Faderman, 1991), the beginnings of contemporary gay liberation movements are generally dated to police raids on the Stonewall bar in the Greenwich Village neighborhood of New York City in 1969, and to resistance shown by members of the gay community to these raids (Adam, 1987; D'Emilio, 1983). In the years since these events at the Stonewall, more and more lesbians and gay men have abandoned secrecy, come out of the closet, and joined the movement for gay and lesbian rights (Blumenfeld & Raymond, 1988).

With greater openness among lesbian and gay adults, a number of family forms have emerged in which one or more of a child's parents identify themselves as lesbian or gay (Allen & Demo, 1995; Baptiste, 1987; Martin, 1993; Weston, 1991). Most are families in which children were born in the context of a heterosexual relationship between the biological parents (Falk, 1989). These include families in which the parents divorce when one or both parents come out as lesbian or gay, and families in which one or both of the parents comes out as lesbian or gay and the parents decide not to divorce. The gay or lesbian parent may be either the residential or the nonresidential parent, or children may live part of the time in both homes. Gay or lesbian parents may be single, or they may have same-sex partners who may or may not take up stepparenting relationships with the children.

In addition to children born in the context of heterosexual relationships between parents, both single and coupled lesbians are believed increasingly to be giving birth to children (Benkov, 1994; Laird, 1993; Lewin, 1993; Martin, 1989, 1993; Patterson, 1994b; Pies, 1985, 1990; Steckel, 1985). The majority of such children are believed to be conceived through donor insemination (DI). Although DI techniques have been known for many years, it is only in recent years that they have become widely available to unmarried heterosexual women and to lesbians (Martin, 1989, 1993; Pies, 1985, 1990). Lesbians who seek to become mothers may also do so by becoming foster or adoptive parents (Laird, 1993; Martin, 1993; Patterson, 1994b, 1995c).

A number of gay men have also sought to become parents after coming out (Bigner & Bozett, 1990; Bozett, 1989; Patterson & Chan, 1996; Ricketts, 1991; Ricketts & Achtenberg, 1990). Options pursued by such gay men include adoption and foster care of children to whom the men are not biologically related (Patterson, 1995c). Through DI or through sexual intercourse, gay men may also become biological fathers of children whom they intend to coparent with a single woman (whether lesbian or heterosexual), with a lesbian couple, or with a gay male partner (Martin, 1993; Patterson, 1994b).

Thus, many children today are being brought up in a diverse array of lesbian and gay families, most of which did not exist as recently as 50 years ago (Allen & Demo, 1995; Benkov, 1994; Laird, 1993; Lewin, 1993; Patterson, 1995a; Weston, 1991). Of the different types of families, those of divorced lesbian mothers living with their children, and those of nonresidential gay fathers, are probably the largest groups. In addition, the numbers of families in which children are now being conceived by lesbian mothers using DI are unprecedented. The birth and upbringing of children in such families provides a unique opportunity to observe the formation, growth, and impact of new family forms.

Although it is widely believed that family environments exert significant influences on children who grow up in them, authoritative scholarly treatments of such influences have rarely considered children growing up in families with lesbian and/or gay parents (e.g., Jacob, 1987; Parke, 1984). Even treatments of nontraditional family forms (e.g., Lamb, 1982) have generally failed to consider lesbian and gay parents and their children. Given the many new family forms among lesbian and gay parents, and in view of their apparent vitality, the experiences of children with gay and/or lesbian parents would seem, however, to be a topic deserving of study. Indeed, newer treatments of parenting and of parent–child relationships are beginning to recognize the existence of lesbian and gay parents and their children (Bornstein, 1995; Gottfried & Gottfried, 1994; Lamb, in press).

To the extent that parental influences are seen as critical in psychosocial development, and to the extent that lesbians and/or gay men may provide different kinds of influences than heterosexual parents, then the children of gay men and lesbians can be expected to develop in ways that are different from children of heterosexual parents. Whether any such differences are expected to be beneficial, detrimental, or nonexistent depends, of course, upon the viewpoint from which the phenomena are observed. For instance, some feminist theorists have imagined benefits that might accrue to children growing up in an all-female world (e.g., Gilman, 1915/1979). Expectations based on many psychological theories are, however, more negative.

2.2. Theoretical Issues

Theories of psychological development have traditionally emphasized distinctive contributions of both mothers and fathers to the healthy personal and social development of their children. As a result, many theories predict negative outcomes for children who are raised in environments that do not provide these two kinds of input (Nungesser, 1980). An important theoretical question thus concerns the extent to which such predictions are sustained by results of research on children of gay and/or lesbian parents.

For instance, psychoanalytic theory places heavy weight on the Oedipal drama, in which children experience very different reactions to their mothers and to their fathers (Bronfenbrenner, 1960). From the psychoanalytic perspective, healthy psychological development is believed to require the child's eventual resolution of Oedipal issues. Factors that inhibit or distort this process are therefore thought to be detrimental to the child's development. Recent writers in the psychoanalytic tradition (e.g., Chodorow, 1978; Dinnerstein, 1976) also emphasize different influences of male and female parents in the socialization of children. From psychoanalytic perspectives, then, when one or more parents are either absent and/or homosexually oriented, disruptions of personality development for their children could be anticipated.

From the point of view of social learning approaches to personality development (e.g., Huston, 1983), children are seen as learning distinctive lessons from the examples and the rewards offered by both male and female parents. For example, fathers are thought to model and reward masculine behavior among sons, and mothers to model and reward feminine behavior among daughters. Predictions based on social learning suggest negative outcomes for children brought up in families that do not provide conventional models or rewards for the acquisition of sexual identities.

There have been significant challenges to these theoretical positions, especially from cognitive developmental theory (Kohlberg, 1966) and from gender schema theory (Bem, 1983), neither of which in principle requires that a child's home environment include both heterosexual male and heterosexual female parents in order to support favorable development. Advocates of cognitive developmental and gender schema theory have not, however, discussed the assumption that children's development is best fostered in families that contain both male and female parents, nor have they challenged the premise that development is optimal in families where the parents are heterosexual.

In short, psychoanalytic and social learning theories of personal and social development during childhood emphasize the importance of children having both heterosexual male and heterosexual female parents, and they predict generally negative outcomes for children whose parents do not exemplify these qualities. Although cognitive developmental theory and gender schema theory do not require such assumptions, proponents of these views have not challenged them. As a result, these perspectives on individual differences in personal and social development are commonly believed to predict difficulties in development among children of lesbian and gay parents. Empirical research with such children thus provides an opportunity to evaluate anew these theoretical assumptions.

2.3. Legal and Public Policy Issues

The legal system in the United States has long been hostile to gay men and to lesbians who are or who wish to become parents (Brantner, 1992; Cain, 1993; Editors of the *Harvard Law Review*, 1990; Falk, 1989, 1994; Hitchens, 1979/1980; Kleber, Howell, & Tibbets-Kleber, 1986; Patterson & Redding, in press; Polikoff, 1990; Ricketts & Achtenberg, 1990; Rivera, 1991). Because of judicial and legislative assumptions about adverse effects of parental homosexuality on children, lesbian mothers and gay fathers have often been denied custody and/or visitation with their children following divorce (Editors of the *Harvard Law Review*, 1990; Falk, 1989, 1994; Patterson & Redding, in press; Rivera, 1991). Although some states now have laws stipulating that sexual orientation is not relevant to determinations of parental fitness in custody disputes, in other states, parents who admit a gay or lesbian sexual orientation are presumed to be unfit as parents (Brantner, 1992; Editors of the *Harvard Law Review*, 1990). In addition, regulations governing foster care and adoption in many states have made it difficult for lesbians or gay men to adopt children or to serve as foster parents (Patterson, 1995c; Ricketts, 1991; Ricketts & Achtenberg, 1990).

One issue underlying both judicial decision making in custody litigation and public policies governing foster care and adoption has been questions concerning the fitness of lesbians and gay men to be parents (Falk, 1989, 1994). In particular, courts have sometimes assumed that gay men and lesbians are mentally ill and hence not fit to be parents, that lesbians are less maternal than heterosexual women and hence do not make good mothers, and that lesbians' and gay men's relationships with sexual partners leave little time for ongoing parent–child interaction (Patterson & Redding, in press).

Although systematic empirical study of these issues is just beginning, results of research to date have failed to confirm any of these fears. The idea that homosexuality constitutes a mental illness or disorder has long been repudiated both by the American Psychological Association and by the American Psychiatric Association (Blumenfeld & Raymond, 1988). Lesbians and heterosexual women have been found not to differ markedly either in their overall mental health or in their approaches to child rearing, nor have lesbians' romantic and sexual relationships with other women been found to detract from their ability to care for their children (Falk, 1989,

1994; Patterson, 1995d). Research on gay fathers has been similarly unable to unearth any reasons to believe them unfit as parents (Barret & Robinson, 1990; Bozett, 1980, 1989; Patterson & Chan, 1996). Studies in this area are still rather scarce, and more information would be helpful. On the basis of research to date, though, negative assumptions about lesbian and gay adults' fitness as parents appear to be without foundation (Cramer, 1986; Crawford, 1987; Falk, 1989, 1994; Gibbs, 1988; Patterson, 1995a, 1995d).

In addition to judicial concerns about gay and lesbian parents themselves, there are three major kinds of fears about the impact of lesbian or gay parents on children that are reflected in judicial decision making about child custody and in public policies such as regulations governing foster care and adoption policies. I outline each of the areas of concern here; in the review of empirical literature which follows, I describe research findings relevant to each of these issues. For further discussion of these issues, see Patterson (1995c) and Patterson and Redding (in press).

The first area of judicial concern is that development of sexual identity will be impaired among children of lesbian or gay parents (Falk, 1989, 1994; Patterson, 1992, 1995a). For instance, it is feared that children brought up by gay fathers or lesbian mothers will show disturbances in gender identity and/or in gender-role behavior. It is also feared that children brought up by lesbian mothers or gay fathers will themselves become gay or lesbian, an outcome that the courts view as undesirable.

A second category of judicial concern about the influences of lesbian or gay parents on their children involves aspects of personal development other than sexual identity. For example, courts have expressed fears that children in the custody of gay or lesbian parents will be more vulnerable to mental breakdown, and/or that they will exhibit more adjustment difficulties and behavior problems. It is also feared that these children will be less psychologically healthy and/or less well adjusted than children growing up in homes with heterosexual parents.

A third category of specific fears expressed by the courts is that children of lesbian and gay parents may experience difficulties in social relationships. For example, judges have repeatedly expressed concern that children living with lesbian mothers may be stigmatized, teased, or otherwise traumatized by peers. Another common fear is that children living with gay or lesbian parents may be more likely to be sexually abused by the parent and/or by the parent's friends or acquaintances.

Because such negative assumptions have often been explicit in judicial determinations when child custody has been denied to lesbian and gay parents, or when visitation with gay or lesbian parents has been curtailed (Falk, 1989, 1994; Patterson & Redding, in press), and because such assumptions are open to empirical test, they provide an important impetus for research. Given the enormous significance of custody determinations in the lives of lesbian mothers, gay fathers, and their children, it is essential that evidence regarding oft-expressed judicial assumptions be examined with care.

2.4. Summary

There are thus a number of perspectives from which interest in lesbian and gay parents and their children has emerged. In the next sections, I review the available research findings on children of lesbian and gay parents. I first describe research on children who were born in the context of heterosexual relationships between parents. In the majority of these families, the parents were married at the time of children's birth or adoption, then divorced after one or both parents came out, and for this reason, I refer to them as divorced lesbian and gay parents and their children. A review of research on children of divorced lesbian and gay parents is followed by a description of work on children born to or adopted early in life by parents who had already identified as lesbian or gay.

3. Children of Divorced Lesbian and Gay Parents

Much of the impetus for early research on children of lesbian and gay parents has been generated by judicial concerns about the psychosocial development of children residing with gay or lesbian parents. Research in each of three main areas of judicial concern, namely, children's sexual identity, other aspects of children's personal development, and children's social relationships, will be summarized here. For other recent reviews of this material, see Cramer (1986), Crawford (1987), Falk (1989, 1994), Gibbs (1988), Green and Bozett (1991), Patterson (1992, 1995a), and Tasker and Golombok (1991).

Reflecting issues relevant in the largest number of custody disputes, most of the research compares development of children with custodial lesbian mothers to that of children with custodial heterosexual mothers. Since many children living in lesbian mother-headed households have undergone the experience of parental divorce and separation, it has been widely believed that children living in families headed by divorced but heterosexual mothers provide the best comparison group. Although some studies focus exclusively on children of gay men or lesbians (Green, 1978; Paul, 1986), most compare children in divorced lesbian mother-headed families with children in divorced heterosexual mother-headed families.

3.1. Sexual Identity

Following Money and Ehrhardt (1972), I considered research on three aspects of sexual identity here: gender identity, gender-role behavior, and sexual orientation. Gender identity concerns a person's self-identification as male or female. Gender-role behavior concerns the extent to which a person's activities, occupations, and the like are regarded by the culture as masculine, feminine, or both. Sexual orientation refers to a person's attraction to and choice of sexual partners (e.g., heterosexual, homosexual, or bisexual). To examine the possibility that children in the custody of divorced lesbian mothers or gay fathers experience disruptions of sexual identity, I describe research findings relevant to each of these three major areas of concern.

Research on gender identity has failed to reveal any differences in the development of children as a function of their parents' sexual orientation. In one of the earliest studies, Kirkpatrick, Smith, and Roy (1981) compared the development of 20 elementary-school-aged children of lesbian mothers to that of 20 same-aged children of heterosexual mothers. In projective testing, as expected, most children in both groups drew a same-sex figure first. Of those who drew an opposite-sex figure first, only 3 (1 with a lesbian mother, and 2 with heterosexual mothers) showed concern about gender issues in clinical interviews. Similar findings have been reported in projective testing by other investigators (Green, 1978; Green, Mandel, Hotvedt, Gray, & Smith, 1986). Studies using more direct methods of assessment (e.g., Golombok, Spencer, & Rutter, 1983) have yielded similar results. No evidence for difficulties in gender identity among children of lesbian mothers has been reported.

Research on gender-role behavior has also failed to reveal difficulties in the development of children with lesbian or gay parents. Green (1978) reported that 20 of 21 children of lesbian mothers in his sample named a favorite toy consistent with conventional sex-typed toy preferences, and that all 21 children reported vocational choices within typical limits for conventional sex roles. Results consistent with those described by Green have also been reported for children by Golombok et al. (1983), Hoeffer (1981), and Kirkpatrick et al. (1981); and for adult daughters of lesbian mothers, by Gottman (1990). In interviews with 56 children of lesbians and 48 children of heterosexual mothers, Green et al. (1986) found no differences with respect to favorite television programs, television characters, games, or toys. These investigators did, however, report that daughters of lesbian mothers were more likely to be described as taking part in rough-and-tumble play or as playing with "masculine" toys such as trucks or guns, but found no comparable differences for sons. In all of these studies, the behavior and preferences of children in unconventional families were seen as falling within conventional limits.

Rees (1979) administered the Bem Sex-Role Inventory to a group of young adolescent offspring of lesbian mothers and a same-aged group of youngsters with heterosexual mothers. Although children of lesbian and heterosexual mothers did not differ on masculinity or on androgyny, adolescent offspring of lesbian mothers reported greater psychological femininity than did their same-aged peers with heterosexual mothers. This result would seem to run counter to expectations based on stereotypes of lesbians as lacking in femininity. Overall, research has failed to reveal any notable difficulties in the development of sex-role behavior among children of lesbian mothers.

A number of investigators have also studied sexual orientation, the third component of sexual identity. For instance, Huggins (1989) interviewed 36 youngsters who were between 13 and 19 years of age; half were the offspring of lesbian mothers, and half had mothers who were heterosexual in their orientation. No child of a lesbian mother identified as lesbian or gay, but one child of a heterosexual mother did; this difference was not statistically significant. Similar results have been reported by Golombok and her colleagues (1983), Gottman (1990), Green (1978), Paul (1986), and Rees (1979), and by Tasker and Golombok (1995); some children of lesbian mothers have identified themselves as gay, lesbian or bisexual, but their numbers did not exceed expectations based on presumed population base rates. Studies of the offspring of gay fathers have yielded similar results (Bozett, 1980, 1982, 1987, 1989; Miller, 1979; Patterson & Chan, 1996).

Despite the consistency of the findings, this research can be criticized on a variety of grounds. For instance, many lesbians do not self-identify as such until adulthood (Brown, 1995; Kitzinger & Wilkinson, 1995); for this reason, studies of sexual orientation among adolescents may count as heterosexual some individuals who will come out as lesbian later in life. Concern has also been voiced that in many studies comparing children of divorced heterosexual mothers with children of divorced lesbian mothers, lesbian mothers were more likely to be living with a romantic partner; in these cases, maternal sexual orientation and household composition variables have been confounded. Although these and other methodological issues still await resolution, it remains true that no significant problems in the development of sexual identity among children of lesbian mothers have yet been identified.

3.2. Other Aspects of Personal Development

Studies of other aspects of personal development among children of gay and lesbian parents have assessed psychiatric and behavior problems

(Golombok et al., 1983; Kirkpatrick et al., 1981), personality (Gottman, 1990), self-concept (Huggins, 1989; Puryear, 1983), locus of control (Puryear, 1983; Rees, 1979), moral judgment (Rees, 1979), and intelligence (Green et al., 1986). As was true for sexual identity, studies of other aspects of personal development have revealed no significant differences between children of lesbian or gay parents and children of heterosexual parents.

3.3. Social Relationships

Studies assessing potential differences between children of lesbian and gay versus heterosexual parents have sometimes included assessments of children's social relationships. Because of concerns voiced by the courts that children of lesbian and gay parents might encounter difficulties among their peers, the most common focus of attention has been on peer relations. Studies in this area have consistently found that school-aged children of lesbian mothers report a predominantly same-sex peer group, and that the quality of their peer relations is described by their mothers and by the investigators as good (Golombok et al., 1983; Green, 1978; Green et al., 1986). Anecdotal and first-person accounts describe children's worries about being stigmatized as a result of their parents' sexual orientation (Pollack & Vaughn, 1987; Rafkin, 1990), but available research provides no evidence for the proposition that the development of children of lesbian mothers is compromised by difficulties in peer relations. In fact, a recent study of adult children of divorced lesbian mothers found that they recalled no more teasing by peers during childhood than did adult children of divorced heterosexual parents (Tasker & Golombok, 1995).

Research has also been directed toward description of children's relationships with adults, especially fathers. For instance, Golombok et al. (1983) found that children of lesbian mothers were more likely than children of heterosexual mothers to have contact with their fathers. Most children of lesbian mothers had some contact with their father during the year preceding the study, but most children of heterosexual mothers had not; indeed, almost a third of the children of lesbian mothers reported at least weekly contact with their fathers, whereas only 1 in 20 of the children of heterosexual mothers reported this. Kirkpatrick and her colleagues (1981) also reported that lesbian mothers in their sample were more concerned than heterosexual mothers that their children have opportunities for good relationships with adult men, including fathers. Lesbian mothers' own social networks have been found to include both men and women, and their offspring as a result have contact with adults of both sexes. Hare and Richards (1993) reported that the great majority (90%) of children living with divorced lesbian mothers in their sample also had contact with their fathers. Overall, results of the meager research to date suggest that children of lesbian parents have satisfactory relationships with adults of both sexes.

Concerns that children of lesbian or gay parents are more likely than children of heterosexual parents to be sexually abused have also been voiced by judges in the context of child-custody disputes. Results of research in this area show that the great majority of adults who perpetrate sexual abuse are male; sexual abuse of children by adult women is very rare (Finkelhor & Russell, 1984; Jones & MacFarlane, 1980). Lesbian mothers are thus extremely unlikely to expose their children to sexual abuse. Moreover, the overwhelming majority of child sexual abuse cases involve an adult male abusing a young female (Jenny, Roesler, & Poyer, 1994; Jones & MacFarlane, 1980). Gay men are no more likely than heterosexual men to perpetrate child sexual abuse (Groth & Birnbaum, 1978; Jenny et al., 1994). Fears that children in custody of gay or lesbian parents might be at heightened risk for sexual abuse are thus without empirical foundation.

In summary, then, results of research to date suggest that children of divorced lesbian and gay parents have normal relationships with peers and that their contacts with adults of both sexes are satisfactory. The picture of children with divorced lesbian and gay parents emerging from this research is thus one of general engagement in social life with peers, with parents, and with adult relatives and friends of both genders.

3.4. Diversity among Children with Divorced Lesbian or Gay Parents

Despite the tremendous diversity of gay and lesbian communities (Blumenfeld & Raymond, 1988), research on individual differences among children of divorced lesbian and gay parents is as yet very limited. Here I focus on the impact of parental psychological and relationship status, as well as on the influence of other stresses and supports.

One important dimension of variability among gay and lesbian families concerns whether the custodial parent is involved in a romantic relationship, and if so what implications this may have for children. Pagelow (1980), Kirkpatrick et al. (1981), and Golombok et al. (1983) all reported that divorced lesbian mothers were more likely than divorced heterosexual mothers to be living with a romantic partner. Huggins (1989) reported that self-esteem among daughters of lesbian mothers whose lesbian partners lived with them was higher than that among daughters of lesbian mothers who did not live with a partner. This finding might be interpreted to mean that mothers who are high in self-esteem are more likely to be involved in romantic relationships and to have daughters who are also high in self-esteem, but many other interpretations are also possible. In view of the small sample size and absence of conventional statistical tests, Huggins's finding should be interpreted with caution. In view of the judicial attention that lesbian mothers' romantic relationships have received during custody proceedings (Falk, 1989; Hitchens, 1979/1980; Kirkpatrick, 1987), however, it is surprising that more research has not examined the impact of this variable on children.

Rand, Graham, and Rawlings (1982) found that divorced lesbian mothers' sense of psychological well-being was related to the extent to which they were open about their lesbian identity with employers, ex-husbands, and children. In this sample, a mother who felt more able to disclose her lesbian identity was more likely also to express a greater sense of well-being. In light of the consistent finding that children's adjustment in heterosexual families is often related to maternal mental health (Rutter, Izard, & Read, 1986; Sameroff & Chandler, 1975), one might expect factors that enhance mental health among lesbian mothers also to benefit the children of these women.

Another area of great diversity among families with a gay or lesbian parent concerns the degree to which a parent's sexual identity is accepted by other significant people in children's lives (Casper, Schultz, & Wickens, 1992). Huggins (1989) found a tendency for children whose fathers were rejecting of maternal lesbianism to report lower self-esteem than those whose fathers were neutral or positive. Due to small sample size and absence of conventional statistical tests, however, this finding should be seen as suggestive rather than definitive. Huggins's results raise questions about the extent to which reactions of important adults in a child's environment can influence responses to discovery of a parent's gay or lesbian identity.

Effects of the age at which children learn of parents' gay or lesbian identities have also been a topic of study. Paul (1986) reported that those who were told either in childhood or in late adolescence found the news easier to cope with than did those who first learned of it during early to middle adolescence. Huggins (1989) reported that those who learned of maternal lesbianism in childhood had higher self-esteem than did those who were not informed until adolescence. Some writers have suggested that early adolescence is a particularly difficult time for children to learn of their parents' lesbian or gay identities (Baptiste, 1987; Lewis, 1980).

As this brief review reveals, research on diversity among families with gay and lesbian parents is just beginning (Freiberg, 1990; Martin, 1989, 1993; Patterson, 1995a). Existing data favor early disclosure of identity to children, positive maternal mental health, and a supportive milieu, but the available data are still limited. No information is as yet available on differences stemming from race or ethnicity, family economic circumstances, cultural environments, or related variables. Because none of the published work has employed observational measures or longitudinal designs, little is known about behavior within these families or about any changes over time. It is clear that much remains to be learned about differences among gay and lesbian families and about the impact of such differences on children growing up in these homes.

4. Children Born to or Adopted by Lesbian Mothers: The Bay Area Families Study

Although many writers have recently noted an increase in childbearing among lesbians, research with these families is as yet very new (Patterson, 1992, 1994a, 1994b, 1995a, 1995e; Polikoff, 1990; Pollack & Vaughn, 1987; Riley, 1988; Weston, 1991). In this section, I summarize the research to date on children born to or adopted by lesbian mothers. Although some gay men are also undertaking parenthood after coming out (Patterson & Chan, 1996), no research has yet been reported on their children.

In one of the first systematic studies of children born to lesbians, Steckel (1985, 1987) compared the progress of separation–individuation among 11 preschool children born via DI to lesbian couples with that among 11 same-aged children of heterosexual couples. Using parent interviews, parent and teacher Q-sorts, and structured doll-play techniques, Steckel compared independence, ego functions, and object relations among children in the two types of families. Her main results documented impressive similarity in development among children in the two groups. Similar findings, based on extensive interviews with five lesbian-mother families were also reported by McCandlish (1987).

Steckel (1985, 1987) did, however, report some suggestive differences between groups. Children of heterosexual parents saw themselves as somewhat more aggressive than did children of lesbians, and they were seen by both parents and teachers as more bossy, domineering, and negativistic. Children of lesbian parents, on the other hand, saw themselves as more lovable and were seen by parents and teachers as more affectionate, more responsive, and more protective toward younger children. In view of the small sample size and the large number of statistical tests performed, these results must be considered suggestive rather than definitive. Steckel's work is, however, the first to make systematic comparisons of development among children born to lesbian and to heterosexual couples.

More recently, Flaks, Ficher, Masterpasqua, and Joseph (1995) compared social and personal development among fifteen 3- to 9-year-old children born to lesbian couples via DI with that among 15 children from matched, two-parent heterosexual families. Across a wide array of assessments of cognitive and behavioral functioning, there were notable similarities between the children of lesbian and heterosexual parents. The only significant difference between the two groups was in the area of parenting skills and practices; lesbian couples revealed more parenting skills than did heterosexual couples.

In this context, I designed the Bay Area Families Study to contribute to understanding of children born to lesbian mothers. In this section, I describe the study itself and its principal results to date; they fall into four major areas. First, I describe demographic and other characteristics of the participating families. Next, I describe assessments of the adjustment of both mothers and children, relative to normative expectations based on large comparison samples drawn from the population at large. In families that were headed by lesbian couples, the study also examined key facets of couple functioning (e.g., relationship satisfaction, division of labor), and I report normative findings in this area. The study also explored individual differences in children's adjustment, and their correlates, and I present these findings next. Finally, the study examined the degree to which children in participating families have contact with grandparents and other members of the extended family, and I present these findings as well. Although I do not provide statistical details here, all findings described as statistically significant were at the $p < .05$ level. The methods and findings are summarized briefly, but additional details and commentary are available elsewhere (Patterson, 1994a, 1995b, 1995f; Patterson & Kosmitzki, 1995). There were no significant sex differences in the data presented here, so my presentation does not consider this variable.

4.1. Description of Participating Families

Families were eligible to participate in the Bay Area Families Study if they met each of three criteria. First, at least one child between 4 and 9 years of age had to be present in the home. Second, the child had to have been born to or adopted by a lesbian mother or mothers. Third, only families who lived within the greater San Francisco Bay Area (e.g., San Francisco, Oakland, and San Jose) were considered eligible.

Recruitment began when I contacted friends, acquaintances, and colleagues who might be likely to know eligible lesbian-mother families. I described the proposed research and solicited help in locating families. From names gathered in this way, I telephoned each family to describe the study and ask for their participation. In all, I made contact with 39 eligible families, of whom 37 participated in the study. Thus, approximately 95% of the eligible families who were contacted did take part. Participation involved a single home visit during which all of the data reported here were collected.

Twenty-six of the 37 participating families (70%) were headed by a lesbian couple. Seven families (19%) were headed by a single mother living with her child. In four families (11%), the child had been born to a lesbian couple who had since separated, and the child was in *de facto* joint custody (i.e., living part of the time with one mother and part of the time with the other mother). In this last group of families, one mother was out of town during the period of testing, and so did not participate.

Sixty-six lesbian mothers took part in the study. Their ages ranged from 28 to 53 years, with a mean age of 39.6 years of age. Sixty-one (92%) described themselves as white or non-Hispanic Caucasian, two (3%) as Afro-American or black, and three (4%) as coming from other racial/ethnic backgrounds. Most were well educated; 74% had received college degrees, and 48% had received graduate degrees.

The great majority of mothers (94%) were employed on a regular basis outside the home, and about half said that they worked 40 hours or more per week. Most (62%) of the women were in professional occupations (e.g., law, nursing), but others were in technical or mechanical occupations such as car repair (9%), business or sales such as real estate (9%), or in other occupations such as artist (14%). Only four mothers were not employed outside the home. Thirty-four families reported family incomes over $30,000 per year, and 17 families reported incomes over $60,000 per year.

In each family, the focal child was between 4 and 9 years of age (mean age, 6 years and 2 months); there were 19 girls and 18 boys. Thirty-four of the children were born to lesbian mothers, and three had been adopted. Thirty of the children were described by their mothers as white or non-Hispanic Caucasian, three as Hispanic, and four as some other racial/ethnic heritage.

Some additional descriptive information was also collected. Mothers were asked to explain the circumstances surrounding the child's conception, birth, and/or adoption. Mothers were also asked about the child's biological father or sperm donor, the degree to which the mothers had knowledge of his identity and/or contact with him, and the degree to which the focal child had such knowledge and/or contact. In addition, mothers were asked to give the child's last name and to explain how the child had been given that name.

The mothers' accounts of the conception, birth, and/or adoption of their children made clear that, in general, the focal children were very much wanted. The average amount of time that it took for biological mothers to conceive focal children after they began to attempt to become pregnant was 10 months. Adoptive mothers reported that, on average, the adoption process took approximately 12 months. In the great majority of cases, these lesbian mothers had devoted considerable time and effort to making the birth or adoption of their children possible.

There was tremendous variability in the amount of information that families had about the donor or biological father of the focal child. In 17 families (46%), the child had been conceived via DI with sperm from an anonymous donor (e.g., sperm that had been provided by a sperm bank or clinic). In these cases, families had only very limited information (e.g., race, height, weight, hair color) about the donor, and none knew the donor's name. In 10 families (27%), the child was conceived via DI, with sperm provided by a known donor (e.g., a family friend). In 4 families (11%), children were conceived when the biological mother had intercourse with a man. In 3 families (8%), the child was adopted. In the 3 remaining families, some other set of circumstances applied, or the parents acknowledged that the child had been born to one of the mothers, but preferred not to disclose any additional information about their child's conception.

Mothers reported relatively little contact with biological fathers or donors. Most of the families (62%) reported no contact at all with the biological father or donor during the previous year. Only 10 families (27%) had had two or more contacts with the biological father or sperm donor during the previous year.

Given that many families did not know the identity of the child's sperm donor or biological father, and that most currently had little or no contact with him, it is not surprising that the donor or biological father's role with the child was described by mothers as being quite limited. In the majority of families (60%), mothers reported that the donor or biological father had no special role *vis-à-vis* the child; this figure includes the families in which the sperm donor had been anonymous. In a minority of families (35%), the biological father's identity was known to parents and children, but he took the role of a family friend rather than that of a father. There were only two families in which the biological father was acknowledged as such and in which he was described as assuming a father's role.

Questions about selection of the child's last name are of particular interest in families headed by lesbian couples. In this sample, the majority of children—26, or 70%—bore the last names of their biological or adoptive mothers; this figure includes children in 4 families in which *all* family members (i.e., both mothers and all children) shared the same last name. In 7 families, children had been given hyphenated last names, created from the two mothers' last names. Finally, in 4 families, children had some other last name.

Thus, the families who participated in the Bay Area Families Study were mostly white, well educated, and relatively affluent. Almost every mother was employed, many in the professions. Most children had been conceived via donor insemination, and most had little or no contact with the sperm donor or biological father.

4.2. Mental Health of Mothers and Their Children

For purposes of presentation, I will refer to the biological or legal adoptive mother in each family as the "biological mother," and the other mother, if any, as the "nonbiological mother." In what follows, I describe first the assessment procedures and results for mothers and then turn to those for children (see Patterson, 1994a, and Patterson & Kosmitzki, 1995, for details).

4.2.1. Assessment of Maternal Self-Esteem and Adjustment

Maternal self-esteem was assessed using the Rosenberg Self-Esteem Scale (Rosenberg, 1979). This scale consists of 10 statements, with four response alternatives, indicating the respondent's degree of agreement with each statement. Results were tabulated to obtain total scores, based upon the recommendations contained in Rosenberg (1979).

Maternal adjustment was assessed using the Derogatis Symptom Checklist—Revised (SCL-90-R; Derogatis, 1983), which consists of 90 items addressing a variety of psychological and somatic symptoms. Each respondent rated the extent to which she had been distressed by each symptom during the past week (0 = *Not at All*, 4 = *Extremely*). Nine subscales (i.e., anger/hostility, anxiety, depression, interpersonal sensitivity, obsessive–compulsiveness, paranoid ideation, phobic anxiety, psychoticism, and somatization) were scored, as well as a global severity index (GSI), which summarized the respondent's overall level of distress.

4.2.2. Results for Maternal Self-Esteem and Adjustment

Total scores on the Rosenberg Self-Esteem Scale were calculated for each mother, following the method described by Rosenberg (1979). The means for both biological and nonbiological mothers were almost identical, and both were well within the range of normal functioning. These results (see Table 1) indicate that lesbian mothers who took part in this research reported generally positive views about themselves.

For the Derogatis SCL-90, nine subscale scores and one GSI for each mother were computed, and then average scores on each measure both for biological and nonbiological mothers were calculated (Derogatis, 1983). Mean scores for biological and nonbiological mothers were virtually iden-

Table 1

Means and T-Scores of SCL-90-R Subscales and
Rosenberg Self-Esteem Scale for Biological and Nonbiological Mothers

	Biological mothers		Nonbiological mothers	
	Mean	T-score[a]	Mean	T-score
SCL-90-R subscales				
Anger/hostility	.36	55	.31	52
Anxiety	.29	52	.24	51
Depression	.40	53	.43	53
Interpersonal sensitivity	.33	53	.36	54
Obsessive–compulsiveness	.31	50	.51	54
Paranoid ideation	.32	52	.25	52
Phobic anxiety	.01	44	.12	53
Psychoticism	.11	53	.11	53
Somatization	.29	50	.32	50
Global severity index (GSI)	.34	53	.38	55
Rosenberg Self-Esteem	16.00		16.10	

[a]T-scores based on norms of nonpatient group according to Derogatis (1983); T-scores for Rosenberg scale were not available. Reprinted from Patterson and Kosmitzki (1995).

tical for most subscales as well as for the GSI, and they were all well within a normal range (see Table 1). None of the scores deviated substantially from the expected mean, indicating that lesbian mothers' reports of symptoms are no greater and no smaller than those expected for any other group of women of the same age. Thus, the results for maternal adjustment revealed that lesbian mothers who took part in the Bay Area Families Study reported few symptoms and good self-esteem.

4.2.3. Assessment of Children's Adjustment

To assess levels of child social competence and of child behavior problems, the Child Behavior Checklist (CBCL; Achenbach & Edelbrock, 1983) was administered (Patterson, 1994a). The CBCL was selected because of its ability to discriminate children in the clinical versus normative range of functioning for both internalizing (e.g., inhibited, overcontrolled behavior) and externalizing (e.g., aggressive, antisocial, or undercontrolled behavior) problems, as well as in social competence. It is designed to be completed by parents. In the present study, all participating mothers completed this instrument.

Norms for the CBCL (Achenbach & Edelbrock, 1983) were obtained from heterogeneous normal samples of two hundred 4- to 5-year-old, and six hundred 6- to 11-year-old children, as well as from equivalent numbers of children at each age who were drawn from clinical populations (e.g., those receiving services from community mental health centers, private psychological and psychiatric clinics or practices, etc.). For purposes of the present research, mean scores reported by Achenbach and Edelbrock (1983, pp. 210–214) were averaged across 4- to 5- and 6- to 11-year age levels to provide estimates of average scores for social competence, internalizing, externalizing, and total behavior problems among normative and clinical populations at the ages studied here. To assess the extent of their resemblance to normal and clinical populations, then, scores for children in the current sample were compared with these figures.

Assessment of children's self-concepts was accomplished using five scales from Eder's Children's Self-View Questionnaire (CSVQ: Eder, 1990). These scales, designed especially to assess psychological concepts of self among children from 3 to 8 years of age, assess five different dimensions of children's views of themselves. The aggression scale assessed the degree to which children saw themselves as likely to hurt or frighten others. The Social Closeness scale assessed the degree to which children enjoy being with people and prefer to be around others. The Social Potency scale assessed the degree to which children like to stand out and/or be the center of attention. The Stress Reaction scale assessed the extent to which children said they often felt scared, upset, and/or angry. Finally, the Well-Being scale assessed the degree to which children felt joyful, content, and comfortable with themselves. Using hand puppets, the CSVQ was administered individually to participating children, and their answers were tape-recorded for later scoring.

Children's sex-role behavior preferences were assessed in a standard, open-ended interview format, such as that employed in earlier research on children of divorced lesbian mothers (e.g., Golombok et al., 1983; Green, 1978; Green et al., 1986). The interviewer explained to each child that she was interested in learning more about the friends and other children that he or she liked to play with, and about his or her favorite toys and other things. She then asked each child to name the friends and other children he or she liked to play with. Following this, each child was asked to name his or her favorite toys, favorite games, and favorite characters on television, in movies, or in books. The interviewer wrote down each of the children's responses. Children's responses were also tape-recorded, and the interviewer's notes were later checked for accuracy against the audiotapes.

After testing had been completed, each child's answers for each of four topics (peer friendships, favorite toys, favorite games, and favorite characters) were coded into one of four categories with regard to their sex-role relevant qualities. The four categories were *Mainly same-sex* (e.g., a boy reports having mostly or entirely male friends), *Mixed sexes* (e.g., an even or almost-even mix of sexes in the friends mentioned by a child), *Opposite sex* (e.g., a girl reports having mostly or entirely male friends), and *Can't tell* (e.g., an answer was unscorable, or not clearly sex-typed—for instance, children saying that playing Chutes and Ladders was one of their favorite games). Because children's play groups are known to be highly sex-segregated at this age, children were expected to give mainly *Same sex* answers to these questions.

4.2.4. Results for Children's Adjustment

As expected, social competence among children with lesbian mothers was rated as normal (see Figure 1). Scores for children of lesbian mothers were significantly higher than those for Achenbach and Edelbrock's (1983) clinical sample, but were not different from those for the normal sample. This was true for reports given by both mothers in the lesbian-mother families (Patterson, 1994a).

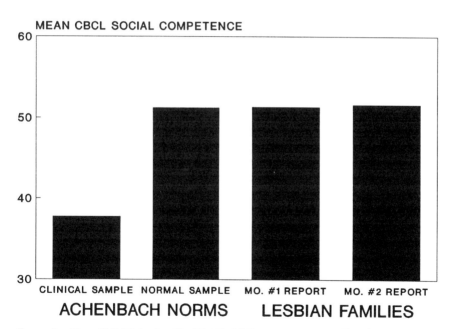

FIGURE 1.   Mean Child Behavior Checklist Social Competence scores (data from Patterson, 1994a).

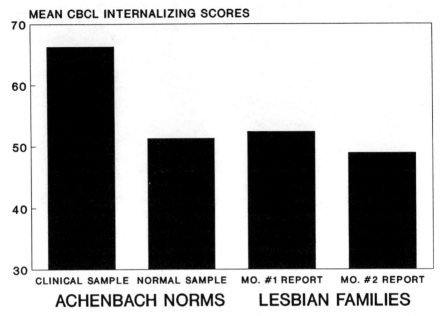

FIGURE 2.   Mean Child Behavior Checklist Internalizing Behavior Problem scores (data from Patterson, 1994a).

Results for behavior problems revealed the same pattern. For internalizing (see Figure 2), externalizing (see Figure 3), and total behavior problems, scores for children of lesbian mothers were significantly lower than those for children in the clinical sample, but did not differ from those in the normal sample. This was true of reports given by both mothers in the lesbian mother families. Overall, then, the behavior problems of lesbian mothers' children were rated as significantly smaller in magnitude than those of children in the clinical sample, and as no greater than those of children in the normal sample.

On three scales of the Eder CSVQ, there were no significant differences between the self-reports of children of lesbian as compared to those of Eder's (1990) heterosexual mothers. Specifically, there were no significant differences between children of lesbian and heterosexual mothers on self-concepts relevant to Aggression, Social Closeness, and Social Potency. Children of lesbian mothers in the present sample did not see themselves as either more or less aggressive, sociable, or likely to enjoy being the center of attention than did children of heterosexual mothers in Eder's sample.

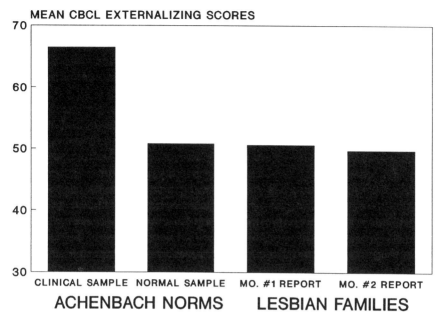

FIGURE 3.   Mean Child Behavior Checklist Externalizing Behavior Problem scores (data from Patterson, 1994a).

On two scales, however, differences did emerge between children of lesbian and heterosexual mothers (see Figure 4). Specifically, children of lesbian mothers reported greater reactions to stress than did children of heterosexual mothers, and they also reported a greater overall sense of well-being than did children of heterosexual mothers. In other words, children of lesbian mothers said that they more often felt angry, scared, or upset, but also said that they more often felt joyful, content, and comfortable with themselves than did children of heterosexual mothers.

The aspect of children's sexual identity studied here was that of preferences for sex-role behavior. As expected (Green, 1978), most children reported preferences for sex-role behaviors that are considered to be normative at this age (see Table 2). For instance, every child reported that his or her group of friends was mainly or entirely made up of same-sex children. The great majority of children also reported favorite toys and favorite characters (e.g., from books, movies, or television) that were of the same sex. In the case of favorite games, a number of children mentioned games that were not clearly sex-typed (e.g., board games such as Chutes and Ladders), and hence were not categorizable; however, the great major-

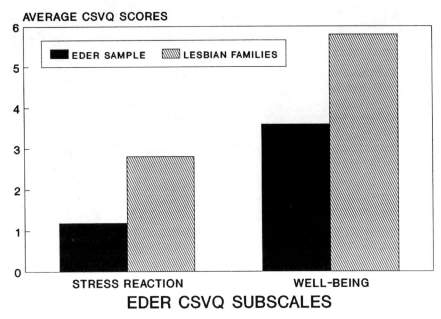

FIGURE 4.   Mean Child Self-View Questionnaire Stress Reaction and Well-Being scores (data from Patterson, 1994a).

ity mentioned games that are generally associated with their own rather than with the opposite sex. In short, preferences for sex-role behavior among the children of lesbian mothers studied here appeared to be quite typical for children of these ages.

4.3.   Couple Functioning

Couple functioning was assessed among the 26 participating families that were headed by a lesbian couple (Patterson, 1995b). In this section, the assessment instruments are described first, followed by results for the couples who took part in the study.

4.3.1.   Assessment of Couple Functioning

To assess division of labor as well as satisfaction with role arrangements in each family, an adapted form of the Who Does What? for parents of 5-year-olds (Cowan & Cowan, 1990, 1992) was administered to each adult respondent (Patterson, 1995b).

TABLE 2
Children's Sex-Role Behavior[a]

	Peer friendships	Favorite toys	Favorite games	Favorite characters
Mainly same sex	35	31	12	24
Mixed sexes	1	0	1	9
Mainly opposite sex	0	1	1	2
Not clearly sex typed	0	4	22	1

[a]Reprinted with permission from Patterson (1994a).

The instrument began with 13 items concerning the division of household labor (e.g., planning and preparing meals, cleaning up after meals). Respondents were asked to decide for each item *How it is now* and *How I would like it to be* on a scale of 1 to 9, in which 1 meant *She does it all* and 9 meant *I do it all*. These are referred to as the "real" and "ideal" divisions of labor, respectively. At the bottom of that page, each respondent was asked to indicate how satisfied overall she was with "the way you and your partner divide the family tasks," and with "the way you and your partner divide the work outside the family"; in each of these two cases, scores ranged from 1 (*Very Dissatisfied*) to 5 (*Very Satisfied*).

The next page contained 12 items about family decision making (e.g., decisions about major expenses, deciding which friends and family to see). Respondents were again asked to indicate the real and ideal division of labor. At the bottom of this second page, each respondent was asked to indicate on a 5-point scale how satisfied overall she was with "the way you and your partner divide family decisions."

The third page contained 20 items about child-care responsibilities (e.g., playing with our child, disciplining our child, picking up after our child). Respondents were again asked to indicate the real and ideal divisions of labor for each item.

The fourth page contained four questions about overall evaluations of child-care responsibilities. Respondents were asked to rate their own and their partner's overall involvement with their child on a scale running from *No Involvement*, to *Shared Involvement*, to *Sole* responsibility. Respondents also were asked to rate their satisfaction with their own and with their partner's involvement in child care responsibilities, from *Very Dissatisfied* to *Very Satisfied*.

To assess satisfaction with couple relationships, the Marital Adjustment Test (Locke & Wallace, 1959) was administered to all adult respondents. The Marital Adjustment Test is a 16-item instrument designed to record in a standardized format the overall satisfaction of spouses with their heterosexual marriages. A handful of small changes in wording (e.g., substituting the word *partner* for the word *spouse*) made the instrument more suitable for use with lesbian couples. Scoring was accomplished using the methods described by the authors.

4.3.2. Results for Couple Functioning

The actual and ideal reported participation of biological and non-biological mothers in each of three domains of family work was compared (Patterson, 1995b; see Table 3). Results showed that biological and non-biological mothers did not differ in their evaluations of ideal distributions of labor in the three domains; most believed that tasks should be shared relatively evenly in all domains. In terms of the actual division of labor, biological and nonbiological mothers did not differ in their reported participation in household labor or family decision making. In the area of child care, however, biological mothers reported themselves as responsible for more of the work than nonbiological mothers. Thus, although lesbian mothers agreed that ideally child care should be evenly shared,

TABLE 3
Parent Reports of Actual and Ideal Division of Family Labor

Division of labor		Report of biological mother	Report of nonbiological mother	$t(25) =$
Actual				
Household tasks	M	5.33	4.80	2.52
	SD	.59	.66	
Child-care tasks	M	5.70	4.35	3.92*
	SD	.90	.92	
Decision making	M	5.14	4.94	1.05
	SD	.65	.42	
Ideal				
Household tasks	M	5.10	4.86	1.55
	SD	.56	.52	
Child-care tasks	M	5.20	4.75	2.42
	SD	.63	.42	
Decision making	M	5.02	4.97	<1
	SD	.25	.23	

Note. Scores of 1 indicate that *She does it all*, scores of 5 indicate that *We both do this about equally*, and scores of 9 indicate that *I do it all*. To protect alpha levels against inflation due to multiple comparisons, the Bonferroni correction has been applied to all *t*-tests. Reprinted with permission from Patterson (1995b).
*$p < .01$.

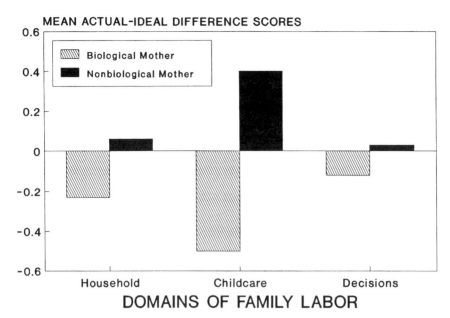

FIGURE 5.   Mean differences between parent reports of actual versus ideal division of labor (reprinted with permission from Patterson, 1995b).

they reported that in their families, the biological mother was actually more responsible than the nonbiological mother for child care.

To assess satisfaction with division of labor, comparisons between actual and ideal divisions of labor were made (see Figure 5). Results showed that biological mothers reported that ideally they would do fewer household tasks and less child care. Nonbiological mothers did not report feeling that they should be significantly more involved in household tasks, but did agree that an ideal allocation of labor would result in them doing more child care. There were no effects for family decision making. Thus, the main result was that both mothers felt that an ideal allocation of labor would involve a more equal sharing of child care tasks between them.

Each respondent also had been asked to provide a global rating of each mother's overall involvement in child care activities. Biological mothers reported on this measure that they were more involved than nonbiological mothers. Reports of the nonbiological mothers were in the same direction but did not reach statistical significance. Global judgments thus confirmed the more detailed reports described earlier in showing that, if anyone, it is the biological mother who takes more responsibility for child care.

In interviews, parents were asked to give estimates of the average number of hours both biological and nonbiological mothers spent in paid employment each week. Results showed that biological mothers were less likely than nonbiological mothers to be working 40 hours per week or more in paid employment (see Figure 6). Thus, whereas biological mothers reported greater responsibility for child care, nonbiological mothers reported spending more time in paid employment.

There were no differences between relationship satisfaction reported by biological and nonbiological mothers (see Table 4). Consistent with expectations based on earlier findings with lesbian mothers (Koepke, Hare, & Moran, 1992), lesbian mothers reported feeling very satisfied in their couple relationships. Overall satisfaction with division of family labor was also high, and there were no significant differences between biological and nonbiological mothers in this regard.

4.4. Parental Division of Labor, Satisfaction, and Children's Adjustment

The study also assessed the strength of overall association between the three measures of child adjustment on the one hand and the four

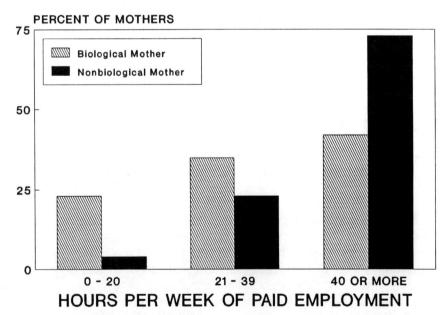

FIGURE 6.   Percent of biological and nonbiological mothers spending 0–20, 21–39, and 40 or more hours per week in paid employment (reprinted with permission from Patterson, 1995b).

TABLE 4
*Parent Reports of Satisfaction with Division of Family Labor
and with Couple Relationships*

Satisfaction with		Report of biological mother	Report of nonbiological mother	$t(25) =$
Division of household tasks	M	3.96	3.88	<1
	SD	.72	.86	
Division of work outside family	M	3.69	3.88	<1
	SD	1.05	.91	
Division of family decisions	M	4.15	4.12	<1
	SD	.78	.71	
Own involvement with child	M	4.38	4.08	1.28
	SD	.98	1.06	
Partner's involvement with child	M	4.58	4.38	1.22
	SD	.50	.85	
Locke–Wallace Relationship	M	118.46	117.42	<1
Satisfaction score	SD	15.70	15.18	

Note. Except for the Locke-Wallace Relationship Satisfaction score, all scores are on a 5-point scale, with higher scores indicating greater satisfaction. None of the comparisons between satisfaction among biological versus nonbiological mothers were significant. Reprinted with permission from Patterson (1995b).

measures of parents' division of labor and satisfaction with division of labor on the other (Patterson, 1995b). Results of multivariate analysis showed a significant association between the two sets of variables. Parent reports of division of labor, satisfaction with division of labor, and measures of child adjustment were significantly associated with one another. When biological mothers did less child care and when nonbiological mothers did more and were more satisfied, children's adjustment was rated as being more favorable.

In this study, then, both children and mothers reported more positive adjustment in families in which the nonbiological mother was described as a relatively equal participant in child care, and in which the biological mother was not described as bearing an unequal burden of child care duties. In other words, the most positive outcomes for children occurred in families that reported sharing child-care tasks relatively evenly between parents.

4.5. Contacts with Members of Extended Family

One common stereotype about lesbian mothers and their children is that they are isolated from extended family networks. In particular, because it is sometimes assumed that lesbian women who are open with parents or siblings about their sexual identities will be disowned or rejected by—and therefore estranged from—their relatives, it is sometimes expected that children of lesbian mothers will have little or no contact with their grandparents, aunts, or uncles. One concern that is sometimes expressed about children growing up in custody of lesbian mothers, then, is that they may be isolated in a single-sex home, without access to heterosexual adults, both male and female, who might serve as role models for them.

To evaluate these possibilities, lesbian mothers were asked to provide information about their children's contacts with grandparents and with any other adults outside the immediate household who were seen by the mothers as being important to their children (Patterson et al., 1995). For each person named, mothers were asked to give the person's relationship to the focal child and an estimate of the person's frequency of contact with the focal child, including visits, telephone calls, cards, and letters.

Results showed that, contrary to the stereotypes, most children were in relatively active contact with grandparents and with other members of their extended families. For instance, mothers reported that more than 60% of children had contact with at least one grandmother, and more than 50% of children had contact with at least one grandfather, once a month or more often. Similarly, mothers reported that many children had such contact with at least one additional adult relative (usually, an aunt or an uncle) and most had such contact with parents' adult friends, both male and female. Clearly, then, the results suggested that children were in active contact with both male and female grandparents and other relatives.

4.6. Summary and Discussion of Bay Area Families Study

The Bay Area Families Study was designed to examine child development and family functioning among families in which children were born or adopted after their mothers had acknowledged lesbian identities. Although findings from this study should be regarded as preliminary in a number of respects, four principal results have emerged to date. The first major finding was that, according to the standardized assessment techniques used here, both mothers' and children's adjustment fell clearly within the normative range. Considering that this result is consistent with the findings of other research on lesbian women in general (Gonsiorek, 1991), lesbian mothers in particular (Falk, 1989, 1994; Patterson, 1992, 1995d), children of divorced lesbian and gay parents (Patterson, 1992), and children born to lesbian mothers (Flaks et al., 1995; McCandlish, 1987; Steckel, 1985, 1987), this outcome was not surprising. Particularly in light of judicial and popular prejudices against lesbian and gay families that still exist in many parts of the country, however, the result is worthy of attention. The present study found not only that lesbian mothers' adjustment and self-esteem were within the normative range, but also that social and personal development among their children were proceeding quite normally.

Although psychosocial development among children of lesbian versus heterosexual parents was generally quite similar, there were nevertheless also some differences among children in the two groups, most notably in the area of self-concept. Even though their answers were well within the normal range, children of lesbian mothers reported that they experienced more reactions to stress (e.g., feeling angry, scared, or upset) and also a greater sense of well-being (e.g., feeling joyful, content, and comfortable with themselves) than did the children of heterosexual parents studied by Eder (1990).

The best interpretation of this difference is not yet clear. One possibility is that children of lesbian mothers report greater reactions to stress because they actually experience more stress than do other children. In other words, children of lesbian mothers may actually encounter more stressful events and conditions than do children with heterosexual parents (Casper, Schultz, & Wickens, 1992; Lott-Whitehead & Tully, 1993; O'Connell, 1993). If so, then their more frequent reports of emotional responses to stress might simply reflect the more stressful nature of their experience. From this viewpoint, however, it is difficult to account for the greater sense of well being reported by children of lesbian mothers.

Another possibility is that, regardless of actual stress levels, children of lesbian mothers may be more conscious of their affective states in general and/or more willing to report their experiences of negative emotional states. If, as some have suggested (e.g., Pollack & Vaughn, 1987; Rafkin, 1990), children in lesbian homes may have more experience with the naming and verbal discussion of feelings in general, then they might exhibit increased openness to the expression of negative as well as positive feelings. In this view, the greater tendency of lesbian mothers' children to admit feeling angry, upset, or scared might be attributed not as much to differences in experiences of stress as to a greater openness to emotional experience and expression of all kinds.

Consistent with this latter interpretation, children of lesbian mothers in the present study reported greater feelings of joy, contentedness, and comfort with themselves than did children of heterosexual mothers in Eder's (1990) sample. Although these findings do not rule out the possibility that children of lesbian women do indeed experience greater stress, they do suggest that these children may be more willing than other children to report a variety of intense emotional experiences, whether positive or negative. Because this study was not designed to evaluate alternative interpretations of these differences, however, clarification of these issues must await the results of future research.

A second main finding was that lesbian couples who took part in this study reported that they divide various aspects of the labor involved in household upkeep and child care in a relatively even manner. The fact that lesbian mothers in this sample reported sharing many household and family tasks is consistent with, and expands upon, earlier findings on the division of household labor among lesbian and gay couples. For instance, Kurdek's (1993) study of lesbian, gay, and heterosexual couples without children found that lesbian couples were the most likely to share household responsibilities such as cooking, cleaning, and doing laundry. In the present study, results showed that lesbian couples with children not only reported sharing such household tasks but also reported enjoying equal influence in family decision making. Thus, even under pressure of child-rearing responsibilities, lesbian couples seem to maintain relatively egalitarian divisions of household responsibilities. In this way, lesbian couples with children resembled lesbian couples without children.

On the other hand, there were also some indications of specialization in the allocation of labor among lesbian couples who participated in this study. Consistent with patterns of specialization in heterosexual families (Cowan & Cowan, 1992), biological mothers reported greater involvement with child care, and nonbiological mothers reported spending more time in paid employment. In accommodating to the demands of child rearing, it would appear that lesbian couples who took part in this research specialized to some degree with regard to their engagement in child care versus paid work. In this way, lesbian couples with children resembled heterosexual couples with children.

It is important, however, not to overemphasize the similarities between division of labor in lesbian and heterosexual families. In an unpublished dissertation, Hand (1991) compared division of labor among lesbian and heterosexual couples with children under the age of 2 years. Consistent with the present findings, she found that household tasks and decision making were shared evenly by both lesbian and heterosexual couples with children, and that biological lesbian mothers reported greater involvement in child care than did nonbiological mothers. She also found, however, that both biological and nonbiological lesbian mothers were more involved in child care than were heterosexual fathers. Thus, even though differences between biological and nonbiological lesbian mothers were significant, both in the present study and in the study by Hand (1991), they were much less pronounced than the differences between husbands and wives in the matched group of heterosexual families studied by Hand (1991). These results are depicted in Figure 7. As can be seen in the figure,

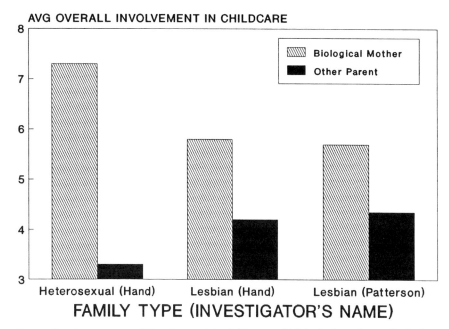

FIGURE 7.   Average overall involvement in child care of biological mother and of other parent (reprinted with permission from Patterson, 1995b).

division of the labor involved in child care was more pronounced among heterosexual than among lesbian couples.

The third major result documented significant associations between division of labor among lesbian couples and psychosocial outcomes for mothers and their children. When lesbian couples shared child care more evenly, mothers were more satisfied and children were more well adjusted. Thus, even within the context of largely egalitarian arrangements, more equal sharing of child care was associated with more positive outcomes among both lesbian mothers and their children.

Mothers' ratings of their children's behavior problems were significantly associated with assessment of the parents' division of labor as well as with nonbiological mother's satisfaction with the allocation of tasks. Especially striking was the extent to which the nonbiological mother's satisfaction with child-care arrangements was associated with children's self-reports of well-being. Even within this well-adjusted nonclinical sample, children with mothers who shared child-care tasks evenly, and who expressed satisfaction with this arrangement, appeared to enjoy the most favorable adjustment.

That equal sharing of child care was associated with favorable adjust-ment among children is a result very much in concert with ideas proposed by Okin and by other scholars working from a feminist perspective (e.g., Hochschild, 1989; Okin, 1989). These writers have suggested that models of fairness in division of labor at home are important influences on children's development, and that children who observe equal division of respon-sibilities between their parents may enjoy developmental advantages. Although this is by no means the only possible interpretation of the present findings, these results are certainly consistent with such a view.

One possible pathway through which benefits of equality in parents' division of labor might accrue to children involves parental satisfaction with their couple relationships. Given the egalitarian ideals expressed so clearly by lesbian couples who took part in this research, higher relation-ship satisfaction was expected among those who succeeded—by equal division of labor—in putting these ideals into action. Whether by its association with the relative absence of conflict between parents or with other aspects of parenting behavior (Belsky, 1984), satisfaction was ex-pected to mediate connections between division of labor and child adjust-ment. Contrary to expectations, however, no consistent association emerged among relationship satisfaction and the other study variables. In retro-spect this may have been due to the global nature of the assessments of relationship satisfaction used here. Ruble, Fleming, Hackel, and Stangor (1988) have reported that some aspects of marital satisfaction are more tied to division of labor than others. Future research employing more detailed measures of potential mediators will, it is hoped, explicate more clearly pathways that link parental division of labor and child adjustment.

Although questions about causal linkages are of great interest, one should keep in mind that the present data are correlational in nature and therefore cannot support causal inferences. Are happy, well-adjusted les-bian families more likely to divide labor evenly? Or does the equal division of labor among lesbian couples with children lead to better adjustment and satisfaction with domestic arrangements? Or both? The present study was not designed to examine such possibilities, and the present data do not allow for their evaluation. Future work employing other kinds of research designs will be needed to disentangle causes and consequences in these domains.

The fourth major finding concerned children's contact with grand-parents and other adult members of their extended families. Common stereotypes suggest that lesbian mothers who disclose their sexual identi-ties to family members may be rejected for that reason, and hence that they and their children may be estranged to some extent from members of their extended families. In contrast to such expectations, results from the Bay

Area Families Study suggested that most children were in relatively active contact with at least some of their grandparents, aunts, and uncles. Far from being isolated from lesbian mothers' families of origin, then, the results suggested that children were actively engaged in relationships with grandparents and other relatives of both sexes.

A number of limitations of this research should be acknowledged. This research relied on mothers' and children's reports as sources of data. The study included no observational assessments, and so the correspondence between parental reports about division of labor and the actual division of labor cannot be determined. Likewise, assessments of children's adjustment completed by independent observers would have been a valuable addition to the study. On the other hand, the use of well-known and widely used instruments such as the Locke–Wallace Marital Adjustment Test and the Achenbach and Edelbrock Child Behavior Checklist enhances the degree to which the present results can be compared with those of other researchers.

Some concerns relevant to sampling issues should also be acknowledged. Most of the families who took part in the Bay Area Families Study were headed by lesbian mothers who were white, well educated, relatively affluent, and living in the greater San Francisco Bay Area. For these reasons, no claims about representativeness of the present sample can be made. The reliability and generalizability of findings would likely be enhanced by the participation of more diverse samples of lesbian families over longer periods of time.

In summary, the Bay Area Families Study was designed to study child development, maternal mental health, and family functioning among the families of the lesbian baby boom. Results to date suggest that maternal mental health is good and that child development is proceeding normally. Lesbian couples described equal sharing of many household and decision-making tasks involved in their lives together, but they also reported that child care and paid employment were specialized to some degree. The more evenly they shared child care, the more satisfied mothers reported feeling, and the better adjusted were their children. In addition, children were reported to be in relatively active contact with their grandparents and with other adult members of their extended families.

5. Conclusions

Overall, results of research on children of lesbian and gay parents suggest that such children develop in a normal fashion. Despite strong legal presumptions against lesbian and gay parents in a number of jurisdictions, despite negative expectations about such children's development drawn from well-known psychological theories, and despite the accumulation of a substantial amount of research in this area, no evidence for significant difficulties in development among children of lesbian or gay parents has been produced. Indeed, the results of research to date are exceptionally clear, and they suggest that home environments provided by lesbian and gay parents are as likely as those supplied by heterosexual parents to support and enable children's psychosocial growth.

Without denying the clarity of the research findings, it is also important to emphasize that this is a relatively new area of study. As the present review of the literature reveals, systematic research on lesbian and gay parents and their children is a phenomenon of the past 20 years, and most of the studies have been published within the last 10 years. Some issues have been studied by many investigators, whereas others have as yet received little attention. Most studies have involved relatively small samples, and the range of methodological approaches has been limited. Questions can be raised about the degree to which various methodological challenges of research in this area have been met, and few studies would be entirely invincible to all criticism. Much remains for future research to accomplish. Despite limitations, however, results of work to date are quite clear, and they merit attention from a number of perspectives.

First, inasmuch as they serve to counter ignorance and prejudice, results of research on children of lesbian and gay parents contribute to ongoing processes of social change. Fears of new or unfamiliar ways of living can characterize lesbian and gay as well as heterosexual individuals, and can lead to negative expectations about the impact of novel arrangements. Just as questions about the impact on children of other kinds of recent social innovations, such as maternal employment (Hoffman, 1984), have often arisen at least in part from lack of information, so it is also the case that lack of familiarity with lesbian and gay parents and their children may lead to unrealistic concerns. Research in this area has already been helpful in addressing many misconceptions that exist about children of lesbian and gay parents.

Evidence from research on children of lesbian and gay parents also has important implications for theoretical accounts of human development. Results of research on children of divorced lesbian mothers or divorced gay fathers reveal that parents' sexual orientation has not proven to be an important determinant of development during childhood or adolescence among the offspring of such parents. Because parents in these studies typically lived together during children's earliest years, however, there is still the possibility that children's normal development should be attributed to this fact. Thus, studies of divorced lesbian and gay parents and their children, although suggestive from a theoretical point of view, are not likely to be definitive with regard to the theoretical significance of parental sexual orientation on human development.

More likely to have definitive theoretical implications are studies of children born to (or adopted early in life by) lesbian or gay parents. In the Bay Area Families Study, for example, most children had little or no contact with the sperm donor or biological father who had made their conception possible; about half of the children did not even know this man's identity (Patterson, 1994a). In these families, then, children have lived their entire lives in custody of lesbian mothers; no heterosexual parent has ever lived in the child's household. To the extent that normal development can be observed within this group of children, then, it cannot be attributed to any social influences from heterosexual parents.

To the extent that the findings from initial studies of children born to lesbian parents (e.g., Flaks et al., 1995; McCandlish, 1987; Patterson, 1994a, 1995b, 1995f; Patterson & Kosmitzki, 1995; Steckel, 1985, 1987) replicate in future research and are extended into adolescent and adult development, they will suggest that important revisions of well-known theories of psychological development may be necessary. If development of children born into lesbian-mother homes is normal, then traditional emphases on contributions of a heterosexual male parent to socialization may need to be reconsidered. If contributions of heterosexual male and female parents are not essential to satisfactory psychosocial development, then it will be necessary to consider alternative formulations.

A number of different approaches might be examined. For example, it might be argued that certain kinds of family interactions, processes, and relationships are beneficial for children's development, but that parents need not be heterosexual to provide them. In other words, variables related to family processes (e.g., qualities of relationships) may be more important predictors of child adjustment than are variables related to family structure (e.g., sexual orientation, number of parents in the home).

A possible analogy in this regard is provided by research on the impact of parental divorce on children. Although early studies of children's reactions to divorce focused on variables related to household composition and family structure (e.g., divorced vs. nondivorced families), more recent research has highlighted the important contributions of variables related to family processes and interactions (e.g., conflict, warmth). For instance, a number of investigators (e.g., Emery, 1982; O'Leary & Emery, 1984) have argued that child behavior problems associated with parental divorce are best understood as the result of interparental conflict rather than changes in household composition or structure as such. Research on divorcing families has thus suggested the preeminence of process over structure in mediating outcomes for children.

Applied to the present concerns, this perspective suggests the hypothesis that structural variables such as parental sexual orientation may be less important in mediating child outcomes in lesbian and gay families than qualities of family interactions, relationships, and processes. Many theoretical perspectives are compatible with an emphasis on function. For instance, attachment theory (Ainsworth, 1985a, 1985b; Bowlby, 1988) emphasizes the functional significance of sensitive parenting in creating secure relationships, but does not require any particular family constellation or structure. Similarly, self psychology (Kohut, 1971, 1977, 1984) describes the significance of mirroring and idealizing processes in human development, but does not require that they occur in the context of any specific family structure. Theoretical perspectives such as attachment theory and self psychology would seem to be compatible with an emphasis on functional rather than structural aspects of family life, and hence to provide promising interpretive frameworks within which to conceptualize further research in these directions.

To evaluate the impact of both process and structural variables on child outcomes in lesbian, gay, and heterosexual families, research would need to assess variables of both types. Research with other kinds of nontraditional families (Eiduson & Weisner, 1978; Weisner & Wilson-Mitchell, 1990) has demonstrated the potential utility of this approach. Most research on lesbian and gay families, however, has focused on structural rather than process variables (e.g., on comparisons between children of lesbian and heterosexual mothers rather than on the qualities of interactions and relationships within these families). An adequate evaluation of the significance of process versus structure in lesbian and gay families therefore awaits the results of future research.

An alternative theoretical response might be to shift the focus of attention away from parental influences on children's development. As Maccoby (1990) has proposed, important forms of learning (e.g., about behavior considered appropriate for members of each sex) may be less dependent on parental input than traditionally believed. Other social influences, such as those of peers, should also be considered. It will also be important to identify and acknowledge contributions of genetic influences (Dunn & Plomin, 1990). By investigating the impact of new family forms on the development of children who are growing up in them, it seems likely that research on children of lesbian and gay parents will provide opportunities to broaden understanding of human development.

Results of research on children of lesbian and gay parents also have significant implications for public policies governing child custody, foster care, and adoption in the United States (Falk, 1989, 1994; Patterson, 1995c; Patterson & Redding, in press; Polikoff, 1986, 1990). Unless and until the weight of evidence can be shown to have shifted, there is no empirically verifiable reason under the prevailing "best interests of the child" standard (Reppucci, 1984; Rivera, 1991) to deny or curtail parental rights of lesbian or gay parents on the basis of their sexual orientation, nor is there any empirically verifiable reason to believe that lesbians or gay men are less fit than heterosexuals to serve as adoptive or foster parents (Editors of the *Harvard Law Review*, 1990; Patterson, 1995c; Ricketts, 1991; Ricketts & Achtenberg, 1990). Existing research evidence provides no justification for denial of parental rights and responsibilities to lesbians and gay men on the basis of their sexual orientation.

Indeed, protection of the best interests of children in lesbian and gay families increasingly demands that courts and legislative bodies acknowledge realities of life in nontraditional families (Falk, 1994; Patterson, 1995c; Patterson & Redding, in press; Polikoff, 1990). Consider, for example, a family created by a lesbian couple who undertake the conception, birth, and upbringing of their child together. Should this couple separate, it is reasonable to expect that the best interests of the child will be served by preserving the continuity and stability of the child's relationships with both parents. In law, however, it is generally only the biological mother who is recognized as having parental rights and responsibilities. From a legal standpoint, the nonbiological mother is generally considered a stranger, with no legal rights or responsibilities with respect to the child. When courts and legislatures fail to acknowledge facts of children's lives in nontraditional families, they experience great difficulty in serving the best interests of children in these families (Polikoff, 1990).

A number of approaches to rectifying this situation have been proposed. For instance, a small number of families have obtained second-parent adoptions (Patterson, 1995c; Ricketts & Achtenberg, 1990), in which a nonbiological parent legally adopts a child without the biological parent giving up his or her legal rights and responsibilities; this avenue is not, however, available in most states. Others (e.g., Polikoff, 1990) have advocated legislative reform, including changes in the standards for legal designation as a parent. As the number of lesbian and gay families with children increase, pressures for legal and judicial reform seem likely to increase.

As this review has revealed, most of the existing research has focused primarily on comparisons between children of gay or lesbian parents and those of heterosexual parents. It has taken this approach in order to address what can be considered heterosexist and/or homophobic questions

(Herek, 1995). Heterosexism reflects the belief that everyone is or ought to be heterosexual. Homophobic questions are those that are based on prejudice against lesbians and gay men, and are designed to raise the expectation that various negative outcomes will befall children of gay or lesbian parents as compared to children of heterosexual parents. Examples of such questions that were considered earlier include the following: Won't the children of lesbians and gay men have difficulty with sexual identity? Won't they be more vulnerable to psychiatric problems? Won't they be sexually abused? Now that research has begun to provide negative answers to such heterosexist and/or homophobic questions, the time has come for child development researchers to address a broader range of issues in this area (Allen & Demo, 1995; Laird, 1993; Patterson, 1995a, 1995d).

Many important research questions can stem from a more positive approach to the concerns of gay and lesbian communities. Such questions may raise the possibility of various desirable outcomes for children of gay and lesbian parents. For instance, won't these children grow up with increased tolerance for viewpoints other than their own? Won't they be more at home in the multicultural environments that almost all people increasingly inhabit? A number of children of lesbian mothers have reported that they see increased tolerance for divergent viewpoints as a benefit of growing up in lesbian mother families (Rafkin, 1990), but systematic research in this area is still lacking. Alternatively, these approaches may suggest study of the great diversity among gay and lesbian families. For example, how does growing up with multiple gay and lesbian parents differ from the experience of growing up with a single parent or with two parents who are a gay or lesbian couple? It will be helpful in future research to explore ways in which family processes are related to child outcomes in different kinds of lesbian and gay families (Allen & Demo, 1995; Laird, 1993; Patterson, 1995a, 1995d).

A few studies that provide information relevant to issues of diversity among children of gay and lesbian parents have already been reported. Results of work with families headed by divorced lesbian mothers suggest that children are better off when their mothers have high self-esteem and are currently living with a lesbian partner (Huggins, 1989; Kirkpatrick, 1987). Research and clinical reports suggest that children in such families also appear to show more favorable adjustment when their fathers and/or other important adults accept their mothers' lesbian identities, and perhaps also when they have contact with other children of lesbians and gay men (Huggins, 1989; Lewis, 1980). In addition, there are indications that those who learn as children that they have a gay or lesbian parent experience less difficulty in adapting to this reality than do those who are not told until adolescence (Paul, 1986). In one study, young children whose lesbian parents shared child care relatively evenly were better adjusted than those whose parents reported less egalitarian arrangements (Patterson, 1995b). Such findings are best regarded as preliminary glimpses of a territory in need of further exploration.

As a number of writers have pointed out (Martin, 1993; Patterson, 1995a, 1995d), much remains to be done to understand differences between and among gay and lesbian families, and to comprehend the impact of such differences on children and youth. It would be valuable to know more about the economic, religious, racial, ethnic, and cultural diversity in gay and lesbian families, and about the ways in which parents and children in such families manage the multiple identities available to them. It would be helpful to learn more about different kinds of parenting experiences— such as noncustodial parenting, nonbiological parenting, coparenting, multiple parenting, adoption, and foster care—and about their likely influences on the children involved. Studies are also needed to explore the nature of stresses and supports encountered by children of lesbian and gay parents—in the parents' families of origin (e.g., with grandparents and other relatives), among parents' and children's friends, and in their larger communities. Research is needed about the ways in which effects of heterosexism and homophobia are felt by parents and children in lesbian and gay families, and about the way in which they cope with ignorance and prejudice that they encounter.

To address these issues most effectively, future research should be conducted from an ecological perspective and should, where possible, employ longitudinal designs. Studies of development over time, especially during middle and later childhood and adolescence, are badly needed. Research should seek to assess not only child adjustment over time, but also the family processes, relationships, and interactions to which child adjustment may be linked. Family processes, in turn, should be viewed in context of the prevailing ecological conditions of family life.

In conclusion, it would seem that research on children of gay and lesbian parents, although still quite new, is well under way. Having begun to address heterosexist and homophobic concerns represented in psychological theory, judicial opinion, and popular prejudice, researchers are now in a position also to explore a broader range of issues raised by the emergence of and increased openness among lesbian and gay parents and their children. Research in this area has the potential to contribute to knowledge about nontraditional family forms and about their impact on children, encourage innovative approaches to the conceptualization of human development, and inform legal rulings and public policies relevant to children of gay and lesbian parents.

ACKNOWLEDGMENTS

Grateful acknowledgment is due to the Society for Psychological Study of Social Issues for support of the Bay Area Families Study. I thank especially Mitch Chyette, Deborah Cohn, Carolyn Cowan, Philip Cowan, Charlene Depner, Ellie Schindelman, and all of the families who participated in the Bay Area Families Study for their support and assistance. I also wish to thank Alicia Eddy, David Koppelman, Meg Michel, and Scott Spence for their efficient work in coding the data for this study, and Sally Hand for her generosity in granting permission to present results from her research. Correspondence should be directed to Charlotte J. Patterson, Department of Psychology, Gilmer Hall, University of Virginia, Charlottesville VA 22903; or via Internet, CJP@VIRGINIA.edu.

6. References

Achenbach, T. M., & Edelbrock, C. (1983). *Manual for the Child Behavior Checklist and Revised Child Behavior Profile.* Burlington: University of Vermont, Department of Psychiatry.

Adam, B. D. (1987). *The rise of a gay and lesbian movement.* Boston: Twayne.

Ainsworth, M. D. S. (1985a). Patterns of infant–mother attachments: Antecedents and effects on development. *Bulletin of the New York Academy of Medicine, 61,* 771–791.

Ainsworth, M. D. S. (1985b). Attachments across the life span. *Bulletin of the New York Academy of Medicine, 61,* 792–812.

Allen, K. R., & Demo, D. H. (1995). The families of lesbians and gay men: A new frontier in family research. *Journal of Marriage and the Family, 57,* 111–127.

Baptiste, D. A. (1987). Psychotherapy with gay/lesbian couples and their children in "stepfamilies": A challenge for marriage and family therapists. In E. Coleman (Ed.), *Integrated identity for gay men and lesbians: Psychotherapeutic approaches for emotional well-being* (pp. 223–238). New York: Harrington Park Press.

Barret, R. L., & Robinson, B. E. (1990). *Gay fathers.* Lexington, MA: Lexington Books.

Belsky, J. (1984). The determinants of parenting: A process model. *Child Development, 55,* 83–96.

Bem, S. L. (1983). Gender schema theory and its implications for child development: Raising gender-aschematic children in a gender-schematic society. *Signs: Journal of Women in Culture and Society, 8,* 598–616.

Benkov, L. (1994). *Reinventing the family.* New York: Crown Publishers.

Bigner, J. J., & Bozett, F. W. (1990). Parenting by gay fathers. In F. W. Bozett & M. B. Sussman (Eds.), *Homosexuality and family relations* (pp. 155–176). New York: Harrington Park Press.

Blumenfeld, W. J., & Raymond, D. (1988). *Looking at gay and lesbian life.* Boston: Beacon.

Bornstein, M. H. (ed.). (1995). *Handbook of parenting.* Hillsdale, NJ: Erlbaum.

Bowlby, J. (1988). *A secure base: Parent–child attachment and healthy human development.* New York: Basic Books.

Bozett, F. W. (1980). Gay fathers: How and why they disclose their homosexuality to their children. *Family Relations, 29,* 173–179.

Bozett, F. W. (1982). Heterogeneous couples in heterosexual marriages: Gay men and straight women. *Journal of Marital and Family Therapy, 8,* 81–89.

Bozett, F. W. (1987). Children of gay fathers. In F. W. Bozett (Ed.), *Gay and lesbian parents* (pp. 39–57). New York: Praeger.

Bozett, F. W. (1989). Gay fathers: A review of the literature. In F. W. Bozett (Ed.), *Homosexuality and the family* (pp. 137–162). New York: Harrington Park Press.

Brantner, P. A. (1992). When mommy or daddy is gay: Developing constitutional standards for custody decisions. *Hastings Women's Law Journal, 3,* 97–121.

Bronfenbrenner, U. (1960). Freudian theories of identification and their derivatives. *Child Development, 31,* 15–40.

Brown, L. S. (1995). Lesbian identities: Concepts and issues. In A. R. D'Augelli & C. J. Patterson (Eds.), *Lesbian, gay and bisexual identities over the lifespan* (pp. 3–23). New York: Oxford University Press.

Cain, P. (1993). Litigating for lesbian and gay rights: A legal history. *Virginia Law Review, 79,* 1551–1642.

Casper, V., Schultz, S., & Wickens, E. (1992). Breaking the silences: Lesbian and gay parents and the schools. *Teachers College Record, 94,* 109–137.

Chodorow, N. (1978). *The reproduction of mothering: Psychoanalysis and the sociology of gender.* Berkeley: University of California Press.

Cole, M. (1988). Cross-cultural research in the sociohistorical tradition. *Human Development, 31,* 137–157.

Cowan, C. P., & Cowan, P. A. (1990). Who does what? In J. Touliatos, B. F. Perlmutter, & M. A. Straus (Eds.), *Handbook of family measurement techniques* (pp. 447–448). Newbury Park, CA: Sage.

Cowan, C. P., & Cowan, P. A. (1992). *When partners become parents: The big life change for couples.* New York: Basic Books.

Cramer, D. (1986). Gay parents and their children: A review of research and practical implications. *Journal of Counseling and Development, 64,* 504–507.

Crawford, S. (1987). Lesbian families: Psychosocial stress and the family-building process. In Boston Lesbian Psychologies Collective, *Lesbian psychologies: Explorations and challenges* (pp. 195–214). Urbana: University of Illinois Press.

D'Emilio, J. (1983). *Sexual politics, sexual communities: The makings of a homosexual minority in the United States, 1940–1970.* Chicago: University of Chicago Press.

Derogatis, L. R. (1983). *SCL-90-R administration, scoring, and procedures manual.* Towson, MD: Clinical Psychometric Research.

Dinnerstein, D. (1976). *The mermaid and the minotaur: Sexual arrangements and human malaise.* New York: Harper & Row.

Dunn, J., & Plomin, R. (1990). *Separate lives: Why siblings are so different.* New York: Basic Books.

Eder, R. A. (1990). Uncovering young children's psychological selves: Individual and developmental differences. *Child Development, 61,* 849–863.

Editors of the *Harvard Law Review.* (1990). *Sexual orientation and the law.* Cambridge, MA: Harvard University Press.

Eiduson, B. T., & Weisner, T. S. (1978). Alternative family styles: Effects on young children. In J. H. Stevens & M. Mathews (Eds.), *Mother/child father/child relationships* (pp. 197–221). Washington, DC: National Association for the Education of Young Children.

Elder, G. H., Jr. (1986). Military timing and turning points in men's lives. *Developmental Psychology, 22,* 233–245.

Emery, R. E. (1982). Interparental conflict and the children of discord and divorce. *Psychological Bulletin, 92,* 310–330.

Faderman, L. (1991). *Odd girls and twilight lovers: A history of lesbian life in twentieth century America.* New York: Columbia University Press.

Falk, P. J. (1989). Lesbian mothers: Psychosocial assumptions in family law. *American Psychologist, 44*, 941–947.

Falk, P. J. (1994). The gap between psychosocial assumptions and empirical research in lesbian-mother child custody cases. In A. E. Gottfried & A. W. Gottfried (Eds.), *Redefining families: Implications for children's development* (pp. 131–156). New York: Plenum Press.

Finkelhor, D., & Russell, D. (1984). Women as perpetrators: Review of the evidence. In D. Finkelhor (Ed.), *Child sexual abuse: New theory and research* (pp. 171–187). New York: Free Press.

Flaks, D., Ficher, I., Masterpasqua, F., & Joseph, G. (1995). Lesbians choosing motherhood: A comparative study of lesbian and heterosexual parents and their children. *Developmental Psychology, 31*, 104–114.

Freiberg, P. (1990). Lesbian moms can give kids empowering role models. *APA Monitor, 21*, 33.

Gibbs, E. D. (1988). Psychosocial development of children raised by lesbian mothers: A review of research. *Women and Therapy, 8*, 55–75.

Gilman, C. P. (1979). *Herland*. New York: Pantheon. (Originally published 1915)

Golombok, S., Spencer, A., & Rutter, M. (1983). Children in lesbian and single-parent households: Psychosexual and psychiatric appraisal. *Journal of Child Psychology and Psychiatry, 24*, 551–572.

Gonsiorek, J. (1991). The empirical basis for the demise of the illness model of homosexuality. In J. C. Gonsiorek & J. D. Weinrich (Eds.), *Homosexuality: Research implications for public policy* (pp. 115–136). Newbury Park, CA: Sage.

Gottfried, A. E., & Gottfried, A. W. (Eds.). (1994). *Redefining families: Implications for children's development*. New York: Plenum Press.

Gottman, J. S. (1990). Children of gay and lesbian parents. IN F. W. Bozett & M. B. Sussman (Eds.), *Homosexuality and family relations* (pp. 177–196). New York: Harrington Park Press.

Green, G. D., & Bozett, F. W. (1991). Lesbian mothers and gay fathers. In J. C. Gonsiorek & J. D. Weinrich (Eds.), *Homosexuality: Research implications for public policy* (pp. 197–214). Beverly Hills, CA: Sage.

Green, R. (1978). Sexual identity of 37 children raised by homosexual or transsexual parents. *American Journal of Psychiatry, 135*, 692–697.

Green, R., Mandel, J. B., Hotvedt, M. E., Gray, J., & Smith, L. (1986). Lesbian mothers and their children: A comparison with solo parent heterosexual mothers and their children. *Archives of Sexual Behavior, 15*, 167–184.

Groth, A. N., & Birnbaum, H. J. (1978). Adult sexual orientation and attraction to underage persons. *Archives of Sexual Behavior, 7*, 175–181.

Hand, S. I. (1991). *The lesbian parenting couple*. Unpublished doctoral dissertation, Professional School of Psychology, San Francisco, CA.

Hare, J., & Richards, L. (1993). Children raised by lesbian couples: Does the context of birth affect father and partner involvement? *Family Relations, 42*, 249–255.

Harrison, A. O., Wilson, M. N., Pine, C. J., Chan, S. Q., & Buriel, R. (1990). Family ecologies of 15ethnic minority children. *Child Development, 61*, 347–362.

Herek, G. M. (1995). Psychological heterosexism in the United States. In A. R. D'Augelli & C. J. Patterson (Eds.), *Lesbian, gay and bisexual identities over the lifespan: Psychological perspectives* (pp. 321–346). New York: Oxford University Press.

Hernandez, D. J. (1988). Demographic trends and the living arrangements of children. In E. M. Hetherington & J. D. Arasteh (Eds.), *Impact of divorce, single parenting, and stepparenting on children* (pp. 3–22). Hillsdale, NJ: Erlbaum.

Hetherington, E. M., & Arasteh, J. D. (Eds.). (1988). *Impact of divorce, single parenting, and stepparenting on children*. Hillsdale, NJ: Erlbaum.

Hitchens, D. J. (1979/1980). Social attitudes, legal standards, and personal trauma in child custody cases. *Journal of Homosexuality, 5,* 1–20, 89–95.

Hochschild, A. R. (1989). *The second shift: Working parents and the revolution at home.* New York: Viking Penguin.

Hoeffer, B. (1981). Children's acquisition of sex-role behavior in lesbian-mother families. *American Journal of Orthopsychiatry, 5,* 536–544.

Hoffman, L. W. (1984). Work, family, and socialization of the child. In R. D. Parke (Ed.), *Review of child development research, Vol. 7. The family* (pp. 223–282). Chicago: University of Chicago Press.

Huggins, S. L. (1989). A comparative study of self-esteem of adolescent children of divorced lesbian mothers and divorced heterosexual mothers. In F. W. Bozett (Ed.), *Homosexuality and the Family* (pp. 123–135). New York: Harrington Park Press.

Huston, A. (1983). Sex typing. In E. M. Hetherington (Ed.), P. H. Mussen (Series Ed.), *Handbook of child psychology: Vol. 4. Socialization, personality, and social development* (pp. 387–487). New York: Wiley.

Jacob, T. (Ed.). (1987). *Family interaction and psychopathology: Theories, methods, and findings.* New York: Plenum Press.

Jenny, C., Roesler, T. A., & Poyer, K. L. (1994). Are children at risk for sexual abuse by homosexuals? *Pediatrics, 94,* 41–44.

Jones, B. M., & McFarlane, K. (Eds.). (1980). *Sexual abuse of children: Selected readings.* Washington, DC: National Center on Child Abuse and Neglect.

Kirkpatrick, M. (1987). Clinical implications of lesbian mother studies. *Journal of Homosexuality, 13,* 201–211.

Kirkpatrick, M., Smith, C., & Roy, R. (1981). Lesbian mothers and their children: A comparative survey. *American Journal of Orthopsychiatry, 51,* 545–551.

Kitzinger, C., & Wilkinson, S. (1995). Transitions from heterosexuality to lesbianism: The discursive production of lesbian identities. *Developmental Psychology, 31,* 95–104.

Kleber, D. J., Howell, R. J., & Tibbits-Kleber, A. L. (1986). The impact of parental homosexuality in child custody cases: A review of the literature. *Bulletin of the American Academy of Psychiatry and Law, 14,* 81–87.

Koepke, L., Hare, J., & Moran, P. B. (1992). Relationship quality in a sample of lesbian couples with children and child-free lesbian couples. *Family Relations, 41,* 224–229.

Kohlberg, L. (1966). A cognitive-developmental analysis of children's sex-role concepts and attitudes. In E. E. Maccoby (Ed.), *The development of sex differences* (pp. 82–173). Stanford, CA: Stanford University Press.

Kohut, H. (1971). *The analysis of the self.* Madison, CT: International Universities Press.

Kohut, H. (1977). *The restoration of the self.* Madison, CT: International Universities Press.

Kohut, H. (1984). *How does analysis cure?* Chicago: University of Chicago Press.

Kurdek, L. (1993). The allocation of household labor in homosexual and heterosexual cohabiting couples. *Journal of Social Issues, 49,* 127–139.

Laird, J. (1993). Lesbian and gay families. In F. Walsh (Ed.), *Normal family processes* (2nd ed., pp. 282–328). New York: Guilford Press.

Lamb, M. E. (Ed.). (1982). *Nontraditional families: Parenting and child development.* Hillsdale, NJ: Erlbaum.

Lamb, M. E. (Ed.). (In press). *The role of the father in child development* (3rd ed.). New York: Wiley.

Laosa, L. M. (1988). Ethnicity and single parenting in the United States. In E. M. Hetherington & J. D. Arasteh (Eds.), *Impact of divorce, single parenting, and stepparenting on children* (pp. 23–49). Hillsdale, NJ: Erlbaum.

Lewin, E. (1993). *Lesbian mothers: Accounts of gender in American culture.* Ithaca, NY: Cornell University Press.

Lewis, K. G. (1980). Children of lesbians: Their point of view. *Social Work, 25,* 198–203.

Locke, H., & Wallace, K. (1959). Short marital adjustment and prediction tests: Their reliability and validity. *Marriage and Family Living, 21,* 251–255.

Lott-Whitehead, L., & Tully, C. T. (1993). The family lives of lesbian mothers. *Smith College Studies in Social Work, 63,* 265–280.

Maccoby, E. E. (1990). Gender and relationships: A developmental account. *American Psychologist, 45,* 513–520.

Martin, A. (1989). The planned lesbian and gay family: Parenthood and children. *Newsletter of the Society for the Psychological Study of Lesbian and Gay Issues, 5,* 6, 16–17.

Martin, A. (1993). *The lesbian and gay parenting handbook: Creating and raising our families.* New York: Harper Collins.

McCandlish, B. (1987). Against all odds: Lesbian mother family dynamics. In F. Bozett (Ed.), *Gay and lesbian parents* (pp. 23–38). New York: Praeger.

McLoyd, V. (1990). The impact of economic hardship on black families and children: Psychological distress, parenting, and socioemotional development. *Child Development, 61,* 311–346.

Miller, B. (1979). Gay fathers and their children. *Family Coordinator, 28,* 544–552.

Money, J., & Ehrhardt, A. A. (1972). *Man and woman, boy and girl: The differentiation and dimorphism of gender identity from conception to maturity.* Baltimore: Johns Hopkins University Press.

Nungesser, L. G. (1980). Theoretical basis for research on the acquisition of social sex roles by children of lesbian mothers. *Journal of Homosexuality, 5,* 177–188.

O'Connell, A. (1993). Voices from the heart: The developmental impact of a mother's lesbianism on her adolescent children. *Smith College Studies in Social Work, 63,* 281–299.

Okin, S. M. (1989). *Justice, gender and the family.* New York: Basic Books.

O'Leary, K. D., & Emery, R. E. (1984). Marital discord and child behavior problems. In M. D. Levine & P. Satz (Eds.), *Middle childhood: Development and dysfunction* (pp. 345–364). Baltimore: University Park Press.

Pagelow, M. D. (1980). Heterosexual and lesbian single mothers: A comparison of problems, coping and solutions. *Journal of Homosexuality, 5,* 198–204.

Parke, R. D. (Ed.). (1984). *Review of child development research, Volume 7: The family.* Chicago: University of Chicago Press.

Patterson, C. J. (1992). Children of lesbian and gay parents. *Child Development, 63,* 1025–1042.

Patterson, C. J. (1994a). Children of the lesbian baby boom: Behavioral adjustment, self-concepts, and sex-role identity. In B. Greene & G. Herek (Eds.), *Contemporary perspectives on lesbian and gay psychology: Theory, research, and applications* (pp. 156–175). Newbury Park, CA: Sage.

Patterson, C. J. (1994b). Lesbian and gay couples considering parenthood: An agenda for research, service and advocacy. *Journal of Lesbian and Gay Social Services, 1,* 33–55.

Patterson, C. J. (1995a). Lesbian mothers, gay fathers, and their children. In A. R. D'Augelli & C. J. Patterson (Eds.), *Lesbian, gay and bisexual identities over the lifespan: Psychological perspectives* (pp. 262–290). New York: Oxford University Press.

Patterson, C. J. (1995b). Families of the lesbian baby boom: Parents' division of labor and children's adjustment. *Developmental Psychology, 31,* 115–123.

Patterson, C. J. (1995c). Adoption of minor children by lesbian and gay adults: A social science perspective. *Duke Journal of Gender Law and Policy, 2,* 191–205.

Patterson, C. J. (1995d). Lesbian and gay parenthood. In M. H. Bornstein (Ed.), *Handbook of parenting, Vol. 3: Status and social conditions of parenting* (pp. 255–274). Hillsdale, NJ: Erlbaum.

Patterson, C. J. (1995e). Sexual orientation and human development: An overview. *Developmental Psychology, 31,* 3–11.

Patterson, C. J., & Chan, R. W. (1996). Gay fathers and their children. In R. P. Cabaj & T. S. Stein (Eds.), *Homosexuality and mental health: A comprehensive textbook* (pp. 371–393). Washington, DC: American Psychiatric Press.

Patterson, C. J., Hurt, S., & Mason, C. (1995). Families of the lesbian baby boom: Children's contacts with grandparents and other adults outside their households. Unpublished manuscript, Department of Psychology, University of Virginia, Charlottesville.

Patterson, C. J., & Kosmitzki, C. (1995). Families of the lesbian baby boom: Maternal mental health, household composition, and child adjustment. Unpublished manuscript, Department of Psychology, University of Virginia, Charlottesville.

Patterson, C. J., & Redding, R. (in press). Lesbian and gay families with children: Public policy implications of social science research. *Journal of Social Issues.*

Paul, J. P. (1986). *Growing up with a gay, lesbian, or bisexual parent: An exploratory study of experiences and perceptions.* Unpublished doctoral dissertation, University of California at Berkeley.

Pies, C. (1985). *Considering parenthood.* San Francisco: Spinsters/Aunt Lute.

Pies, C. (1990). Lesbians and the choice to parent. In F. W. Bozett & M. B. Sussman (Eds.), *Homosexuality and family relations* (pp. 137–154). New York: Harrington Park Press.

Polikoff, N. (1986). Lesbian mothers, lesbian families, legal obstacles, legal challenges. *Review of Law and Social Change, 14,* 907–914.

Polikoff, N. (1990). This child does have two mothers: Redefining parenthood to meet the needs of children in lesbian mother and other nontraditional families. *Georgetown Law Review, 78,* 459–575.

Pollack, S., & Vaughn, J. (1987). *Politics of the heart: A lesbian parenting anthology.* Ithaca, NY: Firebrand Books.

Puryear, D. (1983). *A comparison between the children of lesbian mothers and the children of heterosexual mothers.* Unpublished doctoral dissertation, California School of Professional Psychology, Berkeley.

Rafkin, L. (1990). *Different mothers: Sons and daughters of lesbians talk about their lives.* Pittsburgh: Cleis Press.

Rand, C., Graham, D. L. R., & Rawlings, E. I. (1982). Psychological health and factors the court seeks to control in lesbian mother custody trials. *Journal of Homosexuality, 8,* 27–39.

Rees, R. L. (1979). *A comparison of children of lesbian and single heterosexual mothers on three measures of socialization.* Berkeley: California School of Professional Psychology.

Reppucci, N. D. (1984). The wisdom of Solomon: Issues in child custody determination. In N. D. Reppucci, L. A. Weithorn, E. P. Mulvey, & J. Monahan (Eds.), *Children, mental health, and the law* (pp. 59–78). Beverly Hills, CA: Sage.

Ricketts, W. (1991). *Lesbians and gay men as foster parents.* Portland: National Child Welfare Resource Center, University of Southern Main.

Ricketts, W., & Achtenberg, R. (1990). Adoption and foster parenting for lesbians and gay men: Creating new traditions in family. In F. W. Bozett & M. B. Sussman (Eds.), *Homosexuality and family relations* (pp. 83–118). New York: Harrington Park Press.

Riley, C. (1988). American kinship: A lesbian account. *Feminist Issues, 8,* 75–94.

Rivera, R. (1991). Sexual orientation and the law. In J. C. Gonsiorek & J. D. Weinrich (Eds.), *Homosexuality: Research implications for public policy* (pp. 81–100). Newbury Park, CA: Sage.

Rogoff, B. (1990). *Apprenticeship in thinking.* New York: Oxford University Press.

Rosenberg, M. (1979). *Conceiving the self.* New York: Basic Books.

Ruble, D. N., Fleming, A. S., Hackel, L. S., & Stangor, C. (1988). Changes in the marital relationship during the transition to first time motherhood: Effects of violated expectations concerning division of household labor. *Journal of Personality and Social Psychology, 55,* 78–87.

Rutter, M., Izard, C. E., & Read, P. B. (Eds.). (1986). *Depression in young people: Developmental and clinical perspectives.* New York: Guilford Press.

Sameroff, A. J., & Chandler, M. (1975). Reproductive risk and the continuum of caretaking casualty. In F. D. Horowitz (Ed.). *Review of child development research* (Vol. 4, pp. 187–244). Chicago: University of Chicago Press.

Spencer, M. B., Brookins, G. K., & Allen, W. R. (Eds.). (1985). *Beginnings: The social and affective development of black children.* Hillsdale, NJ: Erlbaum.

Steckel, A. (1985). *Separation–individuation in children of lesbian and heterosexual couples.* Unpublished doctoral dissertation, Wright Institute Graduate School, Berkeley, CA.

Steckel, A. (1987). Psychosocial development of children of lesbian mothers. In F. W. Bozett (Ed.), *Gay and lesbian parents* (pp. 75–85). New York: Praeger.

Tasker, F. L., & Golombok, S. (1991). Children raised by lesbian mothers: The empirical evidence. *Family Law, 21,* 184–187.

Tasker, F., & Golombok, S. (1995). Adults raised as children in lesbian families. *American Journal of Orthopsychiatry, 65,* 203–215.

Weisner, T. S., & Wilson-Mitchell, J. E. (1990). Nonconventional family lifestyles and sex typing in six year olds. *Child Development, 61,* 1915–1933.

Weston, K. (1991). *Families we choose: Lesbians, gays, kinship.* New York: Columbia University Press.

8

Primary Prevention Programs in Schools

Joseph A. Durlak

1. Introduction

The title of Klein and Goldston's (1977) text, *Primary Prevention: An Idea Whose Time Has Come*, was prophetic. Whereas there had been relatively few reports of school-based prevention before the mid-1970s, over the past two decades there has been a surge of interest in such programs. In fact, each year millions of school-children throughout the United States are exposed to programs with a preventive thrust, with many receiving more than one program. For instance, over 90% of all school districts offer services to children who are at risk for academic problems (Slavin, Karweit, & Madden, 1989). Between 72% and 77% of all districts provide programming relevant to smoking, alcohol and other drug use, nutrition, physical fitness, and sex education; between 51% and 67% of districts instruct students on such matters as AIDS, suicide prevention, physical violence, and the use of seat belts and other safety behaviors (Holtzman et al., 1992). There are also many other programs devoted to students' personal growth and adjustment, and specialized interventions to prevent teenage pregnancy, sexual abuse, and school dropouts. Unfortunately, the overwhelming majority of school-based prevention programs have never been systematically evaluated, with the result that students are being exposed to many programs of unknown impact. Because schools are willing to offer prevention programs, it is important to ascertain which programs are effective in achieving which goals.

Although the practice of prevention has greatly outpaced research findings, there is a substantial database on the impact of school-based programs. There have been over 600 published and unpublished reports

Joseph A. Durlak • Department of Psychology, Loyola University, Chicago, Illinois 60626.

Advances in Clinical Child Psychology, Volume 19, edited by Thomas H. Ollendick and Ronald J. Prinz. Plenum Press, New York, 1997.

of academic interventions (Slavin et al., 1989; Slavin, Karweit, & Wasik, 1994), and by the end of 1994, there were about the same number of published controlled outcome studies in other areas of prevention (Durlak, 1995).

I have extensively discussed research and practice in school-based prevention elsewhere (Durlak, 1995). Here, I distill this information in an effort to describe the current status of school-based primary prevention. More specifically, the intent of this chapter is to explain the major conceptual approaches used in school-based interventions, summarize current outcome research, describe several exemplary programs, and highlight some important areas for future research. This chapter is thus intended to serve as an introduction to school-based primary prevention in order to bring readers up to date on developments in this field. Programs conducted in primary and secondary schools are the major focus except to emphasize the need for earlier interventions to prevent learning problems. The term *children* is used generally to refer to all students in primary and secondary schools, and the term *adolescents* is used in reference to specific interventions for those in high school.

1.1. Need for Prevention

There is a clear need for programs that can prevent various types of adjustment problems. Epidemiological surveys indicate that between 17% and 22% of children up to age 18 develop clinical disorders; at the same time, only 10%–30% of this population ever receives any formal mental health treatment (Kazdin, 1990). Treatment, of course, is not effective for all children, and dropout rates from child and family therapy are frequently 50% or higher (Pekarik & Stephenson, 1988). Therefore, as pointed out by Gullotta (1994), primary prevention does not have to be highly successful to be a good social investment. If programs can prevent problems in one out of five children, then prevention can help as many children as are currently being served by all existing mental health channels.

Traditional forms of psychopathology do not include all types of problems affecting youth. Dryfoos (1990) integrated the literatures in four areas: unprotected sexual intercourse, poor academic achievement, delinquent acts, and drug use. Based on past behaviors in these four areas, she estimated that half of all 10- to 17-year-olds (approximately 14 million youth) are at some level or risk (either moderate, high, or very high) for later problems. The observation that so many young people may later develop problems suggests the importance of examining what can be done within schools to prevent negative outcomes.

1.2.   Definition of Primary Prevention

Prevention is a multidisciplinary science that draws upon basic and applied research from numerous disciplines such as psychology, education, medicine, public health, nursing, sociology, economics, health education, communications, and criminal justice. Three major types of prevention are frequently distinguished, depending on the timing and basic goal of the intervention. Primary prevention involves interventions for normal populations in order to prevent the occurrence of problems. Children who participate in primary prevention programs are functioning within the normal range and the goal of intervention is to do something now to prevent the occurrence of future problems. In contrast, secondary prevention involves early intervention for those with subclinical problems to prevent the development of more serious dysfunction. Tertiary prevention is intervention for those with established problems to reduce the duration and negative consequences of existing disorders. This chapter focuses on primary prevention.

Recently, the Institute of Medicine (1994) proposed new terminology for the prevention of mental disorders. Three suggestions were made: (1) Only interventions designed to prevent the onset of new disorders should be considered as prevention, and so the term and concept of tertiary prevention should be discarded; (2) secondary prevention should be renamed *indicated preventive intervention*; and (3) distinctions should be made in primary prevention between *universal preventive interventions* and *selective preventive interventions*. These two categories of primary prevention are discussed, along with a third category that has been used by several preventionists, the transitions or milestone approach.

2.   Conceptual Approaches to Primary Prevention

Conceptual approaches to primary prevention can be divided into six categories based upon the three major ways that populations are selected for intervention and the two major levels of intervention that are emphasized. Figure 1 depicts these distinctions.

A universal strategy targets all available children in the population, such as all children in junior high school, all high school seniors, and so on. The risk or high-risk approach (also called *selective preventive intervention*) focuses only on those in the population who are at risk for eventual problems, but who are not yet demonstrating any difficulties. For example, children of alcoholic or depressed parents are populations at risk for

Focus of Intervention

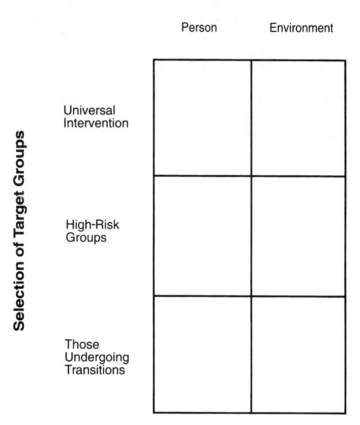

FIGURE 1.   Conceptual overview of approaches to primary prevention. From Durlak, J. A., *School-based prevention programs for children and adolescents*, p. 4, copyright 1995 by Sage Publications, Inc. Reprinted by permission of Sage Publications, Inc.

various forms of maladjustment, and a primary prevention high-risk program would therefore target these children for intevention.

Finally, in a transitions approach (sometimes called a *milestone approach*) children about to experience a particular life transition or a series of stressful life events are targeted for intervention. The rationale behind this strategy is that some transitions or life events can have negative effects, so the intent of the intervention is to help children master or negotiate these transitions or events successfully. Children whose parents are divorcing and those changing schools would be suitable candidates for a primary prevention transitions program.

The two major levels of intervention in primary prevention are person-centered and environment-centered programs (also identified as individual vs. ecological or systems-level interventions, respectively). Person-centered programs attempt to change individuals directly without attempting any major environmental change, whereas environmental programs attempt to influence children indirectly by modifying their environment. Environmental interventions usually focus on the social environment, such as the interactions occurring between children and their peers, teachers, or family members.

Although they are not identified separately in Figure 1, at least four levels of environmental intervention are possible: the familial, the interpersonal (individuals beyond the family such as teachers or peers), the organizational, and the community. For instance, some school programs focus on parents, some on peers or teachers, some attempt organizational change at the level of the classroom or school, and a few include schools as part of more comprehensive communitywide interventions. Program examples illustrating each of these levels of intervention are provided later in this chapter.

The approaches depicted in Figure 1 are by no means mutually exclusive or antagonistic to each other; approaches can be combined in different ways, and some interventions fit into multiple categories. For instance, many environmental programs include an individual-level component. There may be a classroom component for the children that is coupled with a parent intervention. Therefore, the main distinction in terms of level of intervention is whether some type of environmental change is being attempted.

There are numerous questions related to assessment and intervention that must be answered concerning the approaches identified in Figure 1 to make prevention programs maximally effective. For example, person-centered programs must identify which individual characteristics are important to adjustment. Should the intervention target knowledge, attitudes, perceptions, specific behaviors, or all of these? A risk-approach requires reliable and valid methods of identifying risk status: How can we tell who is at risk? Those conducting environmental interventions must determine how to identify, measure, and then modify environmental features at different levels of intervention. Which aspects of family functioning, peer influence, and organizational and community life are most important, and how can they be changed? Finally, transition programs have their own corresponding set of questions. Which events have important implications for adjustment and maladjustment? How does the transition process influence development? How can children be helped to negotiate stress and transition effectively?

Obtaining data related to each of above questions is currently the subject of much attention in prevention research. Moreover, there is unlikely to be a simple and single answer to any of these questions, since additional factors are likely to be important, such as the nature of the problem(s) to be prevented, the developmental status and other characteristics of the target population, and the timing of the intervention.

3. Major Themes in School-Based Prevention

Four major related themes have emerged in prevention research and are useful in understanding the general context for many school-based interventions. These four themes are (1) the assumption of multiple causality, (2) health promotion, (3) attention to risk and protective factors, and, finally, (4) the importance of skills training.

3.1. Multiple Causality

Some early critics of prevention maintained that primary prevention could not be successful unless the cause of pathology was known (Lamb & Zusman, 1979). This criticism rests largely on a medical model paradigm that assumes the presence of specific and different causes for different diseases or disorders. Since the specific causes for most forms of maladjustment are unknown, attempting primary prevention was thought to be premature.

In contrast, most contemporary prevention research rests on the assumption of multiple causality. The general view is that there is no single cause of good or poor adjustment; multiple factors influence development. Longitudinal developmental research illustrating the principles of convergent and divergent development supports the validity of a multiple causality orientation (Sameroff, 1987).

The principle of divergent development states that the same condition or beginning can produce several different final outcomes; the principle of convergent development is that the same final result can develop from a variety of different starting points. The same factors do not always lead to the same results, because developmental discontinuities occur. Discontinuities refer to major breaks or shifts in the developmental process that lead to differential outcomes. In other words, the developmental process is not perfectly linear. If it were, then all normal infants would become normal adults, and all infants with early physical or behavioral problems would develop later difficulties. We know this does not happen.

Therefore, preventionists do not have to search for the single magic bullet or missing link explaining each form of maladjustment before they intervene. Rather, they can mount interventions to modify factors that presumably influence adjustment. Outcome data will reveal if the choices made are good or poor ones.

3.2. Health Promotion

Health promotion refers generally to increasing competencies or coping resources of target groups. The general idea is to promote psychological well-being or mental health in the belief that enhanced mental health will have a preventive function; that is, compared to those who lack such resources, children who have better social skills or coping abilities should be better able to achieve personal goals, deal with stress, and master various developmental tasks. The presence of these new strengths and resources should lessen the likelihood of future problems.

One important rationale for health promotion is that good mental or physical health is not simply the absence of problems or symptoms. For instance, the absence of physical symptoms does not necessarily mean a person is in good physical condition. Similarly, someone without psychological problems may not necessarily demonstrate positive mental health in terms of having good coping abilities or skills. Therefore, some preventionists believe that an effective way to forestall future problems is through health promotion (Cowen, 1994).

Although there is disagreement on the value of health promotion (Institute of Medicine, 1994), many prevention programs seek to improve children's competencies. For example, programs to prevent aggression and serious acting-out problems have trained children in self-control strategies and social skills in order to replace their customary antisocial behavior with prosocial forms of behavior (e.g., Hawkins, Von Cleve, & Catalano, 1991). In other words, these programs promote aspects of mental health as a way to prevent maladjustment.

3.3. Risk and Protective Factors

Risk and protective factors relate to the future probability of negative and positive outcomes, respectively. Risk increases the chances of some negative outcome, whereas a protective factor increases the likelihood of positive outcomes. Some authors only conceive of protective factors in relation to pathology, that is, in terms of reducing the possibility of negative outcome, but protective factors can also be viewed in relation to health promotion.

There are many different type of risk factors. At the individual level, risk can be a demographic characteristic (low socioeconomic status), or a current behavior (child opppositionality or unprotected sexual intercourse); at the family level, it can refer to low maternal education or inconsistent discipline practices; at other levels, risk may include friends who use drugs, the lack of social support, a school with poor levels of achievement and poor pedagogic resources or a public policy that limits access to certain types of care. In other words, risk factors can be present at all levels, and some factors are more amenable to influence than others.

Usually, it is a combination or accumulation of risk factors rather than the presence of any single factor that is associated with negative outcomes. For example, Rutter (1979) studied six risk factors related to child psychiatric disorder. These included severe marital discord, low socioeconomic status, overcrowding or large family size, paternal criminality, maternal psychiatric disorder, and the child's separation from the parents for extended periods. Children exposed to any one of these six risks did not differ from those exposed to none, but those experiencing two or three risks were five times more likely, and those experiencing four, five, or six were 20 times more likely to have a clinical disorder.

The fact that risk factors exist at all levels and that the accumulation of risk potentiates adjustment problems has strong implications for prevention. It may be necessary to mount programs that reduce multiple risk factors present at multiple levels of intervention (the individual, the family, the interpersonal, and so on) in order to achieve maximal success.

In theory, the same general principles that apply to risk factors also apply to protective factors. For instance, protective factors can exist at multiple levels, and the presence of more protective factors increases the likelihood of positive outcomes. However, we currently have much more information about risk than about protective factors. Variables most frequently cited as protective factors include family relationships characterized by warmth and acceptance, the availability of social support beyond one's immediate family, and a positive social orientation, often associated with a temperament or interpersonal style that is outgoing, affectionate, and reinforcing to others (Masten & Garmezy, 1985). Evidence is accumulating to suggest the possibility that certain social skills and good academic performance may also serve as protective factors (discussion to follow).

Risk and protective factors can serve as proximal outcome criteria in preventive trials. For instance, if intervention reduces the immediate level of risk among target populations, then the possibility of future problems is lessened. Follow-up is still needed, however, to document the intevention's subsequent preventive impact.

3.4. Systematic Skills Training

The final important theme in school-based prevention involves a shift in which individual factors are important. Initially, many prevention programs emphasized informational approaches. These interventions were based on the premise that children who have accurate knowledge about drugs or sexuality or nutrition would change their behavior accordingly. Interventions emphasizing informational strategies, however, have not been successful in any area of school prevention in which they have been used (Durlak, 1995). Over time, researchers have recognized that training schoolchildren systematically in different skills is much more likely to be associated with positive program outcomes.

Many programs use social learning principles in training. The target skills are briefly defined, then are effectively modeled by adults or by peers. Children then practice the new skills, receive feedback on their performance, and are reinforced for behavioral improvement. This training loop continues until mastery is achieved. Many different skills have been increased using these step-by-step training techniques, including communication skills, assertiveness, goal setting, various self-control and self-monitoring strategies, and problem solving.

In summary, many contemporary school-based primary prevention programs operate from the assumptions that most forms of adjustment and maladjustment are multiply determined, that multilevel interventions to modify multiple risk and protective factors may be necessary, that health promotion can be one useful form of intervention, and that children need systematic skills training to acquire new behaviors.

4. Current Findings in School-Based Prevention

Several narrative and meta-analytic reviews have evaluated the impact of school programs regarding behavioral and social problems (Durlak, 1995), academic problems (Slavin et al., 1994), drug use (Schinke, Botvin, & Orlandi, 1991; Tobler, 1986), sex education (Kirby et al., 1994), health education (Allensworth, 1993), suicide prevention (Shaffer, Garland, Gould, Fisher, & Trautman, 1989), pregnancy prevention (Miller, Card, Paikoff, & Peterson, 1982), and sexual abuse (Finkelhor & Strapko, 1992).

Although outcome data are not definitive, there is considerable evidence supporting the positive impact of school-based primary prevention (Durlak, 1995), particularly if one concentrates on the better conceptualized and controlled investigations in each area and recognizes the evolutionary character of the field. For instance, school-based prevention is a very young science; 74% of outcome studies have appeared since 1980 (Durlak, 1995). Ordinarily, one would not expect much progress in so relatively short a time. Furthermore, in retrospect, some early attempts at prevention were poorly conceived and implemented and thus unable to achieve their ambitious goals. Preventionists working in the schools have learned quickly from past failures, and research has improved substantially in sophistication and effectiveness over the past few years. Some research areas are now in their third or fourth generation of study as investigators continue to improve and refine school-based prevention.

Not all areas have met with success. Current data are insufficient to claim that efforts to prevent suicide (Shaffer et al., 1989) or sexual abuse (Finkelhor & Strapko, 1992) are effective. There is stronger evidence, however, in terms of eliminating academic and behavioral problems, reducing drug use, and improving children's physical health. For instance, mean effect sizes for prevention studies in these areas frequently range between .30 and .50 (Durlak, 1995).

It is illustrative to compare these outcomes to those produced by other social interventions. Lipsey and Wilson (1993) surveyed findings from 156 meta-analyses evaluating 9,400 studies in the behavioral, educational, and psychological literature. The grand mean effect across all areas was .47, with a standard deviation of .28. Furthermore, the majority of mean effects obtained from a sampling of effective medical treatments were also under .50, sometimes as low as .07 (for the use of aspirin to prevent heart attacks). In other words, comparatively speaking, the results achieved in several areas of school-based primary prevention are similar in magnitude to those attained by many established medical, psychological, and educational interventions.

Since it is impossible to review all school-based prevention, four areas are discussed: prevention of behavioral/social problems, academic problems, drug use, and health promotion, which includes topics such as AIDS education and pregnancy prevention. A few exemplary studies are described within each area to provide some perspective on the approaches taken and results obtained in different programs.

In general, the outcome studies that are cited in the following sections are exemplary in terms of being theory-driven, using randomized designs to study relatively large sample sizes, evaluating outcomes from several perspectives (e.g., child, parent, and teacher), and conducting follow-up, although not every study possesses each of these features. Moreover, many of the following studies are parts of programmatic research efforts in which investigators have replicated their findings.

5. Prevention of Behavioral/Social Problems

A meta-analysis of 131 school-based programs reported through the end of 1991 (Durlak, 1995) indicated that programs with the goals of preventing behavioral and social problems obtained significant positive effects. Mean effect sizes varied from .25 to .50 across different types of programs. Moreover, interventions were successful in terms of significantly reducing children's problems and significantly increasing various competencies. Furthermore, studies appearing after 1991 have continued to confirm the efficacy of school-based programs; however, two important qualifications must be offered: (1) Three-fourths of the studies have not included any follow-up data, and (2) programs have often had the vague goal of preventing school maladjustment, and this construct has been defined in many different ways across studies. In other words, program participants change for the better as a result of intervention, but it is not always clear what specific form of maladjustment has been prevented or for how long.

The following sections describe some interventions to prevent behavioral and social problems using some of the distinctions offered in Figure 1. Examples of person-centered, environment-centered, and transition programs are provided.

5.1. Person-Centered Programs

A frequent strategy in person-centered interventions is health promotion, and researchers have targeted several different competencies for such interventions. For example, Hartman (1979) evaluated an 8-week high school health education class designed to improve adolescents' abilities to deal with stress. Behavioral techniques were used to teach students cognitive restructuring, relaxation, assertiveness, and various anxiety management techniques. On the basis of psychological testing, students were initially categorized as high or low risk for subsequent psychological problems, based on the quality and extent of their coping techniques and the amount of stress they were experiencing (i.e., high-risk students had poor coping skills and were experiencing high levels of stress). Outcome data that included a 5-month follow-up indicated the intervention was successful in improving the psychological functioning of all students, and was relatively more helpful for those at high risk.

Training school-children in interpersonal problem-solving skills has been a particularly popular approach in prevention, based on Spivack and Shure's (1974) theory and early findings that the ability to solve interpersonal problems is important to adjustment. Problem-solving curricula have been developed for students at many different grade levels. Generally, the intent is to help children identify the existence of problems, think through the consequences of different possible solutions, and choose an effective strategy.

Data from several investigations clearly indicate that problem-solving skills in children as young as 4 or 5 years of age can be significantly improved, but the link between problem-solving skills and adjustment remains elusive. For instance, two groups of investigators (Weissberg et al., 1981; Work & Olsen, 1990) conducted careful implementations of problem-solving interventions for third- and fourth-grade students. Children in both studies improved significantly in problem-solving skills and in school adjustment based on teachers' ratings, but gains in these two dimensions were not correlated. Such data raise the question of which factors are responsible for the children's adjustive gains. Since problem-solving training has been added to several multicomponent prevention programs, its specific contribution to outcome needs to be assessed.

5.2. Transition Programs

The two types of transitions most likely to occur among schoolchildren are the divorce of their parents and a change in schools. Projections suggest that between one-third to one-half of all schoolchildren will eventually experience the divorce of their parents by age 18 (Emery, 1988), and each year approximately 6 million children between the ages of 5 and 13 change schools (Jason et al., 1992). Each of these transitions can have both short- and long-term negative effects on children's social, personal, and academic adjustment, and several programs have been developed to help children negotiate these potentially stressful life events.

5.2.1. Children of Divorce

Programs for children of divorce typically consist of short-term group interventions designed to help children talk about their feelings and learn effective coping skills. Group interventions also provide the context for social support. A good example is the Children of Divorce Intervention

Program (CODIP; Alpert-Gillis, Pedro-Carroll, & Cowen, 1989). CODIP helps children to express their feelings about divorce, share common experiences, and includes a skills-building component to teach children how to express anger appropriately and resolve interpersonal problems. CODIP has been used with children from the second through the sixth grades; participating children have reported significantly reduced anxiety, and their parents and teachers have reported significant changes in problems, competencies, and overall levels of adjustment.

5.2.2. School Transitions

The School Transition Project (STP) is designed to help multiethnic children who are entering new inner-city elementary schools (Jason et al., 1992). STP provides social support to transfer students through a brief group orientation program that introduces students to the rules and procedures of their new school, provides opportunities to develop new friendships, and assigns each new student a peer helper ("buddy"). The main focus of the intervention, however, is tutoring, based on initial assessments indicating that many transfer students could benefit from such services. STP outcome data have suggested that the orientation program combined with in-school tutoring conducted by college students, and home tutoring conducted by parents, has produced the best results in terms of improving academic functioning and reducing children's social withdrawal and aggression (Jason et al., 1992).

The School Transitional Environment Project (STEP) focuses on the transition to junior high or high school (Felner et al., 1993). STEP modifies the environment of the receiving school to make the school atmosphere more supportive and less stressful. Specifically, incoming students are placed in homerooms and remain together for classes in core academic subjects. Moreover, teachers assume a counseling and mentoring role for their homeroom students to help them with personal, social, or academic problems. Homeroom teachers also form teams and meet regularly to monitor the progress of students, to intervene if students need additional assistance, and to improve communication between the school and parents.

STEP has been effective in preventing negative outcomes resulting from school transitions. Whereas control students have shown significant decreases in academic performance and self-esteem following their entry into ninth grade, and increased absenteeism, none of these outcomes occurred among STEP students. STEP students have rated their schools as better organized, understandable, and the interpersonal environment as more supportive. A 5-year follow-up indicated significantly higher grades and a 55% lower school dropout rate for STEP students. Furthermore, replication studies have confirmed STEP's positive impact not only in terms of preventing academic problems, but also in reducing emotional and behavioral problems (e.g., depression, substance abuse, and delinquency).

5.3. Environment-Centered Programs

An ambitious effort to change the organizational structure and practices of elementary schools is the Yale–New Haven Primary Prevention Project (Comer, 1985). The basic intent of the program is to respond more effectively to students' academic and social needs by initiating new programs and policies, and developing new forms of school governance. A committee is formed consisting of the principal, teachers, and parents, and these committee members collaborate in developing and enacting school policies, monitoring programs and services, and enhancing staff development. An important feature of the school's restructuring is the active involvement of parents in school activities and decision-making committees. The project began in 1968 in two inner-city schools characterized by low levels of academic achievement and many behavioral problems. Over time, behavioral and attendance problems have virtually been eliminated from these schools, and students' academic performance has skyrocketed from the bottom to near the top of city rankings on academic achievement. A 3-year follow-up indicated students in project schools were performing at grade level and were 2 years ahead of controls; project students also reported significantly improved academic and personal competencies.

The Social Development Program is a multilevel intervention designed to reduce multiple problems in low-income young school children (Hawkins et al., 1991; O'Donnell, Hawkins, Catalano, Abbott, & Day, 1995). Intervention is based on a social developmental model, which emphasizes that children at risk for antisocial behavior, particularly aggression, delinquency, and drug abuse, must form attachments to school and family and receive reinforcement in both settings in order to develop prosocial behaviors that are inimical to later dysfunction.

One 2-year intervention that began in first grade combined parent, teacher, and child training components (Hawkins et al., 1991). Parents learned behavioral child management skills emphasizing reinforcement for appropriate behavior and consistency in disciplinary practices, while teachers were concurrently taught to use new classroom management and interactive teaching methods. The classroom intervention also included interpersonal problem-solving training conducted by teachers. This intervention produced substantial reductions in boys' aggressive behavior and girls' self-destructive behaviors. For instance, the aggressive behavior of only 6% of experimental boys compared to 20% of control boys was in the clinical range of dysfunction at the end of the intervention.

A 6-year-long replication of the social development program indicated program gains at the end of sixth grade for boys, girls, or both sexes in such areas as greater self-reported attachment to school; higher rates of classroom participation; higher levels of school achievement; lower rates of alcohol, marijuana, and tobacco use; less association with deviant peers; and lower levels of delinquency (O'Donnell et al., 1995).

Another environment-centered multilevel program combines intervention at the child, teacher, parent, and schoolwide level to prevent bullying, a form of aggressive behavior in which children are verbally or physically intimidated or abused by peers (Olweus, 1994). Epidemiological data suggest that about 9% of Scandinavian school children are the victims of bullying, approximately 7% initiate such acts, and 1.6% are both victims and bullies.

In general, the program involves careful monitoring of peer interactions to reinforce prosocial behavior and provide immediate nonphysical sanctions for all forms of aggressive behavior, but particularly for bullying. School assemblies and teacher conferences are called to formulate standards for student behavior and to establish clear and consistent prosocial rules on a schoolwide level. Rules are also developed in each classroom, and student meetings are convened to discuss rule infractions. Children receive individual counseling for bullying, if necessary, and consultation is offered to their parents. Several interventions (summarized in Olweus, 1994) have resulted in significant reductions of up to 50% in bullying. Other forms of antisocial behavior, such as vandalism and truancy, have also been reduced. Finally, students in program schools have reported more positive attitudes and greater satisfaction with school, and the general psychosocial climate of program schools appears to have been changed positively in terms of increased order and discipline, and better relationships among students and staff.

6. Preventing Academic Problems

Four major findings in the educational literature are relevant to understanding the context for preventing academic problems:

1. The best general predictor of academic performance before the child reaches first grade is the family's socioeconomic level. Many children from low-income households do not begin first grade ready to profit from formal academic instruction.

2. Most learning problems become evident in the first year or two of elementary school, particularly as the child begins instruction in reading and mathematics.
3. Most children do not outgrow their learning problems and tend to fall further and further behind their peers over time in the absence of intervention.
4. Once the child enters elementary school, the best predictor of future academic performance is current academic performance. For example, one out of every five children is retained (i.e., "flunks" a grade) at least once between grades 1 and 8. Grade retention increases the risk for subsequent academic and psychological problems, regardless of the child's gender, race, or socioeconomic level (Meisels & Liaw, 1993).

In summary, many children at risk for academic problems (i.e., those from low-income households) need intervention before they reach first grade. Once children reach elementary school, it is important they receive assistance in mastering basic academic skills, since early academic performance generally tends to predict later performance. The following two sections briefly discuss successful preventive interventions initiated before the child reaches first grade (called *early childhood programs*) and programs offered during the early elementary school grades.

6.1. Early Childhood Programs

The general intent of early childhood programs is to promote the child's readiness for school. School readiness refers generally to the adequate maturation of linguistic, cognitive, and social skills. Most programs employ an array of academic and social strategies to promote the child's early developmental competencies.

The major question concerning the impact of early childhood programs is their long-term, not their short-term, effects; that is, many programs have produced significant immediate improvements in children's cognitive development and intellectual functioning, but the results for many interventions have tended to fade quickly over time. As research on early intervention has continued, however, it is becoming clearer that high-quality early childhood programs do have significant long-term benefits. Barnett (1990) located 14 studies that provided follow-up data on three key indices of children's later school performance: retention in grade, placement in special education, and high school graduation rates. These studies contained a mix of center- and home-based interventions ranging in duration from 1 to 3 years, begun when the children were from 2 to 5

TABLE 1
*Long-Term Effects of Early Childhood
Interventions on School Functioning*

Program	Percent retained in grade	Percent in special education	Percent high school graduation	Time of follow-up
1	15/20	37/50	67/49	Post high school
2	58/61	5/29	68/52	Post high school
3	23/43	0/13		7th grade
4	38/53	5/6	65/62	Post high school
5	30/52			7th grade
6	26/58	32/63	67/53	Post high school
7	10/16	13/15		7th grade
8	33/47			4th grade
9	16/21	2/5		3rd grade
10	31/45	15/22		4th grade
11	9/12	5/11		8th grade
12	18/35			—
13	51/63	11/25	50/33	Post high school
14	10/22	5/10		6th grade
Overall	26/39	12/23	63/51	

Note. The first data in each column are for the experimental group and the second for the
comparison group. Data are drawn from Barnett (1990). The exact follow-up period was
not noted for program 12.

years old, with follow-ups as long as 14 years. Table 1 summarizes the long-
term results for these programs; not all programs collected data on each of
the three school outcomes.

What is striking about the information in Table 1 is that every data
point favors the experimental children over their respective control group.
Although in some cases the differences are small, the cumulative effects
across all programs are large. During an average follow-up period of over
9 years, 33% fewer children who had participated in early childhood
intervention were ever subsequently retained in a grade, 48% fewer ever
received any special education services, and 24% more eventually graduated from high school. These are impressive figures, indicating that early
preventive intervention has a substantial long-term impact on children's
school careers.

The Perry Preschool Program has become the most famous early
childhood prgram because of the breadth of its long-term effects (Schweinhart & Weikart, 1988). When children from low-income families were 3 to 4
years of age, they became involved in an intensive 2-year preschool intervention. Preschool teachers also made weekly home visits to help parents

promote their child's social and cognitive development, and to secure needed child-care, medical, and social services. Follow-up assessment conducted up to 14 years later indicated that experimental students earned higher school grades and graduated more frequently than control students, spent fewer years in special education, and repeated fewer grades. Comparisons also favored the Perry Preschool graduates on social and vocational outcomes such as arrest rates (31% vs. 51%), welfare status (18% vs. 32%), and pursuit of continuing education after high school (38% vs. 21%).

Data from the Carolina Abecedarian Project (Horacek, Ramey, Campbell, Hoffmann, & Fletcher, 1987) demonstrate how earlier and more intensive intervention leads to better outcomes. Three experimental cohorts and one no-treatment control group were evaluated at the end of third grade. One experimental group received an intensive preschool program only, one received a later less-intensive elementary school program only, and one received both programs. Both the analyses of school grades and grade retentions reflected a linear relationship between school success and the intervention's timing and intensity. For example, only 16% of the children who received both the earlier (preschool) and later (elementary school) programs had repeated a grade; 29% of those receiving the early, but not the later program, repeated a grade; and the corresponding figures for those receiving the later program only, or no program at all, were 38% and 50%, respectively.

6.1.1. Elements of Effective Interventions

Most successful early intervention programs are multilevel interventions targeting individual, family, and interpersonal factors affecting development. The combination of elements make it difficult to discern exactly how different features contribute to outcomes. After extensively reviewing early childhood programs, Slavin et al. (1994) concluded that, in general, programs that were more intensive, of longer duration, and required the active involvement of parents tended to produce the best overall results. In contrast, shorter term programs without high levels of parental participation tended, at best, to produce modest immediate benefits that were likely to dissipate quickly over time.

Many programs involving parents operate according to an ecological model, in the sense that although direct services to children are helpful, ultimately it is believed that program benefits are mediated through the family and the home atmosphere. Generally, parents (often single mothers) receive specific guidance in stimulting their children's linguistic, social, and cognitive development. As the children move from infancy into toddlerhoood and early childhood, parents also receive training in child management skills to deal with common problems and difficult child behaviors. Many programs also offer social support services to parents. The underlying philosophy of such programs is to empower the child's primary caretakers to be effective advocates for their children and families.

6.2. Interventions at the Elementary School Level

6.2.1. Tutoring

One of the most successful primary prevention strategies at the elementary school level is also one of the oldest and most basic educational strategies: tutoring. Several investigators have independently come to the conclusion that tutoring can successfully improve students' academic performance (Slavin et al., 1994; Cohen, Kulik, & Kulik, 1982; Greenwood, Carta, & Hall, 1988). For example, after carefully reviewing the literature on the prevention of academic problems, Slavin et al. (1994) concluded that "one-on-one tutoring is the most effective form of instruction known" (p. 178).

Most tutoring is done in reading and mathematics. Tutoring has been effective when conducgted by teachers, paraprofessional aides, parents, or peers. Peer tutors also benefit academically from their tutoring experiences (Cohen et al., 1982). Tutoring appears to work because its application can be modified to suit the child's needs, and it can provide the intensity of instruction needed to achieve academic mastery.

One highly successful tutoring program is classwide peer tutoring (CWPT; Greenwood, Delquadri, & Hall, 1989). In CWPT, all students from the same class are divided into pairs for weekly tutoring sessions. Each tutee is assigned to one of two classroom teams that can earn points for their team based on their academic performance; teams earn daily and weekly prizes. Teachers organize the academic content for CWPT and monitor the tutoring process. In a 4-year intervention, tutored children from low-income households not only demonstrated substantial improvements in reading, math, and language compared to controls, but also were eventually able to equal the performance of a comparison group of high-achieving, high-SES students (Greenwood et al., 1989).

6.2.2. Success for All

Success for All (SFA) is a program that attempts to combine what is currently known about effective programs at the preschool and elementary school level into a comprehensive approach at prevention and early intervention. The prototypical SFA program begins with a half-day preschool and kindergarten program, focusing on both academic readiness and social development. One-on-one tutoring is used extensively beginning in first grade to promote children's initial success in reading. Trained tutors offer daily 20-minute tutoring to individual students and also assist the regular classroom teacher in daily 90-minute classroom reading periods. A systematic writing/arts program, based primarily on cooperative learning principles, is introduced, beginning in second grade. Finally, family support teams are created at each SFA school to involve parents in their children's education, and to offer social support and parent education as needed.

SFA produces positive results. Data pooled from several program implementations indicate that students demonstrate progressively better academic achievement the longer they are in SFA. SFA students academically outperformed their matched controls by almost 3 months in first grade, 5 months in second grade, and 7 months in third grade. Overall, whereas the reading achievement of just under half of the controls was at grade level, 81.4% of SFA students were at or above grade level. Other findings indicate that students initially at the lowest levels of academic proficiency demonstrate almost twice the benefit from intervention as other students, indicating that SFA is most effective for those at greatest risk. SFA also reduces the number of children retained in a grade or placed in special education (Slavin et al., 1994).

In summary, there have been several preschool and elementary school interventions that have reduced the future incidence of academic problems. Except for tutoring, most of these programs are multilevel environment-centered interventions that target several factors in the home, in the individual, and in the school. Slavin and his colleagues (1994) provide useful details on many of thtese interventions.

6.3. Academic Functioning as a Protective Factor

The importance of children's academic functioning should not be underestimated. Poor academic performance is frequently associated with a variety of negative behavioral and social outcomes, such as discipline problems, poor peer relations, drug use, psychological difficulties (e.g., anxiety and depression), and delinquency. Moreover, growing evidence indicates that good academic achievement may be a protective factor for children, in the sense that the promotion of academic competencies can help prevent other types of problems.

For instance, early intervention to prevent academic problems has sometimes also resulted in later reductions in delinquency, aggression, and other forms of behavior problems (Johnson, 1988; Schweinhart &

Weikart, 1988; Yoshikawa, 1994). Accordingly, more preventionists are now adding academic components to their interventions in an attempt to prevent later psychological and social problems (e.g., Cowen, Hightower, Pedro-Carroll, & Work, 1990; Hawkins et al., 1991; Jason et al., 1992). The positive results obtained in these programs lend support to the view that the academic needs of target populations should be addressed in preventive trials.

7. Health Education and Promotion

Many different types of prevention programs, including drug programs and some of the programs to prevent behavioral and social problems, have been offered under the general rubric of health education. This section, however, describes a few programs devoted to physical health promotion, to AIDS education, and to pregnancy prevention. Table 2 summarizes the characteristics of some exemplary programs in these areas.

7.1. Physical Health Promotion

By far, the largest school-based prevention study has been the School Health Education Evaluation (SHEE; Connell, Turner, & Mason, 1985). Four different health promotion and risk reduction programs with established field-tested curricula were evaluated. Two of these specifically targeted cardiovascular health, whereas two others also included other health areas such as personal safety and drug use. SHEE eventually involved 30,000 children in grades 4 through 7, drawn from 1,071 classrooms in 20 states.

Two findings from SHEE are particularly important. First, two of four health programs had significant behavioral impact (mean effect sizes of .68 and .34), demonstrating that health education can be successfully introduced into many schools across the country. Second, findings clearly carried the implication that preventive programs must be conducted well and for a sufficient length of time to achieve maximum benefits. For instance, program intensity affected outcomes. Students who participated for 2 school years demonstrated more change than those receiving 1 year of instruction. Level of program implementation also had a strong effect on outcomes. For two of the four health programs, significant outcomes were not achieved unless the program was conducted for at least 20 hours and parents were involved, as the program model specified. Across all four programs, when different levels of program implementation were com-

TABLE 2
Exemplary Studies in Various Areas of Health Education

Study	Sample size/ grade level	Program goal	Emphasis of intervention	Significant findings
Connell, Turner, & Mason (1985)	30,000/ 4–7	Develop healthy lifestyles	Classroom instruction	Behavioral lifestyle changes
Walter & Vaughn (1993)	1201/ 9 and 11	HIV risk reduction	Perception of risk and skills training	Fewer unsafe sexual behaviors
Simons-Morton, Parcel, Baranowski, Forthofer, & O'Hara (1991)	4 schools[a]/ 3 and 4	Improved diet and physical activity	Skills training and organizational change	Reduction in sodium and fat; increase in physical activity
Zabin et al. (1986)	1800/ 7–12	Reduce pregnancy rate	Classroom instruction, individual counseling, access to contraceptives	Reduced pregnancies

[a]The exact number of participating students was not provided.

pared, students exposed to full program implementation demonstrated 85% greater behavioral gains than those exposed to average levels of implementation. In general, Connell et al. (1985) concluded that stable and maximum program effects were obtained in SHEE only after 50 hours of classroom instruction. We will return to the importance of program implementation later in this chapter.

The Go for Health Program (Simons-Morton, Parcel, Baranowski, Forthofer, & O'Mara, 1991) has the dual goal of promoting physical activity and healthy food choices in elementary school children. This health program is innovative in integrating classroom-based instruction with organizational changes occurring in both the school's food service and physical education programs. A skills training approach is used in the classroom to teach third and fourth graders how to distinguish healthy from unhealthy foods and what types of physical activity will improve physical fitness. Children then learn how to self-monitor their behaviors in both of these realms and are reinforced for whatever improvements they demonstrate.

The other aspects of the Go for Health Program involve consultation with appropriate school personnel to achieve systemic changes in school practices. A dietician works with the food service managers and cooks to produce more nutritious servings in the school cafeteria. Consultants also work with the physical education staff to provide children with greater opportunities to improve physical fitness through activities such as dancing, aerobic activities, and so on. This latter consultation is necessary, since many school physical education programs often do not promote physical health through conditioning or exercise. Observations suggest that on average elementary students spend only 8.6% of physical education class time in moderate to vigorous physical activity (Simons-Morton, Taylor, Snider, & Huang, 1993). This translates into only 3.5 minutes per class.

Go for Health has been successful for several cohorts of ethnically diverse children. Analysis of school lunches has demonstrated average declines of 13% in total fat, 25% in saturated fat, and 47% in sodium (Simons-Morton et al., 1991). Children have also shown a fourfold increase in the time spent in moderate to vigorous physical activities. Other evaluations reflect that positive changes in program participants are maintained over a 1-year follow-up period (Simons-Morton, Parcel, & O'Mara, 1988).

The Go for Health program illustrates one likely advantage for interventions achieving environmental changes versus those attempting only individual-level change. Once school staff make positive organizational modifications in the food service and the physical education program, these changes continue to affect children year after year. Moreover, spillover effects for the entire school population are possible. All children at the Go for Health schools can benefit from the changes in the school food service and physical education department. Simons-Morton and his colleagues have noted that although the efforts involved in introducing organizational changes into schools are time-consuming and not easy to achieve, the benefits can be substantial and long-lasting.

Although parents are important models and reinforcers for their children's health-related behaviors, school-based programs have not been very successful in securing parental participation in health promotion programs. The Home Team (HT) program developed by Perry and her colleagues (1988) is an exception and has been able to secure high rates of parental participation (77% or more). HT requires that parents help their children complete homework assignments in nutrition. Children receive small rewards at school each week, based on how many homework activities are completed with their parents. Parents are thus motivated to assist their children in securing these incentives. Activities involve assessing the nutritional content of selected foods in the home and planning healthier food purchases.

HT has produced not only positive changes in children's home diets but also has positively affected parental behavior. Parents demonstrate increased knowledge about nutrition, their health communications to their children increase, they give their children greater input into food choices, and they increase their purchase of healthier foods for the family. The applicability of HT for different school populations and the durability of program effects are currently unknown, but HT appears to be a very economic way to modify both parental and child eating patterns. HT costs only $7 per family, including the cost of all incentives.

7.2. AIDS Education

Walter and Vaughan (1993) were the first to demonstrate in a large-scale, controlled fashion that it is possible to reduce risky sexual behaviors relative to HIV infection in adolescents. Several features of this investigation are noteworthy. The researchers first conducted a needs assessment of the target group to identify deficiencies in knowledge, attitudes, and skills. They then designed a brief intervention that was specifically tailored to adolescents' needs and could be offered by regular classroom teachers. Observations conducted during the program confirmed the ability of trained teachers to implement the program as required. A large ($N = 1,201$) multiethnic, inner-city sample of students was studied.

The intervention utilized health belief and social learning principles to teach students about AIDS and safe sexual practices, in particular, the correct and consistent use of condoms during intercourse. Outcome data that included a 3-month follow-up indicated that adolescents in the experimental group demonstrated less risky sexual behaviors. Positive program effects also occurred in adolescents' AIDS knowledge, attitudes, and sense of self-efficacy.

7.3. Pregnancy Prevention

Approaches to adolescent pregnancy prevention have been controversial in terms of whether sexual abstinence should be the major theme of the intervention. Most authorities would agree that the timing of the intervention and the sexual history of the target population are critical. Sexual abstinence may be an appropriate objective for those who are not sexually active, but effective contraceptive behavior is a more realistic and attainable goal for nonvirgins who are not likely to cease their sexual activity completely.

Evaluation of the Self Center (Zabin et al., 1986), a storefront health clinic located in close proximity to an inner-city junior high and high school, indicated that the program was successful in two major respects: (1) delaying the onset of sexual activity among females, and (2) reducing pregnancy rates. There was a 30% reduction in pregnancy rates in the program schools, compared to a 58% increase over a 3-year period in control schools. Nurses, social workers, and carefully chosen peer helpers offered three types of services in the schools (classroom education, informal, small-group rap sessions, and individual counseling) and three at the nearby clinic (informal group education, counseling, and medical services, including access to contraceptives). The ability of the staff to gain the students' trust, offer a range of services, and be accessible when needed seemed a vital aspect of the program; 85% of the students took advantage of at least one of the available services, and the average student had 10 contacts with the Self Center. The informal rap sessions were particularly popular among many of the students and often served as their first introduction to the Self Center and its staff.

8. Drug Programs

Drug programs have undergone extensive procedural and outcome changes within the past two decades. During the 1960s and early 1970s, the results of many interventions were discouraging in terms of their behavioral effects. Many early programs emphasized informational strategies in the belief that providing students with accurate information about drugs would deter drug use. Other programs used strategies to enhance self-esteem in the belief that students who feel better about themselves would not use drugs. Some drug programs combined fear appeals with either of the aforementioned strategies and emphasized the negative side effects and consequences of drug use. By and large, we now know most early programs were founded on incorrect assumptions. Providing new knowledge, improving self-esteem, or simply scaring students about drugs does not lead to significant behavioral change (Schinke et al., 1991).

Contemporary drug programs have been much more successful than earlier programs in changing behavior and now emphasize skills training at the individual level and the importance of social factors affecting drug use. These programs have been guided by a growing research literature indicating that multiple factors in the individual and social environment influence drug use (Hawkins, Catalano, & Miller, 1992). Table 3 summarizes some characteristics of currently successful drug programs.

8.1. Characteristics of Current Programs

Two general types of skills training programs are represented in Table 3. The Life Skills Training (LST) program developed by Botvin and others (Dusenbury, Botvin, & James-Ortiz, 1990) uses social learning principles to systematically teach students a set of skills that may be useful in preventing drug use. For instance, students are taught coping and relaxation techniques to deal with anxiety, how to resist peer pressure, how to communicate effectively, and how to set and maintain personal goals. Evaluations indicate LST has consistently been effective in reducing student drug use, and the program has been successful in several school settings and for ethnically diverse populations.

Another group of skills training programs actively teaches students how to detect and resist peer and social pressures to take drugs (Hansen & Graham, 1991). These programs (often called *resistance* or *refusal skills programs*) frequently focus on assertiveness and communication skills training. Some of these programs also emphasize the importance of social norms affecting drug use. Many students overestimate the extent and acceptability of drug use in their environment, and a social norms approach attempts to correct these misconceptions and develop prosocial (nondrug) behavioral norms.

There has also been a change in the use of mass media approaches to combat drug use. Whereas early programs depended on brief campaigns using public service announcements, later programs have used sophisticated social marketing priniciples to reach the target audience. For instance, the successful mass media campaign developed in one program (Flynn et al., 1994) used over 50 different paid television and radio ads that were broadcast up to 450 times per year to saturate the media with antidrug messages.

TABLE 3
Successful Contemporary Drug Prevention Programs

Study	Sample size/grade level	Target drug(s)	Emphasis of intervention	Significant findings
Botvin, Baker, Dusenbury, Botvin, & Diaz (1995)	3597/ Grades 5 and 6	Tobacco, alcohol, marijuana	Life skills training	Reduced use for all target drugs
Dielman, Shope, Leech, & Butchart (1989)	1505/ Grade 7	Alcohol	Resistance training	Students with prior use show less alcohol use and misuse
Flynn et al. (1994)	5458/ Grades 4–6	Tobacco	1. Resistance training 2. Resistance training and mass media	2 more effective than 1 on smoking
Hansen & Graham (1991)	2135/ Grade 7	Alcohol, tobacco, marijuana	1. Resistance training 2. Social norms 3. Both 1 and 2 4. Information only	Both 2 and 3 more effective than 1 or 4 for all target drugs
Johnson et al. (1990)	1607/ Grade 6	Tobacco, alcohol	Comprehensive: classroom, parents, school, community, and mass media	Reduced cigarette and marijuana use

The Midwestern Prevention Program (MPP) is a model, comprehensive approach to drug prevention and illustrates how a school intervention can be incorporated into a wider community effort (Johnson et al., 1990). MPP targets five levels of intervention—individual, familial, interpersonal, organizational, and community—and is the only school prevention program to have such ambitious goals. MPP program components are added in successive years to the intervention. There is an initial 10-session classroom component conducted by teaches and peer leaders, augmented by five booster sessions the following year. Parents participate in the classroom component by assisting their children with homework assignments, receive training in communication skills, and participate in various prevention activities at school and in the community. At the organizational level, schools initiate antidrug policies and programs. There is a community-based media campaign and, finally, community leaders and agencies are organized to support the other program components and develop and promote health policies at the community level. MPP has been successful in modifying the use of cigarettes, marijuana, and alcohol.

The drug programs listed in Table 3 are impressive in terms of the magnitude of change achieved. For instance, there has been a 33% reduction in the onset of smoking (Flynn et al., 1994), an 87% reduction in the onset of problems associated with alcohol (Hansen & Graham, 1991), reductions of up to 38% in the use of marijuana (Johnson et al., 1990), and reduced odds of smoking, drinking immoderately, or using marijuana of up to 40% (Botvin, Baker, Dusenbury, Botvin, & Diaz, 1995). Furthermore, these findings have been obtained during follow-up periods as long as 3 years (Johnson et al., 1990). Such data reflect the practical and social importance of the effects of successful contemporary drug programs.

9. Directions for Future Research

Although current evidence indicates that school-based primary prevention can produce significant positive outcomes, research is far from definitive, and there are many unknowns. In general, there is a need to answer several basic questions: Who benefits from primary prevention? How long do program effects last? What specific types of problems are being prevented? What accounts for program outcomes? When should interventions be offered for maximum impact? What risk and protective factors are relevant in each situation?

Several authors have provided useful suggestions to improve prevention research (Coie et al., 1993; Heller, Price, & Sher, 1980; Institute of Medicine, 1994; Jason, Thompson, & Rose, 1986; Lorion, 1990; Price, Cowen, Lorion, &

Ramos-McKay, 1989). Rather than repeating all these suggestions, a few important issues are briefly discussed: program implementation, avoiding the uniformity myth, collecting follow-up data, and cost-effectiveness.

9.1. Importance of Program Implementation

Implementation, sometimes referred to as *treatment integrity* or *fidelity*, refers to the extent to which intended program procedures are effectively put into practice. Implementation is not all-or-none, but exists in degrees or levels and may refer to how many components in a multicomponent program are actually conducted, how well each component is administered, or a combination of these possibilities. Two important findings have consistently emerged among studies that have examined the implementation of school-based prevention: (1) Implementation varies across settings and programs; and (2) the level of implementation attained affects outcomes.

For example, across three studies, an acceptable or high level of program implementation was achieved by only 21–46% of participating teachers (Resnicow et al., 1992; Rohrbach, Graham, & Hansen, 1993; Taggart, Bush, Zuckerman, & Theiss, 1990). Outcome data suggest that either significant program outcomes are obtained only when the intervention is appropriately implemented (Ross, Luepker, Nelson, Saaveredra, & Hubbard, 1991; Taggart et al., 1990), or that much stronger effects occur under circumstances of more complete implementation (Botvin et al., 1995; Connell et al., 1985; Tobler, 1986).

These findings have strong implications for evaluation research. Unless care is taken to ensure appropriate levels of implementation, outcomes can be jeopardized. Future studies should routinely monitor the level of program implementation and assess its relationship to outcome. In fact, the term, *Type III error*, has been coined to refer to the evaluation of a program that has not been properly implemented (Scanlon, Horst, Nay, Schmidt, & Waller, 1977). Authors discussing methods to improve program implementation often emphasize the importance of careful preprogram planning and training as well as ongoing supervision, consultation, and troubleshooting to deal with unanticipated problems once a program is launched (Fullan, 1992; Huberman & Miles, 1974).

9.2. Avoiding the Uniformity Myth

Preventionists must avoid the uniformity myth that originally plagued psychotherapy research, that is, the general notion that the same intervention produces similar effects across clients and problems. A good working assumption in prevention, then, is that the same approach will not work equally well for everyone. As a result, program evaluations should be planned to help understand how an intervention affects different program participants. Potentially important individual characteristics to consider include developmental status, age, gender, racial or ethnic status, risk status, and presence of relevant skills. Social and environmental variables of possible significance include family characteristics and functioning, peer behavior, teaching practices, and classroom and school climate, organization, and policies.

9.3. Collecting Follow-up Data

Follow-up information is critical, since the basic thrust of prevention is to intervene now to forestall the future development of problems. Although data suggest that the results of many school-based interventions do not fade over time, only about 10% of all studies have examined the durability of program impact, and follow-up periods have often been brief (less than 6 months).

Nevertheless, some of the strongest evidence for the value of primary prevention has come from a dozen or so follow-up investigations illustrating how program effects eventually generalize to other areas of children's lives. For instance, some early childhood programs have improve not only children's later academic functioning but also their social and personal behavior; the reverse has occurred in some programs originally focused on reducing social and behavioral problems (Durlak, 1995). Some of these findings are only apparent years after the original intervention, however, indicating the importance of long-term follow-up whenever possible.

9.4. Assessing Cost-Effectiveness

A cost-effectiveness analysis (CEA) compares the costs and benefits of a program in an attempt to decide if the intervention is a worthwhile social investment. CEAs can help schools decide if they would be better off with a particular program than without it, or, if a program is to be offered, which alternative is best for achieving specific objectives.

CEAs should be as comprehensive as possible and assume a long-term perspective in order to be fair to prevention programs. A comprehensive cost evaluation would consider all costs and benefits connected with a program and not just those that can be easily translated into monetary terms. Some programs may be costly to conduct but achieve results that are so valued by local citizens that the intervention is nevertheless viewed as worthwhile.

Many of the most important effects from prevention are psychological and social benefits that may be difficult to quantify but should not be overlooked. For example, the reduction of behavioral or academic problems is likely to lessen emotional pain and suffering, stigma, and stress in both children and their families. The effects of health promotion are also important. Enhanced psychological well-being and the improved academic and social performance that can result from preventive programs need to be part of the equation in any cost analysis.

A long-term perspective is important in cost evaluations, because the costs and benefits from prevention tend to occur at different tiimes. Whereas most of the costs of a program are incurred when the program is conducted, benefits may not appear until after the program has ended. In some cases, the longer the follow-up, the more cost-effective a program may appear (Barnett, 1993). Without follow-up, the true benefits from prevention will not be discovered or counted.

Finally, external benefits need to be considered. External benefits are those that occur for society or for others not directly involved in the program. For example, society benefits when people do not smoke, because there are many external costs associated with smoking that are eliminated. External costs from smoking come from such sources as disability insurance, lifetime taxes on earnings, and the effects of passive or secondhand smoke on others. The total lifetime external costs of smoking to society have been conservatively calculated at $1,000 per smoker (Manning, Keeler, Newhouse, Sloss, & Wasserman, 1991). In other words, an intervention that prevents 10 children from smoking yields external benefits for society of $10,000! Considering external benefits can greatly enhance the perceived value of prevention. The following sources contain good discussions of cost analyses of social and medical programs, along with program examples (Barnett & Escobar, 1989; Manning et al., 1991; Russell, 1986; Yates, 1985).

10. Summary

Many outcome studies have otained significant results suggesting the general value of school-based primary prevention. There is still much to be learned, however, about the specificity of program effects, particularly in answering basic questions such as what, who, how, why, when, and where (Gullotta, 1994). The field has come a long way in a short time, and it is up to the next generation of research studies to add to our understanding of how primary prevention programs in schools can be conducted to achieve maximum and enduring effects.

ACKNOWLEDGMENTS

The writing of this chapter was supported in part by a grant (92-1475-92) from the William T. Grant Foundation.
Correspondence concerning this chapter should be addressed to Joseph A. Durlak, Department of Psychology, Loyola University Chicago, 6525 N. Sheridan Road, Chicago, IL 60626.

11. References

Allensworth, D. D., (1993). Health education: State of the art. *Journal of School Health, 63*, 14–20.

Alpert-Gillis, L. J., Pedro-Carroll, J. L. & Cowen, E. L. (1989). The child of divorce intervention program: Development, implementation, and evaluation of a program for young urban children. *Journal of Consulting and Clinical Psychology, 57*, 583–589.

Barnett, W. S. (1990). Benefits of compensatory preschool education. *Journal of Human Resources, 27*, 279–312.

Barnett, W. S. (1993). Benefit–cost analysis of preschool education: Findings from a 25-year follow-up. *American Journal of Orthopsychiatry, 63*, 500–508.

Barnett, W. S., & Escobar, C. M. (1989). Research on the cost-effectiveness of early educational intervention: Implications for research and policy. *American Journal of Community Psychology, 17*, 677–704.

Botvin, G. J., Baker, E., Dusenbury, L., Botvin, E. M., & Diaz, T. (1995). Long-term follow-up results of a randomized drug abuse prevention trial in a white middle-class population. *Journal of the American Medical Association, 273*, 1106–1112.

Cohen, P. A., Kulik, J. A., & Kulik, C. C. (1982). Educational outcomes of tutoring: A meta-analysis of findings. *American Educational Research Journal, 19*, 237–248.

Coie, J. D., Watt, N. F., West, S. G., Hawkins, J. D., Asarnow, J. R., Markman, H. J., Ramey, S. L., Shure, M. B., & Long, B. (1993). The science of prevention: A conceptual framework and some directions for a national research program. *American Psychologist, 48*, 1013–1022.

Comer, J. P. (1985). The Yale–New Haven Primary Prevention Project: A follow-up study. *Journal of the American Academy of Child and Adolescent Psychiatry, 24*, 154–160.

Connell, D. B., Turner, R. R., & Mason, E. F. (1985). Summary of findings of the school health education evaluation: Health promotion effectiveness, implementation, and costs. *Journal of School Health, 55*, 316–321.

Cowen, E. L. (1994). The enhancement of psychological wellness: Challenges and opportunities. *American Journal of Community Psychology, 22*, 149–180.

Cowen, E. L., Hightower, D., Pedro-Carroll, J., & Work, W. C. (1990). School-based models for primary prevention programming with children. In R. P. Lorion (Ed.), *Protecting the children: Strategies for optimizing emotional and behavioral development* (pp. 133–160). Binghamton, NY: Haworth Press.

Dielman, T. E., Shope, J. T., Leech, S. L., & Butchart, A. T. (1989). Differential effectiveness of an elementary school-based alcohol misuse prevention program. *Journal of School Health, 59*, 255–263.

Dryfoos, J. G., (1990). *Adolescents at risk: Prevalence and prevention*. New York: Oxford University Press.

Durlak, J. A. (1995). *School-based prevention programs for children and adolescents*. Thousand Oaks, CA: Sage.

Dusenbury, L., Botvin, G. J., & James-Ortiz, S. (1990). The primary prevention of adolescent substance abuse through the promotion of personal and social competence. In R. P. Lorion (Ed.), *Protecting the children: Strategies for optimizing emotional and behavioral development* (pp. 201–224). Binghamton, NY: Haworth Press.

Emery, R. E. (1988). *Marriage, divorce, and children's adjustment*. Newbury Park, CA: Sage.

Finkelhor, D., & Strapko, N. (1992). Sexual abuse prevention education: A review of evaluation studies. In. D. J. Willis, E. W. Holden, & M. Rosenberg (Eds.), *Prevention of child maltreatment: Development and ecological perspectives* (pp. 150–167). New York: Wiley.

Felner, R. D., Brand, S., Adan, A. M., Mulhall, P. F., Flowers, N., Sartain, B., & DuBois, D. L. (1993). Restructuring the ecology of the school as an approach to prevention during school transitions: Longitudinal follow-ups and extensions of the School Transitional Environment Project (STEP). *Prevention in Human Services, 10*, 103–136.

Fullan, M. G. (1992). *Successful school improvement: The implementation perspective and beyond*. Philadelphia: Open University Press.

Flynn, B. S., Worden, J. K., Secker-Walker, R. H., Pirie, P. L., Badger, G. J., Carpenter, J. H., & Geller, B. M. (1994). Mass media and school interventions for cigarette smoking prevention: Effects 2 years after completion. *American Journal of Public Health, 84*, 1148–1150.

Greenwood, C. R., Delquadri, J. C., & Hall, R. V. (1989). Longitudinal effects of classwide peer tutoring. *Journal of Educational Psychology, 81*, 371–383.

Greenwood, C. R., Carta, J. J., & Hall, R. V. (1988). The use of peer tutoring strategies in classroom management and educational instruction. *School Psychology Review, 17*, 258–275.

Gullotta, T. P. (1994). The what, who, why, where, when, and how of primary prevention. *Journal of Primary Prevention, 15*, 5–14.

Hansen, W. B., & Graham, J. W. (1991). Preventing alcohol, marijuana, and cigarette use among adolescents: Peer pressure resistance training versus establishing conservative norms. *Preventive Medicine, 20*, 414–430.

Hartman, L. M. (1979). The preventive reduction of psychological risk in asymptomatic adolescents. *American Journal of Orthopsychiatry, 49*, 121–135.

Hawkins, J. D., Catalano, R. F., & Miller, J. Y. (1992). Risk and protective factors for alcohol and other drug problems in adolescence and early adulthood: Implications for substance abuse prevention. *Psychology Bulletin, 112*, 64–105.

Hawkins, J. D., Von Cleve, E., & Catalano, H. F., Jr. (1991). Reducing early childhood aggression: Results of a primary prevention program. *Journal of the American Academy of Child and Adolescent Psychiatry, 30*, 208–217.

Heller, K., Price, R. H., & Sher, K. J. (1980). Research and evaluation in primary prevention: Issues and guidelines. In R. H. Price, R. F. Ketterer, B. C. Bader, & J. Monahan (Eds.), *Prevention in mental health: Research, policy, and practice* (pp. 285–313). Beverly Hills, CA: Sage.

Holtzman, D., Greene, B. Z., Ingraham, G. C., Daily, L. A., Demchuk, D. G., & Kolbe, L. J. (1992). HIV education and health education in the United States: A national survey of local school district policies and practices. *Journal of School Health, 62*, 421–427.

Horacek, H. J., Ramey, C. T., Campbell, F. A., Hoffman, K. P., & Fletcher, R. H. (1987). Predicting school failure and assessing early intervention with high-risk children. *Journal of the American Academy of Child and Adolescent Psychiatry, 26*, 758–763.

Huberman, M., & Miles, M. (1984). *Innovation up close*. New York: Plenum Press.

Institute of Medicine (1994). *Reducing risks for mental disorders: Frontiers for preventive intervention research*. Washington, DC: National Academy Press.

Jason, L. A., Thompson, D., & Rose, T. (1986). Methodological issues in prevention. In B. A. Edelstein & L. Michelson (Eds.), *Handbook of prevention* (pp. 1–19) New York: Plenum Press.

Jason, L. A., Weine, A. M., Johnson, J. H., Warren-Sohlberg, L., Filipelli, L. A., Turner, E. Y., & Lardon, C. (1992). *Helping transfer students: Strategies for educational and social readjustment.* San Francisco: Jossey-Bass.

Johnson, D. L., (1988). Primary prevention of behavior problems in young children: The Houston Parent–Child Development Center. In R. H. Price, E. L. Cowen, R. P. Lorion, & J. Ramos-McKey (Eds.), *Fourteen ounces of prevention: A casebook for practitioners* (pp. 44–52). Washington, DC: American Psychological Association Press.

Johnson, C. A., Pentz, M. A., Weber, M. D., Dwyer, J. H., Baer, N., MacKinnon, D. P., Hansen, W. B., & Flay, B. R. (1990). Relative effectiveness of comprehensive community programming for drug abuse prevention with high-risk and low-risk adolescents. *Journal of Consulting and Clinical Psychology, 58,* 447–456.

Kazdin, A. E. (1990). Psychotherapy for children and adolescents. *Annual Review of Psychology, 41,* 21–54.

Kirby, D., Short, L., Collins, J., Rugg, D., Kolbe, L., Howard, L. Miller, B., Sonenstein, F., & Zabin, L. S. (1994). School-based programs to reduce sexual risk behaviors: A review of effectiveness. *Public Health Reports, 109,* 339–360.

Klein, D. C., & Goldston, S. E. (1977). *Primary prevention: An idea whose time has come.* Department of Health, Education and Welfare, Publication No. (ADM) 77-447. Washington, DC: U.S. Government Printing Office.

Lamb, H. R., & Zusman, J. (1979). Primary prevention in perspective. *American Journal of Psychiatry, 136,* 12–17.

Lipsey, M. W., & Wilson, D. B. (1993). The efficacy of psychological, educational and behavioral treatment. *American Psychologist, 48,* 1181–1209.

Lorion, R. P. (1990). Evaluating HIV risk-reduction efforts: Ten lessons from psychotherapy and prevention outcome strategies. *Journal of Community Psychology, 18,* 325–336.

Manning, W. G., Keeler, E. B., Newhouse, J. P., Sloss, E. M., & Wasserman, J. (1991). *The costs of poor health habits.* Cambridge, MA: Harvard University Press.

Masten, A. S., & Garmezy, N. (1985). Risk, vulnerability, and protective factors in developmental psychopathology. In B. B. Lahey & A. E. Kazdin (Eds.), *Advances in clinical child psychology* (Vol. 8, pp. 1–52). New York: Plenum Press.

Meisels, S. J., & Liaw, F. R. (1993). Failure in grade: Do retained students catch up? *Journal of Educational Research, 87,* 69–77.

Miller, B. C., Card, J. J., Paikoff, R. L., & Peterson, J. L. (Eds.). (1992). *Preventing adolescent pregnancy: Model programs and evaluations.* Newbury Park, CA: Sage.

O'Donnell, J., Hawkins, J. D., Catalano, R. G., Abbott, R. D., & Day, L. E. (1995). Preventing school failure, drug use, and delinquency among low-income children: Effects of a long-term prevention project in elementary schools. *American Journal of Orthopsychiatry, 65,* 87–100.

Olweus, D. (1994). Annotation: Bullying at school: Basic facts and effects of a school-based intervention program. *Journal of Child Psychology and Psychiatry, 35,* 1171–1190.

Pekarik, G., & Stephenson, L. A. (1988). Adult and child client differences in therapy dropout research. *Journal of Clinical Child Psychology, 17,* 316–321.

Perry, C. L., Luepker, R. V., Murray, D. M., Kurth, C., Mullis, R., Crockett, S., & Jacobs, D. R., Jr. (1988). Parent involvement with children's health promotion: The Minnesota Home Team. *American Journal of Public Health, 78,* 1156–1160.

Price, R. H., Cowen, E. L., Lorion, R. P., & Ramos-McKay, J. (1989). The search for effective prevention programs: What we learned along the way. *American Journal of Orthopsychiatry, 59,* 49–58.

Resnicow, K., Cohn, L., Reinhardt, J., Cross, D., Futterman, R., Kirschner, E., Wynder, E. L., & Allegrante, J. P. (1992). A three-year evaluation of the Know Your Body Program in inner-city schoolchildren. *Health Education Quarterly, 19*, 463–480.

Rohrbach, L. A., Graham, J. W., & Hansen, W. B. (1993). Diffusion of a school-based substance abuse prevention program: Predictors of program implementation. *Preventive Medicine, 22*, 237–260.

Ross, J. G., Luepker, R. V., Nelson, G. D., Saavedra, P., & Hubbard, B. M. (1991). Teenage health teaching modules: Impact of teacher training on implementation and student outcomes. *Journal of School Health, 61*, 31–34.

Russell, L. B. (1986). *Is prevention better than cure?* Washington, DC: Brookings Institution.

Rutter, M. (1979). Protective factors in children's responses to stress and disadvantage. In M. Whalen & J. E. Rolf (Eds.), *Primary prevention of psychopathology: Volume 3. Social competence in children* (pp. 49–74). Hanover, NH: University Press of New England.

Sameroff, A. J., (1987). Transactional risk factors and prevention. In J. Steinberg & M. Silverman (Eds.), *Preventing mental disorders: A research perspective* (pp. 74–89). Washington, DC: U.S. Government Printing Office.

Scanlon, J. W., Horst, P., Nay, J. N., Schmidt, R. E., & Waller, T. (1977). Evaluability assessment: Avoiding type III and IV errors. In G. R. Gilbert & P. J. Conklin (Eds.), *Evaluation management: A source book of readings* (pp. 71–90). Charlottesville, VA: U.S. Civil Service Commission.

Schinke, S. P., Botvin, G. J., & Orlandi, M. A. (1991). *Substance abuse in children and adolescents: Evaluation and intervention.* Newbury Park, CA: Sage.

Schweinhart, L. J., & Weikart, D. B. (1988). The High/Scope Perry Preschool Program. In R. H. Price, E. L. Cowen, R. P. Lorion, & J. Ramos-McKay (Eds.), *Fourteen ounces of prevention: A casebook for practitioners* (pp. 53–65). Washington, DC: American Psychological Association Press.

Shaffer, D., Garland, A., Gould, M., Fisher, P., & Trautman, P. (1988). Preventing teenage suicide: A critical review. *Journal of the American Academy of Child and Adolescent Psychiatry, 27*, 675–687.

Simons-Morton, B. G., Parcel, G. S., Baranowski, T., Forthofer, R., & O'Mara, N. M. (1991). Promoting physical activity and a healthful diet among children: Results of a school-based intervention study. *American Journal of Public Health, 81*, 986–991.

Simons-Morton, B. G., Parcel, G. S., & O'Mara, N. M. (1988). Implementing organizational changes to promote healthful diet and physical activity at school. *Health Education Quarterly, 15*, 115–130.

Simons-Morton, B. G., Taylor, W. C., Snider, S. A., & Huang, I. W. (1993). The physical activity of fifth-grade students during physical education classes. *American Journal of Public Health, 83*, 262–264.

Slavin, R. E., Karweit, N. L., & Madden, N. A. (1989). *Effective programs for students at risk.* Needham Heights, MA: Allyn & Bacon.

Slavin, R. E., Karweit, N. L., & Wasik, B. A. (1994). *Preventing early school failure.* Needham Heights, MA: Allyn & Bacon.

Spivack, G., & Shure, M. (1974). *Social adjustment of young children: A cognitive approach to solving real-life problems.* San Francisco: Jossey-Bass.

Taggart, V. S., Bush, P. J., Zuckerman, A. E., & Theiss, P. K. (1990). A process evaluation of the District of Columbia "Know Your Body" project. *Journal of School Health, 60*, 60–66.

Tobler, N. S. (1986). Meta-analysis of 143 adolescent drug prevention programs: Quantitative outcome results of program participants compared to a control or comparison group. *Journal of Drug Issues, 16*, 537–567.

Walter, H. J., & Vaughan, R. D. (1993). AIDS risk reduction among a multiethnic sample of urban high school students. *Journal of the American Medical Association, 270*, 725–730.

Weissberg, R. P., Gesten, E. L., Rapkin, B. D. Cowen, E. L., Davidson, E., de Apodaca, R. F., & McKim, B. J. (1981). The evaluation of a social problem-solving training program for suburban and inner-city third-grade children. *Journal of Consulting and Clinical Psychology, 49*, 251–261.

Wolchik, S. A., West, S. G., Westover, S., Sandler, I. N., Martin, A., Justig, J., Tein, J., & Fisher, J. (1993). The Child of Divorce Parenting Intervention: Outcome evaluation of an empirically based program. *American Journal of Community Psychology, 21*, 293–331.

Work, W. C., & Olsen, K. H. (1990). Evaluation of a revised fourth-grade social problem solving curriculum: Empathy as a moderator of adjustive gain. *Journal of Primary Prevention, 11*, 143–157.

Yates, B. T. (1985). Cost-effectiveness analysis and cost–benefit analysis: An introduction. *Behavior Assessment, 83*, 201–206.

Yoskikawa, H. (1994). Prevention as cumulative protection: Effects of early family support and education on chronic delinquency and its risks. *Psychological Bulletin, 115*, 28–54.

Zabin, L. S., Hirsch, M. B. , Street, R., Emerson, M. R., Hardy, J. B., & King, T. M. (1986). The Baltimore Pregnancy Prevention Program for urban teenagers: I. How did it work? *Family Planning Perspectives, 20*, 182–187.

9

Expanded School Mental Health Services

A National Movement in Progress

MARK D. WEIST

1. Introduction

In 1982, Knitzer's compelling *Unclaimed Children* underscored the tremendous gap between the mental health needs of children in the United States and services actually available to them. Throughout the 1980s and into the 1990s, some progress has been made to improve the mental health system of care for youth, as exemplified by national reform efforts that improve the coordinated delivery of services (e.g., the Child and Adolescent Service Systems Program [CASSP]; Day & Roberts, 1991), the growth of family preservation models of treatment (Knitzer & Cole, 1989), and the development of "multisystemic" treatment approaches for youth with severe disturbances (Henggeler & Borduin, 1990). In spite of these improvements, a large gap between youth who need and receive services remains (Duchnowski & Friedman, 1990), mental health services continue to be fragmented and uncoordinated (Burns & Friedman, 1990), and university-based applied research efforts have not been effectively integrated into communities on a wide scale (Weisz & Weiss, 1993).

One method to significantly address gaps in mental health services for youth is to place more of them in schools. Each day during the school year, 40 million children attend one of the 82,000 public elementary and secondary schools in the United States (Dryfoos, 1994). By placing services in

MARK D. WEIST • Department of Psychiatry, University of Maryland, Baltimore, Maryland 21201.

Advances in Clinical Child Psychology, Volume 19, edited by Thomas H. Ollendick and Ronald J. Prinz. Plenum Press, New York, 1997.

them, we are reaching youth "where they are," eliminating many of the barriers that exist for traditional child mental health services (e.g., as provided in community mental health centers and private offices).

Most school-based mental health services are limited to youth in special education (Duchnowski, 1994). However, a national movement is under way to place a full range of mental health services (from primary to tertiary preventive) for youth in schools. This movement is part of a broader effort, now around two decades old, to bring health services to schools. The movement to place "expanded" mental health services in schools offers considerable opportunities for mental health professionals for clinical service, program development, and research. The purpose of this chapter is to provide an overview of expanded school mental health services, with discussion of broad, systems issues, followed by review of challenges confronting individual clinicians working in schools.

2. Limitations in the Mental Health Service Delivery System for Youth

Statistics indicate that many youth who need mental health services are not receiving them. In 1991, the Congressional Office of Technology Assessment (OTA) reported that up to 20% of youth under the age of 20 present emotional and behavioral disorders severe enough to warrant intervention, but less than one-third of these youth actually receive mental health services. Zahner, Pawelkiewicz, DiFrancesco, and Adnopoz (1992) conducted a survey of parents and teachers of 822 children (aged 6–11) who were attending public and private schools in a northeastern city. Based on parent and teacher screening measures, 38.5% of the children were determined to be at risk for developing psychiatric disturbance. However, only 11% of the children determined to be at risk had received treatment in traditional mental health settings (i.e., community outpatient clinics and private offices). Goodwin, Goodwin, and Cantrill (1988) surveyed over 500 personnel from a Colorado school district on the mental health needs of elementary students. Approximately 15% of the students were identified as needing, but not receiving, mental health services.

Dryfoos (1994), a leading researcher on youth at risk, estimated that one in four U.S. youth aged 10 to 17 "do it all," that is, engage in early unprotected sexual activity, use drugs, skip school, and fall behind in their schoolwork. With 40 million children attending U.S. public schools, 10 million could benefit from mental health services, based on her estimate of one in four being at risk.

Children and adolescents from the inner city are in particular need for mental health services, given the high life stress they contend with, including poverty (Duncan, 1991), exposure to crime and violence (Prothrow-

Stith, 1991; Shakoor & Chalmers, 1991), frequent abuse and neglect (Garbarino, 1976), and commonly occurring family problems (e.g., absence of one parent, large family size, substance abuse in the home; Rutter & Quinton, 1977). Related to these conditions, urban youth are evidencing rising rates of troubling problems such as teen pregnancy (Hofferth & Hayes, 1987); sexually transmitted diseases (including HIV infections; Blum, 1987); substance use (Elliott, Huizinga, & Menard, 1989); drug trafficking (Feigelman, Stanton, & Ricardo, 1993); depression, anxiety, and post-traumatic stress (Pynoos & Nader, 1990; Warner & Weist, 1996); school avoidance, poor school performance, and dropout (with rates exceeding 50% in many urban areas; Rhodes & Jason, 1988).

In contrast to the rather significant attention to the plight of urban youth, problems of rural youth have received little attention (Kelleher, Taylor, & Rickett, 1992). Rural areas have more unemployment, 38% of the country's poor, and 67% of substandard housing, although comprising only 25% of the U.S. population (National Mental Health Association [NMHA], 1989). Furthermore, there is evidence that rural children have higher levels of injuries, drownings, and some chronic illnesses than metropolitan children (Kelleher et al., 1992). In terms of mental health status, limited studies indicate that rural youth present lower rates of drug abuse than urban youth, but higher rates of alcohol abuse (Alexander & Klassen, 1988), with urban and rural youth having roughly comparable levels of behavioral and emotional problems (Offord et al., 1987). Impediments for rural youth to receive mental health services are significant, including geography (with fewer clinics and treatment programs spaced farther apart than in metropolitan areas), enhanced stigma for seeking mental health treatment, and significant difficulties in recruitment and retention of adequately trained mental health providers (Kelleher et al., 1992).

Suburban youth (i.e., youth from suburbs and small cities and towns) are a neglected population as well. However, there is evidence that violence and carrying of weapons is increasing among suburban youth (Prothrow-Stith, 1991), and that suburban adolescents may be more prone to abuse of hard drugs (e.g., LSD, methamphetamine) than their urban or rural counterparts (Way, Stauber, Nakkula, & London, 1994).

Thus, across urban, rural, and suburban settings, there is a consensus among mental health providers and analysts that youth with mental disorders are inadequately served in the current system of care. Numerous problems such as fragmentation of services, poor coordination within and between agencies, staff limitations (in numbers and quality), inadequate treatment facilities, and escalating difficulties in paying for services associated with managed care, in combination make the mental health services system for youth a "nonsystem" (Burns & Friedman, 1990; Kelleher et al., 1992). Commenting on the status of children's mental health services, Duchnowski and Friedman (1990) wrote:

> The discrepancy between the conceptual model of what a system of care should be, as embraced by state policy makers and its actual implementation at a grass roots level is, in many cases, enormous. The discrepancy between the numbers of youngsters and families in need of services and the amount of services that is available is also enormous. (p. 5)

Community mental health clinics remain the dominant method of addressing mental health problems in youth. However, there are many barriers that prevent children and adolescents from accessing mental health services in these clinics. These include familial factors such as poor knowledge of mental health services, financial difficulties, transportation problems, and stress in families that often precludes adequate attention to children's emotional difficulties. Barriers also exist in community clinics, including long waiting lists (often 3 weeks or longer), high turnover among staff, long intake procedures, and excessive paperwork to justify even short treatment to insurance companies. These barriers often serve to prevent youth from receiving needed services. Barriers to community mental health services are particularly acute for families from other cultures, who often have little or no conception of these services or how to access them.

An additional issue of importance is that recent analyses have called into question the dominant model of treating children's emotional/behavioral disorders with weekly outpatient therapy visits. For example, Weisz, Weiss, and Donenberg (1992) conducted a meta-analysis of child and adolescent psychotherapy outcome studies and concluded that there is limited evidence for the effectiveness of such therapy as practiced with clinical samples in applied settings. Another side of this issue is that youth often need to act out or show salient symptoms of emotional distress before they receive enough attention to be seen in a community clinic. As such, many youth receiving treatment in these clinics present full-blown diagnoses, meaning that prevention efforts are predominately tertiary (Weist, Myers, & Baker, 1995). Moreoever, the notion of once per week outpatient therapy in an artificial setting (often far removed from the child's natural environment) to address emotional/behavioral problems in youth is questionable at best (Henggeler, 1994).

3. Advantages of School-Based Programs

Related to recognition of inadequacies of community clinics in preventing and addressing emotional and behavioral problems in youth, there has been increasing discussion and action toward expanding mental health services for youth in schools (Adelman & Taylor, 1991). Schools provide a single point of access to services in a familiar, nonthreatening atmosphere, and placing services in them reduces barriers that constrain the provision of community-based mental health services to youth in need. For youth from the inner city, the presence of these services in schools significantly improves their accessibility. For example, in Baltimore schools, we have found that 80% or more of youth referred for services have had no prior mental health involvement, in spite of significant presenting problems (e.g., depression with suicidal ideation; Flaherty, Weist, & Warner, in press).

Other advantages for school-based mental health services include (1) improved capabilities to provide a full range of preventive services from primary to tertiary (see Fleisch, Knitzer, & Steinberg, 1990); (2) significantly enhanced roles of therapists working in schools, for example, being able to see students in multiple settings (e.g., athletic games, assemblies, in the cafeteria) and over long periods of time (e.g., from 9th through 12th grade); (3) reduced stigma of seeking and receiving mental health services, since they are provided in an environment that is natural for the child; (4) reduced referrals to special education by providing mental health services rapidly and to all children, which serves to reduce costs to educational systems, while avoiding the labeling of children as being in "special ed" (Flaherty et al., in press); and (5) opportunities to improve the overall environment in schools through collaborative efforts between health and educational staff (Fleisch et al., 1990).

In spite of these advantages, comprehensive mental health services are still not widely available to youth in schools. Although school psychologists and social workers provide the full array of mental health services to all students (including those in regular education) in some localities, in many others, these professionals work exclusively with youth in special education. In the following sections, I review issues related to these more traditional school-based mental health services for youth. This is followed by discussion of models to expand mental health services in schools to the whole student population.

4. Mental Health Services Offered through Special Education

The mandate for schools to become involved in the physical, mental, and social health of their students initially came from public laws 93-641 and 94-317, enacted in the early 1970s by the United States Congress (Thomas & Texidor, 1987). Public Law 94-142, the Education for All Handicapped Children Act of 1975, mandated that each school system provide an appropriate educational program for all handicapped children (including those "handicapped" by emotional and behavioral disorders) in the least restrictive setting possible. It also required specific assessment approaches (e.g., based on multiple measurement strategies, nonbiased), comprehensive evaluations of handicapped children every 3 years, and adherence to due process in identifying, assessing, and developing interventions for handicapped children (Butler, 1988). Public Law 94-142 was amended in 1990 and renamed the Individuals with Disabilities Education Act (IDEA; Duchnowski, 1994).

There are over 24,000 school psychologists working in school districts across the United States (National Association of School Psychologists, 1995). Since passage of Public Law 94-142, school psychologists (and in many districts, social workers) must spend a large proportion of time in special education screening, assessment, and treatment planning to ensure compliance with its provisions. For many school psychologists, these involvements have increased over the years, leaving less time for prevention and consultation activities for the whole school population (Thomas, 1987).

School psychologists have expressed their desire to move away from extensive involvement in psychological testing, and to be more involved in providing consultation and direct intervention services (Abel & Burke, 1985; Stewart, 1986). Although some have been successful in increasing the amount of time available for consultation (Fisher, Jenkins, & Crumbley, 1986), most still spend only a "very small percentage" of their time in direct therapeutic activities with children or their families (Conoley & Conoley, 1991).

Related to these constraints, some school psychologists are expressing frustration. For example, Johnston (1990) wrote:

> The literature and my experiences suggest that the present system is not working. School psychologists are overburdened with traditional caseloads.... Only the most severe cases receive attention, all others fall between the cracks. Classroom interventions, too, are often not carried out, either because the teacher does not have the skill to implement the recommendations, or because the recommendations are not realistic in terms of the classroom structure or curriculum. Ultimately, many children (and teachers) reach maximum frustration levels and give up. Problems that could be dealt with in the early stages, or even prevented, become magnified, and irreversible damage is done. (p. 51)

The picture that emerges is that traditional mental health services available for children in schools are generally limited to students in special education, and school psychologists (and other mental health staff such as social workers) are overwhelmed with demands associated with Public Law 94-142 (now IDEA) in providing these services. An additional concern is that the availability of special services to address children's emotional and behavioral difficulties decreases as children advance through grades, particularly at secondary levels. As such, services are especially limited for adolescents in regular education.

However, it is important to note that the National Association of School Psychologists (NASP) has strongly endorsed the employment of school psychologists for comprehensive mental health service delivery. Furthermore, in a growing number of school districts in the United States, school psychologists provide a wide range of services including mental health assessment, various therapeutic services, consultation with parents and school personnel, and program planning and evaluation (NASP, 1995). Notwithstanding these developments, there remains a critical need for the expansion of mental health services for youth in schools.

5. Models for Expanded School Mental Health Services

The foregoing discussion suggests a significant need for the provision of preventive (e.g., identification of incipient problems in early elementary youth) and more intensive mental health services (e.g., evaluations; individual, group, and family therapies) to youth in both special and regular education in schools. Across the nation, these "expanded" school mental health services are developing rapidly. In the following sections, I review service delivery models for mental health services for the whole school population.

5.1. Programs Developed by University Faculty

It is important to note that in the academic community, there has been long-standing recognition (e.g., Cowen, 1967) that schools represent a preferred site to provide mental health services to youth, and there are numerous examples of innovative programs that have been developed by university faculty for schools. Prominent examples include (1) the Primary Mental Health Project (PMHP; Cowen et al., 1975; Farie, Cowen, & Smith, 1986), a program that provides supportive services by non- and paraprofessional staff (with professionals in "quarterbacking" roles) to address early behavioral and educational problems in youth identified to be at risk; (2) the Success for All program (Slavin, Madden, Karweit, Dolan, & Wasik, 1992), which provides intensive training in reading skills, one-to-one tutoring, and a range of mental health and social services to impoverished youth in the early elementary grades; and (3) the School Development Model (SDM; Comer, 1988), which espouses a multifaced approach (e.g., creation of school governance teams, parent outreach, curriculum change, mental health prevention, and crisis intervention services) to improve the climate in schools for disadvantaged youth.

Each of these programs is characterized by availability to all students who are determined to be in need, and fairly widespread dissemination in schools throughout the United States. There are numerous other innovative university-based school interventions (e.g., Kellam & Rebok, 1992) that have had more limited dissemination.

5.2. Efforts to Restructure School Mental Health Services

Adelman and Taylor (1993) have recommended a model for allocation of limited school mental health resources. "Mental health specialists," or social workers, psychologists, psychiatrists, and other professionals trained to address emotional, behavioral, or social problems in youth serve as "catalytic agents" within schools. These specialists assist schools in developing programs that will have the broadest impact, given the school's resources. As such, mental health resource development is prioritized, followed by staff development, improving access to community resources, and providing supervision. Provision of direct service (i.e., clinical assessment and treatment) is viewed as a lower order priority "to be pursued as time allows" (p. 36).

Recently, Adelman (in press) has promoted a conceptual model for restructuring traditional school support services (e.g., school-based psychology, social work, guidance counseling, tutoring, and other special support programs) to "enable" (i.e., facilitate, empower) children's learning. A multisystemic approach is recommended, based on resource coordination and involving other elements such as classroom skill training; prevention, crisis intervention, and mental health treatment; supporting students in transition (e.g., from middle school to high school); increasing family involvement in education; and community outreach. The approach is designed to shift the view of school support services (including health and mental health services) from fragmentary and supplemental to foundational to effective learning. Beginning efforts to implement this model in the Los Angeles public schools are underway.

5.3. Collaborative Programs between Schools and Community Agencies

The primary mission of school systems is obviously education, and many do not have the funding or resources to develop comprehensive mental health programs. Community organizations involved in health, including hospitals, community mental health centers, and some universities have the mission and resources to provide these comprehensive services (Dryfoos, 1994). The more effective school-based mental health programs involve the merging of schools and community agencies, with the latter taking primary responsibility for the development and implementation of the services (Fleisch et al., 1990).

Dryfoos (1994) reviewed advantages of school-based programs developed and organized by outside community agencies versus the educational system. These include (1) increased capacity to assume responsibility for organization and delivery of services; (2) greater comprehensiveness of services; (3) knowledge of, and ability to facilitate funding for services (e.g., through Medicaid); (4) independent liability insurance, which relieves schools of a considerable financial burden and risk; and (5) better protection for students' confidentiality, leading to increased comfort by students in seeking services (since staff are viewed as being from an outside agency and not the school).

5.3.1. A Shifting Locus for Primary Mental Health Services from Community Clinics to Schools

These school–community partnerships are leading to progressive growth in expanded school mental health services. For example, in Baltimore in 1987, there were expanded mental health programs involving such partnerships in three schools. In 1994 there were programs in over 30 schools, and in 1995, programs were operating in over 60 schools. Similarly, in the state of Maryland in 1994, there were expanded mental health services in 90 schools; in 1995, this number increased dramatically, to 140. The most significant growth was for programs placed in elementary schools, with an increase from 39 to 78 schools in the 2 years. Only small increases were shown in middle schools (plus 6) and high schools (plus 1; Maryland Department of Health and Mental Hygiene [MDHMH], 1995). Such local growth is congruent with regional and national trends on school-based mental health services (Flaherty et al., in press).

These programs represent a shifting locus of primary mental health care for youth from community clinics to the schools. For example, our School Mental Health Program represents a partnership between the Department of Psychiatry of the University of Maryland School of Medicine and the Baltimore City Public Schools. In this program, therapists provide focused mental health evaluation; psychological and psychiatric consultation; individual, family, and group therapy; and referral of students for more intensive services (e.g., medication, inpatient treatment) in 14 Baltimore City schools (5 elementary, 5 middle, 3 high school, and 1 school for special education students with intellectual handicaps). We also provide a range of preventive and consultative services such as support groups for students in transition (e.g., from elementary to middle school), classroom presentations on mental health issues, and consultation with teachers and health staff regarding child behavioral and emotional problems. Programs sharing this focus of providing intensive and preventive mental health services to youth in schools are operational in many other cities (e.g., Dallas, Texas; Denver, Colorado; New Brunswick, New Jersey; New Haven, Connecticut; Minneapolis, Minnesota; New York City; Memphis, Tennessee), with formal reports on these programs beginning to be circulated at national level planning meetings.

There is a continuum of services developed through these school–community agency partnerships, from augmenting services of existing school mental health staff, to "outstationing" of a mental health provider from a community clinic to a school for a small number of hours per week, to programs that essentially become school-based mental health centers. This latter concept is exemplified by programs in New Brunswick, New Jersey and Orange County, California, in which the majority of mental health services for youth has been essentially shifted away from community sites and into the schools (Dryfoos, 1994). It is important to emphasize that these school–community partnerships to develop mental health services do not seek to supplant those that already exist (e.g., services provided by school psychologists and social workers). Rather, the focus is on establishing collaborative relationships between schools and community agencies to expand the range of school-based mental health services. In fact, school psychologists and social workers can play an instrumental role in ensuring that these expanded services are appropriately developed and well coordinated (cf. NASP, 1995).

5.3.2. Mental Health Services Provided through School-Based Health Centers

A major factor in the development of expanded mental health services for youth in schools has been the growth of school-based health centers (SBHCs). This movement began in relation to general concerns about the health of adolescents, and particular concerns regarding psychological and educational risks associated with adolescent pregnancy and parenting (Dryfoos, 1988). By 1987, there were approximately 150 SBHCs operating in junior and senior high schools throughout the country (Dryfoos, 1988). In 1990, Hyche-Williams and Waszak reported that there were 178 SBHCs operating in junior and senior high schools in 32 states. In 1993, the Center for Population Options reported over 500 SBHCs. In the most recent survey, Schlitt, Rickett, Montgomery, and Lear (1994) reported 607 SBHCs located in 41 states and in the District of Columbia. The report indicated that 46% of the SBHCs were placed in high schools, 28% in elementary schools, 16% in middle schools, and 10% in "other" schools. SBHCs are located primarily in urban, medically underserved areas, but are increasingly being developed in rural and suburban areas (Juszczak, Fisher, Lear, & Friedman, 1995).

Mental health services offered in SBHCs occur in the context of a range of other primary-care health services including medical screening and physical examinations on site, treatment for accidents and minor illnesses, family planning services, immunizations, and a range of health education programs. Commonly, staff in SBHCs include a medical assistant, nurse practitioner or physician assistant, and a mental health professional (usually a master's level social worker) to address the psychosocial needs of the students. SBHCs are almost always run by outside community agencies, such as local health departments. The model SBHC "offers age-appropriate, comprehensive physical and mental health services through a multidisciplinary team of health professionals" (Juszcak et al., 1995, p. 101).

Lear, Gleicher, St. Germaine, and Porter (1991) reported on a project funded by the Robert Wood Johnson Foundation, which assisted in the development of 23 SBHCs in 11 states. Descriptive analyses of the programs indicated that mental health concerns were the second most frequent reason for visits to the health center (21% of visits) behind acute illness or accidents (26% of visits). In addition, the report emphasized awareness of all staff in the centers of the critically important role psychosocial issues have on adolescent health concerns. Dryfoos (1994) noted that providers in SBHCs often refer to mental health counseling as their greatest unmet need. She quoted one provider: "As soon as we open our doors, kids walk past the counselor's office, past the school nurse, past the principal, and come into our clinic to tell us that they have been sexually abused or that their parents are drug users" (p. 52). Across SBHCs, Dryfoos characterized the demand for mental health services as "overwhelming."

Baltimore currently contains 16 SBHCs. It is notable that in this city, these SBHCs were the first sites for expanded school mental health services. Since then, mental health services have been added to schools without health centers, based in large part on lessons learned from the SBHCs. As such, school-based health centers can serve as demonstration sites for expanded mental health services in cities and localities. As the health centers gain experience in the provision of mental health services, their expertise can be shared to promote the development of these services in other schools.

Although there has been growth in mental health services offered through SBHCs, gaps remain. In 1994, Advocates for Youth (formerly the Center for Population Options) reported on a survey of 231 school-based and school-linked (i.e., located off school grounds, but involving collaborative relationships between community health agencies and specific schools) health centers on their 1992–1993 activities and operations. Over 85% of centers offered mental health services to address problems including substance abuse, depression, anger, sexual abuse, and dysfunctional family systems. Approximately 49% of programs offered group counseling; the most common topics were children of substance abusers (25%), self-esteem enhancement (20%), general support (16%), and coping with sexual abuse (15%). Notably, only 36% of programs providing mental health services used mental health professionals in the provision of these services; "remaining respondents used various other staff to fulfill the counseling tasks" (p. 24).

5.3.3. A Growing Movement to Institutionalize School-Based Health and Mental Health Services

As is increasingly evident, expanded mental health services are being developed in schools as part of a broader movement to bring comprehensive health services to youth in schools. Three organizations have played an integral role in this rapidly developing movement:

1. Advocates for Youth (AFY; formerly the Center for Population Options) is a national organization that aims to improve decisions by youth about sexuality. AFY has conducted annual surveys on school health programs and offers a range of technical assistance services.
2. Making the Grade, an organization sponsored by the Robert Wood Johnson Foundation, aims to develop partnerships between states and communities to expand and improve school-based health services.
3. The School Health Policy Initiative (SHPI) of Columbia University has conducted a series of national work group meetings to analyze and make policy recommendations on issues critical to the development of school health services.

These three organizations, along with professional groups such as the American School Health Association (ASHA) and federal agencies such as the Health Resources and Services Administration (HRSA) and the Centers for Disease Control (CDC) played a critical role in the development of the National Assembly on School-Based Health Care (NASBHC).

The NASBHC is a new organization (inaugural meeting in June 1995) developed in response to the increasing growth of school-based health centers and the absence of a large coordinating body. It aims to improve coordination of research, technical assistance, and advocacy for school-based health care and to provide a membership organization for school health providers, planners, and supporters.

The newly formed Psychosocial Services Section of NASBHC includes providers and planners of mental health services in SBHCs. This group has begun efforts to identify a list of school mental health programs, along with descriptions of programs and presenting problems of students to begin to document the constellation of services and problems addressed by expanded school mental health services.

5.3.4. Full-Service Schools

Comprehensive mental health services would be one component of what Dryfoos (1994) refers to as "full-service schools." She wrote:

> The vision of the full-service school puts the best of school reform together with all other services that children, youth, and their families need, most of which can be located in a school building. The educational mandate places responsibility on the school system to reorganize and innovate. The charge to community agencies is to bring into the school: health, mental health, employment services, child care, parent education, case management, recreation, cultural events, community policing, and whatever else may fit into the picture. The result is a new kind of "seamless" institution, a community-oriented school with a joint governance structure that allows maximum responsiveness to the community, as well as accessibility and continuity for those most in need of services. (p. 12)

Dryfoos's (1994) vision for schools to become "hubs" in communities for education, health, mental health, social, and vocational services is stirring enthusiastic discussion around the country. However, very few schools in the United States are approximating this vision (San Diego's New Beginnings Program and Hanshaw Middle School in Modesto, California are exceptions). Instead, there is wide variability, with some schools having no supportive services, others having singular and isolated programs, and still others having multiple service components with multiple agency involvement (Dryfoos, 1994).

As reviewed in the previous sections, expanded school mental health services based on partnerships between school and community agencies offer the best opportunity for institutionalizing these services. Although some of the earlier mentioned university-based programs have produced impressive results (e.g., Success for All; Slavin et al., 1992), these programs are unlikely to become institutionalized on a *national* level. Such university-based programs are usually characterized by adequate research methodology but a failure to extent implementation across heterogenous populations, particularly to address the array of problems of disadvantaged youth (Shoenwald, Henggeler, Pickrel, & Cunningham, in press). In contrast, expanded mental health services provided in the contexts of SBHCs are developing rapidly, with over 600 programs in almost every state of the United States (Schlitt et al., 1994). In essence, the development of SBHCs and their associated services represents a significant national movement to bring health and mental health services to youth "where they are." This movement offers vast clinical, program development, and research opportunities for mental health professionals. In the context of this movement, critical issues attendant to these developments are reviewed next.

6. Broad Critical Issues

6.1. Limited Knowledge of Existing Programs

We conducted a recent literature review (Flaherty et al., in press) on the development of school-based mental health services. This review highlighted that in spite of significant growth, little information on mental health services associated with school health services has been published or disseminated. Considerable activity has occurred to establish school mental health services nationwide, but there are few methods to capture this activity. Thus, planners and analysts of these services must rely on information provided by professional groups such as Advocates for Youth and Making the Grade. The movement to provide expanded school mental health services is so new that we do not yet know where the services are, let alone information in ideal patterns of staffing or service delivery models. Fortunately, efforts are underway through NASBHC to more systematically document the status of school-based mental health services nationwide. These assessments will serve as the preliminary step in planning to develop and improve expanded school mental health services.

6.2. Funding Issues

Funding issues are obviously critical to the development of expanded school mental health services. In Baltimore, these services are funded through at least five different mechanisms. There is considerable overlap in funding sources, and many of the local streams have state or federal support underpinning them. While enabling mental health services in more schools, this mixed funding pattern creates administrative problems related to different contractual and reporting requirements for each of the funding streams (Flaherty et al., in press).

Limited cost-efficiency data that are available suggest costs of around $8,000 per pupil per year for children receiving special education services under the classification "severely emotionally disturbed" (Butler, 1988). Clearly, mental health services provided through school health centers cost much less than this amount, and the diversion of children from special education to these health services is viewed as cost saving by special education administrators. Furthermore, we have seen a decrease in referrals for special education services by about one-third after clinical therapists have been placed in schools (Flaherty et al., in press). Data on cost savings to educational systems can be used by school health centers to lobby communities for funds for the development and/or expansion of mental health services.

Managed care is having a very significant impact on funding for school-based health and mental health services. For example, in Maryland, legislation has passed indicating that students in Medicaid must have a primary, coordinating medical provider. In order for services to be reimbursed, this provider (individual physician or HMO) must authorize the service, and programs are encountering significant problems in obtaining such authorization.

Perhaps more significantly, in Baltimore and other localities, "aggressive strategies" are in place to enroll students with Medicaid in managed care companies (School Health Policy Initiative [SHPI], 1993). Almost uniformly, these companies have been unwilling to authorize school-based mental health services. As more and more students are enrolled in these companies, funding for school-based mental health services can be expected to decrease significantly.

To address these problems, SHPI and other groups have recommended that school health administrators form relationships with managed care companies. This is beginning to occur, and some managed care companies are even funding SBHCs (Rosenthal & Hinman, 1995). Other strategies being discussed to fund school-based health and mental health services include using surplus funds from adult-focused community mental health activities, and developing state financial support for services through excise taxes (Schlitt et al., 1994).

Detailed discussion of funding issues is beyond the scope of this chapter. Needless to say, considerable activity will be needed in this area to ensure that school health and mental health services do, in fact, become institutionalized. In addition, efforts are needed at state and national levels to advocate for support of school mental health services. Unfortunately, children's mental health groups have not had the financial and political resources to significantly impact policymakers in the Administration and Congress (Theut & Bailey, 1994).

6.3. Poor Planning of Services

Although most school-based health and mental health programs are located in lower income, urban areas, services are usually not added based on any systematic strategy (e.g., the percentage of students receiving reduced/free lunches; Dryfoos, 1994). Adelman and Taylor (1993) conducted a survey of all existing mental health programs in a Los Angeles school district. In analyzing 56 programs that targeted student adjustment problems, the most striking issue was that programs seemed to be developed in a "piecemeal" fashion, with no overall plan, and "a great deal of uncoordinated activity" (p. 33). Services were developed at some schools but not at others with seemingly equal need. This is congruent with experiences in Baltimore, where schools appear to obtain mental health programs based on the interest of the principal versus documentation of relative need (some schools with nearly 2,000 students have no expanded mental health services, whereas schools as small as 350 contain them).

A related issue is the control principals and school administrators typically have over services offered in their building. In many school districts, the prevailing view is that education is the primary if not only function, with mental health services being viewed as beyond the reach and scope of an educational institution. One strategy to promote acceptance of mental health services by school administrators is to help them determine how these services can enhance their educational mission (Dryfoos, 1994). However, even with intensive and persuasive efforts, some school administrators continue to be resistant to expanded mental health services in their schools. This means that even with careful planning for allocation of school mental health resources, some of the more needy schools (e.g., as determined by income, unemployment, and crime statistics) will go without mental health services.

6.4. Poor Integration of School and Community Services

A serious problem is the failure of most school-based health and mental health services to be integrated with other services in the local community. Many issues are relevant here. For example, applied research programs are often developed and implemented by university faculty who fail to seek input from community representatives on the intervention. Similarly, health and mental health services are started with little, if any, input from community members. Even when services are developed with community involvement, they are often not effectively integrated into the array of other community resources and programs (Flaherty et al., in press).

Efforts to increase mental health services available to youth in schools are occurring in a broader context of reform of children's mental health services (e.g., the CASSP). These reform efforts seek to change organizational and financial structures to reduce barriers to services, improve coordination between systems, and provide a range of services tailored to the specific needs of children (Henggeler, 1994).

Recently, considerable attention has been paid to developing comprehensive and multiple system approaches to address the needs of youth with severe emotional and behavioral difficulties. For example, multisystemic therapy (MST; Henggeler, Schoenwald, Pickrel, Rowland, & Santos, 1994) is a comprehensive treatment approach involving intervention at individual, family, school, and community levels that has been shown to be effective for delinquent youth (Henggeler, Melton, & Smith, 1992). More recent efforts have extended the model to problems of adolescent substance abuse and severe emotional disturbance, and preliminary findings are encouraging (Henggeler et al., 1994).

In general, the public mental health system has identified as its top priority individuals with severe disorders (Duchnowski & Friedman, 1990), and approaches such as MST (Henggeler et al., 1994) appear to be the most effective for youth with severe disorders. However, it is important to not let attention to the needs of severely disturbed youth preclude the development of preventive programs for youth without, or with incipient, disturbances. Analyzing child health and mental health systems, Weissberg, Caplan, and Harwood (1991) noted that the preponderance of resources were directed at the most ill children and strongly argued for more attention to primary prevention efforts that are system or group oriented and directed toward healthy children.

Analyses are needed that consider the continuum of mental health services for youth from primary to secondary to tertiary preventive activities, and where and in what fashion to provide services at various points on this continuum (see Winett & Anderson, 1994). One plausible schema is reviewed in Table 1. In this scheme, primary, secondary, and some tertiary prevention activities are provided in schools. For example, services in schools would include educational activities on mental health issues; screening of students for emotional and behavioral problems; providing support groups for students under stress (e.g., during educational transitions, to address exposure to violence); assisting in the development of schoolwide programs to address pressing concerns (e.g., conflict mediation training); and individual, group, and family therapy services for

TABLE 1
Schema for Organizing Preventive Child Mental Health Programs

	Prevention continuum		
	Primary	Secondary	Tertiary
School-based programs	▬▬▬▬▬▬	▬▬▬▬▬▬	▬▬▬▬▬▬
Mental health centers		▬▬▬▬▬▬	▬▬▬▬▬▬
Multisystemic programs			▬▬▬▬▬▬

Note. Primary preventive efforts target populations at risk, before the development of the problem of concern; secondary preventive efforts target individuals showing early manifestation of the problem; and tertiary preventive efforts aim to minimize negative sequelae of established disorders (Caplan, 1964).

youth with emotional and behavioral disturbances. These services would be developed to be complementary to services provided by school psychologists and social workers (or, in some communities, would actually be provided by school psychologists and social workers). Generally reflective of their current functions, community mental health centers would provide secondary and tertiary preventive services, such as therapy services for more severely disturbed youth, psychopharmacological assessment and treatment, and referral for more intensive services such as inpatient treatment. Multisystemic programs (as in MST) would provide exclusively tertiary preventive services for youth who meet some cutoff for severity of disturbance (e.g., based on presenting diagnoses, chronicity of disorder). We are using this scheme at the University of Maryland in planning for children's mental health services and have found it useful in attempting to create a true continuum of services.

Recently, the Section on Clinical Child Psychology of the Division of Clinical Psychology of the American Psychological Association (APA) reported on a task force on Innovative Models of Mental Health Services for Children, Adolescents, and Their Families. In this report, Duchnowski (1994) reviewed innovative models of service delivery in education. However, this review was restricted to services available to students in special education, because "very few schools have services for children with serious mental health needs that are part of the regular education program" (p. 13). Thereafter, the report made almost no reference to services available to students in regular education. Reports such as this help to embed the concept that mental health services in schools are primarily for students in special education. For schools to play a significant role in addressing the continuum of children's mental health needs (as mentioned), a more expansive view of the potential for mental health services within them is needed.

6.5. Limited Evaluation of School Mental Health Services

Evaluation of school-based mental health services has been quite limited, with most of these efforts at the descriptive level. For example, the U.S. Department of Health and Human Services (1994) recently reported findings from an evaluation of seven SBHCs in rural and urban areas of the United States. The report highlighted the limited access to health and mental health resources for many of the students, in spite of the high levels of health-related problems found in their communities (e.g., teenage pregnancy, infant mortality, family and community violence, child abuse and neglect). Substance abuse and mental health problems were reported to be particularly prevalent. Importantly, the report underscored the general absence of program outcome data; although there were selected reports of positive impact of the SBHCs (e.g., in reducing teenage pregnancies and school absences), these findings were based on uncontrolled evaluation designs.

Analyzing the state of affairs for assessment of outcomes of school health and mental health services, Dryfoos (1994) commented that "the limitations of published evaluations of the impact of school-based services programs on health and educational outcomes are undeniable" (p. 133). Similarly, Barnett, Niebuhr, Baldwin, and Levine (1992) provided this cautionary note in discussing school-based mental health services: "Outcomes often have been poorly documented because of the public demand for quick remedies. As a result, these programs consume time and energy of school staff without producing convincing results" (p. 246). Adelman and Taylor (1993) characterized evaluations of school mental health services as limited and narrowly focused, and called attention to the negligible research on cost-effectiveness of these services, as well as their possible iatrogenic effects.

Prout and DeMartino (1986) conducted a meta-analysis of school-based psychotherapy programs. Thirty-three studies involving some type of school-based counseling services were evaluted. Results suggested that group therapies were more effective than individual approaches, behavioral approaches were more effective than others, and treatment targets most responsive to intervention were observable behaviors and problem-solving abilities. However, many of the studies cited in this review were not controlled, and a wide number of approaches were reported by relatively few studies, constraining the power of statistical analyses.

Since this review, we identified only two studies involving controlled assessment of the impact of *ongoing* school mental health services (i.e., vs.

those associated with a special program). Lavoritano and Segal (1992) assessed school counseling services provided by master's level school counselors to 141 students (aged 8 to 13) in private schools in Philadelphia and the surrounding county. A comparison of pre- and posttreatment responses on a measure of self-perceived competency revealed that students evidenced gains in scholastic self-perception only, and showed a small *decline* in global self-worth. In a recently completed study, we (Weist, Paskewitz, Warner, & Flaherty, 1996) assessed the treatment outcome of mental health services for ninth graders enrolled in a school-based health clinic in Baltimore. Compared to students receiving no mental health treatment ($n = 34$), treated students ($n = 39$) showed improvements in self-concept and decreased depression scores following the receipt of individual and/or group therapy services.

Numerous issues constrain the ability to track the impact of school-based mental health services in sophisticated fashion. These include pragmatic difficulties of randomly assigning children to treatment versus control conditions; high mobility of students across schools, particularly in urban areas; and difficulty in establishing causes for measured outcomes due to the coexistence of other programs and educational reform efforts (Dolan, 1992).

There is recognition of the need for standardization in descriptive statistics for school-based health programs. Many programs have systems in place to record presenting problems of students and the types of services rendered. Additionally, computerized systems of data collection have been implemented across school health sites in different states such as "School Health Care—On Line!!!" by David Kaplan (see Dryfoos, 1994). However, such systems have generally not been established for mental health services. Programs that have systems in place to describe mental health problems and services are inadequate (e.g., use of idiosyncratic methods to record presenting problems of students). Other mental health programs have no systems in place to track students presenting problems or provided services.

There is a significant need to implement standard measures of psychosocial factors and emotional/behavioral difficulties for students who present for school mental health services. Such efforts are beginning to occur in some school-based programs. For example, clinicians in 12 schools of the University of Maryland School Mental Health Program collected standard measures of life stress, violence exposure, family support, self-concept, and emotional/behavioral functioning for youth aged 11 to 18 who presented for services. Preliminary analyses of these data indicated high levels of violence exposure for referred youth, and expected associations between life stress, violence exposure, and emotional/behavioral problems (Weist, Myers, & Baker, 1995).

Fortunately, developments to organize school health and mental health providers are occurring rapidly. As mentioned, the NASBHC and its Psychosocial Services Section are in the process of planning a survey of mental health service needs and programs for mental health providers from across the country. The Maternal and Child Health Bureau (MCHB) of the Health Resources and Services Administration has funded two national technical assistance and training centers to provide support to school-based health programs in developing and expanding mental health services. These centers, located at the University of Maryland at Baltimore and the University of California at Los Angeles, should be well established in mid-1996.

6.6. Need for Specialty Training in School-Based Mental Health

Juszczak, Fisher, Lear, and Friedman (1995) conducted a survey of training in school health for allied health disciplines in 9 SBHCs funded by the Robert Wood Johnson Foundation. Around half of the programs included traineeships for graduate students in social work, psychology, or psychiatry. Program directors noted generally that trainees were well accepted by students, and the presence of trainees assisted the centers in providing services to more students. The study highlighted other advantages to such training programs, including experience in "front line" clinical services, hands-on exposure to the "complexities" of practicing in a SBHC, expanding the range of offered services, and decreasing feelings of isolation among school health staff.

Graduate training programs for disciplines of clinical psychology, social work, psychiatry, and psychiatric nursing generally do not include systematic preparation for trainees to work in schools as primary clinical sites. As the movement to provide expanded mental health services to youth in schools grows, there will be an increasing need for graduate-level training programs in these related disciplines to prepare clinicians for work in the school setting. The role of school psychologists in providing these expanded mental health services also needs analysis. Issues confronted by mental health professionals working in schools are next reviewed.

7.   Critical Issues Confronting School-Based Clinicians

7.1.   Differences between Services in Schools and Community Clinics

In community mental health centers, a common scenario is for seven or eight children to be scheduled per day for each therapist, and for three to five 50-minute sessions to be actually held. Mental health services usually have a discrete beginning and end, and, related to pressures associated with managed care, services are often limited to six or less sessions. Children require clear diagnoses to be seen, and if they do not present clear diagnoses, they are either "creatively" fit into a diagnostic category or not seen. After termination, the therapist is unlikely to see the child again. Although this may reflect a stereotyping of children's out-patient mental health services, it begins to capture the reality of such services for most therapists.

Mental health services that are provided in schools are often dramatically different from the aforementioned picture of community mental health centers. In most school-based programs, children do not require diagnoses to be seen. Following intake sessions, which may run 50 minutes, students are seen in meaningful therapeutic encounters for briefer periods of time, such as 30 or even 15 minutes. Many of these sessions are scheduled, but others are impromptu, with students stopping in for a brief problem-solving session or to share some news with the therapist. Given that the therapist is where the children are, there is no reason for down time in his or her schedule; if one student does not show for an appointment, usually another one can be quickly found. The school therapist has contact with students not only in the therapy office, but in the hallway, at schoolwide events (e.g., assemblies), athletic games, in the cafeteria, and so on. Given these environmental factors, it is not uncommon for school-based therapists to see 10–12 children in a 7-hour day.

Unlike services provided in community mental health centers, contact with students does not have to end, with some relationships with students lasting from the 6th through 8th, or 9th through 12th grades (and sometimes longer). In such long-term relationships, at times clinicians are providing traditionally conceived therapy services, but at other times (e.g., when there are no clear presenting problems), the therapist becomes more of a mentor to the student (e.g., providing encouragement and practical support). This transitioning back and forth from the role of therapist to mentor is neither possible, nor feasible, in community mental health clinics (or in private practice).

7.2. Intensive Clinical and Administrative Demands

Related to limited funding, many school-based mental health programs are staffed by one (usually master's level) clinician. Funds for mental health services are often limited to salary support, with many funding agencies not paying for supervision or administration of the program. Generally, salary support is inadequate, creating problems in recruitment of skilled and, especially, experienced therapists. Therapists are commonly faced with intensive clinical demands associated with large caseloads and very high mental health encounters. In our program, full-time therapists usually see more than 100 children a year, maintain active caseloads of 40 or more youth, have over 40 clinical contacts (assessment and treatment sessions) per week, and over 800 clinical contacts in an academic year. In addition to clinical services, there are obvious paper-work demands, case management activities, and actions that need to be taken to arrange for contacts with students (e.g., scheduling and finding them). Furthermore, related to demands of managed care and the absence of administrative support, clinicians are forced to contact physicians to gain authorization to see youth. This can be a highly time-consuming and frustrating process.

A related issue is that mental health providers are employees of agencies outside of the educational system. As such, programs commonly need to beg and barter for office space, telephones, and so forth. Clinicians are often moved from one inadequate office space to the next and usually either do not have a phone, or have to share one with numerous other health and/or educational staff.

Low salaries, isolation, absence of support, intensive clinical, case management and administrative demands; poor office space; and limited telephone access combine to make school-based mental health services highly stressful. Clinicians are very susceptible to burnout, and turnover in these positions tends to be fairly high.

7.3. Identifying Students in Need

A challenge for school-based clinicians is developing mechanisms to receive appropriate referrals. Teachers are likely to refer children for mental health services for externalizing behaviors such as talking out of turn, being out of their seats, noncompliance, and disruptiveness (Conoley & Conoley, 1991). In addition, there is a view among school psychologists that teachers are often not requesting assistance to develop interventions when making referrals for mental health services. Rather, the "desired intervention" is removal of the child from the classroom to be placed in special education services (Johnston, 1990).

Related to this, internalizing problems such as depression, anxiety, and social withdrawal do not consistently lead to referral for services by educational staff (Ritter, 1989). However, in programs that operate in conjunction with SBHCs, our experience has been that medical staff (e.g., nurse practitioners) regularly screen youth for depression, suicidal ideation, anxiety, and trauma symptoms, facilitating referral of youth with internalizing problems for mental health services (Flaherty et al., in press). Many SBHCs incorporate formal screening measures for these problems.

Regardless of the school setting (i.e., containing an SBHC or not), mental health staff usually need to conduct educational activities with other staff in the school to assist them in recognizing emotional/behavioral problems in youth and referring them for services.

7.4. Getting Students to Use School Mental Health Services

Lear et al. (1991) documented difficulties in some school health centers in getting students to use medical services. Similarly, many youngsters in need do not utilize mental health services offered through the health center. For example, in a recent study (Weist, Proescher, Freedman, Paskewitz, & Flaherty, 1995), we found that students who used a school-based health center intensively were more likely to report significant emotional distress. However, less than one-third of these distressed students were actually receiving mental health services. This finding highlights the fact that medical staff should consider intensive health center use as a marker of potential emotional/behavioral difficulties, and that staff should attempt to connect intensive users to mental health staff. We also found that students rated as socially withdrawn by their peers were much less likely to seek out the health center than more outgoing youth, pointing to the need for outreach efforts to offer mental health services to such youth.

In a survey of 471 high school juniors and seniors from Los Angeles on their use of school-based mental health services, Barker and Adelman (1994) found "low levels of utilization despite apparently wide spread need." The authors suggested that providing accessible mental health services in schools is "a necessary but insufficient condition for increasing the likelihood that people will seek out professional help when they need it" (p. 261).

7.5. Integrating the Clinician into the School

School health programs implementing mental health services confront obstacles such as poor knowledge of these services and resistance or unwillingness by staff to cooperate with the new clinician. School health staff are often viewed as "outsiders" by staff hired by the Department of Education. This is particularly true for mental health staff. Generally, in the first year of mental health services, considerable efforts are needed by the clinician to meet and form alliances with school staff, and practically demonstrate the benefit of his or her services with a few salient clinical successes.

A related issue is that teachers and school personnel often form "high hopes" after referring a child for mental health services. Despite these high hopes, teachers have reported feelings of disappointment in their relationships with mental health professionals. Problems attributed to mental health staff include failing to seek teacher input, providing "already known" and simplistic formulations of children, making excessively cumbersome or vague recommendations for classroom interventions, and not reporting back to teachers on the progress of the student (Conoley & Conoley, 1991; Lusterman, 1985; Pryswansky, 1989).

Particularly in middle schools and high schools, mental health practitioners will be confronted with stigma and misconceptions about their services by students and faculty. Our experience has been that students generally do not understand the title *psychologist*, associating it with "crazy people." Similarly, the terms *therapist* and *clinician* generally do not have meaning for them. As a result, psychologists in our program refer to themselves as *counselors*, which seems to avoid the pejorative connotation of *psychologist* and is a term that most students understand and accept. However, use of this title creates some problems in distinguishing the role of the school-based clinician from guidance counselors, who also use this title.

7.6. Privacy and Confidentiality Issues

Most middle school and high school students expect their visits to the mental health provider to be kept private, and school clinicians generally do all they can to respect students' desires for such privacy. However, unique confidentiality problems arise in the school setting. There are many opportunities for students to be associated with mental health staff, which can lead to problems with other students (e.g., teasing about "being crazy"). School-based clinicians should attempt to be sensitive to these concerns by arranging for the student to receive services as privately as possible, for example, sending passes for students to attend mental health sessions without providers specified, being careful about talking to treated students in front of other students (and allowing some of them to walk 10 feet behind on the way to the therapy office!).

Most school mental health programs keep records separate from the educational record and the health records in programs having on-site health services. However, there are often requests from teachers and other school staff (including health providers) for information on students who are receiving mental health services. Standards vary across programs, with some strictly not releasing any information to anyone without a signed release of information form from the student and his or her parents, and other programs adhering to a "looser" policy. One approach that is fairly common is for mental health staff to release process information (e.g., whether a student is attending sessions), but not content information, to select staff designated by the student as important. Release of more than process information to these staff would require more formal permission from the student and his or her parents.

7.7. Issues of Race and Cultural Sensitivity

As reviewed earlier, expanded school mental health services are more likely to be found in urban, economically deprived areas, in which Caucasians are a racial minority. However, programs often have difficulty in recruiting staff of the predominant racial/cultural background of their district, or there is such heterogeneity in racial/cultural backgrounds that it would be difficult for staff to be reflective of the community. Although progress is this area has been made, a common scenario remains for a Caucasian therapist to be placed in a school that is primarily African-American. Most programs learn that issues of racial differences are relatively minor, provided that school-based clinicians are nonprejudiced, demonstrate that they truly care about their work, and are knowledgeable and sensitive about issues of cultural diversity (see Lee, 1995; Sue & Zane, 1987). However, even given these qualities, a reality is that a relatively small proportion of students and staff will avoid the clinician because of his or her race. This reality points to the need for the clinician to directly address issues of racial awareness in interactions with students and teachers, but also to accept an unfortunate limit to the boundaries of his or her work.

7.8. Coordinating Mental Health Services within Schools

As reviewed by Adelman and Taylor (1993) and Flaherty et al. (in press), mental health services within schools are often not coordinated with each other. This leads to duplication of some services (e.g., one student seeing multiple providers) and gaps in others (e.g., the absence of substance-abuse services). Commenting on services provided in a Los Angeles school district Adelman (in press) wrote, "The ad hoc way in which programs were developed was reflected in the fragmented, piecemeal function in which they operated."

As noted earlier, there are a number of disciplines that may be involved in providing mental health services to students. In most school districts (with many exceptions) assessment-oriented mental health services are provided by social workers and school psychologists to students in special education. Most districts also contain guidance counselors in middle and high schools who provide academic and career guidance, as well as some counseling for personal issues. However, most guidance counselors have responsibility for hundreds of students, which severely limits their accessibility. Also, there is variability in training background, with some guidance counselors not trained to address complex psychosocial issues (Dryfoos, 1994).

"Clinical" staff brought in to provide more intensive services (including treatment) to the whole school population must integrate their services with services provided by "traditional" mental health staff as mentioned earlier. Most commonly, these clinical staff are licensed social workers and clinical psychologists, but staff from other disciplines such as psychiatry, counseling psychology, marriage and family therapy, psychiatric nursing, and addictions counseling may be involved in the provision of expanded mental health services in a school.

There is considerable variability in mental health staffing across schools. Some may have essentially no mental health staff, some have only guidance counselors, and others have a range of traditional and clinical staff. Regardless of how limited or comprehensive mental health services in a school area, it is important for mental health staff to work closely together. In one high school in our program, the "Mental Health Team" comprises staff from the disciplines of clinical psychology, school psychology, school social work, and guidance counseling, who work closely together to avoid duplication in services, plan for difficult issues (e.g., how to handle crisis), and initiate schoolwide interventions to address pressing problems. In the past year, this team has initiated a program to promote sexual responsibility (and abstinence) for high school students, implemented a crisis-intervention plan, initiated a peer counseling program, and conducted a range of classroom presentations, assemblies, and group therapies aimed at preventing and coping with violence. Teachers have expressed appreciation for these activities and have requested the development of support groups for them to assist in stress management. These efforts have served to improve the integration of mental health staff into the school, and have also contributed to global positive impacts in the school climate.

It is important for staff from various disciplines to work together collegially, without preconceived perceptions of superiority of one discipline over another (referred to as "professional arrogance" by Conoley and Conoley, 1991). For example, clinical psychologists, psychiatrists, and social workers need to be careful to not disparage the abilities of other disciplines such as school psychology and guidance counseling to provide intensive services such as individual therapy for troubled students. Rather, discussions should be held with representatives from these disciplines in which respective roles are defined. Such discussions usually lead to deference by staff such as guidance counselors to clinical staff when faced with issues such as suicidal ideation in students.

Negotiating "turf" issues is also a challenge (Dryfoos, 1994). For example, in Baltimore, a common scenario has been that outside clinical therapists are placed in schools to provide more intensive services including individual, group, and family therapy. School social workers and psychologists are tired down with administrative and assessment tasks, primarily with students in special education, and may resent the relative freedom of the clinical therapist, as well as his or her opportunity to provide treatment services. In these situations, considerable efforts are needed by the new clinical therapist to establish relationships with existing school staff, and to mutually plan for the expansion of mental health services (see Conoley & Conoley, 1991).

7.9. Involving Families in School Mental Health Services

Lack of meaningful involvement of families has been a complex issue for school-based programs. In many cases, expanded health and mental health services are placed in schools in economically disadvantaged areas. Families in the surrounding area typically must contend with a range of stressors associated with economic hardship, nonoptimal living conditions, crime, and so on. In the context of these stressors, it is often difficult for families to come to the school to work with health and mental health providers in treatment of their children. A frequent lament of health and mental health practitioners concerns the serious difficulties encountered in involving families in services, resulting in minimal or absent involvement by most families.

Difficulties in involving families are not limited to school health and mental health services. Education staff often have very limited relationships with families, with communication limited to report cards and telephone calls around specific problems. Most schools do not have established methods for schools and parents to systematically share information, and parents generally play a very limited role in educational decision making for their child. This lack of information flow can contribute to an adversarial quality between parents and school staff (Conoley & Conoley, 1991). Efforts to involve parents as collaborators with school staff can assist with this problem. For example, some school systems have involved parents in decision making regarding school social services, outreach efforts into the community, and advocacy efforts for students (Dryfoos, 1994).

With regard to school health and mental services, there are differences in involving families of elementary versus high school aged youth (Dryfoos, 1994). Generally, involving families in mental health services is more necessary and easier with younger youth (e.g., parents are more likely to bring them to, and pick them up from, school). Mental health efforts with adolescents are often based on their choice to initiate services, and in some cases, a goal is to foster independence from a dysfunctional family. As such, services can be provided relatively independent of family involvement, which is much more difficult in traditional community settings (e.g., community mental health centers).

8.   Concluding Comments

Although mental health services have been available in schools for more than four decades (Conoley & Conoley, 1991), it is only recently that a full range of services (from primary to tertiary preventive) have become available to youth in special *and regular* education in primary and secondary schools throughout the country. For the most part, these expanded school mental health services have resulted from partnerships between schools and community agencies, with primary responsibilty for the services taken by the latter. Exemplifying these partnerships are SBHCs, which are developing rapidly across the country, based on widespread support for the concept of schools as sites for primary health care for youth. Mental health services are developing lock step with SBHCs, with health staff identifying mental health problems as "overwhelming" and treatment services for them as their "greatest need." In essence, there is a significant national movement under way to "institutionalize" school health and mental health services, as provided by local community agencies working in schools. However, much activity related to this movement has not been published, and there is a prevailing view that mental health services in schools are assessment oriented and limited to students in special education. In reality, if trends continue, primary mental health care will begin to shift from community mental health centers and private offices to the schools, offering vast opportunities for those who are interested in improving mental health services for children. This review has attempted to capture this movement, its opportunities, and its limitations.

ACKNOWLEDGMENTS

Appreciation is extended to Lois Flaherty and Beth Warner for ideas generated in an earlier paper and to Nicole Dorsey for assistance in identifying and reviewing the extant literature.

This research is supported in part by Project #MCJ24SH02-01-0 from the Maternal and Child Health Bureau (Title V, Social Security Act), Health Resources and Services Administration, Department of Health and Human Services.

9. References

Abel, R. R., & Burke, J. P. (1985). Perceptions of school psychology services from a staff perspective. *Journal of School Psychology, 23,* 121–131.

Adelman, H. S. (in press). Restructuring education support services: Toward the concept of an enabling component. *American School Health Association Monograph.*

Adelman, H. S., & Taylor, L. (1991). Early school adjustment problems: Some perspectives and a project report. *American Journal of Orthopsychiatry, 61,* 468–474.

Adelman, H. S., & Taylor, L. (1993). School-based mental health: Toward a comprehensive approach. *Journal of Mental Health Administration, 20,* 32–45.

Advocates for Youth. (1994). Unpublished survey of school-based and school-linked health services. Washington, DC: Author.

Alexander, C. S., & Klassen, A. C. (1988). Drug use and illnesses among eighth grade students in rural schools. *Public Health Reports, 103,* 394–399.

Barker, L. A., & Adelman, H. S. (1994). Mental health and help-seeking among ethnic minority adolescents. *Journal of Adolescence, 17,* 251–263.

Barnett, S., Niebuhr, V., Baldwin, C., & Levine, H. (1992). Community-oriented primary care: A process for school health intervention. *Journal of School Health, 62,* 246–248.

Blum, R. (1987). Contemporary threats to adolescent health in the United States. *Journal of the American Medical Association, 257,* 3390–3395.

Burns, B. J., & Friedman, R. M. (1990). Examining the research base for child mental health services and policy. *Journal of Mental Health Administration, 17,* 87–97.

Butler, J. A. (1988, August). *National special education programs as a vehicle for financing mental health services for children and youth.* Paper presented at the workshop, The Financing of Mental Health Services for Children and Adolescents, National Institute of Mental Health, Washington, DC.

Caplan, G. (1964). *The principles of preventive psychiatry.* New York: Basic Books.

Center for Population Options. (1993). Unpublished survey of school-based and school-linked clinics. Washington, DC: Author.

Comer, J. (1988). Educating poor minority children. *Scientific American, 259,* 42–48.

Conoley, J. C., & Conoley, C. W. (1991). Collaboration for child adjustment: Issues for school- and clinic-based child psychologists. *Journal of Consulting and Clinical Psychology, 59,* 821–829.

Cowen, E. L. (1967). Emergent approaches to mental health problems: An overview and directions for future work. In E. L. Cowen, E. A. Gardner, & M. Zax (Eds.), *Emergency approaches to mental health problems.* New York: Appleton-Century-Crofts.

Cowen, E. L., Trost, M. A., Lorion, R. P., Dorr, D., Izzo, L. D., & Isaacson, R. V. (1975). *New ways in school mental health: Early detection and prevention of school maladaptation.* New York: Human Sciences Press.

Day, C., & Roberts, M. C. (1991). Activities of the Children and Adolescent Service System Program for improving mental health services for children and families. *Journal of Clinical Child Psychology, 20,* 340–350.

Dolan, L. J. (1992). *Models for integrating human services into the school* (Tech. Rep. No. 30). Baltimore: Johns Hopkins University, Center for Research on Effective Schooling for Disadvantaged Students.

Dryfoos, J. G. (1988). School-based health clinics: Three years of experience. *Family Planning Perspectives, 20,* 193–200.

Dryfoos, J. G. (1994). *Full-service schools*. San Francisco: Jossey-Bass.

Duchnowski, A. J. (1994). Innovative service models: Education. *Journal of Clinical Child Psychology, 23,* 13–18.

Duchnowski, A. J., & Friedman, R. M. (1990). Children's mental health: Challenges for the nineties. *Journal of Mental Health Administration, 17,* 3–12.

Duncan, G. (1991). The economic environment of childhood. In A. C. Huston (Ed.), *Children in poverty* (pp. 23–50). New York: Cambridge University Press.

Elliot, D. S., Huizinga, D., & Menard, S. (1989). *Multiple problem youth: Delinquency, substance abuse, and mental health problems*. New York: Springer-Verlag.

Farie, A. M., Cowen, E. L., & Smith, M. (1986). The development and implementation of a rural consortium program to provide early, preventive school mental health services. *Community Mental Health Journal, 22,* 94–103.

Feigelman, S., Stanton, B. F., & Ricardo, I. (1993). Perceptions of drug selling and drug use among urban youths. *Journal of Early Adolescence, 13,* 267–284.

Fisher, G. L., Jenkins, S. J., & Crumbley, J. D. (1986). A replication of a survey of school psychologists: Congruence between training, practice, preferred role and competence. *Psychology in the Schools, 23,* 271–279.

Flaherty, L. T., Weist, M. D., & Warner, B. S. (in press). School-based mental health services in the United States: History, current models, and needs. *Community Mental Health Journal.*

Fleisch, B., Knitzer, J., & Steinberg, Z. (1990). *At the schoolhouse door: An examination of programs and policies for children with behavioral and emotional problems*. New York: Bank Street College of Education.

Garbarino, J. (1976). A preliminary study of some ecological correlates of child abuse: The impact of socioeconomic stress on mothers. *Child Development, 47,* 178–185.

Goodwin, L. D., Goodwin, W. L., & Cantrill, J. L. (1988). The mental health needs of elementary school children. *Journal of School Health, 7,* 282–287.

Henggeler, S. W. (1994). A consensus: Conclusions of the APA Task Force Report on Innovative Models of Mental Health Services for Children, Adolescents, and Their Families. *Journal of Clinical Child Psychology, 23,* 3–6.

Henggeler, S. W., & Borduin, C. M. (1990). *Family therapy and beyond: A multisystematic approach to treating the behavior problems of children and adolescents*. Pacific Grove, CA: Brooks/Cole.

Henggeler, S. W., Melton, G. B., & Smith, L. A. (1992). Family preservation using multisystemic therapy: An effective alternative to incarcerating serious juvenile offenders. *Journal of Consulting and Clinical Psychology, 60,* 953–961.

Henggeler, S. W., Schoenwald, S. K., Pickrel, S. G., Rowland, M. C., & Santos, A. B. (1994). The contribution of treatment outcome research to the reform of children's mental health services: Multisystemic therapy as an example. *Journal of Mental Health Administration, 21,* 221–239.

Hofferth, S., & Hayes, C. (1987). *Risking the future: Adolescent sexuality, pregnancy, and childbearing: Statistical appendices*. Washington, DC: National Academy Press.

Hyche-Williams, J., & Waszak, C. (1990). *School-based clinics: 1990*. Washington, DC: Center for Population Options.

Johnston, N. S. (1990). School consultation: The training needs of teachers and school psychologists. *Psychology in the Schools, 27,* 51–56.

Juszczak, L., Fisher, M., Lear, J. G., & Friedman, S. B. (1995). Back to school: Training opportunities in school-based health centers. *Journal of Developmental and Behavioral Pediatrics, 16*, 101–104.

Kellam, S. G., & Rebok, G. W. (1992). Building developmental and etiological theory through epidemiologically based preventive intervention trials. In J. McCord & R. E. Tremblay (Eds.), *Preventing antisocial behavior: Intervention from birth through adolescence.* New York: Guilford Press.

Kelleher, K. J., Taylor, J. L., & Rickert, V. I. (1992). Mental health services for rural children and adolescents. *Clinical Psychology Review, 12*, 841–852.

Knitzer, J. (1982). *Unclaimed children: The failure of public responsibility to children and adolescents in need of mental health services.* Washington, DC: Children's Defense Fund.

Knitzer, J., & Cole, E. (1989). *Family preservation services: The policy challenge to state child welfare and child mental health systems.* New York: Bank Street College of Education.

Lavoritano, J., & Segal, P. B. (1992). Evaluating the efficacy of a school counseling program. *Psychology in the Schools, 29*, 61–70.

Lear, J. G., Gleicher, H. B., St. Germaine, A., & Porter, P. J. (1991). Reorganizing health care for adolescents: The experience of the school-based adolescent health care program. *Journal of Adolescent Health, 12*, 450–458.

Lee, C. C. (1995). *Counseling for diversity: A guide for school counselors and related professionals.* Needham Heights, MA: Allyn & Bacon.

Lusterman, D. D. (1985). An ecosystem approach to family school problems. *American Journal of Family Therapy, 12*, 22–30.

Maryland Department of Health and Mental Hygiene. (1995). *School-based mental health: Charting program development and exploring issues in service delivery.* Baltimore: Author.

National Association of School Psychologists. (1995). *School psychologists: Helping educate all children.* Bethesda, MD: Author.

National Mental Health Association. (1989). *Invisible Children Project: Final report.* Alexandria, VA: Author.

Office of Technology Assessment. (1991). *Adolescent health.* Congress of the United States, Washington, DC: U.S. Government Printing Office.

Offord, D. R., Boyle, M. H., Szatmari, P., Rae-Grant, N. I., Links, P. S., Cadman, D. T., Byles, J. A., Crawford, J. W., Blum, H. M., Byrne, C., Thomas, H., & Woodward, C. A. (1987). Ontario child health study. *Archives of General Psychiatry, 44*, 832–855.

Prothrow-Stith, D. (1991). *Deadly consequences: How violence is destroying our teenage population and a plan to begin solving the problem.* New York: HarperCollins.

Prout, H. T., & DeMartino, R. A. (1986). A meta-analysis of school-based studies of psychotherapy. *Journal of School Psychology, 34*, 285–292.

Pryzwansky, W. B. (1989). Private practice as an alternative setting for school psychologists. In R. C. D'Amato & R. S. Dean (Eds.), *The school psychologist in nontraditional settings* (pp. 76–87). Hillsdale, NJ: Erlbaum.

Pynoos, R. S., & Nader, K. (1990). Children's exposure to violence and traumatic death. *Psychiatric Annals, 20*, 334–344.

Rhodes, J. E., & Jason, L. A. (1988). *Preventing substance abuse among children and adolescents.* New York: Pergamon Press.

Ritter, D. R. (1989). Teachers' perceptions of problem behavior in general and special education. *Exceptional Children, 55*, 559–564.

Rosenthal, B., & Hinman, E. (1995, June). *Negotiating relationships between managed care and SBHCs.* Paper presented at the first annual meeting of the National Assembly on School-Based Health Care, Washington, DC.

Rutter, M., & Quinton, D. (1977). Psychiatric disorder: Ecological factors and concepts of causation. In H. McGurk (Ed.), *Ecological factors in human development*. Amsterdam: North Holland.

Schlitt, J. J., Rickett, K. D., Montgomery, L. L., & Lear, J. G. (1994). *State initiatives to support school-based health centers*. Washington, DC: Making the Grade.

Schoenwald, S. K., Henggeler, S. W., Pickrel, S. G., & Cunningham, P. B. (in press). Treating seriously troubled youths and families in their contexts: Multisystemic therapy. In M. C. Roberts (Ed.), *Model programs in service delivery in child and family mental health*. Hillside, NJ: Erlbaum.

Shakoor, B. H., & Chalmers, D. (1991). Co-victimization of African-American children who witness violence: Effects on cognitive, emotional, and behavioral development. *Journal of the National Medical Association, 83*, 233–238.

School Health Policy Initiative. (1993). *Ingredients for success: Comprehensive school-based health centers*. Bronx, NY: Author.

Slavin, R. E., Madden, N. A., Karweit, N. L., Dolan, L. J., & Wasik, B. A. (1992). *Success for All: A relentless approach to prevention and early intervention in elementary schools*. Arlington, VA: Educational Research Service.

Stewart, K. J. (1986). Innovative practice of indirect service delivery: Realities and idealities. *School Psychology Review, 15*, 466–478.

Sue, S., & Zane, N. (1987). The role of culture and cultural techniques in psychotherapy: A critique and reformulation. *American Psychologist, 42*, 37–45.

Thomas, A. (1987). School psychologists: An integral member of the school health team. *Journal of School Health, 57*, 465–468.

Thomas, P. A., & Texidor, M. S. (1987). The school counselor and holistic health. *Journal of School Health, 57*, 461–463.

Theut, S. K., & Bailey, H. G. (1994). What is the outcome for children's mental health needs in national health care reform? *Journal of the American Academy of Child and Adolescent Psychiatry, 33*, 1219–1222.

U.S. Department of Health and Human Services. (1994). *School-based clinics that work*. U.S. Department of Health and Human Services, Public Health Service, Bureau of Primary Health Care. Rockville, MD: Author.

Warner, B. S., & Weist, M. D. (1996). Urban youth as witnesses to violence: Beginning assessment and treatment efforts. *Journal of Youth and Adolescence, 25*, 361–377.

Way, N., Stauber, H. Y., Nakkula, M. J., & London, P. (1994). Depression and substance abuse in two divergent high school cultures: A quantitative and qualitative analysis. *Journal of Youth and Adolescence, 23*, 331–357.

Weissberg, R. P., Caplan, M., & Harwood, R. L. (1991). Promoting competent young people in competency-enhancing environments: A systems-based perspective on primary prevention. *Journal of Consulting and Clinical Psychology, 59*, 830–841.

Weist, M. D., Myers, M. P., & Baker, M. E. (1995, June) *Violence exposure and behavioral functioning in inner-city youth*. Paper presented to the Maryland Psychiatric Research Center, University of Maryland School of Medicine, Baltimore.

Weist, M. D., Paskewitz, D. A., Warner, B. S., & Flaherty, L. T. (1996). Treatment outcome of school-based mental health services for urban teenagers. *Community Mental Health Journal, 32*, 149–157.

Weist, M. D., Proescher, E. L., Freedman, A. H., Paskewitz, D. A., & Flaherty, L. T. (1995). School-based health services for urban adolescents: Psychosocial characteristics of clinic users versus nonusers. *Journal of Youth and Adolescence, 24*, 251–265.

Weisz, J. R., & Weiss, B. (1993). *Effects of psychotherapy with children and adolescents*. Newbury Park, CA: Sage.

Weisz, J. R., Weiss, B., & Donenberg, G. R. (1992). The lab versus the clinic. *American Psychologist, 47,* 1578–1595.

Winett, R. A., & Anderson, E. S. (1994). HIV prevention in youth: A framework for research and action. In T. H. Ollendick & R. J. Prinz (Eds.), *Advances in clinical child psychology, Vol. 16* (pp. 1–44). New York: Plenum Press.

Zahner, G. E., Pawelkiewicz, W., DiFrancesco, J. J., & Adnopoz, J. (1992). Children's mental health service needs and utilization patterns in an urban community: An epidemiological assessment. *Journal of the American Academy of Child and Adolescent Psychiatry, 31,* 951–960.

Author Index

Subject Index